Cruising the Performative

for Carlos
as a token
of future collaboration!

Philip.

Unnatural Acts: Theorizing the Performative

Sue-Ellen Case
Philip Brett
Susan Leigh Foster

The partitioning of performance into obligatory appearances and strict disallowances is a complex social code assumed to be "natural" until recent notions of performativity unmasked its operations. Performance partitions, strictly enforced within traditional conceptions of the arts, foreground the gestures of the dancer, but ignore those of the orchestra player, assign significance to the elocution of the actor, but not to the utterances of the audience. The critical notion of performativity both reveals these partitions as unnatural and opens the way for the consideration of all cultural intercourse as performance. It also exposes the compulsory nature of some orders of performance. The oppressive requirements of systems that organize gender and sexual practices mark who may wear the dress and who may perform the kiss. Further, the fashion of the dress and the colorizing of the skin that dons it are disciplined by systems of class and "race." These cultural performances are critical sites for study.

The series "Unnatural Acts" encourages further interrogations of all varieties of performance both in the traditional sense of the term and from the broader perspective provided by performativity.

CRUISING THE PERFORMATIVE

*Interventions into the Representation
of Ethnicity, Nationality, and Sexuality*

edited by
Sue-Ellen Case, Philip Brett,
and Susan Leigh Foster

Indiana University Press

Bloomington and Indianapolis

The paper used in this publication meets the minimum
requirements of American National Standard for Information
Sciences—Permanence of Paper for Printed
Library Materials, ANSI Z39.48-1984.
Manufactured in the United States of America

Library of Congress Cataloging-in-Publication Data

Cruising the performative : interventions into the representation
of ethnicity, nationality, and sexuality / edited by Sue-
Ellen Case, Philip Brett, and Susan Leigh Foster.
p. cm. — (Unnatural acts)
Includes index.
ISBN 0–253–32901–9 (alk. paper). — ISBN 0–253–20976–5
(pbk. : alk. paper)
1. Gays in popular culture—United States. 2. Sexuality in
popular culture—United States. 3. Homosexuality in art—United
States. 4. Homosexuality in literature—United States.
5. Performance art—United States. I. Brett, Philip. II. Case,
Sue-Ellen. III. Foster, Susan Leigh. IV. Series
HQ76.3.U5C78   1995
305.9′0664—dc20
94–47062
1 2 3 4 5   00 99 98 97 96 95

Contents

Introduction   *vii*

Instrumental Accompaniments

1

Who's Been in My Closet? Mimetic Identification and
the Psychosis of Class Transvestism in *Single White Female*
Ellen Brinks   *3*

2

Michael Jackson's Penis
Cynthia J. Fuchs   *13*

3

The Telephone and Its Queerness
Ellis Hanson   *34*

4

John Rechy and the Grammar of Ostentation
Ricardo L. Ortiz   *59*

5

Homodevotion
Richard Rambuss   *71*

Inter-Nationalist Interventions

6

Deviance and Dissidence: Sexual Subjects of the Cold War
Katrin Sieg   *93*

7

As the Master Saw Her
Parama Roy *112*

8

Tango and the Postmodern Uses of Passion
Marta E. Savigliano *130*

9

Hyphen-Nations
Jennifer DeVere Brody *149*

Community Cruises

10

"We Are Family": House Music and Queer Performativity
Brian Currid *165*

11

Compulsory Homosociality: Charles Olson, Jack Spicer, and
the Gender of Poetics
Michael Davidson *197*

12

Performing "Nature": Shamu at Sea World
Jane C. Desmond *217*

13

"If We Could Talk with the Animals": Elephants and
Musical Performance during the French Revolution
Michael E. McClellan *237*

Notes on Contributors *249*
Index *251*

Introduction

A CTS HAVE A long subversive history in Western cultures. From Plato's *Republic* onward, the "unnatural" quality of acting was condemned by numerous
philosophers and state officials alike. Theaters have been closed by the state and
actors' bodies, such as Molière's, rejected at the cemetery gates as polluted by the
"art."

Music as performance (rather than metaphysical speculation) has also lurked
on the verge of the unacceptable. Whether it is St. Augustine entertaining moral
qualms about his attachment to boys' voices, Tolstoy violently condemning the
effects of Beethoven's Kreutzer Sonata, or Allan Bloom becoming hysterical over
adolescents' addiction to popular music in modern times, musical activity is
regularly perceived in Western societies as a threat—to be labeled as such in the
case of pop records or to have its effects emasculated by the trappings of a Western concert hall or opera house. Likewise, dance has had its history of blame in
the Christian world, ever since Salomé secured the head of the first martyr with
her pagan undulations. Consistently aligned with the feminine via the categories
of intuition, sensuality, and the nonverbal, dance nonetheless perambulates
through the masculine domain of public space, turning those who perform it into
varieties of public women or effeminate men. Dance's lack of a literature, its painful preoccupation with THE BODY, its late and hardwon entrance into the academy, all confirm its status on Protestant, Catholic, as well as intellectual scales.

Trained in theater, music, and dance, the three editors of this volume, with
a developed sense of the shame, but also of the subversive potential of our professions, found ourselves together in Riverside. A place poised precariously on
the edge of the desert, it burgeons only at the expense of vast acre-feet of water
nervously distributed on its suburban lawns in an unending dance of sprinkler
systems. Such an environment intensified our sense of the social code which
regulates performativity and designates only those things it can control as "performances." On the one hand, we shared a desire to examine the partitions
within our own arts that localize performance in, for instance, the body of the
dancer, the voice of the singer, the aura of the actor. On the other, we were involved in the debate in feminist and lesbian and gay studies concerning the pres-

sure that surrounds the roles that gender and sexual practices entail. The walls and partitions of our own departments, we also thought, were only too ready for a trumpet blast of joint performativity. Prompted by the demise of an annual conference and book series entitled "Themes in Drama" (Masterpiece Theatre for us) we got together to organize "Unnatural Acts."

The poster announcing the call fleshed out in intentional and accidental ways what we had been moving toward. A long list of gerunds was meant not only to reassure those who couldn't see themselves as involved in "performance," but opened up our own ideas of what constituted the performative: dog racing and nipple piercing accompanied choreographing and cruising. Moreover the images we selected—the frontal embrace of a violoncello by a bare-chested African American male, a fifties white family enacting a domestic scene, a lesbian melodrama—were not mounted or framed as "performances" but presented (by accident) in the rude cuts made by Sue-Ellen's shears—possibly too rude, since one addressee secured a formal prohibitory order against the delivery of further documents from the conference.

The favorable response to this call, which went out to a wide variety of people and institutions, was so encouraging that three concurrent sessions were necessary to accommodate even a fair representation of the papers. Many of the participants rose to the challenge of the performative in the very act of presenting their papers. Sandy Stone's was a performance of the transsexual at the computer, performing gender in her voice and gestures with the computer as aid. She performed herself as vampire, in the darkened room incorporating threat and allure as part of her delivery. A pair of "queer twins," Anneliese and Stephanie Heyl, broke the tradition of the single voice along with the taboo against incestuous desire. Gordon Simpson chewed his way through a mix of scholarly voices on the semiotics of cereal packaging.

If the papers broke traditional conference bounds, so too did those events designated as performances. The opening Unnatural Buffet was carefully staged. The naugahyde doors parted to reveal three gently revolving steam tables, manipulated by Susan Rose and her dancers, choreographing the presentation of food, and later caricaturing the bodily discomforts of conference attendance to the accompaniment of a tango. Lois Weaver and Peggy Shaw, in their *Lesbians Who Kill*, staged the virtual nature of radio, the car, the woman serial killer, and the way lesbian is marked semiotically as violence and is also the site of potential violence, as Weaver ran into the audience waving a revolver and yelling, "all the men up against the wall!" Carmelita Tropicana, in her elevator shoes, her flounce, and her bilinguality, leveled a joke-cracking deconstruction of the "Conquest of Mexico." As finale, Jeff Tobin's chocolate pig-cake, a representative of his theory of chocolate and deconstruction, brought climactic squeals of delight. And as these performances penetrated the conference, so an awareness was formed of other spectacles—the people who had come to "cruise" the lesbian and gay speakers, the adulation of graduate students for the glamorous authors, the polite but hurried visits of liberal academics.

UC Riverside grew from an experimental citrus station—"Pest Management" still abuts "Philosophy" in the campus catalog and down the road stands the "Mother Navel" tree, imported into Southern California and altered by campus scientists. The local citizenry never quite noticed the transition, but on this occasion the press responded with its own sense of the spectacular. As luck would have it, the poster, which managed to obscure many of the participant's more provocative titles, sported "Michael Jackson's Penis" in a prominent place on a white background. A columnist in the *Press-Enterprise* questioned how we, a state university, could afford, both morally and financially, to run such a thing. Of course the question later became, how could Michael Jackson. Then a Professor of Philosophy entered the fray across the Sunday editorial page, labeling us both old-fashioned for following outworn French intellectual styles (boring old Barthes) and "chic and trendy" for including popular culture. He also complained of our lack of involvement with the community (as one might imagine, philosophy is celebrated in Riverside for its shelters for the homeless). The Dean of Humanities took our part with firm arguments about the university as a place of free inquiry. Such a dramatic representation of institutional and community themes was more than we had bargained for, and yet also an integral part of the conference, where a public reading of the newspaper articles brought the issues home.

We present in some detail a description of the weekend where the essays in this volume made their first appearance because it vivifies the issues that they address and that give them a collective coherence. Some of the essays, for example Desmond's Shamu or McClellan's elephants (unnatural acts by large mammals), push the limits of the species-specific boundaries of performance and audience. Roy's Vivekananda and Rambuss's naked Christ reveal the heterosexualized, national bodies of "pure" metaphysical adoration, while Hanson's hymns are the "phone noir's" live connection to virtual erotics and paranoid surveillance fantasies. Brinks brings a lot of class to her reading of *Single White Female*, but Sieg illustrates how socialist anti-class ideology enforced homophobia in the GDR. Sieg's "hyphen-nation" is Germany's own national one, but Brody's is of ethnic and sexual "passing." Savigliano tangoes her way in and out of postmodernist strategies exported into the "Third World" and Currid dances to "house music" in gay bars that digitizes ethnicity and history.

Whether at the bar, or Black Mountain poetry readings, a field trip to Sea World, an orchestra concert at the zoo, the closed borders of the GDR, or in the prayer closet, these essays address issues of communal identity—its fragility and transitoriness, as well as its legacy of endurance. We have divided them into three parts—an ancient custom since Caesar took Gaul. Yet the multiple intersections of critical theories, social concerns, and cultural inscriptions that operate among them might have produced various other arrangements. This proliferation of commonalities across the broad terrain of cultural artifacts is what "Unnatural Acts" celebrates.

Instrumental Accompaniments

1

Who's Been in My Closet?

Mimetic Identification and the Psychosis of Class Transvestism in *Single White Female*

Ellen Brinks

Barbet schroeder's 1992 film *Single White Female* features a lesbian gripped by psychosis who almost beats a gay actor to death before she turns to murder the roommate and "double" that she desires.[1] The Hollywood film industry seems to be redefining the psychological horror flick as the genre in which parasitic lesbianism, murderous violence, and "family values" are contested through their hyperbolic conjunction. And if this fantastic coincidence is not ludicrous enough in one film, then we note that *SWF* appeared at the same cultural moment with other similarly unreal films such as *Poison Ivy* and *Basic Instinct*. (Perhaps it is the synchronicity of these Hollywood films that truly warrants the diagnosis of psychosis.) Reviews by gay and lesbian critics and activists alike justly attack the film for its potent misogyny and homophobia. Such queer criticism is psychologically and politically necessary, given Hollywood's inability and unwillingness to imagine positive gay and lesbian characters. Yet limiting their focus solely to the ways the representation of lesbian sexuality wreaks violence upon the film's audience and the queer community, these same critics do not go far enough. They fail to examine the equally salient forms of "economic violence" that transect the film's sexual politics.[2] This essay attempts to explore the ways *SWF* imagines sexual identities as economic identities: those points where forms of erotic desire, homophobia, and market-violence make contact in a series of terrorizing exchanges and constitute an uncanny sexual subject.

SWF enacts sexual and class identities along the same trajectory, one that could be called "mimetic performance." Hedra (nicknamed "Hedy"), responding to Allie's ad for an apartment share, aims to be more than a roommate, friend, or lover. An identical twin who lost her sister in a childhood accident, Hedy tries to recover an imaginary, twin identity in her relationships with women. She gradually transforms her appearance and manner, assuming an identity difficult to differentiate from her roommate's. She attempts to pass as Allie. For Hedy, "to look like" is a way "to become" or share a twin/dual identity. Instead of the purely acquisitive desire *to have* the clothing or the man that Allie possesses or enjoys (something which would assume an already constituted *subject* who desires some *thing* or *object*), Hedy "does the double" in order to create a subjective identity for herself. She desires *to be, to be like,* or *to become* Allie.[3]

Communicated above by her appearance or "look," Allie's identity belongs to the professional class, a membership that positions subjectivity within a socio-economic context.[4] As Hedy will show us, the emergence of her subjective identity is not only heavily invested with the kinds and expenditures of labor, as well as the material signifiers of class difference, but it is sexualized as well. More specifically, mimetic desire in *SWF* deconstructs a naturalized sexual identity through its materialist emphases. Along an economic axis of values—of exchange and commodification—the brutality of class distinctions and the unequal right to identity as private property emerge concomitantly with a struggle to define female sexuality.

One way to simplify the film's narrative trajectory is to say that Hedy insatiably desires—and works to wear—Allie's clothes. If Hedy wants to be Allie, then her emergent female subjectivity depends upon replicating Allie's look, a look that bears a particular intelligibility. Looking at Allie, the viewer sees a socially privileged norm of identity. By desiring to wear her clothes, Hedy desires to participate in this normativized meaning.[5] For these women, then, dressing affixes the cultural codes and status that define the professional. Transgressing the boundaries of an apartment share, Hedy and Allie's shared living space expands to enfold embodied and psychic spaces as well. Hedy cannot project an "ego-surface" with a different legibility.[6] When Hedy first appears, for example, she wears what are clearly secondhand clothes. (Without a retro-chic appeal, she merely looks drab and faded next to Allie's exclusive prerogative—an effortless style.) Even here, however, Hedy remains consistent. With clothing or ego-identity, Hedy gets it secondhand. The refusal of singular ownership acknowledges that clothes and their identifiable subjects pass from one person to another. What is important is that this transitivity goes in a single direction, from Allie to Hedy. Prior to assuming Allie's look, Hedy's "invisibility" marks her social "inscrutability." Outside fungibility, with no exchange value on (Allie's) market of style, Hedy makes a fashion statement when she first appears.[7]

In Allie's mind, Hedy's facile appropriation of her look becomes an all-too-facile assumption of what should count as her singular and proper identity. By disrupting the boundaries of self and other through the violated sartorial boundary of the closet (Hedy's "one-way" transgression), mimesis induces a paranoia with its psychosomatic transvestism. How can Allie "own" her identity—owned as her look—if Hedy can so easily take it? Even more unsettling, how can Allie reclaim her identity by dispossessing her double, Hedy, since dispossessing the double means that she dispossesses herself? Whether moving into her apartment, going through her closet and borrowing clothing, visiting Allie's salon for a makeover, or seducing Allie's male lover in an attempt to pass in bed as Allie, Hedy *creates* Allie and herself through the mimetic, restructuring power of her gaze. By being able to see Allie and, consequently, allow her to be seen (the "inside-out" structure of Lacan's mirror stage), Hedy reveals the sociocultural stakes of rendering Allie accessible to herself and to others. Visibility is at the expense of another's prior invisibility. Put somewhat differently, Hedy is necessary to propel Allie into the "universalizing" nature of the symbolic. Indeed, because cultural signs are collectively defined, there is no private property in the symbolic. Semiotically, mimetic identification is the mode of language *and* a mode of vicariousness. Dispossessing by appropriating everything "proper" to culture's "universal" subject (in this case, Allie), mimesis displaces and jeopardizes the idea of the subject as private or as property.

Hedy's mimetic facility turns "psychotic" because it undermines Allie's fantasmatic class stability. Itself a symptom of Allie's "bourgeois (or professional) panic reaction," the film spins into a place where psychoanalysis performs its own materialist critique. To begin with, Hedy and Allie are divided by clearly legible class lines. Allie is a fashion consultant and computer programmer, one whose career is being launched with a software program she designs and markets. She lives in an immense turn-of-the-century apartment on Manhattan's Upper West Side. (It might be plausibly argued that the real tragedy of *SWF* is the loss of this beautiful, rent-controlled apartment.) Hedy, on the other hand, is a clerk in a bookstore, a wage-earner, with no immediate prospects for advancement. Further, she bears the stigma of a lower class status through her transience. Moving from place to place, she has been in similar situations before. Hedy's past history is known to the audience but not to Allie, raising the spectre of previous uncooperative roommates, all sacrificed to Hedy's repetitive, deadly dynamic. Finally, with parents from rural Florida and a pronounced southern drawl, she articulates, literally, the mainstream stereotypes of southern inferiority.

Within the apartment, there is a telling division of labor. Resembling a personal's listing, Allie's ad for an apartment share thwarts critical readings of the film that separate the private from the public, the sexual from the economic. Hedy finds herself relegated to, and accepts being the laborer within the household. Not only does she secure the roommate position with a "hands-on" demonstration of her plumbing skills, but she cooks and cleans the apartment, playing the subservient "wife" to the ambitious, self-confident careerist Allie. Here, the identification of a domestic partner with an unpaid laborer exposes the underlying conditions and guarantees that are necessary to maintain Allie's comfortable domestic fiction. As Hedy puts it to Allie in one of the film's most telling moments: "Did you know that identical twins are never really identical? There's always one who's prettier. And the one who's not does all the work."

The work we do defines and shapes who we become: how we look, how we live, how we relate to one another. Paid for her intelligence, training, and personality, the professional (as a person and as a class) markets this identity.[8] Allie's look, as the commodified signifier of this identity, is marketed within the culture at large, and thus to Hedy. Inscribed as sartorial style, professional power and privilege act as a class-prerogative, a way of dominating rather than surrendering to the gaze of the class-other. It is along these lines that the history of fashion can be understood as class competition, in which the proletariat competes with the middle and upper classes for access to and ownership of styles.[9] Complicating and capitalizing on this struggle, the fashion industry—of which Allie is a part—succeeds in a market-driven economy only through the *mass* production and replication of such looks, or identities, as Allie's. As Kaja Silverman notes, fashion is always at the behest of capital and in the interests of surplus capital.[10] The commodity aims at a universal appeal and an expanded access. Floating fashion is floating subjectivity. Hedy's desire and ability to assume Allie's look marks its success as a commodity.

The commodification of identity, in fact, is elevated to hysterically sublime proportions by Allie herself. Working within the marketing sector of the fashion industry, she creates and sells a software that proliferates and disperses identity as "a look." In addition, Allie's software program is *user-activated*. The users dress and undress a "universalized," that is, generic, image of a female body with the clothing and accessories of the professional woman: allowing the consumer/software-user to "try on and on and on," as it were, Allie's look. Thus, *what* Hedy does within their shared apartment is no different than what Allie *sells* to others. Allie markets *the concept of exchangeable identity* through the mixing and matching of fashion separates.

The concept of exchangeable identity resembles the seriality of late capitalism, as Jean Baudrillard describes it:

> In the series, objects are transformed indefinitely into simulacra of one another and, with objects, so are the people who produce them. Only the extinction of original reference permits the generalized law of equivalence, which is to say, the *very possibility of production*.[11]

As a mode of operation, serial production affects not only the identity of the objects produced but their producers. They stand under a law of equivalence which reduces them to indistinguishable producers, destroying once and for all the fiction of an original, unique, and authentic source or reference. *SWF* takes this mode one step further. The produced object (here, Allie's look as a commodity) and the producer (Allie) collapse into simulacra, literally *simulacra of each other*. Deftly figured in the film through a narrative equivalence, the temporal moment where Allie's software self-erases coincides with the imminent external threat to her life.

By universalizing herself as a commodity, Allie loses the ability to define herself as a *particular* subject. And as the commodified object of desire, her illusory privacy and containment scatters in objectified replication. The Foucaultian lesson Allie fails to learn is that such a loss of self offers other forms of power and privilege. Being the commodity found everywhere and fixed nowhere (like ideology), her power to control also expands. In other words, the extent of her subjective dispersion is also a potential measure of her ability to determine it as an object. Homogenized identity does not necessarily restrict or obliterate Allie's exercise of power. Allie, however, desperately wants to maintain and assert certain class distinctions in the wake of the sartorial homogenization she has produced. She secures a copyright on her line of software, attempting to control it (and its profits) by exclusive, legal ownership. This includes a built-in mechanism that allows Allie alone to erase the program, at any time she desires.

Hedy's "lesbian" desire for Allie comes out most tellingly in her (and the camera's) frequent ventures into Allie's closet. We might say that any woman's closet, framed within the context of another woman's desire to enter into it, provokes an unavoidable pun on that metaphorical, sexual closet. Whose clothes and whose sexuality belong to whom, anyway? If Hedy's desire for the clothing in the closet is also coded as the desire for another woman, then the attraction of the commodity suggests the secret attraction of lesbian desire. Tracking the vicissitudes of lesbian desire (its production, dispersal, and kind of effacement) becomes a way of mapping the contradictions of late capitalism.

As mentioned earlier, Hedy's mimetic urge pushes her to want to be or to be like her roommate Allie. Mimesis takes a desire to a place where being and wanting become indistinguishable. Paradoxically, the "difference" that defines a lesbian is her compulsive, parasitic tendency to make her subjectivity into a reversion to sameness—precluding difference.[12] Assimilated into another (in this case, heterosexual) identity, the *lesbian* Hedy immediately drops out of sight. According to *SWF*, then, a lesbian would not only be everywhere but nowhere in "doing the double," she produces her invisibility. Hedy's mimetic performance *as a lesbian subject* must fail insofar as *she* will always remain invisible, i.e., the lesbian subject is irreproduceable. Psychic mimesis or the obsession to play the double implicitly becomes a way to play out, that is, to exhaust lesbian desire. For a homophobic audience, and for Allie, it becomes a perverse way to recognize *and* recuperate lesbianism.

Hedy's lesbianism, effaced as soon as it appears, seems to lie in the proximate cause of Allie herself. If Hedy wants to be Allie, then it seems she wants to be straight, too. If Hedy's self-consciousness depends upon her ability to replicate Allie's "look," then Allie's fashion sensibility, not surprisingly, articulates heterosexual subjectivity as *the* culturally meaningful form. Dressing is not only a way to come out professional, but a way to come out straight. Yet in *SWF*, the equivalence of "coming into being" and "coming out" unsettles the originary fiction of an ostensibly always already heterosexual female subject. Instead, Hedy's ability to see Allie's look marks a gaze that, although invisible, occurs in the powerful (and controlling) "no-place" of *butch voyeurism*: a place where Allie's stylish exhibitionism is seen and made intelligible through its play to another woman's desiring gaze. It is Hedy's way to come out on top. Allie's concern, "How do I look?" is generated by Hedy's prior concern, "How do I see?": a prior concern which the camera identifies with as well. Like Hedy, the camera makes Allie the preferred object of its adoring gaze.[13] Unseen, lesbian desire creates and directs the narrative. The conventional heterosexual organization of the voyeuristic or filmic transaction shifts to one between women. While this shift carries a truly subversive potential, *SWF* works to negate it. Hedy's voyeuristic, lesbian gaze produces a normative female identity—the heterosexual, professional Allie.

Hedy threatens Allie because her mimetic proclivities create uncontained, shifting subject/object positions. Her mobile and uncanny sexuality is at home everywhere and *not* at home anywhere. ("Hedy" is actually an alias for her "proper" name, Ellen. A disavowal of a fixed, singular name, the alias literalizes Hedy's affinity for polymorphous, unstable identities. Further, Hedra-Hedy puns on Hydra, the many-headed regenerating monster, and on "heady," the inebriating experience of being "outside" oneself.) Allie, the would-be proprietrix of her sexuality, spins into a "homosexual panic reaction" under Hedy's desiring and (de)constitutive gaze.

Allie's terror surfaces with the double's appearance on the scene. The double traditionally unleashes illicit desires: ones that are repressed or hidden, ones that disturb generative sexuality and, most threatening of all, ones that "oust" the heterosexual love object by ushering in an all-consuming *autoscopia*.[14] Once seen, the double becomes the sole object of attention. Figured as uncanny or monstrous, the double increasingly takes over and commands the subject's desires. Hedy's lesbian compulsion "to do the double" means Allie's vision is full of—and restricted to—her own self, making homoeroticism a dangerous, narcissistic desire. If one's ego-identity depends upon what the double reveals, then Allie's heterosexual identity is upset by her vision of homoerotic desire.

As Allie's psychic energies collect and intensify around the desire to uncover her double Hedy's secret past, they register a drive to self-knowledge. The transitivistic contagion of mimesis suggests that Allie's obsession with Hedy's secret signals an obsession with her own unacknowledged lesbianism. As long as this secret is maintained, it reflects Allie's false consciousness. By a heady series of displacements, however, Allie's visibility to and for herself is paid for at a "horrendous" price: she recognizes the desire for another woman. As Allie says to Hedy, "I'm not like your sister anymore, Hedy. Not anymore. *I'm like you now.*" This insight must stay hidden, or better yet, erased. And in fact, that is where the movie takes us. Allie finally murders Hedy. In *SWF*, to know oneself is to desire oneself is to recognize (and kill) a lesbian.

With homosexuality reduced to the replicative, deadly, and all-absorbing energy of narcissism—the obliteration of differences between women[15]—it is not surprising that the film's heterosexual men wind up as Hedy's and Allie's first victims. Hedy murders Allie's lover Sam, and Allie symbolically castrates the other man who comes on to her sexually before Hedy finishes him off. The film's *survivors* include the gay Graham, who, as an actor and the film's other "homosexual," by definition fluctuates in his identifications, manifesting the same performative lubricity as Hedy. The other survivor is Allie, now a replicant of Hedy doing Allie ("I'm like you now"), who is "homeless" and will presumably soon be looking for an apartment share. One might speculate whether what makes *SWF* a horror film in our homophobic society is its blatant refusal of Freud's comforting developmental fiction—the progression from homosexuality to heterosexuality.[16] From the movie's first scene where Allie and Sam fuck and discuss marriage, we wind up at a place where all the heterosexual partners are dead, and Allie is Hedy's clone. If homosexuality is the threat, it is also the film's legacy. The polymorphous perversity of Hedy's "infantile," mimetic fixation triumphs over the heterosexual, vaginally-oriented, and "mature" femininity of Allie, leaving only the endlessly proliferating identities that Hedy engenders.

What perhaps makes Hedy's desire most terrifying for Allie is the impossibility of controlling its dispersal. In one scene, Allie stalks Hedy passing as Allie and winds up in an s/m leather bar where a woman immediately tries to pick her up. Instead of a *specific* desire for a *particular* person, Hedy's desire (and by extension, Allie's) is pushed into a generalized sector by cathecting it to the commodity. And as a good capitalist, Allie knows that a commodity's value is always abstract and general. It goes everywhere because it compels a universal appeal that cannot be resisted. Hedy's desire *to be* Allie operates like the universalizing desire that makes Allie's professional investment in commodity capitalism so successful. Hedy's specific desire for a particular woman named Allie disperses and metonymically slides, as it were, into a desire for a universalized commodity: the professional identity that Allie is/markets. Lesbian desire, like commodity desire, goes everywhere.

Effacing the differences between desiring subjects and the things or persons that they desire, *SWF* has Hedy becoming what she desires, literally. Here mimetic performance makes its commodified subjects and objects interchangeable.

The film exacerbates the contamination of lesbian desire by hitchhiking a specific subjectivity and/or desire onto the perceived dangers of a similarly uncon-
strained commodity desire. As Allie's professional success and survival at the
film's conclusion makes clear, the triumph of the commodity, its omnipresence,
is perversely equivalent to the triumph of lesbian desire. The danger is not laid
to rest. If such a triumph is synonymous with the horrific in this film, it is because Allie fails to resist or deny the implications of serial production. She is like
Hedy now.

This intersection of economics and sexuality weirdly seems to justify the
film's misogyny and homophobia as a critique of serial capitalism. This critique,
however, results in a conservative backlash. In a panic, Allie attempts to restrict
class mobility and reassert her status as a singular subject, as private property
that she can own and control. The "psychotic" Hedy, on the other hand, manipu-
lates class conventions in order to restructure economic and sexual relations between women. At the film's beginning, she catches Allie snooping around in her
room, picking up and examining her possessions. As Hedy undresses, she casually mentions: "Anything of mine that you want—just go ahead—share and share
alike." Allie, on the other hand, futilely tries to control both the distribution and
her ownership of the clothing passing from hers to Hedy's closet, while Hedy's
communal approach to bodies and things marks a political commitment to a leveling of class distinctions. It ends up wildly exacerbating Allie's proprietary impulses. Whether she searches for a missing garment or discovers that Hedy has
obtained a piece identical to her own, Allie barely controls her exploding, aggressive energy. Hedy "improperly" violates Allie's claim to private property.

The difference between those who survive and those who don't, between Allie and Graham on the one hand and Hedy on the other, I would argue, is that
Allie and Graham have learned to make a career out of—in other words, *to professionalize*—the "psychotic" principle of mimetic identification. Graham, Allie's
gay friend upstairs, more conventionally embodies identity as mimesis through
his profession as an actor, one whose assumed roles signify multiple identities.
Hedy turns to "revolutionary" violence as Allie prevents her from crossing a professional and class divide. Her attempt to share Allie's status, beauty, and intelligence—in other words, her class transvestism—is considered psychotic by Allie.
The extent of Hedy's violence can be measured by the extent of her inability to
professionalize (to own, control, and market) a self mimetically multipliable.
Hedy only *shares* it. Mimesis, without such professional containment, represents
the potent threat of communally held, circulating property and class mobility as
visible forms of lesbian identity and desire.

Hedy becomes a lesbian scapegoat or proxy, made to take responsibility for
capitalism's violence. Allie's murder of Hedy is the (temporary) sacrifice that
would recuperate stable distinctions between classes and sexual identities. The

concluding soundtrack of the film, ironically, is titled "The state of independence shall be." Yet the reconstitution of Allie's exclusive right to her identity as singularly held private property, or to use John Locke's words, "property in the person," is a fiction that Hedy renders only too transparent. Hedy, in other words, embodies mimetic performance as a site of ideological distortion. Within her figure we find a conjunction of opposites condensed and blurred—the excesses of serial capitalism as well as its potential proletarian subversion. Hedy refuses to make invisible the social antagonisms which underlie class or sexual desire or to pave the way for an imaginary solution.

Notes

1. While describing Hedy as a lesbian may not seem self-evident to some readers, this chapter will attempt to clarify just how that identity is constituted within the film. Further references to the film will appear as *SWF*.

2. I am indebted to Adrienne Donald for the term "economic violence" ("Working for Oneself: Labor and Love in *The Silence of the Lambs*," *Michigan Quarterly Review* 31.3 (1992), p. 347).

3. For psychoanalytic theories of mimesis and the constitution of subjective identity, see in particular: Mikkel Borch-Jacobson, *The Freudian Subject*, trans. Catherine Porter (Stanford: Stanford University Press, 1988) and "The Oedipus Problem in Freud and Lacan," *Critical Inquiry* 20.2 (winter 1994), pp. 267–82; Jacques Derrida, "Desistance," in Philippe Lacoue-Labarthe and Jean-Luc Nancy, *Typography: Mimesis, Philosophy, and Politics*, ed. Christopher Fynsk (Cambridge: Harvard University Press, 1989), pp. 1–42; and Ruth Leys, "The Real Miss Beauchamp: Gender and the Subject of Imitation," in *Feminists Theorize the Political*, ed. Judith Butler and Joan Scott (New York: Routledge, 1992), pp. 167–214.

4. For the notion of a social class, like the professional, that goes beyond traditional Marxist definitions of class, see Philippe Bourdieu, *Language and Symbolic Dominance*, trans. Gino Raymond and Matthew Adamson (Cambridge: Harvard University Press, 1991), esp. pp. 229–51.

5. Kaja Silverman's "Fragments of a Fashionable Discourse" calls attention to Éugenie Lemoine-Luccioni's argument that clothing allows the body to be seen and articulated as a meaningful form within culture. In *Studies in Entertainment: Critical Approaches to Mass Culture*, ed. Tania Modleski (Bloomington: Indiana University Press, 1986), p. 145.

6. For ego-identity as the projection of an ego-surface, see Sigmund Freud, *The Ego and the Id*, in vol. IX of *The Standard Edition of the Complete Psychological Works of Sigmund Freud*, trans. James Strachey (London: Hogarth Press, 1953–66), p. 26.

7. Hedy obviously came too early to profit from the "lesbian chic" phase that followed on its footsteps.

8. Donald, p. 348.

9. Quentin Bell, *On Human Finery* (London: Hogarth, 1976), p. 155.

10. Silverman, p. 148.

11. Jean Baudrillard, "The Structural Law of Value and the Order of Simulacra," trans. Charles Levin, in *The Structural Allegory: Reconstructive Encounters with the New French Thought*, ed. John Fekete (Minneapolis: University of Minnesota Press, 1984), p. 63.

12. Along these lines, the reactionary Christopher Lasch claims that the homosexual pervert "erases the more fundamental distinction between the self and the non-self, the source of every other distinction." (Quoted in Michael Warner, "Homo-Narcissism; or, Heterosexuality," in *Engendering Men: The Question of Male Feminist Criticism*, ed. Joseph A. Boone and Michael Cadden (New York: Routledge: 1990), p. 199.)

13. For the fantasy domination of the butch gaze from a Derridean *non-lieu*, see Blakey Vermeule's reading of *All About Eve* in "Is there a Sedgwick School for Girls?" in *Qui Parle* 5.1 (1991), pp. 64 and 66. Vermeule's intelligent article argues that the price of displacing (and equating) lesbian desire with the affective bonds between women is to enfold homosexuality into homosociality: in other words, a "non-genesis" of the lesbian subject. In terms of a mimetically driven economy of lesbian desire (and invisibility) as dependent upon female worship and rivalry, *Single White Female* easily reads as a 1990s remake (or should I say "double"?) of *All About Eve*.

14. Mladen Dolar discusses the double's disturbance in his essay " 'I shall be with you on your wedding night': Lacan and the Uncanny," *October* 58 (1991), p. 14.

15. For the classic argument of homosexuality as narcissism, see Freud's "Leonardo da Vinci and a Memory of His Childhood," vol. XI of *The Standard Edition*, and "On Narcissism," in *The Standard Edition*, vol. XIV. Collapsing narcissism and homoeroticism, the desiring gaze of the lesbian would be the desire for an *autoscopia*. Michael Warner challenges the homophobic conclusions this line of thought has generated (in Lacan and other post-Freudian theorists). Instead, in a subtle and differentiated essay, he recuperates narcissism as fundamental to eroticism. Far from obliterating the difference between self and other, Warner argues that Freud's secondary narcissism and the dynamics of the ego ideal (both of which, in Freud, slip into homoeroticism) have a "proleptic and utopian" function, making the subject truly social. Further, this homoerotic narcissism is the unexamined foundation of heterosexual love. See "Homo-Narcissism; or, Heterosexuality," pp. 190–206.

16. Freud, *Three Essays on the Theory of Sexuality* (1905a), vol. VII of *The Standard Edition*.

2

Michael Jackson's Penis

Cynthia J. Fuchs

Michael Jackson continues to transform his face so that he can be a different
person, a perfect person, perhaps one with an ideal life, and then he looks in the
mirror after each surgery to see if things have changed yet . . . but they don't
change. Nothing changes, because, *inside*, Michael Jackson is troubled.

—J. Randy Taraborrelli, *Michael Jackson: The Magic and the Madness*

One is no longer aware of the Negro, but only of a penis; the Negro is eclipsed.
He *is* a penis.

—Frantz Fanon, *Black Skin, White Masks*

Would it seem so odd that he slept in the same bed with children
if he were a woman?

—Letter to *Newsweek*, 27 Sept. 1993

Dangerous

"MICHAEL JACKSON'S PENIS is a problem."

When I wrote a first version of this chapter for the Unnatural Acts conference, I began with the above observation. A little more than a year later, this
opening seems less "cute" or comic than hopelessly understated. Since the beginning of what now seems to be a lifelong project for me—an investigation of
the various cultural anxieties over race and sex embodied by Michael Jackson—
he was accused of child molestation (August 1993), went into serious seclusion,
suffered accusatory insinuations from his sister LaToya, settled out of court for
multiple millions of dollars (February 1994), married Lisa Marie Presley in the
Dominican Republic (May 1994), and returned to a semi-public life, mostly
through photo-ops on balconies and in windows. It's safe to say that even when
he's in "seclusion," the public life of Michael Jackson is incessant, and frankly, at
this point everything that he does or says seems directed at me and my project:
friends and colleagues tend to check in with me regarding all "latest develop-

ments." In fact, this effect—that "Michael" performs for me personally—is not unusual. Much of his success as a performer, as I understand it, has to do with his intimate (and well-orchestrated) appeals to a variety of fans.

Given that most of this audience remains quite young—at least according to publicity photographs—the child-abuse charges are important for the following discussion of Michael Jackson. Even the term "penis," initially somewhat unsettling for at least some members of his and my audiences, is now in common usage, post-Bobbitts: Jackson himself pointedly used the word when describing, on national television, the "embarrassing" police search and photography of his body.[1] But such gestures toward disclosure hardly quiet the anxieties compelled by the charges, not to mention his unstable public persona. For example, the financial settlement with his accuser, the thirteen-year-old son of a Beverly Hills dentist, has only encouraged ongoing speculation regarding Jackson's "guilt." According to the tabloid press which dedicatedly tracked the story—from *The National Enquirer* to the *New York Post* to the syndicated television show *Hard Copy*—Michael Jackson's penis remains a problem of exponentially expanding dimensions.[2] At the same time, other media sources—including *New York* magazine, ABC's *Nightline*, *Time*, the *Washington Post*, and PBS's *Frontline*—continue to treat the Michael Jackson story as an object lesson in cultural hysteria, indicting mass media as its chief instigators and perpetrators.[3]

The continuing story of Michael Jackson's penis seems simultaneously to be shifting and confirming any initial notion I may have had regarding its broad social, psychosexual, or political import. That the investigation into the abuse charges was conducted by the Los Angeles Police Department even as its most infamous officers, Stacey Koon and Lawrence Powell (convicted of denying Rodney King his civil rights when they beat him in 1991), were removed from prison in order to shield them from possible inmate violence, is disturbingly ironic.[4] For now, and particularly as it has been re-informed by the coverage of the O. J. Simpson case (presently he's represented by one of Jackson's lawyers, Johnnie L. Cochran), at least one chapter of the ongoing crisis of African American masculinity will be written in the city—Los Angeles—renowned as much for its hyperbolic fictions of American dreaming and social climbing as for its fixed, reductive distinctions between people of color and Caucasians, victims and aggressors, men and women, under and upper class, gays and straights, public and private rights. These are precisely the fictions and distinctions which are problematized by the phenomenon called "Michael Jackson."

This phenomenon is based in the narrative of Jackson's victimization and isolation, his blackness and his child-ness. His is the story of an African American male perpetually rising triumphant and (mostly) guiltless from an unhappy personal—and always very public—past. Just months before the child-abuse charges were brought, he was briefly ubiquitous in 1993, hawking his *Dangerous* album, tour, and video singles at the Superbowl, in a widely promoted television interview with Oprah Winfrey, at the Grammy Awards with his photogenic, straight, and eminently safe sister Janet. While never quite absent from the popular cultural arena, Jackson has long been represented as a shy recluse ensconced within the confines of "Neverland," the 27,000 acre ranch where, according to *Life* magazine, Jackson is "ever striving to reclaim the youth he lost in pursuit of celebrity."[5] (That he is now striving for a version of adulthood, through marriage, is tempered by the types of appearances he and Presley-Jackson are making—at the bedsides of ailing children in Budapest, at EuroDisney, and Toys Я Us.)

This particular loss of a childhood is the often-repeated rationale for Jackson's idiosyncratic and much-publicized affections for Bubbles the chimpanzee and Diana Ross the icon. It functions as well as an explanation for his social clumsiness and lack of control over his career; his well-known passivity makes him ostensibly nonthreatening, even endearing (to the point that his publicists have suggested that his increased visibility had nothing to do with the poor initial sales of *Dangerous*; Jackson attorney Burt Fields claimed that Jackson "simply stumbled onto this burst of exposure"[6]). The mythic proportions of Jackson's purity have continued to buoy his international reputation as "pop idol" throughout the child abuse scandal.[7] The representational contradictions sustained by such mythology are significant. Most reductively constructed as Jackson's simultaneous ultrasexuality and asexuality, these contradictions mark simultaneously his art and his awkwardness. A dazzling dancer and choreographer, his sexualized moves may threaten social conventions; yet his recent musical output has been markedly banal, no threat to anyone except perhaps his corporate investors.

Despite erratic performances, his appeal continues, suggesting that dominant cultural, racial, class, and sexual anxieties—certainly complicated in his particular black maleness—have been, at least until August 1993, somewhat diffused in the figure of Michael Jackson. And the marriage to Presley appears to allay them once again, while at the same time troubling traditional gender and race categories: in a "Kudzu" comic strip (25 August 1994), one character remarks that there has been "a lot of criticism of Michael and Lisa Marie marrying. If I heard it once, I heard it a thousand times. That skinny white girl doesn't know what she's doing." Here comes the punchline: "And you should hear what they say about Lisa Marie!" Indeed, next to the more aggressively styled figures of Rodney King, Clarence Thomas, Magic Johnson, Wilt Chamberlain, Mike Tyson, Ice T, and Wesley Snipes, the representational problem Michael Jackson poses seems remarkably self-contained, domesticated, comically weird, and, above all, marketable. His sexualized performances are recuperated by their sentimentality, their appeal to emotional memories of "little Michael Jackson," and their fictionality (the assumption that the man has no sex life offstage).[8] But, I think, by incarnating unstable "limits" to black male sexuality and (an always implied and related) violence, Jackson also challenges such easy containment, exposing the flimsiness of the categories of race, sexuality, and gender even while appearing to reinforce their boundaries.

Given the lasting cultural salience of black male genitalia, Michael Jackson's penis's ambiguous status (its doubled service as reference point and absence) ironically italicizes the importance of addressing the intersections of race, gender, and sexuality. In other words, the representational space where this penis *should be* seems an apt metaphor for the current theoretical gap between essentialist and constructionist versions of identity. My conclusions about this penis remain tentative, however.[9] Jackson seems to me to be most useful not as a means to read the binary ends of excess or constraint, but as a means to read and understand what Homi Bhabha calls a "*productive* ambivalence," to think through the cultural split-self created by the intersections of audiences, social forces, and political mechanisms that construct and contest Michael Jackson.[10]

The Wrong Body

Bhabha writes that the "colonial subject" is produced in discourse, articulated through "forms of difference—racial and sexual" (313). The subject that is Michael Jackson is painfully and erratically "colonial": To the extent that he is, in the words of *Nightline*'s Chris Bury, "a human conglomerate, the Jackson Complex," he is simultaneously a precious "property" and an extravagant "consumer."[11] That is, the "forms of difference" he articulates are multiple and interdependent: continuums of race, class, sexuality, gender, and age inform the ambivalent representation known as "Michael Jackson." And as the emergent "scandal" over child molestation charges suggests, the focus of this ambivalence is "always already" his penis.

The object of his own performative sexuality, fans' obsessions, music video imagery, and tabloid titillations, this penis resists easy representation or comprehension.[12] Rather, it inspires varieties of stories and identifications. For example, shortly after the Superbowl a friend of mine e-mailed me to tell me how she spent her Super Sunday: she said she had watched the game with friends. I said I didn't watch football (I believe I called it "men beating each other up"), but had watched the halftime show because I was writing about Michael Jackson. She told me that she watches football because she used to *be* one of those men who were beating each other up. She is, by the way, a transsexual. And she went on to say that she had also watched Jackson's performance, and that when she saw him she turned to her friends and said, "He's a transsexual."[13]

My friend's (inside) joke speaks directly to Jackson's mutable body and its (un)representability. As transvestism and transsexualism gain currency within gender and queer studies, our understanding of what constitutes (and politicizes) identity becomes increasingly complex: Michael Jackson's wealth and personal peculiarities allow uncommon (read: expensive) surgical transformations which betray common assumptions regarding the construction of identity. As the J. Randy Taraborrelli quotation above suggests, Jackson notoriously obsesses over his imperfect "wrong body," approximating the narrative of self-hate which has historically been ascribed to transsexual subjects. Physically reconstructed, he publicly rejects his past and maintains a nearly anti-masculine voice and demeanor. The problem of his penis remains, of course, continually cited by his own choreographed crotch-grabbing. A sign of autoerotic sexuality (read: perverse, unreproductive, and homosexual), his unseen penis resists visibility, that prevailing emblem of Western cultural Truth.

Post-operative male-to-female transsexuals are traditionally instructed to "lose" their histories along with their penises, to situate new identities in post-operative bodies.[14] Jackson's body, which I would describe as perpetually pre- and post-operative, is quite incapable of such forgetting. Whenever he appears in public—say, on stage for "Motown 25," on television with Oprah Winfrey for their momentous interview, in Monte Carlo at the 1993 World Music Awards[15]— his history is recounted through video imagery, reconfirming that his body is the site of a visibly changing identity, an effect of erasure, repetition, and resurrection. Black or white, male or female, young or old, sexed or not, Jackson's image refuses knowable, previously constituted subjectivities.

That this sexuality exploded into tabloid headlines and television talk shows in late August 1993, generating vehement public exchanges over his "guilt" or "innocence" begins to suggest the depth of cultural sex-anxieties Jackson embodies.[16] That his performances are so insistently masturbatory, so repetitive and nostalgic for previous performances, and yet so perfectly pathological in their self-denial and self-desire, underlines the mutual anxiety concerning his body revealed in the relation between Jackson and his audience. Again and again, in concert footage—and this imagery, such as the scandal coverage, is always about marketing—his young fans sob and clutch their chests; they mouth the familiar words and sway to the familiar rhythms. Yet Jackson himself (if such a concept is possible) offers only uncertainty: as he confessed to Oprah, "I can't say I know anything for sure."

This uncertainty echoes what Eve Kosofsky Sedgwick has usefully termed the "epistemology of the closet," an uncertainty over public and private identity which is manifest as "a chronic, now endemic crisis of homo/heterosexual definition."[17] Jackson offers a kind of paradigm for this crisis. Despite or because of the sad story rehearsed by Taraborrelli—where "nothing changes"—*everything* changes in the ever-proliferating image of Michael Jackson. While he is defined by promotional material in hard numbers—the dollars reaped by *Thriller*, the tonnage of equipment for the *Dangerous* tour, the number of viewers for the Oprah interview—his physical amorphousness, his lack of (sexed) definition, clearly remains troubling. For example, his habitual transmutations seem to belie his claim that he's "proud to be a black American"; yet he complains to Oprah— who would understand what he was talking about—that his audience is to blame, in their need to stabilize him.[18] "The public," he says, "wants to keep you young forever." His perpetual self-imitation both answers and confounds these demands, consummately; he changes his body to maintain its fixed agelessness. It's the same show, same moves, but in different body-drag.

Being E.T.

Jackson's performative instability is explained (and transmutated) as his victimization, a story that solicits viewer sympathy and negates the threat of his peculiar sexuality.[19] This narrative is rehearsed primarily through public apologies/accusations directed at his famously abusive father;[20] the narrative is familiar, enlisting a history of legally and socially regulated black male sexuality, which is in turn italicized by Jackson's familiar gestures—crotch-grabbing, chest-touching, hair-smoothing—signs of a self-contained, self-recuperating body. Could he have considered Grace Jones's explicitly politicized threat to a white, male, heterosexual music industry when he explained his moves with her words, "I'm 'slave to the rhythm' "?[21]

Refusing responsibility for his actions is the Jackson Machine's hugely successful marketing strategy. Judith Butler writes that "the order of sexual difference is not prior to that of race or class in the constitution of the subject";[22] as Jackson's sexuality is raced (for instance, in the often-made observation that Little Michael mimics James Brown), it is also sensationally performative, its artifice denying the efficacy of any "real" sexuality. In other words, Jackson's (disappearing) blackness doesn't define him; it reframes his transformations as more victimization.[23] Because he is a "proud" African American, the story goes, his incurable skin disease (vitiligo) makes him cry on television, in front of Oprah and millions of viewers, as he denies culpability for plastic surgery and chemical skin treatments.[24] Jackson's claimed lack of will, his inexplicable drive to accommodate his audience, his father, and his music, constructs his black masculinity as an act which is dislocated from sex, since any "original" body has long been supplanted by what Kobena Mercer calls "a spectacle of racial and sexual indeterminacy," a promotional synthesis of exaggerations, inaccuracies, and denials.[25]

This indeterminacy is exacerbated by images of Jackson's erstwhile blackness and childishness, snapshot-signs of identity that both recede and advance in the unnegotiable past that reshapes his and his audience's present. Always framed and followed by that parade of small, dark-skinned Michael Jacksons, he appears simultaneously as public property and private empire, victim and perpetrator. As Robert Scheer describes the phenomenon, Jackson embodies "self-hatred," evidenced by the repeated plastic surgery and skin-bleaching. Asserting that Jackson's submission to dangerous procedures "in hopes of becoming the universal child mocks rather than celebrates the innocence of youth," Scheer goes on to observe, after all, that he is a paradoxically complicit victim: "What *is* clear is that he is neither a boy nor a man but rather a product . . . marketed energetically by avaricious adults who condoned his weirdness as long as it was marketable."[26]

As an updated, rather cynical, and often lucrative version of Bhabha's "split subject," this product is "the embodiment of rampant sexuality and yet innocent as a child; he is mystical, primitive, simple-minded and yet the most worldly and accomplished liar, and manipulator of social forces" (328). Weird and wonderful, Jackson's ambivalence makes explicit the colonial fantasy even as it implies that his race and sexuality are unimportant, even nonexistent. Consider his appearance at the 1994 MTV Music Video Awards: he and the silent Lisa Marie pose prettily on stage, he suggests that the marriage will "last" and secures this with an extravagant kiss before millions of people. That the kiss secured nothing is my point: immediately, viewers (including Madonna, in an interview after the show) began questioning the performance, its explicitness, its authenticity, his excessiveness, her passivity. The question of explicitness surfaces as well in a moment from *Michael Jackson: The Legend Continues. . . .* Punctuated by a series of celebrity genuflections to Jackson, the video-biography traces his career from Gary, Indiana talent shows to his current status as multimillion-dollar industry and personification of the American Dream. After several attempts to articulate a passion which is clearly beyond words, Elizabeth Taylor finally gushes, "Michael is E.T.!"[27]

Even amid the myriad overstatements assembled in this video, this observation by Jackson's close friend and role model stands out as hyperbolic nonsense. Yet, it also makes a singular, tacky, and unreconstructed sense. Linking Michael and E.T.'s similar representations for childlike "magic," Taylor alludes as well to their mutual alien-ness, their distance from the planet earth, their ambiguous sex. And this problematic sex could hardly be more startlingly displayed. The publicity still accompanying Taylor's emotional assertion—Michael with his arm around E.T.—resembles nothing so much as a boy and his oversized penis. Read along with Taylor's commentary, the image offers an oddly split but clearly sexed and raced subject. Arguing that the psychic subject is constituted as it suffers loss and so incorporates an other, Judith Butler writes that "the disruption of the Other at the heart of the self is the very condition of the self's possibility."[28] The Michael Jackson portrayed with/as E.T. is possible only in such disruption. His is an uneasy incorporation of otherness, disguised and disjunctive like the various machines, special effects, and the woman-in-a-rubber-suit who created the image of E.T. The character at the center of *Michael Jackson: The Legend Continues . . .* creates his variously heterosexual, homosexual, homophobic, and sexophobic personae as a process of effects, a performative set of losses.

Seen in this way, the visible split in this picture of the penis as alien—between a contained subject and an uncontained sex—also disrupts the binary narratives of subjection emphasized in narratives of gender dysphoria: the "wrong body" narratives or the cultural insistence that an individual "be" one sex or the other. But this incorporation also complicates and denaturalizes the idea of sexual difference by revealing its reproducible sign. June Reich, in her essay on the subversions available in genderfuck, argues that the dildo, "as a phallus . . . assures difference without essentializing gender."[29] If we reimagine Jackson's pose with E.T. as a pose with a big plastic dildo, it shifts what Reich calls the libidinal paradigm from "gender-identity to sexuality-performance" (121). With this shift, we might begin to dismantle the cultural apparatus which frames Jackson's conflicted masculinity.

Multiple Orgasms

Such a "sexuality-performance" is typically visible (and confused) at the Superbowl halftime show, where Jackson appears as a series of ejaculative bodies. The much-anticipated display (heavily promoted for several weeks beforehand) begins with a megamonitor image of Jackson's face as it materializes over the stadium. Cut to a full body shot, which then launches itself rocketlike—with smoke and sound effects—up through the top of the screen to transform into Jackson in the flesh, offering as sign of his "Michaelness" a familiar (but awkwardly executed) dance step. This event is repeated, twice, the third Michael leaping up, with smoke, from beneath the stage at the center of the football field. The television "effect" of simultaneity is achieved by quick cuts from one Jackson-clone to the next, in long, somewhat anonymous shots, so that he seems to be in three places at once: multiple Michaels, dressed alike, grabbing their multiple crotches. That the Michael on the midfield stage adds lip-synching to his stepping suggests that he is the final and authentic Michael.

But such a presumption is also impossible to make, at such a distance, in such a crowd, with such inadequate sound equipment. What can terms like "final" or "authentic" mean under these circumstances? Their irrelevance and meaning are secured by the third Michael Jackson's "effect": as he stands erect and immobile, confirmation of his singular identity erupts as the crowd's affirming roar. The stadium full of football fans (now transformed into Michael Jackson fans), the hundreds of eager LA children (dressed in their eerie "It's a Small World"-style international costumes), and the backup band.[30] The Superbowl show reduces the *Dangerous* tour to some twelve minutes, which repeat previous Michael Jackson tours, which repeat Jackson Five tours. Yet the Superbowl show also repudiates this repeatable history as ground for identity, in its insistence on one Michael's status as "real" and original. The very extravagance of the display names its artifice. As Butler writes, "Part of what constitutes sexuality is precisely that which does not appear and that, to some degree, can never appear"; what remains invisible at the Superbowl (in the extreme scale, distance, and special effectedness of the show) is Michael Jackson's sexuality, the signs of which are multiply overstated.

In *Bodies that Matter*, Butler argues further that the "normative force of performativity—its power to establish what qualifies as 'being'—works not only through reiteration, but through exclusion as well" (188). Overpresent and so excluded in the Superbowl show's finale is the economy of victimization which drives Jackson's performative history: the local children are dressed in international costumes, repeated as gigantic images constructed by the stadium audience brandishing colored placards, a sign which assimilates, reproduces, and finally makes invisible the "actual" children who are deployed here as ever in Jackson's universe, as victims (of hunger, war, abuse). Shot from the Goodyear blimp, the scene at the Superbowl is an infinite regression of repetition and imitation.

Butler writes that the subversive possibility of repetition comes in the intervals "between the acts . . . in which risk and excess threaten to disrupt the identity being constituted" (1991: 28). Available only *as* repetition (how many times will we watch him toss his hat, stand on his toes, and moonwalk for the "kid [who] is not [his] own"?), Michael Jackson cannot help but expose his intervals, the past images where his blackness and sex are less invisible, where a "real" self might emerge. But is this realness also an effect?[31]

Moonwalk like a Man

Jackson's narrative of black maleness—implied and renegotiated, for example, by appearances in "Jam" by famous (real) black male co-stars like Michael Jordan, Heavy D, and Kriss Kross—depends entirely on its management of counter-narratives. In "Jam," Jackson instructs Jordan in the art of "moonwalking," receiving in return lessons on basketball shooting. That Jackson makes an impossible (from the window of another building!) basket while Jordan never quite masters walking backwards suggests that Jackson's magical "effect" is limitless. The sexual and racial fantasy (which is perhaps more flamboyantly embodied by "Air Jordan," though equally under institutional and promotional control), is not threatening, even when Jackson renames it, variously and at different moments, "bad," "off the wall," or "dangerous."

The fantasy is repeatedly recuperable, made more strange as well as more contained, by his well-known psychic instability, produced by his victimization (by father and fans) and catalogued in the video "Leave Me Alone," which refers to the infamous hyperbaric sleeping chamber and his obsessions with the Elephant Man and Elizabeth Taylor. Rumors of freakishness, which clearly compel Jackson's (self-)interest as well as that of his audience, reproduce boundaries between spectacle and spectator. In "Speed Demon" (like "Leave Me Alone," part of the feature-length video *Moonwalker*), frantic fans chase Jackson, who becomes Sheer Effect, a rabbit, whose identity-as-Jackson is designated as dance steps and costume details, codes of an identity.

As trickster rabbit and claymation whirlwind (which momentarily assumes the shape of Pee-Wee Herman, of all people), a succession of Jacksons eluding his menacing fans here poses what Susan Willis calls "transformation as the site at which desire for black cultural autonomy coincides with the fetishization of commodity capitalism."[32] But while Willis sees in "Speed Demon" a critical interrogation of dominant, racist culture by traditional black images (like Brer Rabbit), it seems to me that the video's constant renegotiation of Jackson's body denies the essential identity necessary for such an incursion, leaving only the comprehension of Michaelness to viewers familiar with the codes: he is a set of acts and intervals, available for reading. Without an original, Jackson can only be an inexact copy of himself.

That is, rather than fixed identity Jackson offers something closer to drag, a show which resists normalization as it ironically observes it, exposing the seams of the display and the specific boundaries being crossed (this is opposed, for example, to passing, which would conceal the crossed boundaries of race, sex, or gender boundaries). The (not-real) threat of Jackson's drag rests with what Carole-Anne Tyler refers to as the "big bad dick," the appendage which "has figured so prominently in the history of race relations structured by fantasies of miscegenation and all too real lynchings."[33] The not-realness of Jackson's imitation of black male sexuality is related to the expressly oversized spectacle of the seven-foot-tall black drag queen RuPaul: both are clearly performing (a) sex and, in so doing, shift sites of audience identification; yet their acts do not significantly disturb the dominant "forms of difference" which designate self and other.[34]

As the name implies, the *Dangerous* album and tour over-inscribe these forms (sex and race) as hazards to normative structures. In particular, the show draws a difference between Jackson and his audience. On stage, he repeats "I love you," yet he remains resolutely removed, surrounded—even shielded—by hunky dancers on stage.[35] At the same time, however, the show from Bucharest, televised on HBO, progressively dismantles the distinction between Jackson and his nearly all-white, largely female audience, revealing his similarity to them, their shared emotions and shared spectatorship. Yet, as Nadja Tesich (reporting for *The Nation*) suggests, the very real war-zone "danger" of Bucharest made Jackson's "prancing" on stage seem quite "chilling."[36] His out-of-placeness in this milieu of ongoing (real) victimization is underlined by his difference from his fellow performers. Dressed in a gold bodysuit over his black trousers (a crotch-accentuating outfit recalling the most flamboyant of Madonna's Gaultier ensembles), Jackson is easily the whitest, femmest person on stage. His interracial, macho-male backup dancers wear military uniforms and carry guns, alternately emulating Public Enemy's well-trained S1Ws and Blond Ambition's well-muscled ironworkers.

Here his exorbitant strangeness might approximate what Donna Haraway has called "the promises of monsters," or the "empty space, the undecidability, the wiliness of other actors, the 'negativity,'" that challenge the conventional presumptions of representability.[37] At the same time, however, Jackson's privilege, however monstrous (and this recalls his transformations for *Thriller*[38]), sets him apart (more other?) from the "in/appropriated other" Haraway theorizes. His otherness is a trick, but not unfamiliar enough (the show, after all, is always the same: "Billie Jean" and "Bad"). As even a Caucasian dancer looks "blacker" than Jackson, his body-whitening produces an interminable "moment of undecidability" ("the legend continues . . . "). Mercer asserts that such a moment is "rarely experienced as a purely textual event; rather it is the point where politics and the contestations of power are most felt to be at their most intense" (1991b 191). "Most felt," that is, by Jackson's audience, eager to feel, briefly, the danger that Jackson acts and recuperates for them.

"I ain't scared a no sheets"

The contestations of power most evident in the original seven-minute version of "Black or White" (which aired 15 Nov. 1991) have to do with race; in this strenuously well-intentioned call to worldwide racial harmony, however, these tensions are displaced onto sexuality. The first five minutes of the video construct a series of narrative conflicts which are eventually resolved: father and son, imperialist invasion and native peoples, urban traffic and traditional ritual. Once-young rock fan Macaulay Culkin blasts his oppressive father (George Wendt) literally through the roof of their suburban home and we see a sequence of multicultural, international communities from which Jackson remains removed (as a technologically advanced visitor to various spectacularly "other" sets in Africa, the southwest U.S., and Russia, he appears to be in a different visual register altogether).

The first section's finale features Jackson atop a highly stylized Statue of Liberty, full of expansive bravado: "I ain't scared a no sheets," he sings, granting Klan sheets and bedsheets as equal threats. The artifice of the set suggests less that Jackson is an emblem of freedom than a product of non-choices. Despite the lyrics' expressed sentiment that it "don't matter if you're black or white," Jackson's own blackness is clearly effaced by his light skin contrasted to other nonwhite figures, and at the same time reconfirmed by his difference from Culkin's synched "rap" performance. (Culkin's lip-synching of "I'm not gonna spend my life bein' a color" is tempered, of course, by the fact that he's a blond 12-year-old billionaire who doesn't have to.)

"Black or White" 's justly famous morphing sequence digitally erases racial and sexual differences in favor of like rhythms and head-bobbings; most of the faces lip-synch to Jackson's voice, allowing a contradiction like that posed by the Statue of Liberty sequence: this techno-blending emphasizes Jackson's surgical and "otherworldly" differences, especially in his own morphing. He's transformed from a black panther (an icon which surely carries a specific U.S. mass-cultural reference to threatening black masculinity), indicating that his version of street violence and sexuality results from a kind of elaborate cultural dysphoria: his unstable body confuses personal history, public mythology, and social realities.

While the video doesn't confront the sexual-political significance of Jackson's metamorphosis—from panther to post-*Thriller* gangsta-monster—it imagines him as an angry urban youth who leaps to the roof of an American car, wrecks it with a crowbar, then zips up his fly, this last image in close-up. The public uproar over this part—or "Michael Jackson's Video Nightmare," according to *Entertainment Weekly*—erupted in the guise of "Simpsons" viewers' alarm at the explicit masturbation sequence. (The most obvious problem with citing this particular group's outrage is the assumption that "Simpsons" viewers are committed to the right-wing version of "family values"; see Homer Simpson's coda to the video, when he turns his cartoon remote control at the "camera" and zaps *us* out of existence.[39])

According to *Entertainment Weekly*, one viewer exclaimed "He wasn't just grabbing his crotch—he was *rubbing* it."[40] That there is no penis in sight during this sequence is clearly beside the point of the outrage: the implication is enough, the penis is assumed. Coming three months after Pee-Wee masturbated in a Sarasota porn theater and a year after Madonna performed masturbation on stage while singing "Like a Virgin," the uproar seems inordinate unless recontextualized by his blackness. In Jackson, the constructedness of racial difference is uniquely transparent: his is an always potentially violent body, temporarily tamed by his subscription to regulatory schemas, but also anticipating the angry chaos of the LA Uprising, and the legal and sexual threats posed by Supreme Court nominee Clarence Thomas (the hearings being a lengthy televisual spectacle which seemed particularly fraught precisely with what remained unspoken: Thomas's blackness ["the best man for the job"]).

Jackson's subsequent decision to cut the video's "offending" portion, to excise the masturbatory member that remains not-seen, imitates his continuing surgical reconstruction. (At the time, he read from a prepared statement: "I deeply regret any pain or hurt that the final segment of 'Black or White' has caused children, their parents, or any other viewers" [quoted in *ET* 42].) So the painful, aching, unseen penis is now publicly *removed*, capitulating to fear of violent black male sexuality even in its representational absence.

Closets

This absence is reworked in the second video single from *Dangerous*, "In the Closet." The irony of its title is underlined by the penis problem, and the "danger" he poses seemed to implode when the child-abuse charges were made public, which compounded the problem of categorization: if it was always clear that he wasn't quite "straight," now it appeared that his sexuality was more transgressive than absent. As Jackson began the album tour overseas, events in California plagued him. Continuing to perform an ambiguous but ever-lustful sexuality (recoded as that "slave-to-the-rhythm" autoeroticism), he ignored and then denied the allegations. In this context, the question of his possible homosexuality became inflammatory; gayness was attached to perversion and abuse. The possibility that he was not heterosexual had never been quite repressed, despite his repeated denials that he was homosexual. Even his mother joined the discussion: "He is not gay," Katherine said, "It's against our religion."[41] Jackson's "not-gayness" has become another, more convoluted, phobic drag: he drags as "not-gay," or as not-"in the closet."

The video of "In the Closet," from *Dangerous*, incarnates the problems unanswered by repetition—difference and history—not in Jackson but in his designated other, the dark-skinned, full-lipped Naomi Campbell. First, some questionable history in the interest of reconstructing false origins: when Jackson conceived the title "In the Closet," according to unreliable narrator Madonna, he asked for her collaboration on the lyrics. She suggested that he didn't understand the full meaning of the phrase, but he insisted that he did. She agreed to write lyrics. But the explicit lyrics she composed, says Madonna, shocked Jackson, who rejected them for the normative heterosexual romance of the produced song: the chorus repeats that "She wants to give it, ahh she wants to give it."

Not surprisingly, even in Herb Ritts's vision of hetero heaven, the problem posed by Jackson's closeted penis keeps coming up, almost like that haunting process that Sedgwick calls "de-negation." Unresolvable, the difference between Jackson and his audience, Jackson and Campbell, Jackson and his deracinated heterosexual self-image continues. The extremely pale and t-shirted Jackson (perhaps the most skin he has revealed in a video to date) dances with himself, accompanied only in different frames by the darker, taller supermodel Campbell (who is also visible kissing Madonna in the *Sex* book), both offset by a brief sequence featuring earnest "native" women. The editing is fast and on-beat, the shots are sharply angled, the bodies are hot.

But the sex is expressly single—save for Jackson and Campbell's repeated, mutual masturbation, and the climactic zoom to Jackson diving feet first through Campbell's legs. Naomi rolls in the dust. Michael dances in doorways, in closets. He sings, passionately, " 'Cause if it's aching, you gotta rub it." This narrative of pain and pleasure (not to mention cause and effect) emphasizes the video's concern with indistinct boundaries, and the political evacuation of the phrase "in the closet." What is repressed here? If the meaning of "it"—in "If it's aching"—is clear (but unseen) in this context; not so the meaning of "you." Given previous references to the black heterosexual "she" played by Campbell, Jackson's lyric would seem to address young "men" like himself; but who would that possibly be? Masturbating men? Gay men? Black men? For that matter, could he be singing to me? As whom and for whom is Michael Jackson constructing himself, or passing in and out of this closet? And would these all be the same, unseeing audiences?

The skeletal appearance of Jackson's silhouette in the (closet) doorway further suggests both a loss of identity and a renegotiation of body boundaries to confirm identity. In her essay, "The *Empire* Strikes Back: A Posttranssexual Manifesto," Sandy Stone writes, "Under the binary phallocratic founding myth by which Western bodies and subjects are constituted, only one body per gendered subject is 'right' " (297). But Jackson never gets it "right." Indeed, the not-male Jackson repeats the body of the not-female Jackson, as the not-gay Jackson repeats the body and narrative of the not-straight Jackson—inexactly, it is not quite "right," not quite gendered, not quite a subject either. Instead, this auto-erotic body offers explicit signs of gender, a technically refitted girlish voice (compared throughout to Campbell's husky whispers) and an increasingly white and unformed physique.

Indeed, the "intervals" exposed by Jackson's self-repetition are his own history and difference: the whiteness, the narrow nose, the cleft chin, the lipstick, and the eyeliner; his embodiment of an anti-essentialist argument becomes tenuous when compared to earlier, "essential" self-images. This troubling disjunction was assailed by Arsenio Hall last summer, during an opening monologue when he "spontaneously" ran an Elvis-stamp-like competition, encouraging viewers to vote on their preference for the younger Michael or the new, "aerodynamic model." The predictable results (favoring the younger, blacker Jackson) imply that the changes in Jackson's body, his repeated denials that he has undergone any surgery or chemical processes, and his radical repression of racial and sexual definition, offend the majority of hip, aggressively stylish Arsenio-watchers, who have politicized both blackness and sex.

The same ambiguity and indecision receive more sympathetic treatment in the Oprah interview, where Michael's calculated vulnerability was witnessed by an estimated 90 million viewers. His publicist affirmed, "He exposed himself to the world. He showed the world that he's a very articulate, normal, loving, caring human being." As his public mothers comforted him—Liz Taylor asserted his normalcy, saying, "He is the least weird man I have ever known," and Oprah granted him the televisual space to reclaim his victimhood—Jackson seemed unbelievably stiff and uncomfortable (the illusion of victimization remained intact), surrounded by signs of his wealth and isolation, closeted even as he "exposed himself."

As I suggested earlier, I'm left with more questions than answers about Michael Jackson and his penis. These questions and the masturbatory effects he shares with his audience are amplified and refracted in the Oprah interview, then multiplied in the news and tabloid coverage of the sexual abuse charges. Oprah mirrored Michael, they shared the television frame as larger-than-life, too-public bodies, de- and re-constructed perpetually, for the entertainment of their watchers. Holding court as media royalty, the Queen of Daytime and the King of Pop assuage each others' anxieties about their imperfect, black, and sexed bodies. And at last—after the nighttime tour of "Neverland," the brief glimpse at the Ferris wheel and the Oscar-flanked theater—came the much-anticipated question, the ritual of "truth" pledged by the interview's promotional apparatus. Oprah asked not "Are you gay?" or, "Are you a transsexual?" The question was transformed before our eyes: "Are you a virgin?" He giggled and might have blushed (though under the television lights and his white makeup it was difficult to gauge his response). "I'm a gentleman," he said. "And I'm embarrassed."

Embarrassed, innocent, alienated.

And now, married. The legend continues. The merger with Lisa Marie, *Jet* magazine reports (after mentioning that "*Thriller* is still the largest-selling album"), means that Michael wants something more: "children of my own."[42] And yet, perhaps despite this most recent gesture toward domestic normalcy, sexual containment, and cross-racial identification, the problem that Michael Jackson embodies continues to excite his watchers. "Michael's fans are among the most loyal," asserts *Entertainment Weekly*. "People feel he's a victim." And the "*EW* poll" suggests that Jackson's popularity has risen since the charges were made: "sympathy seems to have bought Jackson *more* fans."[43] Bought, ready, and desirous, fans continue to thrill to the excesses of Michael Jackson's penis.

Notes

1. Michael Jackson's address to the "nation," undertaken shortly after Johnnie Cochran came on as his lawyer, was disseminated "live" from his Neverland Ranch; as Jackson spoke, he was clearly close to tears (this particular performance is a standard sequence from his stage show) and outraged by the emotional abuses he suffered at the hands of authorities. In its various repetitions over the week that followed, the sections from the transmission which were most frequently rerun had to do with the search and documentation of his "body."

2. The *National Examiner*'s front page when the story broke was particularly exclamatory, featuring a row of seven photos of children with *Court TV*-style anonymous blue dots on their faces, against the screaming headline: "Kids & Sex: Jacko Tells All! His Side of the Story" (*National Examiner*, 21 Sept. 1993); the comparably more sedate and insidious *New York Post* headline, "Peter Pan or Pervert?" is accompanied by a typically scary (here called "animated") image of Jackson in performance and the subheadline, "Michael Jackson on kid-sex allegations: 'Horrendous'" (*New York Post*, 25 Aug. 1993). The syndicated television shows *Hard Copy*, *A Current Affair*, and *Inside Edition* covered the scandal with a much contrived pseudo-breathlessness, from August 1993 through January 1994 on a day-to-day basis, including stories on the

boy's parents, Jackson's security chief Anthony Pellicano's denials of Jackson's wrongdoing, the Jackson family's news conference, Elizabeth Taylor's trip to Taiwan to comfort "Michael," and the "diary" produced by Jackson's ex-housekeepers, Mark and Faye Quindoy. And indeed, the apparent sign of Jackson's heterosexual normalcy—his marriage—was almost immediately challenged as illegal and illegitimate. See for example, *Hard Copy*, 15 and 16 August 1994, which featured an interview with a "detective" who claimed that Lisa Marie's divorce from Danny Keough was not properly announced in Dominican newspapers; and the *National Globe*: "Lisa Marie and Jacko's Marriage is a Sham! Judge who performed the ceremony reveals: 'When I pronounced them man & wife they sort of brushed cheeks. . . . You call that a kiss? There was no passion there' (and, the most damning of evidence, also from the judge: 'He wore a lot of makeup—much more than Lisa Marie') " (6 Sept. 1994: 17).

   3. *New York*'s Edwin Diamond wrote, "Whatever the outcome, the fingerprints of one culprit are already on this sordid story. The press, mainstream and tab, high and low, helped in the creation of the character named 'Michael Jackson' " ("We Are the Weird," *New York*, 13 Sept. 1993: 28); *Nightline* took the journalistic high road, investigating the impact of the accusations on the international business world, specifically Jackson's pricey contracts with Pepsi and Sony ("Star-Making, Star-Breaking," *Nightline*, 26 Aug. 1993); and Richard Corliss listed multiple examples of tabloid hysteria, observing that "show biz is part of every scandal," and closing with this moralizing caution to his subject: "The children are watching, Michael. They want to believe that you'd never hurt them—that you are their best, sweetest, secret friend" ("Who's Bad?" *Time*, 6 Sept. 1993: 54, 56). PBS's *Frontline* ran a special report, "Tabloid Truth," chronicling (and indicting) the media frenzy, on 15 February 1994.

   4. Richard Corliss observes that the Los Angeles Police Department was brandishing its own grim irony. When asked when the results of their investigation would be available, LAPD spokesman Arthur Holmes declared, "It could be tomorrow, it could be two months from now. We solve no crime before its time" ("Who's Bad?" *Time*, Sept. 1993: 54).

   5. David Friend, "Michael in Wonderland," *Life* 16.7 (June 1993): 54.

   6. Alan Light, "Jackson's Most Dangerous Game," *Rolling Stone* (Feb. 1993).

   7. See, for example, *People*, 15 August 1994: "Now, though criminal charges could still be brought against him [the private settlement did not, ostensibly, deter the LAPD investigation into the allegations], Michael Jackson is once again the sweetly smiling pop idol who can draw adoring fans to a steamy New York City street corner on the chance that they might catch a glimpse of him and his bride" (34).

   8. A typical Jackson performative ploy (which has been part of the stage act since at least 1987) is his seemingly spontaneous invitation to a young (preferably sobbing with uncontrollable passion) female audience member to join him onstage: they embrace, he is also overcome with emotion and stops singing, they part, they embrace again, she is dragged from the stage by a crew member. Michael, overwhelmed, must bow his head, catch his breath, and only after some minutes of this display, returns to the vigorous rhythms of the show.

   9. Since I have been working on this project and the child-abuse charges have been made, I have been asked repeatedly, "Did he do it?"; my "expertise" on the subject of Michael Jackson apparently suggesting that I would "know." My answer is usually a reframing of the question: the generalized concern with Jackson's sexual identity and activity (often voiced by people who have no interest in his music or performances) seems directly to the point of my argument that he embodies specific and topical cultural anxieties.

   10. Homi K. Bhabha, "The Other Question: The Stereotype and Colonial Discourse," in *The Sexual Subject: A Screen Reader in Sexuality*, ed. Mandy Merck (New York: Routledge, 1992): 313. Further references will be made in parentheses in the text.

   11. Chris Bury's report on the impact of child-abuse allegations on Jackson's contracts

with Pepsi and Sony/Epic Records preceded Ted Koppel's interviews with Jay Coleman, founder and CEO of Entertainment Management and Communications Inc. (EMCI, which brokered a deal between Pepsi and Jackson), advertising executive Jerry Della Femina, and gossip columnist Liz Smith. The report included an interview with Jordan Goodman of *Money* magazine, who assessed Jackson's $65 million contract with Sony as proof that the star is "really such an important property that if he in fact implodes based on all these allegations, that would have a major impact on Sony" ("Star-Making, Star-Breaking," *Nightline*, 26 August 1993).

12. This penis (at least in representation) also proved to be the subject of controversy when it served as the title of this essay, first presented at the Unnatural Acts Conference at the University of California, Riverside. At the time (12–14 Feb. 1993), local newspaper editorials and accounts of conference funding debates cited this title as exemplary of the conference's general concern with "deviant" objects. And afterwards, this mention appeared in *The Advocate*'s "Dossier" section:

"Here, courtesy of the journal *Heterodoxy*, is a partial agenda for this semester's Unnatural Acts Conference, sponsored by the College of Humanities and Social Sciences at the University of California, Riverside: 'Taking on the Phallus,' 'Boys Will Be Girls,' 'Michael Jackson's Penis,' 'Amelia Earhart in Drag,' and 'Lesbians Who Kill.'

"Including, presumably, lesbians who have to listen to a discussion about Michael Jackson's penis" ("Whatever Happened to ECON 101?" *The Advocate*, 628, 4 May 1993: 7).

13. Jackson has been quoted: "I get so many letters asking if I had a sex change or if I go with guys or thinking I'm married to Clifton Davis" (Catherine Dineen, *Michael Jackson: In His Own Words*, London: Omnibus, 1993: 25).

14. See, for example, Marjorie Garber, *Vested Interests: Cross-Dressing and Cultural Anxiety* (New York: Harper Perennial 1992); Moe Meyer, "Unveiling the Word: Science and Narrative in Transsexual Striptease," in *Gender in Performance: The Presentation of Difference in the Performing Arts*, ed. Laurence Senelick (Hanover, NH: University Press of New England, 1992); and Sandy Stone, "The *Empire* Strikes Back: A Posttranssexual Manifesto," in *Body Guards: The Cultural Politics of Gender Ambiguity*, ed. Julia Epstein and Kristina Straub (New York: Routledge, 1991).

15. The World Music Awards, broadcast on ABC, 1 June 1993, included lifetime achievement presentations for Luciano Pavarotti and Tina Turner, but it was evident that the occasion was mounted for the worship of the "King of Pop," who appeared in the credits sequence apart from the other luminaries and sat in the front row all evening beside Prince Albert of Monaco, honored repeatedly for his financial successes ("Best Selling American Artist," "Best Selling Pop Artist," and "World's Best Selling Artist of the Year"). That he also had the boy who would three months later accuse him of molestation on his lap during part of these proceedings is, to say the least, ironic. His last acceptance speech ends with the mispronunciation, "Mercy, mercy, beaucoup." It seems appropriate.

16. In an exemplary display of unrelated emotional responses, *Newsweek* readers wrote letters in response to a cover story—categorized under "Lifestyle"—called "Michael's World" (6 Sept. 1993), which underlined his "eccentricities." Letter-writers argued that *Newsweek*'s coverage was "a glitzier form of the pseudojournalism found in the *National Enquirer*" or unfair; berated parents for letting their children sleep over at Jackson's house; and that "the gloved one needs to open his eyes" and not sleep with children ("Letters," *Newsweek*, 27 Sept. 1993: 14).

17. Eve Kosofsky Sedgwick, *The Epistemology of the Closet* (Berkeley: University of California Press, 1990): 1. She goes on to say that "the relations of the closet—the relations of the known and the unknown, the explicit and the inexplicit around homo/heterosexual definition—have the potential for being peculiarly revealing, in fact, about speech acts than more generally" (3). Further references will be made in parentheses in the text.

18. Certainly Oprah Winfrey has undergone her own battery of publicized self-transformations, from weight loss (her talk show promotional stills no longer attempt to keep up with her drastic changes in appearance), to marital status (the on-again, off-again wedding date), to personal history (a survivor of child abuse). All of these changes are extremely public, the topic of common discussions.

19. This question of self-exploitation comes up more often in the case of Madonna, who appears to display herself as an untraditional female "sex object." Related questions include: Does she exploit her black dancers? Does making exorbitant amounts of money from the performance preclude being exploited? For an incisive discussion of Madonna's exploitations and appropriations, see Amy Robinson, "Is She or Isn't She?: Madonna and the Erotics of Appropriation," in *Acting Out: Feminist Performances*, ed. Lynda Hart and Peggy Phelan (Ann Arbor: University of Michigan Press, 1993). And again, the narrative of victimization is familiar within debates over African American identities. For a recent and controversial consideration of this narrative's relation to affirmative action and other social and political conditions, see, for example, Shelby Steele, *The Content of Our Character: A New Vision of Race in America* (New York: St. Martin's Press, 1990).

20. In the ABC miniseries, *The Jacksons: An American Dream* (which aired in December 1992), Lawrence Hilton Jacobs plays Joseph Jackson as a kind of stock villain, beating his sons, driving them to practice, demanding unreasonable sacrifices from his daughters and wife (Angela Bassett; also an abused wife, Tina Turner, in the theatrical release, *What's Love Got To Do With It?* [1993]). LaToya Jackson claims that her father sexually abused her as well, and has gone on in various interviews since the child-abuse allegations to hint that Michael's "eccentric" behaviors are linked to Joseph's habitual offenses. Like Michael, LaToya is committed to playing the victim. For example, speaking by remote with Katie Couric on *Today* (2 Sept. 1993), LaToya (whom Couric calls "perhaps the most outspoken of the Jackson family") is visibly frustrated, unable to deny the possibility that the allegations are "true": "I'm not a judge, and I really don't know." Couric, on the same/other hand, has no "hard news" basis for the interview; all she can ask is what LaToya thinks "might be true." LaToya, however, does charge the family for "condoning" child abuse.

21. Jackson used this phrase during his interview with Oprah, when she asked him, in the name of "concerned parents," why he grabs his crotch on stage.

22. Judith Butler, *Bodies that Matter: On the Discursive Limits of "Sex"* (New York: Routledge, 1993): 130. Further references will be made in parentheses in the text.

23. One of the most famous instances of Jackson's invocation of victim status is the "Message from Michael," sent to *People Weekly* in 1987. His hand-scrawled note is reproduced in full, with misspellings: "Like the old Indian proverb says, do not judge a man until you've walked 2 moons in his moccosins. Most people don't know me, that is why they write such things in wich most is not true. I cry very often because it hurts and I wory about the children all my children all over the world, I live for them. If a man could say nothing against a character but what he could prove, history could not be written. Animals strike, not from malice, but because they want to live, it is the same with those who criticize, they desire our blood, not our pain. But I still must achieve I must seek truth in all things. I must endure for the power I was sent forth, for the world for ~~my~~ the children. But have mercy, for I've been bleeding a long time now." The images (blood, animals, vampires, "Indians") here are suggestive of a very conventional world order, where Michael remains faultless and abused and the rest of the world violates him (William Small, "Michael's First Epistle." *People Weekly* 28.15, 12 Oct. 1987: 102).

24. The revelation on the Oprah interview (10 February 1993) that he has a disease which causes his skin to change color and appear blotchy was immediately followed up by stories in the tabloids about other victims of such a disease. For example, the *Globe* ran a story with the

headline, "I Watched Wacko Jacko Turn White Before My Eyes," supported by a lie detector "analysis" of his voice as recorded from the broadcast interview (the "I" of the headline is the perennial "one of the singer's aides"; this report is accompanied by a story about a man, Jaron Yaltan, who "turned white in just six days" because of virtiligo [*Globe*, 2 Mar. 1993: 20–21]).

25. Kobena Mercer, "Monster Metaphors: Notes on Michael Jackson's *Thriller*" in *Stardom: Industry of Desire*, ed. Christine Gledhill (London: Routledge, 1991): 302. Further references will be made in parentheses in the text, designated Mercer 1991a.

26. Robert Scheer, "Mega-Michael," *The Nation* 257.11 (11 Oct. 1993): 376. Further references will be cited in parentheses in the text.

27. Taylor made a second remarkable evaluation, when, as she faced Oprah with Jackson standing uncomfortably behind her, she declared, "Michael is the least weird man I have ever known."

28. Judith Butler, "Imitation and Gender Insubordination," in *Inside/Out: Lesbian Theories, Gay Theories*, ed. Diana Fuss (New York: Routledge 1991): 27. Further references will be made in parentheses in the text.

29. June Reich, "Genderfuck: The Law of the Dildo," *Discourse* 15.1 (fall 1992): 120. Further references will be made in parentheses in the text.

30. The band includes a black rapper, because any nebulously black singer must have one (see also Prince and Mariah Carey) and an amazonian bassist with a white punk mane, whose masculine aggressiveness makes Jackson look slight and feminine by comparison.

31. Here I would again offer Madonna as Jackson's reverse-image, the anti-Michael; responses to *Truth or Dare* typically include frustration that there is no "truth" in sight. The point for both Madonna and Jackson is that the promise of "truth," the suggestion that it might be there, underneath, waiting to be exorcized, is exactly what sells one million copies of *Sex* or grants the Oprah interview an enormous Nielsen rating.

32. Susan Willis, *A Primer for Daily Life* (New York: Routledge, 1991): 129.

33. Carole-Anne Tyler, "Boys Will Be Girls: The Politics of Gay Drag," in *Inside/Out: Lesbian Theories, Gay Theories*, ed. Diana Fuss (New York: Routledge, 1991): 62.

34. See, for example, RuPaul's performance on MTV's "Beauty and the Beach" (spring 1993). His expansive, clearly-defined-as-drag performance before a nearly all-white teenage audience hardly upsets the boundaries of sex, gender, race, and class that enables these students to travel to Florida during "spring break." The audience responded to RuPaul with something less than enthusiasm. Andrew Ross, writing on gangsta and diva "realness," observes that the crowd responded with "seriously muted applause—a reaction that was probably part embarrassment, part homophobia, and part jaw-dropped amazement at just how damned good she was" ("The Gangsta and the Diva," *The Nation* 259.6 (Aug. 22/29, 1994: 191). For a more recent and even more disturbing performance, see RuPaul at the 1993 MTV Music Video Awards, where she read her co-presenter Milton Berle. After he made remarks and gestures about her body, she insinuated that he was wearing "diapers."

35. Jackson's verbal devotion to his fans is well known. The 1993 World Music Awards offers one example of the elaborate staging of these declarations of "love." As he came to the stage three times, white girls in expensive evening dresses squealed, jumped, and tittered. Each time Jackson says, like a mantra, "I love you, I love you." They squealed again.

36. Nadja Tesich, "Belgrade: Theater of War," *The Nation* 256.5 (8 Feb. 1993): 176.

37. Donna Haraway, "The Promises of Monsters: A Regenerative Politics for In/Appropriated Others," in *Cultural Studies*, ed. Lawrence Grossberg, Cary Nelson, and Paula Treichler (New York: Routledge 1992): 313.

38. See Mercer, "Monster Metaphors."

39. We might also note that Jackson "appeared" on "The Simpsons" in 1992, as a white

(yellow) male character whom Homer meets in an insane asylum. The joke is that the character believes himself to be Michael Jackson, as he is "acted" or "voiced" by the ever-invisible Michael Jackson.

40. David Browne, "Michael Jackson's Black or White Blues." *Entertainment Weekly* 29 (1991): 40.

41. In J. Randy Taraborrelli, *Michael Jackson: The Magic and the Madness* (New York: Ballantine, 1991).

42. Robert E. Johnson, "Michael Jackson and Lisa Marie Presley 'Look Forward to Raising a Family and Living Happily,'" *Jet*, (22 August 1994): 60.

43. Dana Kennedy, "Is This the End?" *People Weekly*, 187 (10 Sept. 1993): 22–23. The observation has been made that if Jackson were proved innocent of all child-abuse charges, if he were proved to be a victim of extortion, as his public relations team maintains, that Jackson might emerge "triumphant." On *Nightline*, Daniel Goldberg of Atlantic Records says, "This is not an elected official or somebody like that, this is somebody whose job it is to sing and dance and make records and do shows. And unsubstantiated rumors are completely irrelevant." To which reporter Chris Bury adds, "Relevant or not, in show business rumors can take on a reality of their own" ("Star-Making, Star-Breaking," *Nightline*, 26 Aug. 1993).

Bibliography

Bhabha, Homi K. 1983, 1992. "The Other Question: The Stereotype and Colonial Discourse." In *The Sexual Subject: A Screen Reader in Sexuality*, ed. Mandy Merck. New York: Routledge.

Browne, David. 1991. "Michael Jackson's Black or White Blues." *Entertainment Weekly* 29: 38–44.

Butler, Judith. 1993. *Bodies that Matter: On the Discursive Limits of "Sex."* New York: Routledge.

———. 1991. "Imitation and Gender Insubordination." In *Inside/Out: Lesbian Theories, Gay Theories*, ed. Diana Fuss. New York: Routledge.

de Lauretis, Teresa. 1987. *Technologies of Gender: Essays on Film, Fiction, Theory.* Bloomington: Indiana University Press.

Diamond, Edwin. 13 September 1993. "We Are the Weird." *New York.*

Diawara, Manthia. 1988, 1992. "Black Spectatorship: Problems of Identification and Resistance." *Screen*, 29.4: 66–76, reprinted in *Black American Cinema*, edited by Manthia Diawara. New York: Routledge.

Dineen, Catherine. 1993. *Michael Jackson in His Own Words.* London: Omnibus.

Fanon, Frantz. 1970. *Black Skin, White Masks.* London: Paladin.

Friend, David. June 1993. "Michael in Wonderland." *Life.*

Garber, Marjorie. 1992. *Vested Interests: Cross-Dressing and Cultural Anxiety.* New York: Harper-Perennial.

Haraway, Donna. 1991. "A Cyborg Manifesto: Science, Technology, and Socialist Feminism in the Late Twentieth Century." *Simians, Cyborgs, and Women: The Reinvention of Nature.* New York: Routledge.

———. 1992. "The Promises of Monsters: A Regenerative Politics for In/Appropriated Others." In *Cultural Studies*, edited by Lawrence Grossberg, Cary Nelson, and Paula Treichler. New York: Routledge.

hooks, bell. 1992. "Reconstructing Black Masculinity." *Black Looks: Race and Representation.* Boston: South End Press.

Jackson, LaToya, with Patricia Romanowski. 1991. *LaToya: Growing Up in the Jackson Family.* New York: Dutton.

Jackson, Michael. 1988. *Moonwalk.* New York: Doubleday.

———. 1992. *Dancing the Dream: Poems and Reflections.* New York: Doubleday.

Johnson, Robert E. 22 August 1994. "Michael Jackson and Lisa Marie Presley 'Look Forward to Raising a Family and Living Happily.' " *Jet.*

Kennedy, Dana. 10 September 1993. "Is This the End?" *People Weekly*, 187.

Lewis, Lisa. 1990. *Gender Politics and MTV: Voicing the Difference.* Philadelphia: Temple University Press.

Light, Alan. February 1993. "Jackson's Most Dangerous Game." *Rolling Stone.*

Mercer, Kobena. 1991. "Monster Metaphors: Notes on Michael Jackson's *Thriller.*" In *Stardom: Industry of Desire*, ed. Christine Gledhill. London: Routledge.

———. 1991. "Skin Head Sex Thing: Racial Difference and the Homoerotic Imaginary." In *How Do I Look? Queer Film and Video*, ed. Bad Object-Choices. Seattle: Bay Press.

Meyer, Moe. 1992. "Unveiling the Word: Science and Narrative in Transsexual Striptease." In *Gender in Performance: The Presentation of Difference in the Performing Arts*, ed. Laurence Senelick. Hanover, NH: University Press of New England.

Reich, June. Fall 1992. "Genderfuck: The Law of the Dildo." *Discourse*, 15.1: 112–27.

Robinson, Amy. 1993. "Is She or Isn't She?: Madonna and the Erotics of Appropriation." In *Acting Out: Feminist Performances*, ed. Lynda Hart and Peggy Phelan. Ann Arbor: University of Michigan Press.

Ross, Andrew. 22/29 August 1994. "The Gangsta and the Diva." *The Nation*, 259.6.

Sedgwick, Eve Kosofsky. 1990. *The Epistemology of the Closet.* Berkeley: University of California Press.

Small, William. 12 October 1986. "Michael's First Epistle." *People Weekly*, 28.15.

Steele, Shelby. 1990. *The Content of Our Character: A New Vision of Race in America.* New York: St. Martin's Press.

Stone, Sandy. 1991. "The *Empire* Strikes Back: A Posttranssexual Manifesto." In *Body Guards: The Cultural Politics of Gender Ambiguity*, ed. Julia Epstein and Kristina Straub. New York: Routledge.

Taraborrelli, J. Randy. 1991. *Michael Jackson: The Magic and the Madness.* New York: Ballantine.

Tesich, Nadja. 8 Feb 1993. "Belgrade: Theater of War." *The Nation*, 256.5: 174–76.

Trinh T. Minh-ha. 1992. *When the Moon Waxes Red: Representation, Gender, and Cultural Politics.* New York: Routledge.

Tyler, Carole-Anne. 1991. "Boys Will Be Girls: The Politics of Gay Drag." In *Inside/Out: Lesbian Theories, Gay Theories*, ed. Diana Fuss. New York: Routledge.

Wallace, Michele. 1990. "Michael Jackson, Black Modernisms, and 'The Ecstasy of Communication.' " *Invisibility Blues: From Pop to Theory.* London: Verso.

Willis, Susan. 1991. *A Primer for Daily Life.* New York: Routledge.

3

The Telephone and Its Queerness

Ellis Hanson

Bad Connections

I'll tell you right out, I'm a man who likes talking to a man who likes to talk.

—Sydney Greenstreet in *The Maltese Falcon*

WHILE JULIA KRISTEVA's attitudes towards homoeroticism, not to mention illness, are rarely revolutionary, one passage from her essay on AIDS and Eros resonates in my mind: "There is, too, the possibility of discovering new erogenous zones, the arousal of tenderness, and (at last!) the erotic use of speech. Could the threat of AIDS be the harbinger of a new libertine practice, one less performative but more diverting, more narcissistically perverse?"[1] One such erotic use of speech, no doubt suitably perverse by her standards, is phone sex, an industry which has been booming in response to the demand for varieties of safe sex that in some way preserve the sexual liberation of the seventies. But other questions remain: How is the experience of desire between men transformed by the telephone? What is the psychic significance of telephone eroticism in the epidemic that is in large part responsible for its sudden popularity? In psychoanalytic literature, the telephone has had a lively history and there is already a considerable canon of writing on the disembodied voice. My own focus here will be on the relationship of mourning and paranoia to the telephone, especially with regard to queer people confronted with AIDS.[2]

Phone sex has a number of drawbacks, so I am told. Susan Sontag, in her book *AIDS and Its Metaphors*, sets the tone for the many critiques of phone sex when she refers to it as "commercially organized lechery."[3] Surely *lechery* is one of those quaint terms that the metaphor maven would have done well to retire, but her comment points to a more widespread panic about the relationship of sex to commerce. There is an assumption running rampant in our midst that sex can be cordoned off as some sort of transcendent phenomenon, a pure expression of nature that is, or ought to be, innocent of politics and commercial exchange. This edenic illusion seeks to deny the myriad ways in which commercial organization and libidinal organization tend to complement each other, whether one is

34

having sex in a real bedroom or a virtual one. Phone sex as perverse commerce poses a challenge to this illusion, however, and the response is often panic. The most paranoid one I have yet encountered occurs in Philip K. Dick's 1974 science fiction novel, *Flow My Tears, the Policeman Said*:

> Your—everybody's—sexual aspects are linked electronically, and amplified, to as much as you can endure. It's addictive, because it's electronically enhanced. People, some of them, get so deep into it they can't pull out; their whole lives revolve around the weekly—or, hell, even daily!—setting up of the network of phone lines. It's regular picture-phones, which you activate by credit card, so it's free at the time you do it; the sponsors bill you once a month and if you don't pay they cut your phone out of the grid.

In this novel, phone sex is likened to drug addiction and it leaves one looking "debauched, old, fat, listless—the latter between the phone-line orgies, of course."[4] Sex becomes decadent, artificial, even degenerate, as soon as one picks up the phone. In Dick's novel, the technical and the commercial fasten onto sexual desire like vampires, hooking people into an insidious system of exploitation. His concern is admirable but, implicit in this deliciously exaggerated sci-fi scenario, I find a familiar paranoid fantasy of sexual desire out of control, in need of discipline and punishment, transgressing its proper social limits. Through technology, desire makes brazen its age-old love affair with capital. So beware the queer cyborgs! Like Donna Haraway's cyborg feminists, they are bodies without organs, discursive phenomena, chips in the integrated circuit. They have no truck with innocence. They have always viewed sex as a site of political and economic negotiation. They place in doubt the conventional distinctions between human and machine, desire and commerce. Through the voice of the queer cyborg on the telephone, desire suffers a fall from nature into politics, only to find it has been there all along.[5]

But the woes of phone sex are many, and I should not be a judicious observer if I ignored a single complaint. Phone sex is said to be limited in its overemphasis on masturbation and fantasy. It is said to commodify sex by calculating pleasure in terms of dollars per minute and by dividing sex into highly fetishized behaviors or object choices (fisting, hairy men, twins . . . I am always surprised). Some readers and potential advertisers used to complain that trashy phone-sex ads crowd the pages of some queer magazines, but that was before all those magazines went upmarket. More disturbing than these complaints, I think, is the fact that phone sex clearly exposes its enthusiasts to further sexual harassment and surveillance by the government. As Avital Ronell has pointed out, this curious legislative prudery about the telephone is almost as old as the phone itself: "The courts had to determine whether the telephone amounted to an instrument of seduction and entry. Thus, in New England, a group of Puritans fought to have its material placement legally restricted. They sought law enforcement for the telephone's eviction from the bedroom."[6] In a more recent case James A. Maxwell, the commander of Goodfellow Air Force Base in Texas, was dismissed from the Air Force because his e-mail messages included sexually explicit language and graphics. The scary part is the role played by the FBI, which informed the Air Force of Maxwell's communications and which kept a record of all his e-mail (12,000 computer pages) and all his GIF files (39 floppy disks). There have been numerous efforts recently to legislate phone sex, primarily by way of the dubious argument that it will corrupt children. Gay men are still frequently victimized as a group by fallacious accusations of child abuse, but in legislation that seeks to curb commercial phone sex the telephone itself is the site of sexual panic, figured as a queer child-molester with his foot already inside the nursery door of every bourgeois home.

Phone sex certainly has its charms, though one would not know it from most of the accounts I have read. Despite its power to incite sexual panic, phone sex is a relatively safe and harmless pastime. Indeed, I cannot imagine a safer form of safe sex. One can transmit a great many things by telephone, but HIV is not one of them. Although a computer can catch a virus through a phoneline, a queer cyborg cannot. Phone sex is also safe in that, if someone is violent or offensive, I can always hang up. Or I can enjoy it, without getting killed. Phone sex allows for the promiscuity and anonymity often attributed to urban queer sexuality, though few have found it an adequate substitute for promiscuity in person. I would not exaggerate the virtues of phone sex as some sort of desperate sanctuary from the threat of HIV or as a guilty withdrawal from bodily contact, especially since such attitudes have been rendered unnecessary by, among other things, the invention of latex. I would argue, rather, for phone sex as a peculiar mode of queer pleasure, one which has obliged me to rethink the very category of the erotic in my own experience.

First of all, there is the ear. The eroticization of the ear has not gone unnoticed. In fact, not long ago, by dialing 1-800-FON-4-VOX one could hear a recorded sales pitch for Nicholson Baker's hetero phone-sex novel, *Vox*, asserting in a breathy voice that, "In the 90s, the most erogenous zone may be the human ear." In phone sex, after all, beauty is in the ear of the interlocutor. For those of us who do not yet have one of Philip K. Dick's picture-phones, what we hear is what we get. The telephone, because of its disembodiment of the voice, invites a polymorphous play of bodies and identities through description and narrative. The identity of a stranger on the phone is communicated entirely through electric speech. Race is particularly interesting in phone sex, since one cannot see the color of the other's skin. And yet, if the advertisements for commercial lines are any indication, race remains an important issue with many callers, such that some lines even claim that their operators or clientele are of African or Asian descent. If the callers have never seen each other, then race is communicated not through the visual spectacle of the body, which is problematic in itself, but through a promise, sometimes explicit, sometimes not. More so than ever, race becomes a discursive phenomenon, wholly a matter of confession, suggestion, presumption, accent, idiom, or other verbal cues that associate the caller with a particular racial subculture—but even then the potential for masquerade is enormous. The gender of the other is also determined by the voice. With the introduction of technology that disguises the voice, that raises or lowers its pitch, my perception of the gender of my interlocutor is more doubtful than ever. Nor is sexual orientation a given. I was struck by an account given by a lesbian phone-sex worker who found her straight male clients not only more attractive over the phone but also more open to sex roles that otherwise would embarrass them: "So I always try to stick my fingers up their ass, and I find that 90 percent of them are very relieved that I brought it up. . . . They have a way to get fucked, to be taken in, to be passive and to be receptive. But they've always been told that it's not OK, that they have to be the aggressor. It's not so much about fear as about letting go of power and about allowing yourself to surrender."[7] Is this a description of a hetero phone-sex line? Phone sex challenges the imagination and it privileges a renewed narrativity of desire and a renewed eroticization of the voice. It makes me peculiarly aware of the discursive limits of sex. The illusion of a body and a sexuality without language becomes difficult to sustain. The body as *imago*, as social and psychological construction, is nothing new but phone sex makes it difficult for me to deny the status of bodies and desires as narrative performances, as the phantasmatic effects of conversation with my new friend. The most attractive person is the one who spins the most intriguing tale, who speaks in the most disarming and uncanny voice. A beautiful voice incites in me a new dream of my own body, perhaps a new illusion of presence for the lost scene of desire, the lost purity of touch and gaze, at once reproduced and alienated in the very act of speaking or phoning. Eden returns again, but only as a phone message.

The telephone as an important mechanism of fantasy and pleasure in modernity is attested to by the burgeoning canon of psychological case studies on so-called telephone neuroses, compulsive telephoning, and perverse telephoning. Avital Ronell imagines "the eventual need, therefore, for a Psychoanalysis of the Telephone whose range of material symptomatologies would involve hang-up calls, obscene phone calls, phobias, compulsions (including telephone 'sex'), minitels, pregnaphones, car telephones, and other drives."[8] Her list does not include the pleasures of message machines, voice mail, computer conferencing, or telephone personal ads, nor for that matter the sadomasochistic thrills of telemarketing. For those who subscribe to Manhattan cable, there are also the queer amusements of "public access" stations with their hilariously cheesy late-night phone-sex commercials, a sort of backroom version of the Home Shopping Network. Ronell also neglects another new cyborg phenomenon: "phone phreaks," social outcasts turned cyberpunks who break into phone-company computers in order to pirate long hours of anonymous intimacy and subversive tinkering.[9]

There is also that favorite form of AIDS activism and queer protest known as the phone zap or FAX zap, made notorious by ACT UP when they assaulted the phone lines of homophobic businesspeople and journalists, tying them up for hours. There are a number of phone services that seem to be thinly disguised displacements of phone sex—for example, the confession line and dial-a-pope. The confession line allows one to call up and give a confession or hear one, while dial-a-pope gives one an ear to the Holy See with messages from Pope John Paul II in various languages (I have been warned, however, that the Pope's English is vaguely reminiscent of Henry Kissinger after Novocaine). In a similar vein, there is the Mary line, a hotline to the Holy Virgin herself, complete with a billboard campaign that depicts a Renaissance Madonna on the end of an umbilical phone cord, chatting with a blissful expression.[10] On a similarly maternal note is the crisis hotline, or more specifically the AIDS hotline, seducing the caller with promises of reassuring human contact: "for the suicidally depressed patient, the desperate pregnant teenager, the rape victim, and the panicky drug user, the phone can be the carrier of hope, of a friendly and empathic voice, and can bring about a much-needed revival of positive experiences with original objects."[11]

The telephone, by its very shape and function, is a semiotically loaded device, though psychoanalysts do not agree whether Ma Bell is a good breast or a bad breast. Some analysts have stressed the phallic quality of the telephone receiver,[12] and in most clinical essays on the subject the disembodied voice itself is thought to have a certain bisexual or phallic-maternal *je ne sais quoi* that is rumored to be irresistible. In fact, one psychoanalyst, in what must be the most extraordinary case study of an opera queen ever written, describes a man sexually obsessed with phonograph records of his favorite divas, women whose disembodied voices are at once feminine and phallic.[13] In much clinical literature, the telephone is seen not only as a bisexual symbol, in that it "possesses both a receiving and a sending apparatus," but also as a symbol for solitary masturbation.[14] Freud himself wrote of the telephone as a metaphor for transference, the way in which the analyst "must adjust himself to the patient as a telephone receiver is adjusted to the transmitting microphone."[15] Martin Silverman writes about the telephone with respect to the importance of the disembodied voice in the production of the superego, telephonic speech in this case representing the insufficiently internalized "inner voice" of conscience or religious duty whose origin is in the chastising voice of the parent.[16] Again and again, case studies of telephone perversions return to the theme of masturbation and anal eroticism, especially in regard to the mother. Robert Altman turns this maternal trope into comedy in his film *Short Cuts*, when he depicts a phone-sex operator as a jaded working-class mother who spins lurid sexual fantasies over the telephone while diapering her baby. Turning Freudianism into camp is a perennial strategy of postmodern art, though at times it hardly requires an effort. Even in the 1950s, an analyst named Herbert

Harris could write with evident professional solemnity that "telephone anxiety," as he called it, arises from the fear of castration—the fear, as it were, of "getting cut off."[17] Whatever the scientific value of these various treatises, they nevertheless reveal the telephone as a popular site of erotic play. Furthermore, while recent studies of telephone neuroses indicate certain patterns in erotic telephone behavior, it must also be remembered that they have revealed at least one important paradox. The telephone is seen in psychoanalytic discourse as a mechanism for polymorphous play and as its opposite, a mechanism that aids the subject in self-restraint and the internalization of the master's voice. This paradox suggests that the telephone, as a sexual prosthesis, is a device of both control and uncontrol, sexual displacement and sexual intimacy.

Psychoanalytic phone literature often limits itself merely to repressed homosexuality. The one study of an openly gay man that I have found engages some of the same spirit of erotic play and childhood memory as those I have just cited. Leonard Shengold has published a case study of a man he describes as homosexual. This man's first experience of phone sex generated a thrilling but strangely disorienting feeling, not to mention what appears to be a powerful transference. While on the phone, this man's lover started "talking sexually: I want to kiss you, suck you, fuck you." The analysand became excited and started to masturbate. In recounting the incident to his analyst, however, he felt "wrong" and "humiliated." In the course of his account he likened his experience of phone sex to sex with a child, group sex with a child, getting caught having sex by a parent, having sex with a parent, and having an erection during the analytic hour. In other words, for this man the telephone became a transferential hand-grenade. He exclaims, "I have the feeling of becoming so sexual that it's out of control; there is too much feeling. There is just something about the telephone that makes it so wrong. Holding a wire to your [sic] ear while masturbating. I don't want to be telling you about it. I don't want to show how excited I was and might get. I feel so vulnerable." For this particular man vulnerability appears to have its up side: "Excited as I was, I screamed when I came. And I don't know why."[18]

The notion of phone sex in itself as a transgression is qualified in this case study with evidence that phone sex is merely the means to a more radically transgressive act that, in the intensity of its excitement and the peculiarity of its account of itself, gestures toward a lost sexual scene even more effectively erased from cultural consciousness than this man's relationship with his lover. On the phone this lover loses his visible specificity as the other and takes on the noncountenance of a disembodied voice within an intense autoerotic fantasy. The shadowy figures of the parent and the child in this case study point to the volatile function of memory and regression, a function which has profound implications for all queer men, especially in the era of AIDS. Homosexuality has always borne a special relationship to the psychoanalytic theories of regression, narcissism, perversion, and paranoia. In the era of AIDS, this relationship has been transformed or, rather, intensified.

After the Beep

If I didn't hear your voice, I'd be lost in a world of silence.
—Maurice Ronet on the phone with Jeanne Moreau in *Elevator to the Gallows*

The telephone is an oddly powerful trope through which to theorize mourning, especially mourning in the time of AIDS, given the role of phone sex in combatting the spread of HIV. The AIDS crisis has been especially cataclysmic within communities of queer men, bringing news of the deaths of friends, lovers, sometimes dozens of people of one's own acquaintance. It has excited the homophobia of "AIDS hysteria" and an increase in queer-bashing. It has inspired a dread of sex that is difficult to confront and eradicate. It has challenged the often utopian spirit of sexual liberation, and some have made the unlikely assertion that queer men now live a monastic existence of sorts. This confrontation with violence and loss, for which none of us can have been prepared, presses our experience of memory ever into mourning, the inability to mourn, and beyond. The appearance of numerous counseling services to deal with various aspects of the crisis, services specifically for people affected by HIV and AIDS, people who are ill or terrified or despairing or all three, attests to the psychological burden of the epidemic. In this time of incalculable loss, queer sexual identity is itself met at every turn by the threat of its own annihilation.

I sense a tone of immediacy in many of the theoretical discussions I have heard regarding AIDS and queer mourning. First of all, there is a pressing need to define mourning with respect to the specificity of the communities hardest hit. I find, therefore, that the most useful theoretical discussions of queer mourning are by queer people who are insistently self-referential: this is happening to *me*, to *us*, and until you find out about me and people like me you can never really know what it means for us to mourn. Furthermore, I find an impetus to reclaim the psychoanalytic discourse of mourning for queer theory and to conceive of it as "productive" in the Foucauldian sense. How has the experience of mourning transformed queer culture? And how has queer culture transformed the experience of mourning?

In his remarkable essay "Mourning and Militancy," the very title a hopeful revision of Freud, Douglas Crimp discusses the importance of mourning in the time of AIDS. He emphasizes from the beginning the importance of queer mourning, queer activism, and queer sex, and this emphasis alone makes his essay a rare accomplishment. Crimp goes so far as to claim that we are not just in mourning for people, but in mourning for sex itself—sex on the pier, in the dunes, in backrooms, in short the sex by which the gay movement is said to have defined itself in the years after Stonewall. One might reasonably question Crimp's tendency to "mourn" what he calls a "lost sexual ideal" of "untamed impulses" that are now "shielded from us by latex."[19] Not every self-respecting queer is quite this nostalgic for the seventies, not even the romanticized version that Crimp re-enacts for us. His claim that queer sex has died also seems a bit melo-dramatic, especially coming from the man who taught us "how to have promis-cuity in an epidemic."[20] More interesting, I think, is the connection that he makes between mourning and activism. He figures mourning as a repressed Other against which queer militancy has defined itself. Criticizing Larry Kra-mer's distaste for "ghoulish" candlelight rituals and his call to turn mourning into militancy, Crimp describes the process by which militancy becomes an in-ability to mourn in the face of overwhelming loss. Mourning is sacrificed to mili-tancy—or, in Crimp's words, "mourning *becomes* militancy" (9). Activism, in lo-cating all violence in the outside world, denies the internal, unconscious violence that mourning helps to confront. Crimp insists, however, upon a questionable dichotomy between mourning and militancy and makes a plea for both as dis-tinct activities: "Militancy, of course, then, but mourning too" (18). In reading this essay, I lose the sense by which mourning really does become militancy, much as it becomes Electra. Mourning becomes militancy in both senses of the word *becomes*. Like mourning, AIDS activism is an *activity* deeply involved in the loss of the desired object, the loss of beautiful people. Militancy is susceptible to unconscious drives and to the processes of denial, repetition, and idealization that are characteristic of mourning. Militancy has its own dress black, and I should think anyone who has participated in an ACT UP demonstration is aware of the extent to which a funeral is being celebrated. The "die-in" in which AIDS activ-ists pretend to drop dead in politically strategic locations, is especially suggestive in this regard. Beyond the considerable media savvy of this particular form of demonstration, what of the transferential possibilities for the activist? The mass identification with lost friends and lost lovers, the re-enactment of the scene of loss recontextualized as the scene of political struggle, the irrational guilt of sur-vival, the irrational guilt of sexual transgression, the incremental horror of acting out a fantasy of one's own impending death—all are possibilities. Mourning functions as the return of the repressed not only within ACT UP militancy, but also within queer sexuality. Sex, for me, has not died. It is as good and as bad now as it ever was. But sex is different, desire itself is different. Desire has become afflicted, or rather inflected, in the epidemic; desire has been transformed, redi-rected, even rendered frantic, by a symbolic confrontation with this sublime ob-ject, this virus and its enormous devastation.

    The telephone has become part of the circuitry in this contemporary linkage of sex and death. Phone sex may be seen as a metaphor for the vicissitudes of desire and the dissemination of its peculiar voice, a metaphor for how we mourn and how we refuse to mourn in the time of AIDS. To what extent is phone sex both an act of mourning and a radical reassertion of sexual pleasure? I will begin with the first part of the question. The telephone as a mechanism of mourning hit home for me recently. A week after the funeral of my friend Paul who died with AIDS, I called David, his lover, to ask how he was faring. I got instead a message machine with Paul's cheerful voice still on it, inviting me to leave a message and promising to get back to me. After the beep, I was unable to speak. The clinical term "aphonia," what we might call the inability to complete a call, resonates for me now with a peculiar irony. It is impossible to have a rational response to this experience. Confusion, grief, and pleasure all converge in a fantasy of speaking with the dead, a dream of telling a lost friend all the things you forgot to say, a communication not without its sexual significance. I also thought of his lover and felt an immediate identification with him, an affection as yet difficult for me to name for a man who would leave behind this emotional landmine to explode over and over in the faces of friends who call to commiserate.

I would venture to say, moreover, that the function of memory, already an accomplice with desire and speech in the construction and subversion of the subject, veers toward mourning whenever one picks up the phone. In a Demanian sense, death is a linguistic predicament, and the speaking subject is always "celebrating some funeral."[21] But the telephone excites this linguistic dialectic of life and death to a more feverish pitch. As Avital Ronell has pointed out, the telephone belongs to the mechanical and technical and is therefore already on the side of death. Furthermore, she adds, the telephone "flirts with the opposition life/death by means of the same ruse through which it stretches apart receiver and transmitter or makes the infinite connection that touches the rim of finitude."[22] This rimming of finitude, itself oddly analinguistic, no doubt has something to do with the technification of the fantasy of speaking with the dead and the similar fantasy of communing, perhaps by umbilical phone cord, with the dead mother of personal prehistory. Cocteau is not far off the point when he depicts the voice of the dead in its recital of enigmatic poetry to Orpheus over the car radio. I am also reminded of Drew Barrymore, as she communicates with the dead through her television in the film *Poltergeist*. The telephone is a semiotic device of control and uncontrol: my call to another man for sex is always in danger of becoming a return call to my dead lover for love. Is there a fiberoptic beyond? The telephone may be a denial of separation, as Roland Barthes has said in his discussion of the "fade-out," the anxiety of losing the loved and exhausted voice on the other end of the line. The phone wire is charged with meaning, but a meaning "which is not that of junction but that of distance. . . ."[23] Consider Rossellini's film version of Cocteau's telephone drama, *The Human Voice* (*Una Voce Umana*, 1948), and the expressions of loss and desperation on the face of Anna Magnani—no one was ever a mess more exquisitely than Anna Magnani—as she collapses on the bed and cries and pleads over the telephone to the lover who has left her. She is enlivened by her loss, even as it renders her suicidal. The telephone generates an absence acutely felt, and silence on the line makes her panic. When the line is broken, she hears her own neighbors, the eerie laughter of some celebration that penetrates the walls, along with the tinny music of a phonograph that renders every sound mechanical and ghostly. Even when a connection is made, she panics . . . she is suspicious . . . she hears music, and she is told it is coming from next door. She hears other voices on the line. I watch Anna Magnani string out her sentences, wearing the tether thin with conjunctions, dashes, ellipses, question marks, speaking in fragments, incantatory, summoning a lover, speaking from a fear of silence, deferring the inevitable click.

The telephone invites a flirtation with melancholia. Indeed, the whole phone-sex industry strikes me sometimes as an elaborate and relentless mourning ritual attended every hour by thousands of strangers. For those who are convinced that queer sex itself is dead, the telephone becomes a device to wail the Kaddish for it. The advertisements for the all-male sex-lines present an idyll of sexual abandon, which is precisely what all those panicky gay men are running from. The ads are full of idealized sexual imagery, humpy healthy boys posing with telephones—"Talk live!" they exclaim, apparently without irony—and yet they often depend for their appeal on another body, an absent one, that of the gay man dying with AIDS. They are a paradox, these ads, at once a denial of death and an insistence upon it. They never speak of AIDS, but they could hardly speak as they do without the threat of it. AIDS is an essential yet inadmissible word in these ads; it is the unmentioned discourse that nevertheless structures the whole industry around an erotics of loss. Not everyone is in mourning for sex, of course; but even for those who are only in mourning for people, for friends and lovers who have died with AIDS, phone sex can be spiked with memory. With every call to these electric voices, whether intriguing or insufficient, uncanny or just canned, I risk recalling from deep within me the love of men now dead. I risk recalling in myself a history of losses, "preserved in a crypt like a mummy, maintained as the binding around what is not there."[24] To whom am I speaking?

Robert Chesley's play *Jerker*, despite its blandness, demonstrates an instance of the sort of mourning I mean. The title refers to tear-jerkers, since Chesley intended to write a "sex-positive" version of Larry Kramer's weepy play, *The Normal Heart*; and it also refers to jerking off, since the play concerns itself only with the telephone relationship of two men. One, named Jake (played by Joseph Stachura in the 1991 film version), is a Vietnam veteran who feels isolated and lonely. The other man, Bert (Tom Wagner), is not at a loss for lovers but has HIV and later dies with AIDS. We ourselves are a sort of third party on the line, silent voyeurs with the benefit of filmic images; in fact, I believe *Jerker* first raised a scandal as a radio play, a form in which it would no doubt succeed better than the film at giving full rein to the mystery and ambiguity of the disembodied voice. We are privy to about twenty attempts at connection between the two men, many of which are messages left on a machine. Their first exchanges are brief and anonymous—we do not even see much of their bodies. In later calls, like a striptease, we see a flash of cock, we see more of their bodies, more of their apartments, we learn what may or may not be their names and occupations. Their interactions grow longer and more complicated. They lie to each other, withhold information, reveal information, play at different roles, and talk each other through different sexual acts. The telephone becomes a device not only for emotional defense, but also intimacy and emotional vulnerability, control and uncontrol. Their highly contrived conversation gives way to more spontaneous outbursts of fantasy, anxiety and affection. Their erotic conversations lead, perhaps inevitably, in the direction of memory, trauma, and childhood. We learn of Jake's bitter memories of Vietnam and Bert's fears about his health. The earlier calls establish a sense of fraternity through fantasies of childhood sexual experience, especially a fantasy of two young brothers alone in the woods. Childhood attachments are apparent from the very beginning, when we see Bert with his stuffed bear on the bed, and they culminate in Jake's elaborate childhood fantasy, a queer fairy-tale of an enchanted palace where the two brothers are taken to bed by their magical host, who is in a sense our own incarnation as third party to the exchange. During the fantasy Jake's body duplicates itself and lends flesh to his disembodied voice as he attempts a mystical telephonic communion with Bert, who is curled up naked in bed, suffering from a nightsweat. Bert says, "It's been a long time since anyone told me a bedtime story, not since I was a kid." The rest of the film consists of messages left on a machine, while Bert's death becomes apparent and his apartment empties out. The sense of loss, already inherent in the distancing effects of the telephone, lends a powerful ambivalence to sex, reaching deeper into the past, into childhood, and into the present, for experiences that can be as disturbing as they are erotic. In the end, there is no mourning for Bert, apart from the desperate and despairing phone messages left by Jake.[25]

Phone Noir

"I bet each one of these mystical spheres has a little window in it with a little
Levelor blind that's down almost but not quite all the way, right, that you creep up
to and peer into, am I right?"

—Nicholson Baker[26]

Ten-number speed dial and automatic paging have their place. But when it's time
to dial M for murder, make mine black, heavy and rotary.

—William Grimes

But there was a second part to my question: To what extent is the telephone a radical reassertion of queer pleasure in the time of AIDS? Phone sex may be an act of mourning for an idealized sexual freedom rumored to have now disappeared; on the other hand, it may be a refusal to mourn and a challenge to the validity of the loss itself. The telephone calls up an electrical space that becomes a queer space, a new space of sexual play and sexual imagination. After the fashion of Kristeva in her more perverse moments, I rediscover a pleasure supposedly lost to history on the inverted helix of language run through with imagination and jouissance. Even beyond the recollection of old stories and familiar scenes, there is a jouissance of the telephone that is scarcely ever mentioned. This is the same phone, after all, that I use to call my friends, my lovers, my parents, and my analyst, not to mention the pope. This is the phone whose number is disseminated through many lists, through many black books, and my voice is disseminated, re-embodied in countless forms through countless contexts, now master now slave, now garrulous exhibitionist, now silent voyeur.

The telephone sings sometimes, as in Kafka, with an uncanny voice of its own. The pleasures of paranoia are not to be underestimated. I have spoken of a romance between human and machine, each losing its boundaries in an integrated circuit, but we should not lose sight of the terror in this romance. There still remains our paranoid defense against the disruptive erotics of machinery, a defense against the technological voice that seems at times to mimic the alienated, disembodied voices heard by the schizophrenic. I sense a cruelty in electric speech, a cruelty that crackles with desire. Cocteau knew this: the heroine of *The Human Voice* moans into the transmitter, "If you didn't love me but were clever, the telephone would become a terrifying weapon, noiseless and leaving no trace."[27] Pedro Almodóvar, in revising Cocteau's play in his films *Law of Desire* and *Women on the Verge of a Nervous Breakdown*, preserves this sense of desire and persecution as Carmen Maura (in both films) is driven to hysterical rage and cathartic violence by her telephone.[28]

Hollywood, in fact, thrives on the paranoid pleasure of the telephone. If you ever find yourself in a movie, don't answer the phone. Nearly every film that takes the telephone as its central trope is a film of suspense or horror, whether it be *Sorry, Wrong Number*, *Dial M for Murder*, *The Manchurian Candidate*, *Klute*, or *The Conversation*—or lesser known films, like *When a Stranger Calls*, in which a nervous babysitter is harassed by mysterious phone calls, or *Call Me*, in which a woman's first foray into phone sex leads to murder and mayhem. I also recall certain scenes from classic paranoia films where terrified women go crazy in telephone booths. I am thinking of *The Birds*, in which Tippi Hedren tries to hide in a glass phone booth as manic seagulls attack her from all sides; or the vampire movie *The Hunger*, in which Susan Sarandon, in a fit of lesbian panic, gets vamped by Catherine Deneuve at a pay phone; or *Rosemary's Baby*, in which a panicky Mia Farrow, for whom the course of motherhood has never run smooth, tries to explain to her obstetrician that the witches next door are after her unborn child.

The technoculture dream of AT&T, that the telephone will let you reach out and touch someone, invariably gives way in these films to the nightmare that someone awful is going to reach out and touch you back.

As Kaja Silverman makes clear, all the great telephone films mimic the paranoid sensation of persecution by a disembodied voice whose ambiguous origins threaten the certainty of "inside" and "outside," spilling over "from subject to object and object to subject, violating the bodily limits upon which classic subjectivity depends, and so smoothing the way for projection and introjection.[29] Most of these films depict a sexually transgressive woman or a mother-identified man who is terrorized and infantilized by a telephone voice. *Klute* is extraordinary in this respect because the woman, a prostitute named Bree Daniels (Jane Fonda), finds herself accosted by the sound of her own seductive voice played back to her over the phone by a client. In classic cinema, to place a call is masculine aggressive and to answer one is feminine submissive; but the telephone itself, that volatile high-tension wire between self and other, raises the possibility of the queer, the erotic signifier at play, the voice misdirected, the subject, as it were, mislaid. In telephone thrillers, what we might call *phone noir*, desire itself is figured as a tangled network with a great many loose wires, though in the end the call to queerness, the call to sexual transgression, is almost always violently disconnected. This telephonic connection between persecution and maternal desire is suggested by the opening text of *Sorry, Wrong Number*:

> In the tangled network of a great city the telephone is the unseen link between a million lives. . . . It is the servant of our common needs, the confidant of our inmost secrets . . . life and happiness wait upon its ring . . . and horror . . . and loneliness . . . and death.

In the film, Leona (Barbara Stanwyck), a neurotic woman who dominates her husband, overhears a conversation on her telephone. Someone is plotting a murder—Leona's murder, as she later learns. Now an invalid confined to her bed with a "cardiac neurosis," she tries to exercise control over the outside world through the telephone. But the aggression of her desire returns to haunt her as, in a fit of panic, she learns bit by bit the facts of the plot to kill her, and even learns from a click on the line that her murderer is *inside the house*, in the kitchen downstairs. Similarly, in *Dial M for Murder*, a woman's adultery motivates her husband to have her murdered while they talk together on the telephone. As she answers the phone, the man who wants to strangle her—who has been hiding *inside the house*—steps out from behind the curtain. The husband's controlling desire is represented by the gadgetry shifting into place inside the phone as he dials, but as always this symbol of technological control is also a symbol for uncontrol: the murder goes awry.

When a Stranger Calls renders the connection between the feminine, the maternal, and the domestic sphere especially pathological. The girlish babysitter—

sexually inexperienced, overwhelmed by the enormous house where she sits alone, anxious about her own maternal capacity to take responsibility for children—is a classic trope for a woman out of sync with the gender role she has been assigned. Jill (Carol Kane), the babysitter in this film, is harassed by phone calls from a weird man who repeatedly asks her if she has checked the children. She secures the house against intruders, but the telephone itself is an intruder, the ideal metaphor for the symbolic permeability of that not-so-hermetically sealed space, the bourgeois home. In an ironic play of inside and outside, the police trace the calls and discover they have been coming from *inside the house*. The stranger was upstairs all along, chopping up the kids, and now he is coming down the stairs to get her too. She survives but years later a similar scene is replayed, in which the intruder kills her husband and children. He then disguises himself as her husband and waits for her in bed. She is never secure, always powerless. Her household, like her frightened and hysterized body, is always under a paranoid threat of invasion, a threat rendered palpable in the narrative by a psycho-killer outside and inside the house at the same time.

The sequel, *When a Stranger Calls Back*, is all the more disturbing, since it is a feminist narrative gone awry. A babysitter, Julia, goes through the same scenario as Jill. This time the phone cord has been cut and a man whose car has allegedly broken down asks her through the door if he can use her phone. She fakes the call for him, talking into the dead phone, suggesting the hysterized ineffectuality of the female voice in the home. Later, we discover that the stranger has been in the house all along. He is a ventriloquist who has thrown his voice outdoors. Like the voice on the phone, the ventriloquist voice is unlocatable. He also knows the house better than Julia, and even knows her name. This aggressive, intrusive, pathological, all-knowing male voice is likened to the voice of rape culture, whose terrorism succeeds precisely through paranoia, through an excessive fear generated by a pervasive, unlocatable threat that may or may not be real. When the stranger returns to harass her years later, he terrorizes her by altering her dorm room in subtle but noticeable ways. The police think she is "hysterical," but she finds support in Jill, who is now a counselor in a campus women's center. The psycho-killer plot is refigured in the language of rape or incest survivor narratives, the story that only another woman is willing to believe. The paranoid threat of a male intruder is displaced by a far more positive paranoid fantasy of uncanny empathy. Jill is the feminist who appears out of nowhere to help Julia cope and defend herself, the woman who already knows Julia's name and knows what she went through because she went through it herself. The two women keep in contact over the phone, and Julia learns to take control of her own domestic space. Nevertheless, in a bizarre scene, the ventriloquist paints his body to blend with the walls of Jill's apartment. He is the voice of that space in all its paranoid aggression and unlocatability, and the women are always victims precisely because of their status as women in a rape culture. The feminist narrative falls apart when he manages to attack both Julia and Jill and their efforts at self-defense fail. Although he is dead in the end, the final scene is of the two women, side by side in hospital beds, always victims even if they are also always survivors.

The male version of these paranoid telephone narratives is no less volatile. Maternal fixation is usually the hero's tragic flaw. *When a Stranger Calls Back* is a good example. The stranger is a ventriloquist who works in a topless bar; his psychotic self-alienation is articulated through his aggressive fixation on breasts, children, disembodied voices, and a babysitter—in other words, the Lacanian mother. *The Party Line* is an even better example: it is an insipid phone-sex thriller where one of the villains is a man who likes to hang around the house in his dead mother's wedding gown. You would think that alone would make the film worth watching, but it does not. The film is a virtual laundry-list of human sexuality, and all the laundry is dirty: phone sex, sex with a minor, group sex, lesbianism, transvestism, adultery, rape, father-daughter incest, mother-son incest, brother-sister incest—the film is so desperate to shock, not even labeling it camp would redeem it. The plot centers around three women who have all been raped or sexually harassed by men and who are therefore understandably disenchanted with them. As the film progresses all three women are thrown into peril, so that they can be rescued by the hero or killed off, depending on how sexually unconventional they are. All the murders in the film are linked together by the same phone-sex line. And who are the villains to be annihilated? The male mother-identified serial killer and his butch sister. Again, the telephone excites sexual panic and motivates a violent paranoid defense against disruptive sexuality.

The Manchurian Candidate is far more subtle, but follows a similar paranoid logic. A soldier (Laurence Harvey) who has been brainwashed returns home, only to find himself peculiarly susceptible to assassination orders delivered to him by Communists over the telephone. The gender play in the film is most apparent in the famous scene where, in the subjective reality of the brainwashed soldiers, Communist military men appear as bourgeois ladies attending a gardening lecture in New Jersey. The distinctive paranoid gesture, however, comes with the realization that the soldier's mother (Angela Lansbury), with whom he enjoys one of the most intense Oedipal fixations in the history of cinema, is a spy who betrayed him. In this film, the incestuous maternal menace and the ideological red menace go arm in arm in the articulation of paranoid defense. Having resisted the Communist voice on the telephone, the soldier shoots his mother and stepfather through the head, then kills himself.

Another film, *The Conversation*, articulates a similar feeling of paranoia about an all-knowing voice on the telephone. Harry Caul (Gene Hackman) makes his living by surveillance, but he seems strangely desperate to keep his own emotions well hidden and his own apartment perfectly secured. He is especially anxious about his telephone, and in the end it is by phone that he learns he himself is under surveillance. He is feminized by the assault of his own music played back to him over the phone. In a rage he strips his apartment in search of the surveillance device, but fails to find it. His sanctum sanctorum has been penetrated by his own gaze turned back upon him, it has been savaged by his own panicking hands, his inside has been turned inside out. The numerous casual references to homosexuality in this film, always held anxiously at bay in jokes or terms of abuse, come home to roost in the implied feminization of this man's solitary surrender. To quote Kaja Silverman, "He has been displaced from the position of 'bugger' to that of 'buggee.' "[30]

I speak of these various telephone films at length in order to demonstrate in some way how the telephone as a paranoid device is already an established trope in modernity. Frederic Jameson makes a similar point when he speaks of the "high-tech paranoia" genre and the technological sublime. He argues that technology presents the postmodern subject with a vast and tangled network that boggles the mind and excites fantasies of persecution; furthermore, he sees these representations of technology as symbols for the material reality of multinational capitalism, the socioeconomic behemoth that is at once our own creation and our own worst enemy.[31] I would add that this high-tech paranoia has a psychosexual dimension as well as an economic one, and there is a perennial and fascinating queerness to both its horror and its pleasure. Like the failure to mourn, paranoia engages desires, anxieties, even pleasures, that are radically subversive. We should get used to it, since paranoia is one of the defining characteristics of our age. Just as homosexuality started out as a sin, then became a pathology, and is now a lifestyle, so paranoia has enjoyed a similar genealogy: it started out as demonic possession, then became a psychosis, and now it is just a way of life. The connection between paranoia and homoeroticism in psychoanalytic theory is at least as old as the connection between paranoia and the telephone. With the Schreber case in 1911, Freud asserted that repressed homosexuality was at the very root of paranoia, and his colleague, Sándor Ferenczi, went so far as to suggest that paranoia is homosexuality in disguise.[32] Schreber's *Memoirs of My Nervous Illness*, not to mention Freud's interpretation of it, merit a great deal of attention in this respect: nowhere in literature do paranoia, homosexuality, and the telephone converge in so articulate a fashion. I would say that Schreber's memoirs provide a veritable manifesto for the specifically queer desire I have been discussing here. Schreber is hearing voices, uncanny voices, hostile voices, divine voices, that seem foreign to him though they are in a sense issuing from his own head.

Schreber's High-Wire Act

If gaining control, self-mastery, and some dominion over alterity motivate original toolmaking, would this schema suitably define the electric speech of the telephone? Would it too constitute a thing carried into some identifiable inside to

subdue the tongues of exteriority—for example, those still heard by
schizophrenics, paranoiacs, or prophets in the desert?

—Avital Ronell[33]

"I wonder if the pigeon on my windowsill knows what I'm doing," she said, when
she caught her breath.

—Andy Warhol[34]

I confess that Schreber is an absurd and unlikely hero. I might as well call
him a hero, for there seems to be little agreement about what else to call him.
Freud's belief that homosexuality causes paranoia has often been questioned or
revised. For example, Jacques Lacan emphasizes the foreclosure of the paternal
metaphor in Schreber and sees his "delusional homosexuality" and "trans-sexual-
ist jouissance" as an effect rather than a cause of his psychosis.[35] More recent research into Schreber's life suggests that Freud is at least correct in suspecting a
homosexual fixation on the father, Daniel Gottfried Schreber, whose sadistic interest in childhood sexuality and development—his use of physical restraints, his
strict discipline, his horror of masturbation—has led some to suppose that Schreber was abused as a child.[36] If the origin of Schreber's "nervous illness" has been
a matter for dispute, so has the diagnosis. Freud himself questions whether
Schreber is in fact paranoid, and he speaks of Jung's "dementia praecox" and
Bleuler's "schizophrenia," not to mention his own preferred term, "paraphrenia."
Schreber has even more descriptions for himself. According to his memoirs, he
was at various times in his life a *Senatspräsident*, Miss Schreber the harlot of God,
a leper, a martyr, a seer of spirits, and the Prince of Hell.

Whatever the clinical terminology, Schreber is most definitely queer, and in
ways that immediately excite my identification. The question for me here is not
just what is the nature of Schreber's psychosis? but also, why do I, a mere pervert,
identify with him? What is this fascination I have with his protean identity?
What is this familiar feeling of panic I have when I read his book, this sense of
entrapment in an institution or a symbolic order singularly hostile? I do not want
to trivialize or romanticize Schreber's "nervous illness" and his very real suffering, nor do I want to propose paranoid schizophrenia as an alternative sexual
identity; however, I do find in Schreber a model for the experience of a certain
paranoid fear, perhaps even paranoid jouissance, which is already associated culturally, even clinically, with desire between men.[37] I am drawing out a single implication of Freud's reading of Schreber: paranoia is the affliction proper of the
queer body in rebellion against a symbolic order that is loath to speak its name.
In my use of the term *paranoia*, I do not wish to imply that queer people have
nothing to be afraid of. Our fears are often well justified, especially in the present
climate where sexual violence against queer people is an everyday occurrence.

This paranoid rebellion of the queer body, this homosexual panic, is felt no less, it seems, in people who claim to be heterosexual. We have often found ourselves the targets of other people's paranoia: the Christian who thinks AIDS is a punishment from God, the president who thinks we need to secure our national borders against invading hordes of people with HIV, or the Pentagon official who panics at the thought of "feeling watched" by a gay soldier in the shower. Beyond my justified fears, however, is a far less rational panic, my fear of desire itself. I find my various sexual pleasures everywhere transfigured into unmentionable peculiarities, inexplicable compulsions, or dangerous pathologies. It is a wonder I ever recognized them at all. They return to me as the enemy in the language of another, even in my own language. With the AIDS crisis, I learned to think of sex with a dread that exceeded any reasonable concern for HIV transmission. I have experienced sexual pleasure all too often in paranoid fashion as a threat. But that threat has always borne within it, as though in disguise, a pleasure all but lost to consciousness. I want to turn the tables on this tendency to paranoia. I find in Schreber a radical queer ancestry, however ironically I may claim it as my own. Hélène Cixous and Catherine Clément make much the same claim when they discover the roots of their feminism in the incantations of the sorceress and the bodily histrionics of the hysteric. I have through Schreber an odd inheritance. Here is a man who is continually troubled by little people who sit on his left ear or loiter on his head. He makes up homophonic words to confuse the birds who come to talk to him. He launches a plate of sausage through a closed window, and cannot remember why. But he excites my identification. He comes to me like a voice on the telephone, for his body knows no boundaries. He can feel the nerves of voluptuousness under his skin, he can feel them "cord-like" in his sister-in-law's arm, and he can see the nerves of God entering him from the sky. His body has been riddled with the signs of plague, "the blue plague, the brown plague, the white plague, and the black plague."[38] At times he has female genitalia. Schreber makes me peculiarly aware of my body as a subjective experience, a symbolic and imaginary construction, a protean phantasm bearing enigmatic messages.

Freud's case study is legendary, and certainly his theory of paranoia as a defense against repressed homosexuality is important here. Briefly, Schreber experiences a transference of homosexual desire from his father or brother to his doctor Flechsig and finally to God. He writes of being half awake in bed when an idea occurs to him: "It was the idea that it really must be rather pleasant to be a woman succumbing to intercourse." Of course, he is appalled by the notion: "This idea was so foreign to my whole nature that I may say I would have rejected it with indignation if fully awake; . . . some external influences were at work to implant this idea in me" (63). Farther along, in a similarly defensive tone, he describes another of his "ideas": "The most disgusting was the idea that my body, after the intended transformation into a female being, was to suffer some sexual abuse, particularly as there had even been talk for some time of my being thrown to the Asylum attendants for this purpose" (101). Only through God can he finally acknowledge his "ideas": his shame turns to pride as he describes a mystical communication, a divine "nerve contact" and "nerve language." God in effect commands him to act out the desire he has been fending off and Schreber's submission is nothing short of Wagnerian as the rays of God curve through the sky and enter his body. Ferenczi's notion of paranoia as homosexuality in disguise is especially resonant here: Schreber acts out a host of homoerotic and transsexual fantasies under the guise of nervous illness, religious martyrdom, and mystical transformation into a woman.

Schreber's guilty projection onto God reminds me of the paranoid relationship with science and religion in many a gay apologia. The "etiology" question is always a politically volatile one in any society where sexual freedom is routinely denied. "Why are you queer?" is less a question than a challenge to one's civil rights. One is not permitted to answer casually and say, "Because it feels good" or "Because no one is stopping me." One must look desperately to scientific and religious theories that are often no more plausible than Schreber's God. Like Schreber, one finds oneself playing paranoid martyr and paranoid detective. One says: I can't help it. Because God loves me. Because the devil is real. It was my mother, my father, my brother, my teacher, the man next door. It was a fatal book I read once. It's hormonal. It's in my genes. I have a teeny weeny hypothalamus and it keeps whispering in my ear, "It really must be rather pleasant to be a woman succumbing to intercourse." Why do you ask?

Schreber's memoirs read oddly like a coming-out story gone mad. Several passages resonate with this curious irony. Consider the silence and self-castigation in his account of the rays that leave out words: " '*Why do you not say it?*', the word '*aloud*' necessary to complete the sense being omitted, and the rays giving the answer themselves as if it came from me: 'Because I am stupid perhaps' "(70). Or his homophobic sense of indignity and shame, as ascribed to the voices: "Fancy a person who was a *Senatspräsident* allowing himself to be f. . . . d" (148). I should think just about anyone who has ever been queer and sixteen has an intuitive understanding of clinical paranoia, if only for the experience of having one's persecution redefined as a mere figment of one's imagination or, even worse, as therapy. In fact, Schreber's concept of the "not-thinking-of-anything-thought," which he engages as a defense against the voices, sounds curiously like my experience of high school. And let us not forget that the principal motivation for Schreber to write his memoirs was to persuade the authorities that he is no madman and to obtain his release from the asylum. Like much queer writing, his memoirs are about incarceration of a sort and the search for a liberating voice.

One of the most extraordinary passages in Schreber's memoirs is his apologia for his sexual "ideas." It reads oddly like the first feelings of self-acceptance in coming-out stories:

> Since then I have wholeheartedly inscribed the cultivation of femininity on my banner, and I will continue to do so as far as consideration of my environment allows, whatever other people who are ignorant of the supernatural reasons may think of me. I would like to meet the man who, faced with the choice of either becoming a demented human being in male habitus or a spirited woman, would not prefer the latter. (149)

Rather tricky, the wording of that last sentence. Perhaps he *would* like to meet that man. In fact, I think I *am* that man. I myself am taken with the idea that it really must be rather pleasant to be a demented human being succumbing to intercourse and yet retaining a male habitus. The idea is not "foreign to my whole nature," certainly not anymore, however contrary the idea may be to those who do not suspect my "supernatural" intentions. But whatever his reservations, I am struck by Schreber's pride, his sense that all is perfectly rational and clear now that he has made his strange peace with his god, with social prohibitions, and with his own desires. In short, he seems to have found a sexual identity that he thinks he can live with, which is what being "in" or "out" of the closet is all about. The peace he has made plays havoc with the notion of a stable or natural sexual identity: Schreber demonstrates, perhaps unconsciously, how any sexual identity is not an immutable essence, but a performance, a negotiation, "peace talks" of a sort.

To be queer is to hear strange voices, to answer an obscene call, to answer several different calls in the course of one's life. Schreber's pathology, whether he is responding to "repressed homosexuality" or not, translates well into the historically pathologized outsiderhood of being queer. To come to an understanding of oneself as queer is often to hear voices inside one's own head, voices which have been effectively excluded from anything one has ever heard before. Uncanny voices, for surely they are not one's own, and yet one cannot imagine voices more personal or more intimate. And what is most distressing, these voices, which are the voices of an unspeakable desire projected onto the face of the world and returning with foreign accents, seem always to be saying precisely what one needs most to hear. Distressing, of course, because they also seem to be saying what is most terrifying to think about. Nor are they especially polite, as voices go. More often than not, they are exceedingly hostile, as Schreber was quick to discover. His persecutors are always endowed with terrifying power, terrifying knowledge. They have unseated the symbolic father with a father of a very different sort, the anal father, the exacting father of enjoyment. In this sense, Schreber's persecutors are all invisible or they have an evil side that no one else can see. They are all to some extent strangers in the symbolic order, but they are the strangers who know all about him, they know things about him no one else knows, they know things about him that even he does not know. They are the strangers with strange intentions who command him to do strange things. And Schreber is always dependent on the unkindness of these strangers. He may let the phone ring for a while, but eventually he answers the call. And the very pleasure of doing so, however psychotic, finds its manifesto, as I have said, in his memoirs.

I hope it is clear, then, why I dwell on the telephone in speaking of paranoid pleasure and in speaking also of queer people who are exploring the possibilities of promiscuity in an epidemic. The telephone is certainly a symbolic presence in the memoirs. Schreber even had a "writing-down-system," like a telephone message machine or dictaphone, to be sure he did not lose anything or forget that he was repeating himself. He was forever answering calls, repetitive calls, responding to changing voices and messages, and doing so with his entire body. And there are also those networks of "rays" and "filaments" that enter him as the presence of God. Like those mysterious phone wires belonging to AT&T, "the nerves of God are infinite and eternal. They possess the same qualities as human nerves but in a degree surpassing all human understanding." And what marvelous new technology! "They have in particular the faculty of transforming themselves into all things of the created world" (46). Unable to sleep at night, Schreber hears a "recurrent crackling noise" (64) that follows him everywhere he goes. Electrical static, perhaps? A wire in search of its connection? The telephone is as much a psychostructural phenomenon as a machine. It has universal access, and its ringing will not be ignored. It is like the devil at the keyhole, it crawls through: "In my opinion this belief is correctly based on the fact that no mechanical obstacle made by man can prevent the entry of the rays. I experience at every moment on my own body that this is so; no wall however thick, no closed window can prevent the ray filaments penetrating in a way incomprehensible to man and so reaching any part of my body, particularly my head" (242). The rays, like "long drawn out filaments" do not come straight at him, but move in an arc, approaching his head from some distant spot on the horizon, for if they did simply shoot down into his body, the pleasure would be so devastating that, well, "God would hardly be able to contain Himself in heaven, if I may so express it" (229). The rays are visible as bright spots, they are particles broken off the nerves of the upper God, Ormuzd. Spermatic, but with a voice, for in their fabulous freefall they cry out in terror for help. They dial 911 and get Schreber on the line and cry out for help. They call for no one else. "It is presumably a phenomenon like telephoning," the madman observes; "the filaments of rays spun out towards my head act like telephone wires; the weak sound of the cries of help coming from an apparently vast distance is received *only by me* in the same way as telephonic communication can only be heard by a person who is on the telephone, but not by a third person who is somewhere between the giving and receiving end" (229).

There is no such thing as a wrong number for Schreber, or for that matter an illicit wiretap. To paraphrase Lacan, the phone message always arrives at its proper destination.

Where does this leave me, then, when I put aside this manifesto? I recall once staying at the home of a friend who was away. His phone frequently rang—it would not be ignored—and the different voices were surprisingly confident of my alleged propensity for obedience and submission. The commanding masculine tones assured me of who I was, what I was, what I liked. I had been placed, re-placed, found out . . . I am reminded of one of Jung's case studies of a paranoid woman: "Before admission she had, for several years, heard voices that slandered her. For a time she contemplated suicide by drowning. She explained the voices as invisible telephones. They called out to her that she was a woman of doubtful character."[39] The devil is at my keyhole again. The dialectic of private and public is put in play. "Technoculture can barely abide an outside."[40] I am reminded of Carol Kane again in the film *When a Stranger Calls*. So tenuous is my own perception of inside and outside that I am never quite sure who to identify with, the frightened woman or the psychotic stranger. The stranger knows who she is and where she is. He wants to feel her blood all over his body. She locks the doors and the windows, but his calls have been traced and they are coming from *inside the house*. Paranoia takes great pleasure in the futility of locking the doors and locking the windows.

I am alone in this house, and yet I have so many visitors. Depending on whom I call, even the phone company knows my business, not to mention the government and American Express. There is no such thing as privacy when one is talking on the telephone. As on the confessional line, where strangers call to hear my sins, curious filaments like the nerves of God unfurl toward my telephone from divers sources that I regard with suspicion. "Information control is the contemporary version of God's eternal knowledge of each individual's ultimate damnation or salvation; and both theology and computer technology naturally produce paranoid fears about how we are hooked into the System, about the connections it has in store for us."[41] On Manhattan cable late at night there is a trendy black-and-white commercial that plays over and over and over, advertising a phone-sex number. Some guy bolting through the dark in his underwear, locking the door behind him, wrapping himself with the phone cord, and stroking himself with the receiver. He locks the door! Doesn't he know he's on TV? Doesn't he know his privacy is a function of his publicity? His body is presented for my perusal, his behavior for my surveillance. But perhaps he understands my own pretense to privacy and the vulnerability of this position of surveillance where I sit alone at night with the door locked, the television beaming blue across my body. No wall however thick, no closed window can prevent the ray filaments penetrating in a way incomprehensible to man and so reaching any part of my body, particularly my head. I am his intended partner—I need only dial the number on the screen. His seductiveness is designed to appeal to my private desire, to be a mirror of it, in fact. And so I do not know who is really on TV, he or I, and if I pick up the phone to dial, I confess to an identification, a nerve-contact, and I go public with my desire in the privacy of my own home. A magazine by my bed is open to an advertisement, "1-900-963-6363, real people ltd. (subject to change)." Forget the number, it is the ad that intrigues me. It says, "I *WANT* YOU!" with a picture of a naked guy with attitude and big shoulders, presumably my ideal ego, the man I am and am not, eyeing me unkindly through venetian blinds.[42] Like Schreber's God, he is exacting in his call for pleasure, he bears the grimace of my anal dad. He is Uncle Sam gone queer: he says, "I *WANT* YOU!" I find myself interpellated by my own gaze. "As a rule, one focuses on the horror of being the object of some invisible, unfathomable, panoptical gaze (the 'some-one-is-watching-me' motif)—yet it is a far more unbearable experience to find oneself at this very point of a pure gaze."[43] The venetian blinds, like the telephone, foreground the seductive dialectics of gaze and object, self and other, possession and loss, presence and absence, exhibitionism and concealment, already at work in all of these ads. That sense of control in wielding the telephone receiver is already slipping away before I pick it up. And what is most uncanny, as in a mirror, I cannot tell whether I am inside looking out at him or he is inside looking out at me or we are both inside looking in at each other.

And I am always tempted to talk to a guy who looks at me like that.

Notes

1. Julia Kristeva, "AIDS and Eros," trans. Leon S. Roudiez, *Harper's*, 275 (1987): 25.

2. I am using the word *queer* here in the sense of "odd" or "strange." More importantly, of course, I am using it in the sexual sense, as a term of abuse reclaimed and redeployed by queer activists. In this sense, it is virtually synonymous with "lesbian and gay," but much more politically confrontational and emotionally charged. Furthermore, it is wonderfully suggestive of a host of sexual possibilities that play havoc with the conventional distinction between normal and pathological, heterosexual and homosexual, masculine and feminine.

3. Susan Sontag, *AIDS and Its Metaphors* (New York: Farrar, Strauss and Giroux, 1989), 79.

4. Philip K. Dick, *Flow My Tears, the Policeman Said* (1974) (New York: Vintage, 1993), 153–54.

5. On cyborg politics, see Donna Haraway, "A Manifesto for Cyborgs," *Socialist Review*, 15 (1985): 65–107. On the "body without organs," see Gilles Deleuze and Félix Guattari, *Anti-Oedipus* (1972), trans. Robert Hurley et al. (Minneapolis: University of Minnesota Press, 1983).

6. Avital Ronell, *The Telephone Book: Technology—Schizophrenia—Electric Speech* (Lincoln: University of Nebraska Press, 1989), 104.

7. Arlene Stein, "On the Line: Lesbians in the Phone-Sex Industry," *Outweek*, 101 (1991): 35.

8. Ronell, *The Telephone Book*, 424.

9. See Katie Hafner and John Markoff, *Cyberpunk: Outlaws and Hackers on the Computer Frontier* (New York: Simon and Schuster, 1991).

10. This particular image reminds me of Ernest Jones's assertion that the Madonna's legendary "conception through the ear" is a sublimating displacement upward of anal eroticism; her ear is the alternative orifice for penetration by the divine Word or the seminal dove. See his essay, "The Madonna's Conception through the Ear" (1914), *Essays in Applied Psycho-Analysis*, 2 (New York: International Universities Press, 1964).

11. Renato Almansi, "On Telephoning, Compulsive Telephoning, and Perverse Telephoning: Psychoanalytic and Social Aspects," *The Psychoanalytic Study of Society*, 11 (1985): 234.

12. See Wilhelm Stekel, *Sex and Dreams* (1911) (Boston: Badger, 1922); and, more recently, Arlene Kramer Richards, "A Romance with Pain: A Telephone Perversion in a Woman," *International Journal of Psycho-Analysis*, 70 (1989): 153–64.

13. Henry Alden Bunker, Jr., "The Voice as (Female) Phallus," *Psychoanalytic Quarterly*, 3 (1934): 391–429. One might also consider Wayne Koestenbaum's various writings on operatic divas.

14. See Peter Hobart Knapp, "The Ear, Listening and Hearing," *Journal of the American Psychoanalytic Association*, 1 (1953): 672–89; Leonard Shengold, "The Symbol of Telephoning," *Journal of the American Psychoanalytic Assocation*, 30 (1982): 465; and Martin A. Silverman, "A Nine Year Old's Use of the Telephone: Symbolism *In Statu Nascendi*," *Psychoanalytic Quarterly*, 51 (1982): 607. On the telephone as a symbol of solitary masturbation, see especially Robert Fliess, *Symbol, Dream and Psychosis* (New York: International Universities Press, 1973), 95–99.

15. Sigmund Freud, "Recommendations to Physicians Practising Psycho-Analysis" (1912), *The Standard Edition of the Complete Psychological Works of Sigmund Freud*, ed. James Strachey (London: Hogarth Press, 1953–74), 12: 115–16.

16. Martin A. Silverman, "The Voice of Conscience and the Sounds of the Analytic Hour," *Psychoanalytic Quarterly*, 51 (1982): 196–217.

17. Herbert I. Harris, "Telephone Anxiety," *Journal of the American Psychoanalytic Association*, 5 (1957): 342–47.

18. Shengold, "The Symbol of Telephoning," 468–69.

19. Douglas Crimp, "Mourning and Militancy," *October*, 51 (1990): 11.

20. Crimp, "How to Have Promiscuity in an Epidemic," *AIDS: Cultural Analysis/Cultural Activism* (Cambridge: MIT Press, 1988), 237–70.

21. Paul de Man, *The Rhetoric of Romanticism* (New York: Columbia University Press, 1984), 81.

22. Ronell, *The Telephone Book*, 84.

23. Roland Barthes, *A Lover's Discourse: Fragments* (1977), trans. Richard Howard (New York: Hill and Wang, 1978), 115.

24. Ronell, *The Telephone Book*, 341.

25. James Carroll Pickett's play, *Dream Man*, follows a similar plot device in which a phone-sex worker whose lover has left him uses the phone to articulate a paradox of connection and loss, safety and violence, idyllic childhood memory and adult alienation.

26. [Nicholson Baker, *Vox* (New York: Random House, 1992), 62. The speaker is a woman on a phone-sex line with a man who has just told her about his fantasy that all women's orgasms are eternally preserved in mystical "ovums" that he can go back to and visit.

27. Jean Cocteau, *The Human Voice* (1930), trans. Carl Wildman (London: Vision Press, 1951), 31.

28. [On Almodóvar and paranoid pleasure, see my essay, "Technology, Paranoia, and the Queer Voice," *Screen*, 34.2 (1993).

29. Kaja Silverman, *The Acoustic Mirror: The Female Voice in Psychoanalysis and Cinema* (Bloomington: Indiana University Press, 1988), 80.

30. Ibid., 97.

31. See Fredric Jameson, *Postmodernism, or The Cultural Logic of Late Capitalism* (Durham: Duke University Press, 1991), 37–38.

32. Sigmund Freud, "Psycho-Analytic Notes on an Autobiographical Account of a Case of Paranoia (Dementia Paranoides)" (1911), *Standard Edition*, 12: 59; Sándor Ferenczi, "On the Part Played by Homosexuality in the Pathogenesis of Paranoia" (1912), *Sex in Psychoanalysis*, trans. Ernest Jones (New York: Dover, 1956), 133.

33. Ronell, *The Telephone Book*, 94.

34. Andy Warhol, *The Philosophy of Andy Worhol* (1975) (New York: Harvest/HBJ, 1977),224–25. This line comes near the end of a long phone-sex chapter in which B is on the phone with A, telling him about her day (cleaning the house, going to the deli) in breathless and interminable detail while apparently masturbating.

35. Jacques Lacan, "On a Question Preliminary to Any Possible Treatment of Psychosis" (1955–56), *Écrits: A Selection*, trans. Alan Sheridan (New York: W. W. Norton, 1977), 179–225. See also Ida Macalpine's introduction to her English edition of Schreber's memoirs.

36. See Part II of William G. Niederland's book, *The Schreber Case* (New York: Quadrangle, 1974); see also Morton Schatzman, *Soul Murder*; Han Israëls, *Father and Son*.

37. Eve Kosofsky Sedgwick has initiated a similar project in her critique of "homophobia" and "homosexual panic" in English literature. As her terminology suggests, Sedgwick maintains a critical distance from Freud and the pathological implications of terms like "paranoia," though she notes that the homoerotic plots of many Gothic novels "might be mapped almost point for point onto the case of Dr. Schreber." Furthermore, drawing on Guy Hocquenghem, she notes that the psychoanalytic conception of paranoia has almost always been used against homosexuals "on account of an association between 'homosexuality' and mental illness." Like Sedgwick, I engage the term "paranoia" as part of an anti-homophobic critical project. See *Between Men: English Literature and Male Homosocial Desire* (New York: Columbia University Press, 1987), 20, 91.

38. Daniel Paul Schreber, *Memoirs of My Nervous Illness* (1903), trans. Ida Macalpine and Richard A. Hunter (Cambridge: Harvard University Press, 1988), 98. All further references appear within the essay.

39. C. G. Jung, *The Psychology of Dementia Paranoides* (1907), trans. R. F. C. Hull (Princeton: Princeton University Press, 1974), 99.

40. Ronell, *The Telephone Book*, 94.

41. Leo Bersani, *The Culture of Redemption* (Cambridge: Harvard University Press, 1990), 184.

42. In fact, this ad is a lot like the cover of Peggy Kamuf's anthology of Jacques Derrida's essays, in which we get a seductive photographic glimpse of the man himself through something like half-closed blinds. Derrida does not, however, provide a 900 number that I can call, which is probably just as well.

43. Slavoj Žiežk, *Enjoy Your Symptom!* (New York: Routledge, 1992), 126.

4

John Rechy and the Grammar of Ostentation

Ricardo L. Ortiz

> The pornography of a work does not derive from the nakedness of bodies, from
> the obscenity of exposed "parts"; rather, it depends on the discourse which is
> implied, that relating to the right of inspection over the body or corpus of the
> other ... to the constant interchange of subjects, and thus to the law of the
> market, to the escalation and outbidding which governs everything, including us
> who speak here.
>
> —Jacques Derrida, "Right of Inspection"[1]

1. Showing

LITERALLY SPEAKING, John Rechy's *Numbers* may be said to demonstrate, indeed
to enact, the old adage of etiquette, that it is impolite to point.[2] Rechy's rag-
ing exhibitionism characteristically manifests itself in early texts like *Numbers*
precisely in its frequent pointing to itself. *Numbers* betrays its dissatisfaction with
simple, narcissistic self-exposure through the recurrence of some very stagy
graphic marks, marks at once remarkable and redoubtable in their making-appar-
ent Rechy's flexing of tight, textual muscle. This should not, however, be taken
to describe a simply closed model of self-reference; textual economies in Rechy
insist on their openness, on the uneasy accommodation of excess, on a certain
appreciation of waste, of trash, of the trashy. Rechy's readers often trash Rechy,
indeed, because of this false move, this faux pas. His texts, especially early porn
like *Numbers*, symptomatically risk impoliteness in the indiscretion with which
they point; they are often "read" as impolitic, unpolished, woefully apolitical,
politically indiscreet, incorrect.

   In writing, however, there are many ways to show, and therefore many ways
to show too much, and to show off. Rechy's indiscretions may begin with the
manner in which he details the sexual encounters of his string of male-hustler
protagonists, but they end elsewhere, in another space of inter-coursing bodies.
In order to "show" us the figure of Johnny Rio in *Numbers*, for example, Rechy
seems to need to show himself showing us Johnny. Look at these two instances
early in *Numbers*:

As he speeds ineluctably to the foggy city of dead angels . . . ,
Johnny Rio appears moody, almost sinister, like an angel of dark
sex, or death.
   He looks like this:
   He is very masculine, and has been described recurrently in
homosexual jargon as "a very butch number." . . . [3]

and later:

And so, that evening, he went to Pershing Square.
He's dressed like this:
In a thin, pale-yellow silk shirt, perfectly tailored to show
off his body (even his nipples are slightly outlined)[4]

No one "sees" Johnny approach Los Angeles in his car, but, thanks to Rechy's narration, he "looks" at himself, offers himself as something to be looked at, for the voyeuristic pleasure of the "invisible" reader. Simultaneously, of course, Rechy gets in on the act; he steals the show from Johnny, upstages him by showing himself showing in the two indicative phrases, "He looks like this: . . . He's dressed like this:" which in turn point both to and away from their own bodies, their own material, graphic substance. The proximate demonstrative "this" in both cases shows out the representational problematic of pornography, as well as the "pornographic" problematic of representation, this latter especially if we take the epigraph from Derrida at its word.

   When the demonstrative "this" gets too close to its referent or antecedent, it cannot help but fold back into the mark itself, the "this" which allows it to appear and mean, point to, indicate, make appear some other "this," which is (il)logically always a "that." At this level, the argument is equally about the ostentation of grammar as it is about the grammar of ostentation. To look like "this" is then always to look like words, to enjoin substantial bodies; in the case of pornographic writing, to give way to "naked" words or marks or images. "This" in the first instance thus points to "number," the insistently "recurrent" term in "homosexual jargon," the central, organizing metaphor of the text, and one of many instances of the text's indulgent self-naming. "This," in the second instance, addresses itself in/to the dress of its textuality; Johnny's nipple (outlined by the thin fabric of pale-yellow silk) protrudes from Rechy's "thin" prose in the parenthetical phrase devoted to it.

   A more pointed mark for pointing occurs, of course, in the punctuational mark of the colon (":") following the two pronouns. The colon, at once the graphic marker of indication, identification, and renaming, figures at once all the most poignant crises implicated in, say, Lacan's theorizing of the mirror-stage in the psychic career of the subject. Often Johnny finds himself redoubled in a mirror-image marked graphically by the colon. Johnny's flight to Los Angeles begins on "that day" when "as he stood looking at himself in the mirror, he felt curiously that he had ceased to exist, that he existed only in the mirror," and he becomes nostalgic for his days as a male hustler, his personal, irretrievable "before," when "others had confirmed his existence with admiration."[5] His interminable sexual game finally dissipates, suggestively, in the public restroom of the Griffith Park Observatory, where, as Johnny stares at his impossibly alienated image in the mirror, Rechy's colons proliferate, play a promiscuous, graphic game of see/saw with his periods:[6]

> It began then.
> Like this:
> A coldness in his heart . . .
>
> All the symptoms of fear. Yes. And of terror.
> Except that: In Johnny they became a craving to be
> desired. All those manifestations flowed into a starved longing
> which burrowed insistently into his groin: a fire there: a harsh
> demand for sex: a self-contradictory *cold* excitement.
> He set his suitcase aside. He got into his car, and it was
> suddenly as if a force beyond himself was pulling him physically
> into the Park.
> And he felt:
> That coldness. And:
> A sadness.[7]

Johnny's body, however heavenly, experiences here the mortification of the gaze mediated by the colonizing effect of the mirror, and the mirroring effect of the colon. What telescoping Rechy manages here is as much an effect of the dispersal of desire into the "jungle" (and no "Park") of visible, innumerable signs eroticizing *Numbers*, as it is an effect of Johnny's despairing submission to his "ineluctable" self-alienation.

Rechy's text thus displays itself most indiscreetly as it plays with its own material, graphic substance. It is also in this motivated manner of play that it performs its own curious colonization, its rendering of itself as pornographic object. I will have occasion later to analyze the colonizing of Johnny's ethnicity in *Numbers*, where his impolitic pointing borders on the politically incorrect. Here it suffices to say that, as pornography *Numbers* both exploits an image of the eroticized (presumably) gay man and takes upon itself the status of pornographic object or image. In doing so, it rehearses Rechy's self-pornographing gesture in his cultivation of the "hustler" persona as the paradigmatic structure of his own authorship. Rechy's insistence on representing himself as the available street-cruiser in his jacket-cover photographs betrays the depth of the pornographic conceit in his writing, and begins to create a different relation between author, text, and audience in the space of pornographic representation.

This is most directly illustrated in the manner in which Rechy inscribes himself into the text of *Numbers* as a ghostly mark: an old queen recognizes Johnny upon his return to Pershing Square, and she tells Johnny of the "stir" created by "a young number" who "used to hang around the bars and Pershing Square" and "wrote about Main Street and hustling."[8] "Can you imagine?" the old queen goes on, "I knew him—the author . . . why, he looked like any other young vagrant. . . . Now, every time I pick up a hustler, I wonder if I'm going to end up between the sheets of a bed, or the sheets of a book." Rechy thus swells the ranks on each side of the mark of pleasurable transaction; Johnny the hustler evokes the memory of the hustler as author, while the queen is the john is the "daddy" or patron, and by extension the reader.[9] But in doing so Rechy exposes the double falsehood, the bad faith at the heart of the logic of this dichotomy; each figure is caught in the pornographic act of figuration. The book and the bed collapse into one another, and in that intimate space "between the sheets" simultaneously woven of text and textile, "john," John, and Johnny meet, fuse in the interminable echo of the author's name, in the abysmal inscription of his "signature" style.

2. Numb(er)ing

In another book of numbers, Jacques Lacan resituates the subject in the place of the *objet a* through the mathematical analogue of the Cartesian "zero." While numeration is not nomination, certainly *de*nomination plays a role in the function of numerical formulae, especially those involving the fragmentation of integers into fractions. It is here, where the zero threatens to take its place as the denominator, that mathematical language speaks impossibility, where even the Cartesian cogito confronts the fracture of its integrity. "Everyone knows," Lacan submits, "that if zero is placed in the denominator, the value of the fraction no longer has meaning, but assumes by convention what mathematicians call an infinite value." He continues:

> In a way, this is one of the stages in the constitution of the subject. In so far as the primary signifier is pure non-sense, it becomes the bearer of the infinitization of the value of the subject, not open to all meanings, but abolishing them all, which is different. . . . It constitutes the subject in his freedom in relation to all meanings, but this does not mean that it is not determined in it. For, in the numerator, in the place of the zero, the things that are inscribed are significations, dialectized significations in the relation of the desire of the Other, and they give a particular value to the relation of the subject to the unconscious.[10]

Rechy's text intuits this relation between nomination and denomination; Johnny's tricks are named as numbers, as determinate quantitative values which accumulate as the hollow of Johnny's desire expands. Implicit in Rechy's inscription and narration of Johnny's erotic quest is the understanding that, rather than begin-ning *from* zero, we count in the course of our lives *to* zero, (just as Johnny's own name "ends" with an "o") though always with hope of never arriving at the end-term. Johnny's challenge to himself of turning thirty tricks in ten days is sym-bolically a challenge to arrive at such an end-term, specifically "The (graphic) End" of a printed text. As a writer friend tells him (and us), "your . . . goal—30 . . . is a printer's term for The End," something Johnny should have known, given that he worked as "a copy boy" for a newspaper in his youth.[11]

I have already remarked on one instance of Johnny's being a copy, an echo of both "John" the author and the "john"-like reader of porn. Johnny's counting, though, is also relegated to an unproductive, unprofitable act of copying. Johnny's tricks, all anonymous, accumulate no value, compose nothing but a se-quence of zeroes in Johnny's account-books. This is Johnny counting:

> He counted: the thin youngman in the balcony, one; the guy in the men's room, two; the weird fucker in MacArthur Park, three; the two trunks this afternoon, four and five; the man who licked me all over, six. Six. I must've forgotten one; I'm sure it's seven. Let's see: one, two, three, four, five, six, and— . . . just six. No, seven! Yeah!—I forgot the man in the movies!—the first one who sat next to me. He didn't really suck me, just tried to through my pants—but he did grope me earlier and took out my cock. I forgot to count him.
>
> "Count"?
>
> The word, looming large in his consciousness, startled Johnny. Oh, it's not that I'm counting. . . .

And he's right. The whole point of turning tricks, some might argue, is that they don't count. Especially when they occur outside the manifest economy of pros-titution, they have a funny tendency of disappearing as quickly as they appear in the field of the subject's vision; mere pulses on one channel of a latent economy of pleasure, they might as well take the nebulous form of the "first" man "in the movies," figures projected on a screen long since faded to dark.[12]

Numbers counts to zero in at least two other significant ways. It works di-rectly against the sensationalism of its own pornography by performing a kind of an-aestheticization on its hero, and on its own textuality. Past the point of any hope, Johnny submits to the doom of endless repetition, chanting "Numbers, numbers, numbers, numb—"[13] This punning on Rechy's part both fragments the subjectivity of his protagonist in the suggestion of his desensitization, and frag-ments his text: as *Numbers* accumulates signs in the headlong flight to its end, it takes itself up short in a number of ways. The graphic sign of "The End," as we have seen, occurs well before its time, in the explanation of the symbolism of thirty. The text unnames itself, relegates itself to the anonymity symptomatic of its symbolic life, in the failure to complete the final "numb—". In so doing, it also anaesthetizes itself, takes itself out of the register of the aesthetic, positions itself in an altogether different, an-aesthetic textual space. This space is best described as that occupied by the minimalist fiction from which Rechy takes many stylistic cues. *Numbers* is the style which thrives on the illusion of the absence of style. It is the verbal equivalent of the cinematic "look" which foregrounds, and indeed guarantees, the pornographic content of a film by not distracting the audience with too much "style." This gesture, I would argue, constitutes what we might term the "numbing sensationalism" of porn.

3. Gendering[14]

Rechy's text is woefully bereft of flourishes, of the flowers of rhetoric which traditionally mark "literary" language, and which abound in his one true "literary" success, *City of Night*. Language in *Numbers* tends to the status of "mere" language; as such it re-poses (in a field of flowers) the question Derrida asks of Genet's more florid style, that, "If . . . there is no language of flowers, if the flower is in (the) place of zero signification, how can this symbolic zero take hold in a jungle of signs and figures belonging to the natural tongue, to nature, to the physical tongue, as a mother tongue that is necessarily foreign to it?"[15] Flowers, anatomically, are genitals. Clearly, references to Johnny's cock abound in the text of *Numbers*; it is repeatedly taken hold of, and thus takes its hold as one of the odd "flowers" of Rechy's language. The hands which grasp, which apprehend and comprehend the shaft, the thrust of Rechy's language, recur symbolically in Johnny's references to other men as *mano*, the shortening of the Spanish *hermano*, brother, which verbally reduces all Johnny's "brothers" to the function of their hands. For a contact to constitute a trick according to the rules of Johnny's game, he must touch Johnny's cock with either his hands or his tongue. Tongues therefore play as freely with the one flower in Rechy's text as hands do.

This play of tongues is not, however, without further complication. Johnny's occasional reversion to his mother's Spanish, to the mother tongue foreign both to him and to the language in which *Numbers* is written, speaks to the profound repression of linguistically, oedipally motivated desire in Rechy's writing. Johnny's alienated desire for the desire of an endless string of "daddies," that desire which animates *Numbers*, clearly displaces onto text, onto the graphic mark, that unnameable pleasure bodied forth in the physical tongue's contact with the lips, the teeth, the palate, and all other organs of sensation.[16]

What there is of nature in the strictly urban space of Rechy's imagination suffers a similar blight. "Years ago," he tells us, "a great fire swept Griffith Park in Los Angeles. It had been a dry, hot season; and the soil panted for water. Flames clutched greedily at the dry brushes, the trees, the sun-seared grass. . . . The blaze left horrid scars. Brown ashen patches, black skeleton trees—like something out of a dream of desolation. . . . Now the wounds, almost completely healed, have become a part of the vicissitude of the landscape. New trees, new brush, new grass, even new soil cover the razed terrain."[17] But no flowers, not on the anthropomorphic body of nature; they remain the "zero," the absence in Rechy's signification. Except: that when a "blond youngman" encounters Johnny in one of the brushy enclosures of the park and "reaches out—tentatively—to touch Johnny's chest, lightly," Rechy allows something to flourish:

> His fingers brush lower, to the edge of his pubic hair, brush his balls, touching Johnny's cock, holding it while (an)other sucks it.
> Then the blond head bends toward Johnny—and Johnny, thinking the youngman wants to kiss him on the lips, draws back quickly, a knife of fear wrenched into him. But he's wrong . . . what the youngman wants to do is this —and he lets him: At the same time that he continues the light movements with the fingers of one hand and holds Johnny's prick with the other for the dark youngman to suck, he laps at Johnny's nipples with his tongue. . . .
> After long moments during which he felt that, for whatever strange reason . . . he wouldn't be able to make it—Johnny knows he'll come. His body stiffens. Alerted, the dark youngman plunges more rapidly with his mouth; the blond one cups Johnny's balls in his hand, his tongue flits in moist circles about his nipples.
> In one sudden, jetting thrust, Johnny comes.

This scene, like numerous staged in the theatre of the park, shows Rechy performing his characteristic transformation. The blond trick "brushes" Johnny's body in the park's brush, naturalizing one "body" as the other is de-naturalized. The simultaneous stimulation of Johnny's nipples and cock also suggests something that the literary pornographic imagination has sensed at least since Cleland's writing of *Fanny Hill*, that is, the interchangeability in fantasy of the penis and the breast.[18] Johnny's manic psychic passivity belies his ostensibly macho, "top" posturing; in the play of the gaze, he is more seen than seeing, certainly more sucked than sucking. His "jetting thrust" is as much a sign of helpless depletion as it is of active satisfaction; in the park, between the trees, in the play of dark and light signaling competing male desires, Johnny has become the all-giving maternal source. He has, in his absolute phallicization, become his mother.

Johnny's repeated "macho" sexual performances thus constitute his acting in bad faith. Lacan observes at the very conclusion of "The Signification of the Phallus" that, as "the function of the mask . . . dominates the identifications through which refusals of love are resolved," and as "femininity" in particular therefore "takes refuge in this mask," then even "virile display itself" as a performance of gender-identification hinging on the effect of masquerade, "appears as something feminine."[19] At this point we find ourselves well within the theoretical territory recently explored by Judith Butler in *Gender Trouble: Feminism and the Subversion of Identity*.[20] Clearly Butler's central argument for a performative basis to the subject-forming effect of gender can go a long way to explicate Johnny Rio's unstable gendering. Not that Rechy himself had not already theorized this point, had not already tested it on the terrain of Johnny's textual body. "Johnny's is an easy masculinity," Rechy tells us:

> —not stiff, not rigid, not blundering nor posed . . . [and] as with all truly sexually attractive men, there is something very, very subtly female about him; and only at first does that seem a semantic contradiction . . . the "femaleness" has to do with the fact that he moves sensually, that his eyes invite, that he is constantly flirting . . . and that he is extremely vain. . . . And, also, it has to do with a harrowing sensitivity about age.[21]

It is thus that Rechy inscribes an unstably gendered identity onto the surface of his protagonist's body, and thereby performs, in Butler's words, the "gender border control that differentiates inner from outer, and so institutes the 'integrity' of the subject."[22] We have already seen how Rechy's text enacts the dis-integration of its operative subjectivities on all levels, authorial, narrative, and readerly. Butler's work will help us, though, to understand the relation between this performativity, its reliance on a repetition which is not cumulative, and the problem of temporality.

Butler argues that "gender [as] an act . . . requires a performance that is repeated," which in turn renders it "an identity tenuously constituted in time, instituted in exterior space" and explains the emphatically "social" nature of that temporality. Clearly Johnny's counting of his repetitive sexual encounters can be read as the text's way of telling time, of organizing its own temporal extensions, of articulating its own "harrowing sensitivity" about time. On the other hand, *Numbers* also exhibits the odd atemporality conventional to pornography. Time does not seem to pass because Johnny's anonymous, furtive, indistinguishable tricks do not mark progress, regress or any sort of temporal motion. Johnny has taken himself out of the register of narrative, of the story, and by extension of the historical, by coming too soon, and too often. As I have already observed twice before, *Numbers'* "The End" occurs well before it "ends," (typo)graphically guaranteeing it never will. *Numbers* stops with the image of Johnny Rio leaning "against the trunk of a tree," as yet another "man bends down before him," and exclaiming *"Thirty-seven!"* to himself. Johnny's failure, therefore comes in the form of a failure *not* to repeat; he misses what Butler terms "the possibilities of gender transformation . . . to be found . . . in the possibility of a failure to repeat, a de-formity, or a parodic repetition that exposes the phantasmatic effect of an abiding identity as a politically tenuous construction."[23] Johnny's career is certainly *too* "true to form" in the way that it conforms to pornographic convention; this confirms the tragic cast of his fate as a character. On the other hand,

Johnny's hyper-machismo, coupled with Rechy's hyperbolic sense of the dramatic, could be said to allow *Numbers* some limited critical power as precisely a *parodic* re-inscription of some of mainstream pornography's most oppressively gendered codings.

4. Passing

The most disappointing aspect of Rechy's limited critique of gendered identity is that it repeats the sin often ascribed to his apprehensive inscription of his ethnic identity, especially in his early fiction. Johnny Rio thus represents the space of two simultaneous "border" skirmishes, one sexual and the other ethnic or cultural.[24] Johnny's "failure" not to repeat keeps him not only out of time, but also out of history, especially one that is specifically politicized. Rechy has recently given significant attention to Chicano culture in his fiction, but he continues to resist being labelled a "gay" writer; he feels that his career has been hurt by this "ghettoizing" label, and that his pre-Stonewall fiction received a fairer, more disinterested reception, regardless of its explicit homosexual content, when his authorial identity was more difficult to categorize.[25] It is this troubling positioning of Rechy's which has provoked the charges of political indifference, of impolitic, showy self-indulgence with which I played in my opening paragraph. It resituates the question of identity and its construction as an especially tricky one for politically marginalized groups whose assertion of marginalized status is a matter of choice because we can, indeed, pass for mainstream.

It is not my aim here to defend or rescue Rechy politically. Derrida's argument in "Right of Inspection" suggests the need for a different kind of "political" vigilance in reading: the language of law and governance in the epigraph raises the question of critical interpretation as a kind of police work, a "correctional" institution of reading which would always seem to position the reader on the "right" side of some suspiciously tricky law. Such a "right" of inspection implies a "right" of judgment inimical to Rechy's self-styled brand of "outlaw" textuality. As an implicit analysis of the problem of political correctness in the context of presumably "free" intellectual exchange, this essay will not serve me as an occasion to take on the burden of policing what I read, or myself in reading. I thus take a complementary "outlaw" position in my reading; I am the john solicited by Rechy's text into a pleasurable transaction. I must, as an avowed practitioner in pornocriticism, and complicit therefore in an act of pleasuring defined by its odd illegality, take responsibility for a pleasure I hope to have confessed to enjoying in my reading of *Numbers*.

Roland Barthes finds the "pleasure of the text [in] that moment when my body pursues its own ideas—for my body does not have the same ideas I do."[26] For this reason, what pleasure I derive from *Numbers* has little to do with my *conscious* awareness that "in the text . . . I desire the author," that "I need his figure

. . . as he needs mine"[27] for the purpose of confirming something I wish to assert about myself, the cues for which I wished to find in Rechy. My own choice not to pass as straight, or as "non-ethnic," imposes no limit on what Rechy, despite his different choices, can do to please me, to satisfy my desire for, say, a gay latino "father."[28]

Notes

1. Jacques Derrida and Marie-Françoise Pissart, "Right of Inspection," trans. David Wills in *Art and Text* 32 (autumn 1989): 19–97.

2. John Rechy, *Numbers* (New York: Grove-Weidenfeld), 1984. First published in 1967.

3. *Ibid.*, p. 16.

4. *Ibid.*, p. 27.

5. *Ibid.*, p. 23.

6. Rechy's unpunctual use of periods often plays with the complex temporality of grammar, with the way syntax depends on a diachronic exfoliation of meaning. When an old john spots Johnny back in Los Angeles, Rechy has him ask, "Now tell us: Where? have? you? been?" his eyes blinking "as he punches each word out lightly" (*Numbers*, p. 22). Dividing each word from the others not only turns each word into a question, but it disrupts the sequential, metonymic link of semantic values which propels the question to expression, to the momentous articulation of desire. Later, Rechy repeats the (dis)play of periods in Johnny's observation that the absence of the black woman preacher usually (and punctually) portending doom in Pershing Square "Doesn't. Mean. Anything." (*Numbers*, p. 227). As the recurrent chorus-like image of apocalypse in the text, the woman and her repeated chant of "We awll doomed" operates very much like the rest of Rechy's "periods," his abundant signing of ends.

7. *Numbers*, p. 243.

8. *Ibid.*, pp. 25–26.

9. I will return to my own position as reader in the last paragraphs of this chapter. Let it suffice for now to say that Rechy's prostitutive model of literary transaction exhibits an odd symmetry. "John" the hustling, solicitous writer renders the reader structurally "john"-like in his response to that solicitation. But if the reader occupies the position of patron or daddy, this relation folds in on itself to the extent that the author is traditionally said to "father" a text, or even to father comprehension (and pleasure) in the reader. Rechy serves me like/as a father in important ways, both culturally and politically, regardless of the manner in which I patronize him (commercially, and otherwise) as a reader of his texts. "Fathering" each other in this way certainly sends us into a vertiginous, anti-oedipal spin, one which expands even further the rich potential for obscenity in our intercourse.

10. Jacques Lacan, *The Four Fundamental Concepts of Psychoanalysis*, ed. Jacques-Alain Miller, trans. Alan Sheridan (London: Penguin, 1979), pp. 251–52. The more specific discussion of the analogous place of the subject in Cartesian mathematics occurs on pp. 224–26 of the same volume.

11. *Numbers*, p. 231.

12. This particular observation I owe to Roland Barthes, who, in theorizing the "asocial

character of (textual) bliss" in *The Pleasure of the Text*, trans. Richard Miller) New York: Noonday Press, 1975), argues that it admits no "recurrence" even "to the subject"; in it *"everything is lost, integrally."* Bliss thus occupies a constitutively obscene space, described as the "Extremity of the clandestine, the darkness of the motion-picture theatre" (Barthes, p. 39).

13. *Numbers*, p. 249.

14. Stemming from the ongoing discussion of aesthetics, this break should be read doubly; it signals the continuation of the discussion of style as a question of genre, as well as moving into an analysis of Rechy's construction of gender. I take my cues here from French theory's always fertile punning of gender and genre. See, for example, Derrida's argument in "Right of Inspection" that "the question of genre poses and develops sexual difference in its most precise and unstable form, as a difference which actually wavers and not as a binary opposition. What wavers here," Derrida concludes, is constitutively "the law of genre" ("Right of Inspection," p. 40).

15. Jacques Derrida, *Glas*, trans. John P. Leavey, Jr., and Richard Rand (Lincoln: University of Nebraska Press), 1986, p. 31. It is worth noting in passing that Rechy's shift in style from *City of Night* to *Numbers* parallels a shift in literary and philosophical interest from Genet to Camus. *Numbers's* existential minimalism certainly silences what echoes of *Notre-Dame des Fleurs* reverberate through *City of Night*.

16. The split here between written and spoken language, between father and mother tongues, leaves its profound mark on all of Rechy's writing. See especially Rechy's foreword to the 1984 edition of *City of Night* (New York: Grove-Weidenfeld, pp. x–xiii), where he recounts his early life in El Paso. Rechy spoke only Spanish until he entered school, where, presumably, he learned both to speak and write in English; his Mexican mother never learned English, so he would translate his work for her in the course of writing it. It is suggestive, too, that the inspiration for *Numbers* came after a visit to Los Angeles with his mother. In the foreword to the 1984 edition of *Numbers*, Rechy tells us that his mother held the notepad on the dash of his Mustang on which he jotted the preliminary notes for his second novel. In more ways than one, therefore, his mother "had a hand" in the composition of the novel. See *Numbers*, p. 2.

17. *Numbers*, pp. 108–109.

18. Witness the following passage from Cleland, which brings Fanny back to her one "true" lover, Charles: " . . . my lover, lavish of his stores and pleasure-milked, overflowed me once more from the fulness of those his oval reservoirs of the genial emulsion; whilst, on my side, a convulsive grasp . . . rendered me sweetly subservient at once to the increase of his joy and of its effusions, moving me so as to make me exert all those springs of the compressive exsuction, with which the sensitive mechanism of that part thirstily draws and drains the nipple of love, with much such an instinctive eagerness and attachment as, to compare great with less, kind nature engages infants at the breast, by the pleasure they find in the motion of their little mouths and cheeks to extract the milky stream prepared for their nourishment." See John Cleland, *Fanny Hill, or Memoirs of a Woman of Pleasure*, ed. Peter Wagner (London: Penguin: 1985), p. 221. See also Freud's essay on Leonardo da Vinci (*Standard Edition*, vol. XI, pp. 57–137), where Freud explains the recurrence of hermaphroditic images in mythology and childhood fantasy as follows: "What has happened . . . is that the male organ has been added to the breasts which are the mark of a mother, just as it was present in the child's first idea of his mother's body" (Freud, p. 98).

19. Jacques Lacan, *Écrits*, trans. Alan Sheridan (New York: W. W. Norton), 1977, p. 291. In the *Four Fundamental Concepts of Psychoanalysis*, Lacan also offers an interestingly gendered explication of the subject's career in the register of fantasy: "What the voyeur is looking for," Lacan argues, "is merely a shadow, a shadow behind a curtain. There he will fantasize any magic of presence, the most graceful of girls . . . even if on the other side there is only a hairy athlete. What he is looking for is not, as one says, the phallus—but precisely its absence, hence the

pre-eminence of certain forms as objects of his search" (*Four Fundamental Concepts*, pp. 182–83). An interesting recent application of Lacan's idea to the larger problem of gay male sexual identifications can be found in the last chapter of Kaja Silverman's *Male Subjectivity at the Margins* (New York: Routledge, 1992), pp. 339–88.

20. Judith Butler, *Gender Trouble: Feminism and the Subversion of Identity* (New York: Routledge, 1990). See esp. pp. 136–41.

21. *Numbers*, p. 17.

22. Butler, p. 136.

23. Butler, p. 141. Barthes's comments on the effect of repetition on text augment Butler's, and illustrate what many readers find so compelling in what otherwise might seem to be the interminable repetition of sexual scenes in porn. Barthes argues that repeating "excessively," in the way Butler terms "parodic," "is to enter into loss, into the zero of the signified . . . in order for repetition to be erotic, it must be formal, literal . . . [which] in our culture reverts to eccentricity, to marginality" (Barthes, p. 41).

24. This is best exemplified in the punning of Johnny Rio's name. See *Numbers*, p. 18, for an explanation of Johnny's self-nomination. "Johnny Rio" is a pseudonym, reminiscent of the dark, exotic male romantic lead in B-grade Hollywood films. As such, it reflects Johnny's willingness to stereotype himself. On the other hand, it names precisely the problem of borders, as it echoes the "*río*" separating México and the U.S. in southern Texas. So while "Rio" has no familial derivation, its plural cultural derivations send it on a rather complex, connotative drift.

25. I base these observations on remarks Rechy made in person to an undergraduate gay fiction class at UCLA in the spring of 1990. And yes, his nipples were quite apparently "outlined" underneath the tight T-shirt he wore over a tight pair of Levis.

26. Barthes, p. 17.

27. Ibid., pp. 26–27.

28. Read: daddy.

5

Homodevotion

Richard Rambuss

Let me be manly. Let me commit myself to my merciful Creator.

—James Boswell, *London Journal*

Oᴺᴇ ᴏғ ᴛʜᴇ most highly praised gay porn videotapes of recent years, director Jerry Douglas's 1990 *More of a Man* begins, as these things go, with its leading man Vito on his knees.[1] In front of him is a naked male form. Vito, still kneeling, to the same: "You name it, I'll do it." The setting for this alluring scene of submission is an empty church, and the denuded male form Vito addresses is an effigy of Jesus on the cross, dangling from the rosary bead bound up in his hands—thereby offering Christ's as the first of the unclothed male bodies to appear within the pornographic field of vision. This staging of a porno film in church, to a backdrop of votive candles and cathedral bells, means more, however, than simply a gay male recasting of the devotional chic of Madonna's "Like a Prayer" video, the sacrilegious sensation of a few years before.[2] Indeed, allotting Christ his place among the desired and desiring bodies of gay pornography is a "scandal" arguably elicited, as I want to explore here, by Christianity's own libidinal structures. "Christianity may be near-ubiquitous in modern European culture as a figure of phobic prohibition," Eve Kosofsky Sedgwick has noticed in *Epistemology of the Closet*, "but it makes a strange figure for that indeed." Sedgwick continues:

> Catholicism in particular is famous for giving countless gay and proto-gay children the shock of the possibility of adults who don't marry, of men in dresses, of passionate theatre, of introspective investment, of lives filled with what could, ideally without diminution, be called the work of the fetish. . . . And presiding over all are images of Jesus. . . . The scandal of such a figure within a homophobic economy of the male gaze doesn't seem to abate: efforts to disembody this body . . . only entangle it the more compromisingly among various modern figurations of the homosexual.[3]

The final shot of *More of a Man* graphically testifies to the sort of entanglement Sedgwick uncovers here, offering us in freeze-frame the bedside image of Vito's rosary beads next to a spent condom.

Narrativized as the coming-out story of a conflicted Italian Catholic construction worker (played by porn star of the moment Joey Stephano), *More of a Man* undertakes a reconciliation of Vito's devotion to Christ, his correspondingly fervent desire for the bodies of other men, and his emphatically maintained identity as a man who is "more of a man." Thus the solicitation that opens the tape ("You name it, I'll do it") comes in the course of Vito's prayer to be saved from what he calls "all these crazy thoughts . . . okay, okay, these impure thoughts." As if in response to his supplications, he is led, however, through a series of increasingly public homosexual encounters; all the while he carries with him the rosary beads of the opening scene—a token, as I see it, of Christ's sanctioning accompaniment. In the scene that sets up the conclusion of the narrative, we find Vito now "out" enough to ride shirtless atop a float in the L. A. Gay Pride parade, before he heads right inside the float itself accompanied by Duffy—an equally butch L. A. Dodger fan, but also, it turns out, an ACT-UP activist. Their coupling not only brings off the boys' standing flirtation; this final sexual number also emblematizes how devotion, activism, and homosex can come together in the end.[4] Redemption is thus wrought for the symbolically as well as ethnically named Vito, but not at all in the terms he expects at the beginning of the tape— terms which would have kept in opposition his religious devotion and his homosexuality, but also his virility and his sexual desire for the bodies of other men. In *More of a Man*, redemption at last arrives, but it does so in terms of both a coming out and a cum shot, each performance in the service, as I will discuss, of "reforming" Vito as a *butch* gay man, a new gay clone for the '90s.

I will return to *More of a Man* at a later point in this chapter. In the meantime, I want to shift my focus from the contemporary media of video pornography to another, in this case early modern, technology for processing desire and subjectivity in the form of religious lyric poetry. Here, within the amorously accentuated devotional expressions of such seventeenth-century male poets as John Donne, George Herbert, and Richard Crashaw, one finds enactments of erotic desire and gender, all performed in cathexis to a viscerally rendered body of Jesus, that are hardly less spectacularized than those which comprise the redemption-minded pornography with which I began.[5] By juxtaposing that video text with this corpus of sacred verse I want first to claim for the kind of homodevotional pleasure offered in *More of a Man* a canonical pedigree in terms of these metaphysical poets, poets who hold a central position in the period widely esteemed as the apex of religious literature in English. Second, by means of this "unnatural" association I hope to set in a different kind of relief the much-remarked corporealities, as well as vulgarities, of metaphysical verse itself. Posited as analogous to *More of a Man*'s (only apparently) conflicting mise-en-scènes of religious devotion (the rosary beads, the crucifix over Vito's bed, the plastic Virgin Mary on his dashboard) and gay butch masculinity (Vito's pickup truck, baseball cap, and levis, his and Duffy's short haircuts, muscles, and tattoos), metaphysical religious poetry, notorious for its own colliding decorums of the sacred and the sensual, thus becomes a culturally canonic site at which the arcings of male same-sex desire as they travel through and across the body of Jesus can be, but have yet to be, recovered into view.

Christ's body—"This sweeter BODY," as Crashaw's English rendering of the "Office of the Holy Cross" terms him[6]—becomes deeply, sometimes extravagantly corporealized in seventeenth-century devotional literature, where it is recurrently imagined in its arresting nakedness and vulnerability. Thus to cite from any of his numerous lyrics on the crucifixion, we find Crashaw presenting Christ's Passion as a spectacle of bodily penetration:

> Wicked soldier, you will see there the wounds you inflicted
> through whatever skill your madness tricked you with.
>
> Whether at your finger's prodding the *thorny laurel* drank
> from his temples, or the spear drank from the holy side,
>
> or the nails grew cruelly red under your blow,
> or the scourge was ashamed to act at your command.
>
> (Lines 11–16)

This particular epigram, titled "Luke 24:38–40. On the wounds of the Master still present," is just one version of a poem on the manifold violations of Jesus's body that Crashaw seemed never to want to stop writing, a prolix text which exists in the Crashaw corpus in multiple versions, both English and (as in the case above) Latin.[7] In this one, the body of Christ is pierced by the implements of a "Wicked soldier" ("*Improbe . . . miles*"), and it is a wrenching sight. But Christ's body is also subject at the same time, we are shown here, to a second form of penetration. Though performed by another "*miles*," it bears a quite different valence:

> You see the weapons: the bows, the quiver and the light
> darts;
> and—by whatever name—the soldier was Love [Amor].
>
> Love used these things: but also he was these things
> himself.
>
> (Lines 1–3)

With this amatory conceit, Crashaw condensed divine and sensual love in the figure of Amor (Christ himself), equipping the Savior with Cupid's tools of the trade. Recurring throughout Crashaw's crucifixion poems, the Christ-as-Cupid

trope thus suffuses the scene of the Passion with erotic as well as spiritual meaning. Nor is Jesus's the only body to be subject to Amor's darts here, as the poem
bestows upon the very sight of the Passion a piercing power: "To see the wound
you inflicted will be your wound" (line 18). Here, as addressed to the Roman
soldier, the promise comes as a fearful retaliatory threat. More commonly in
Crashaw's poetry, however, penetration is regarded as a rapturous pleasure, as it
is in his most famous poem, "A Hymn to Sainte Teresa": "How kindly will thy
gentle HEART / Kisse the sweetly-killing DART! / And close in his embraces
keep / Those delicious Wounds . . . " (lines 105–108). What excites devotion for
Crashaw, what elicits that notorious "metaphysical shudder" here, as well as in
his many crucifixion epigrams, is the discovering of the Savior's as a (male)
body that is at once penetrating and penetrable: "he was these things himself:
both his / dart and he himself the quiver for his darts" ("On the wounds,"
lines 3–4).

As part of an efflorescence of scholarship on the cultural history of the body,
a number of historians and critics have been attending to the restoration of the
body to its rightful place at the core of pre- and early modern religiosity.[8]
Caroline Walker Bynum, for example, argues persuasively that we should recon-
sider the typically extravagant endeavors of medieval female saints to discipline
and manipulate the body (prolonged fasts, extended trances and fits, self-mutilation, and so on) "more as elaborate changes rung upon *possibilities* provided by
fleshiness than as flights from physicality."[9] In this respect, my reading of metaphysical devotional lyric harmonizes with the aims of other cultural historians
to recorporealize our understanding of the practice and doctrines of Christianity. At the same time, however, I want to use the poetry of Donne and Crashaw
to interrogate and to critique the terms under which the devotional body is being
restored to us. For, despite the talk of extending corporeal possibilities, there
seems to be a recurring impulse in scholarship on the sacred body to police the
more manifold libidinalities of the very "fleshiness" (to use Bynum's term) this
work has itself brought back into view. Furthermore, this policing of erotic possibilities shows up most stridently, as I have detailed elsewhere, when the libidinalities in question appear to be other than straight.[10]

Contrary to this impulse, then, I want to argue that the performances of
Christian devotion, enacted in what early modern devotional literature terms
"the prayer closet," are often homoeroticized in ways that have thus far gone un-
remarked or have even been obfuscated. The effectively pitched—or as Henry
Vaughan is wont to say "love-sick"[11]—pinings of these male poets for union with
Christ constitute a body of erotic verse that, in the domain of the prayer closet,
makes the male form visible to desire. Furthermore, as Crashaw's cupidinous epigram on Christ's opened body suggests, and as I will be discussing at length here,
the bodies one finds imaged in the prayer closet, whether Christ's or the wor-

shipper's, tend to be multiply eroticized bodies—queer bodies, one could say—rendered in this verse as at once penetrable and penetrating, ravished and ravishing, active and passive. Thus for Crashaw, Christ's body holds both a dart and a quiver for the darts of others. Similarly, Herbert's poem "Artillerie" figures God and the poet who "wooes" him with love lyrics as "shooters both."[12]

As the central mystery of Christianity, but also its most spectacular piece of theater, the crucifixion naturally claims center-stage in seventeenth-century devotional poetry. In Robert Herrick's "Good Friday. *Rex Tragicus*, or Christ going to his Crosse," Jesus is thus cast "this day [to] act the Tragedian / To [the] wounder and affrightment" of "we (thy lovers)": "The *Crosse* shall be Thy *Stage*; and thou shalt there / The spacious field have for Thy *Theater*."[13] No event in the life of Christ is more written about in this verse, reflection on the exposed and opened body of Jesus being an indulgence de rigueur in the performance of Christian devotion. Donne thus tells us that he keeps a "picture of Christ, crucified" stored in the cabinet of his heart in place of "all my profane mistresses" ("What if this present were the world's last night?").[14] But no English poet is more transported by the image of Jesus on the cross than Crashaw, who, as I noted, composes dozens of epigrams and lyrics, as well as numerous hymns and devotional offices, to hold in view this body and its often astonishing somatic operations. The nexus of interest in these poems, indeed the trigger of their effusive devotion, is, however, not simply the show made of Christ's body, but, as we have already glimpsed, the discovery of that body as penetrable: "Now you lie open. A heavy spear has thrown back the bolt of your heart. / And the nails as keys unlock you on all sides" ("John 10:7–9. I am the door."). Here Christ's body is figured as a kind of opened closet. This architectural metaphor receives further elaboration in "On our crucified Lord Naked, and bloody," undoubtedly one of Crashaw's most bizarre poems. There we are asked to see that body as a "purple wardrobe" (line 4), a sort of clothes-closet, which is thrown open to produce a viscid garment of blood, a lamentable covering for a body the poet would prefer to envision as wholly naked: "Th' have left thee naked Lord, O that they had" (line 1).

Penetrated "on all sides," Jesus becomes, as Herbert entitles him with apparent envy, "King of wounds!" ("The Thanksgiving," line 4). An apt phrase for what the Savior's body undergoes in Crashaw's verse in particular, even when its ostensible subject is something other than the crucifixion. For in addition to epigrams on the whips, thorns, nails, and lance at Calvary, Crashaw also lyricizes sundry other tools employed at one time or another to enter Jesus's body—the circumcising knife the high priest took to the Infant Christ, the searching finger of Doubting Thomas, even the poet's own pen. A stanza he adds to his Englishing of the "*Dies Irae*" takes us inside Christ's body and its redemptive operations, however, in a way that is perhaps unique to Crashaw, incorporating scatology into theology:

> O let thine own soft bowells pay
> Thy self; And so discharge that day.
> If sin can sigh, love can forgive.
> O say the word my Soul shall live.   (stanza xii)[15]

As I read them, these corporeal probings suggest an impetus in Crashaw's early modern devotional imaginary akin to contemporary cinematic pornography's graphic will-to-knowledge of the body, of its otherwise occluded operations, its secret spaces and its orifices.[16] Indeed for Crashaw to represent—or, as he puts it in an epigram "On the still surviving markes of our Saviours wounds," to make "legible"—Christ's body is to remark its permeability, its portals of penetration.

Robert Martin Adams wryly noted years ago in an essay on taste and bad taste in metaphysical poetry that Crashaw "has a sometimes disturbing way of dealing with orifices, which he likes to dwell upon."[17] As we have seen, he is most devoted to dwelling upon the orifices opened in the literally vulnerable body of Jesus. But beyond this, what I find not so much disturbing as arresting in Crashaw's treatment of that body is his tendency to represent it as nothing but orifices and valves:

> Whether I call your wounds *eyes* or *mouths*—
> surely everywhere are mouths—alas—everywhere are eyes!
>   . . .
> Magdala, you who were accustomed to bring tears and kisses
> to the sacred foot, take yours in turn from the sacred foot.

> The foot has its own *mouths*, to give your kisses back:
> This clearly is the *eye* by which it returns your tears.
>   ("On the wounds of the Lord hanging")[18]

Here the body of Jesus is exposed to be all openings; no surface on it is closed off. Everywhere enterable, this body offers no fixed boundaries of permeability and impermeability.

In texturing the body of Jesus as a surface of multiple, sentimentally rendered openings, as so many mouths to kiss and so many eyes to shed tears, Crashaw likewise presents the uncovered male body as a site of proliferating secretionary valves: "O streams of blood from head, side, hands, and feet! / O what rivers rise from the purple fountain! / . . . / O too much *alive* [are] the *waters* in those precious streams! / Never was he more truly the *fountain of life*" ("*In vulnera Dei pendentis*," lines 1–2, 15–16). The penetrated male body thus turns liquescent, a site of utter ejaculatory excess. Correspondingly, Crashaw's poem is itself little more than an accretion of reiterating ejaculations: "O streams of blood"; "O what rivers"; "O side, o torrent!"

Crashaw's verse is of course notorious for its (too) capacious and (too) extreme figures of liquefaction, as well as for the remarkable transitivity of the effluvia that stream and pool therein. In "The Weeper," to take a much reviled but consistently anthologized example, Mary Magdalen's copious tears swell into "milky rivers" before they somehow (in an image that begins to regender the body of the weeper) shoot heavenward to supply the "cream" upon which "Every morn from hence / A brisk Cherub something sippes" (stanzas 4, 5). In the poem on Christ's wounds cited in the paragraph above, Jesus's body, awash "in its own streams," verges on being entirely liquefied. Those "rushing waters" are a confluence of blood and tears (what Crashaw elsewhere terms "an amorous floud / Of WATER wedding BLOOD"),[19] and possibly eucharistic wine as well, but they are also "holy dews," a fecund discharge prized here as "the fountain of life." These liquids likewise flow through Crashaw's long poem *Sospetto d'Herode* ("The Suspicion of Herod"), where they are even more forthrightly eroticized. Happily ringing erotic changes on yet another traditional image of devotional literature—this time that of Christ as honey—Crashaw brings us to another kind of closet, an occluded, indicatively all-male space called the "Hive of Loves" (stanza 3). Inside, Christ offers "hidden sweets," a fructifying discharge of "the deaw of Life" to be imbibed, sucked from his body by those the poem terms his "Heav'n-labouring Bees," his "smiling sons." The erotic operations Christ performs in his "Hive of Loves" on these male bodies are moreover to be carefully distinguished, the poet instructs, from the mortal "deflowering" wrought by the change of seasons. For only the kind of insemination Christ offers can effect a "deathlesse spring."

Like so much seventeenth-century devotional expression, Crashaw's verse has no inclination to leave behind the flesh; rather, it *insists* upon the bodily, intent on opening up its many possibilities. Crashaw's often exorbitantly rendered, unblushingly eroticized epigrams on Jesus's body and what is discharged from it stimulate Christian devotion in terms of a sustained, palpable meditation on the permeabilities of bodies, the male body in particular. These lyric performances are rhapsodies rung on what is outside Christ's body that can be used to enter it (nails, spears, knives, Crashaw's own pen), as well as what can be made to flow out from it, once penetrated, in unending streams (blood, tears, wine, ink, honey, cream, an inseminating dew of life). To represent Christ as a somatic field generative of countless kissing mouths and tearing eyes, of points of penetration and dilated valves, is to open devotion to the affective, even homoerotic possibilities for the coming together of one's own body and Christ's. Such are Crashaw's favored figures for styling the desired devotional merging with Jesus, for making what is evocatively termed his Passion physically commutable from the Son of

Man to man. The fluid permeabilities of Christ's own male body, localized around the physical wound, the hole in the body, become so many opportunities for staging identifications with him and for an ecstatic union with his saving flesh.

This is by no means to suggest, of course, that such excitations are relics belonging only to a more baroque early modern religious expression. For the filibrations of same-sex desire that are spun out from and around Christ's body continue to cast a queer erotic nimbus over Christian prayer closets. In Pedro Almodóvar's film *Law of Desire*, for example, that queerness—no less efficacious for being recognized as such—shows up in the sentimental, but powerful devotion of Carmen Maura's Tina, a one-time favorite altar boy who has grown up to be a leading lady of the Madrid stage. John Waters, who has remarked that "Being Catholic always makes you more theatrical," similarly exploits Christian homodevotion in his early film *Multiple Maniacs*.[20] Offered as a perverse kind of "homage" to the Manson murders and positing Divine as their real perpetrator, the film is structured as another conversion narrative. What isn't clear, however, is whether conversion is here pointed toward a rapturous experience of Christian salvation for Divine, the convert in question, or toward the bestowal upon her of a voluptuous, homicidal career as a mass murderer—or indeed whether there is meant to be any meaningful difference between these two kinds of ecstasies. Divine is set on the path to redemption when she is guided by an apparition of the Infant of Prague from the scene of her back-alley rape to St. Cecilia's Church in downtown Baltimore. "The more you honor me," the Infant promises her as he departs, "the more I will bless you." Once inside the church and at prayer, Divine finds herself being cruised by Mink Stole, a self-identified "Religious Whore," who, Divine reports in an excited voice-over, threw her "a lewdly religious glance." "She kissed as if Christ himself had ordered every move of her well-practiced tongue," Divine continues. The scene culminates when, exhorting her repeatedly to reflect upon the Stations of the Cross, Mink Stole brings Divine to a moaning climax by inserting a rosary crucifix into what Divine terms one of "my most private parts"—all of which is intercut by Waters with a reenactment of Christ's own Passion, station by station. The ritualistic "rosary job" Divine receives from Mink Stole thus effects twin epiphanies in which she finds Jesus and comes out as a lesbian all by means of the same act. And it is from this scene of conversion that Divine takes the inspiration to bring vengeance on all those who have provoked or even irritated her, climaxing in an orgasmic massacre: "I'm a maniac at last!" she screams, having dispatched her philandering husband, daughter, even newfound female lover.

Not altogether unlike what we have seen in Crashaw's provocative lyric poetry, *Multiple Maniacs* graphically tropes on the cross as a device of spiritual delirium and simultaneous physical ecstasy. In thus tracing the enmeshments of

religious and erotic desire from Crashaw's raptures in probing Christ's wounds
to the pornographic conversion setpiece in Waters's film or the devotional trajectories of the hardcore videoporn of *More of a Man* (arcings that travel there
and back from affective Christian devotion to homosexuality; from religious
commitment to political activism), my approach here aims to depart even further
from the protocols governing current historicizing work on the devout body.
That is, it diverges from what I find there to be a censoring impulse under the
guise of a rigorous—indeed, "pure"—historicism ("in those days—i.e., before
Freud—they couldn't have meant *that*"—"that" being the sexual, and more usually the sexually excessive or perverse) inasmuch as I look to interpolate an early
modern cultural form with a contemporary one, to imbricate my readings of the
canonical religious poetry of the Renaissance with a body of queer filmic narrative that ranges from camp to hardcore. I do so because at the juncture of these
admittedly disparate cultural sites—one high, the other low, one early modern
and the other contemporary—the prayer closet might be rendered at its most pel-
lucid. To be sure, these devotional formations are, as Foucault and other historians of sexuality have taught us, metaphorized according to different organizations of sex. Whereas we tend to experience our sexuality as an identity or a
particular orientation, early modern conceptions turn more on the notion, not
of someone as *a* homosexual or *a* heterosexual, but of a range of erotic activities,
some acceptable and others not, but more or less performable by just about anyone.[21] Thus all men (and not simply those of a certain sexual type) were exhorted
from the early modern pulpit to be vigilant against temptations of sexual un-
naturalness with other men. Without minimizing the differences between the
early modern and the modern sexual subject, I nonetheless want to suggest that
both cultural forms—the devotional pinings of the metaphysicals and our own
homodevotional porn—together "know" what prevailing accounts of the deep
embodiedness of Christian piety have not yet faced—know, that is, that the
prayer closet has been and continues to be structured by queer kinds of desire.

Nor is the association of the poetry of Crashaw, Donne, and other religious
poets of the period with homodevotional camp and pornography as incongruous,
as unnatural an act, as it at first may appear. All these forms are exhibitionist in
their drive to bring the body and its most extreme performances and paroxysms,
whether of pleasure or devotion or both, ecstatically into view. Furthermore,
metaphysical verse, characteristically achieving its effects with a rhetoric of ex-
tremities and a jolting confluence of the carnal and the spiritual, of the profane
and the sacred, has accrued from its own time down into ours more charges of
excess, vulgarity, and even queerness than one finds imputed to any other early
modern literary "school." Indeed, the imputation of gross indecorousness and an
excessiveness bordering on the perverse are among the formative features of Samuel Johnson's construction (following Dryden) of a metaphysical school of poetry: "The most heterogeneous ideas are yoked by violence together; nature and

art are ransacked for illustrations, comparisons, and allusions. . . . What they wanted however of the sublime, they endeavored to supply by hyperbole; their amplification has no limits."[22] Donne and Crashaw, the two poets I am most concerned with here, have been particularly singled out as bearers of these charges.[23] And even more so than is the case with Donne, reading Crashaw has been constituted as something of a dirty pleasure. Here is T. S. Eliot: "Crashaw's images, even when entirely preposterous . . . give a kind of intellectual pleasure—it is a deliberate perversity of language."[24] William Empson similarly finds, and enjoys, "Something weird and lurid" in Crashaw's verse.[25] Commenting on the protean liquids of Crashaw's "The Weeper," Robert Martin Adams likewise remarks that "The transformation of salt tears to milk is queer; raising the butterfat content to make cream is odder yet."[26] And so on.

That is to say, of course, that the encouplement of the spiritual and sexual I am discussing here has seldom passed unnoticed. Yet the recent scholarship that has been so successful in bringing back into focus for us the vivid corporealities of early and early modern devotional performance seems to have worked out the erotics of the prayer closet only insofar as they can be normalized in conformance with a heterosexualized erotic schema. Moreover, one finds this straightening of devotional desire unfortunately no less prevalent in feminist work on the devout body—a critical endeavor which, I would maintain, should have no investment in the enforcement of scenarios of compulsory heterosexuality, even when those scenarios are played out "only" on the level of a religious imaginary.

As an example of this normativizing critical practice, I want to return to a text I have discussed elsewhere, John Donne's "Batter my heart three-person'd God," possibly the best known of his Holy Sonnets:

> Batter my heart, three person'd God; for, you
> As yet but knock, breathe, shine, and seek to mend;
> That I may rise, and stand, o'erthrow mee,' and bend
> Your force, to breake, blowe, burn, and make me new.

(lines 1–4)

Donne begins impudently by revealing the inadequacy of God's endeavors on his behalf thus far, and then he calls for more intense measures, measures that would culminate in him being forcefully carried off and ravished:

> Take mee to you, imprison mee, for I
> Except you'enthral mee, never shall be free,
> Nor ever chaste, except you ravish mee.

(lines 12–14)

Remarkably, it isn't enough for the poet to be ravished, to be raped by Jesus alone, as Crashaw's christocentric poetics would probably have it; pursuing his own fantasia of erotic excess, Donne instead insists the whole Christian Godhead be enlisted in the task: "Batter my heart *three person'd* God"—a trinitarian gang-bang.

Elsewhere I have discussed how critical accounts of Donne's shocking, exciting poem have taken the voicing of a desire to be ravished by God as not only effeminizing the poet but also as (metaphorically) regendering him from male to female.[27] Thus Stanley Fish: "Donne now assumes the posture of a woman . . . and spreads his legs (or cheeks)"; "the woman is now asking for it."[28] What I want to point out in this chapter is how sex change seems also to be the preferred operation in gender-oriented criticism concerned with Donne's Holy Sonnets. Debora Kuller Shuger, in an essay chiefly about the vicissitudes of female sacred eroticism, thus finds Donne's structuring of subjectivity to be "erotic, transgressive, abandoned, and female."[29] Ann Baynes Coiro, in a more explicitly feminist account, notes that Donne "usually talks to his God as one aggressive guy to another," only to shy away from her own aptly-put recognition when the scene turns erotic: "The most complete self-abnegation he can imagine is, in 'Batter my heart,' to place himself before God as a woman, a woman begging to be raped."[30] The direction Coiro sets for a reading of Donne's sonnet is especially interesting in that it is offered in the course of her contribution to a recent MLA *Approaches to Teaching the Metaphysical Poets* volume. Coiro's essay works successfully to recuperate these poets, whose misogynist sexual politics have come under attack over the past two decades, as tools in the service of establishing the classroom as a space where all sorts of gender constructions and deployments can be interrogated: "We need to talk to our students about the gender of any persona, about how we as readers form the persona's gender, about how the gender forms the poem, and about the implied but silent other who is also shaped by the gender of the speaker and by us" (p. 84). Missing in Coiro's useful pedagogical concatenation, however, is any analytical trajectory that would specifically raise questions of sexuality, of those erotics not wholly subsumed under the model of marriage and its metaphorics. Thus, while the approach Coiro suggests here would allow us and our students to map a number of gender-marked axes leading in and out of Donne and the other metaphysicals, its elision of other kinds of erotics unwittingly produces its own "silent other," its own acts of effacement. Let me be more specific. Coiro determines that Donne must now be placing himself before God abjectly as a woman because he voices a desire to be taken and ravished. What undergirds this perceived traversal of gender lines, however, is an uninterrogated presumption that such a desire could find only one form, namely a heterosexually modelled one: if the would-be ravisher (God) is male, then the would-be ravished (Donne) must be seen as female. Someone must be assigned the woman's part here, even if all the players are male.

Coiro knows that "Donne intended to shock" (p. 85). I want to suggest that in "Batter my heart" he may be more (or at least differently) shocking than this

gender-bending reading allows, that the poem's shock waves crest beyond the admittedly transgressive enough image of a man assuming the position of a woman
in order to be ravished by another man or male figure. Instead, the sonnet shows
Donne wanting to take it like and as a man. For, to return to Fish's formulation,
though he may be spreading his legs and/or cheeks ("I . . . / Labour to'admit you,
but Oh, to no end" [lines 5–6]), the poet punningly figures himself here as no
less phallicized: "That I may rise, and stand, o'erthrow mee" (line 3). What is
"shocking" then is that in terms of the poem's erotics, being ravished by one's
male God doesn't necessarily entail effeminization or castration. Indeed, as
Donne presents it here, he needs to be ravished in order to be rendered potent,
erect. It also should be said that the power dynamics in play in "Batter my heart"
are more multivalent than the various abjection readings, feminist and non-femi-
nist alike, have hereto allowed. Though he calls out for enthrallment, indeed demands to be enslaved to divine love, Donne never relinquishes his pushy imperatives: "Batter my heart"; "bend your force"; "Take mee to you, imprison mee";
"untie, or breake that knot againe" (line 11); etc. Instructing his master every
step along the way in what he wants to bring him off to spiritual satisfaction,
Donne, from the bottom, calls all the shots.

In his twice reprinted essay "Coming to Terms: Gay Pornography," media
theorist Richard Dyer determines that all-male porn has blunted its subversive
edge by means of its devotion to a certain kind of narrativity, one Dyer sees as
monolithically in the service, just like its hetero counterpart, of producing the
closure of the visibly rendered male orgasm and little more.[31] Apparently it
doesn't count for much here that gay porn's means for achieving that end mostly
lie outside those forms sanctioned in a culture of compulsory heterosexuality. In
any event, much to be preferred by Dyer as a counter-model of narrative organization—or as he sees it, more a *non*-narrative model—is something like the lesbian sexual number at the end of Chantal Akerman's film *je tu il elle*; here Dyer
finds a representation of "sexuality as more dissolving and ebbing than a masculine thrusting narrative." Dyer then goes on to complain that "narrative [in gay
male porn] is never organized around the desire to be fucked, but around the
desire to ejaculate"—though I can't help hearing this call for a narrative restructuring of porn around the pleasure of being fucked as rather at odds with Dyer's
announced distaste for "masculine thrusting narratives."[32] But even if we bracket
that matter, along with the question of whether or not one sort of sexual desire
or pleasure is always to be honored above another—whether, that is, it is more
counter-hegemonic to be a man who is fucked by or who fucks other men[33]—as
well as any problems one should have here with the soft contours of Dyer's notion
of a non-narrativized, non-penetrative, non-orgasmic lesbian sexuality: even if
we hold at bay all this, one still has to wonder about the simple accuracy of Dyer's
binarized claim that gay porn is never structured around the desire to be fucked

but always in terms of wanting to ejaculate. Certainly such reductivist terms do not encompass all the ambitious cultural work *More of a Man*, to which I now return, has in mind to undertake.

Jerry Douglas's videotape takes on as part of its relatively ambitious cultural work a working through of just what isn't envisioned in the hetero-normativizing imaginary of the critical readings of Donne's sonnet I have been discussing here—namely, that one can be fucked (maybe needs to be fucked) and turn out to be "more of a man." As I indicated earlier, *More of a Man* is integrally concerned with the performance of masculinity, particularly gay butch masculinity (though one might argue that butch masculinity is always gay). The tape, of course, also concerns itself, like most (but not all) hardcore porn, with the performance of fucking. But beyond this, I see it taking up in a nearly metacritical way the question of who will penetrate whom and how such positionings function in according one his place within the ranks of virility. What's more, the videotape makes the act of homosexual fucking the cynosure of its chiasmas of erotic, religious, and political devotional vectors. In its opening moments, Vito, dressed in his levis, construction boots, and hardhat, goes from his private prayer closet to another kind of closet, one which is a setpiece of gay porn—that is, the water closet or public restroom. There he fucks and gets fucked by another man, acts which are athletically performed through an orifice in the water closet door, commonly termed in slang, incidentally, a "glory hole," a naming that itself accords the scene something of the nimbus of the sacred. Aside this opening, moreover, is an ACT-UP "Silence = Death" decal. It's while getting fucked that Vito, the tape's "star," cums, a matter I take as significantly intended and one that signals a narrative organization of pornographic pleasure that diverges from Dyer's paradigm.[34] When Vito's trick suggests that they enjoy a second round back in his apartment, however, the scene disturbingly shifts in register: "What the fuck do you think I am?" is Vito's response. "Well, for one thing you're a natural born piece of ass. Man, you were born to be fucked," comes the admiring reply. At this point, Vito turns on the "faggot" (as he calls his trick) and gaybashes him.

More of a Man's other narrative line involves the breakup of Vito's boyfriend-to-be Duffy and Duffy's current lover. That separation is triggered by Duffy's growing devotion to gay and AIDS activism, a competing commitment seen by his boyfriend to short shrift their sex life: "You're so goddamn busy being a professional homosexual," he complains to Duffy, "it's a miracle you find time to suck cock at all." Yet an extended, though interrupted sexual number between the two (Duffy's activist buddy telephones *in medias res*) makes it clear that their breakup is also predicated on Duffy's reluctance to roll over and let his boyfriend have his turn fucking him. Both Duffy's macho reticence about being penetrated and Vito's violently homophobic repudiation of his own pleasure in the same are dissolved when the two are at last brought together inside the gay pride float in the scene which, I noted earlier, is offered as the narrative's climactic sexual coupling. Here Vito is finally able to voice his desire to be fucked, but Duffy answers it by instead taking a condom from a bedside pile and unrolling it on Vito's dick. Vito: "Hey, that's against my religion." Duffy: "It's not against mine." Duffy is thus the first man to give up his ass, though he does so from a position on top, before swapping places, donning his own condom and fucking Vito in turn. In this carefully choreographed, final sexual number, the body of the man who is "more of a man" happily performs according to pluralized, shifting eroticizations: it is both phallic and anal, penetrative and receptive to penetration, ravishing and ravished, but it is never anything less than virile.[35]

Interestingly, looming muse-like over *More of a Man*'s fashioning of a gay virility, along with the icon of Christ on the cross, is the figure of a woman (or so the naive Vito believes for most of the film), a nightclub drag singer named Belle Zahringer. Played by drag performer (and a gay porn director in her own right) Chi Chi Larue, Belle serves as a kind of mentor, even stand-in mother, for Vito in his coming-out process. Indeed, Belle is an actual parent in the film, and we see her fingering a photograph of the absent child she has fathered. Belle introduces Vito and Duffy, and later, holding court atop the parade float that carries them inside, she quite literally presides over their culminating sex play. It is also Belle who sings the tape's title song in a bar scene which at last opens Vito's eyes, as well as the way for his consummation with Duffy:

> And folks you can take it from me.
> This incredible creature you see
> Has the best of both worlds, yes siree.
> I'm more of a woman than you'll ever have,
> And more of a man than you'll ever be.

Planting the voice of its eroticized hyper-virility ("I'm . . . more of a man than you'll ever be") in Belle, the figure Merck calls the tape's Tiresias (p. 232), saves *More of a Man* from any unqualified proscription of butchness as the single or proper "truth" of the male body. Belle's presiding presence in the narrative as both operative mother and biological father registers other performative possibilities for that body, some of which crisscross lines of gender. Thus, if gay butch masculinity is the privileged male performance in *More of a Man*'s endeavor to style a new form of nineties gay male clone—one who is young, undeviatingly virile in whatever erotic posture he takes up, and of course devoted (religiously, politically)—it also knows this is hardly the only show in town.[36]

Similarly, to return to the metaphysicals, my criticism of the governing practice of making sure that the prayer closet presents one body that is encoded "male" and one that is encoded "female"—even if both belong to men—is not meant to suggest that one never finds these poets envisioning the body in ways which traverse or problematize gender. Indeed, a remarkable lability of gender effects often characterizes what the body performs as it performs devotion. Thus Crashaw's headnote to his "A Hymn to Sainte Teresa" extols this model of piety on the basis of her performative double-genderedness: "a woman for the angelli-cal heighth of [her] speculation, for masculine courage of performance more than a woman." What I am contending, however, is that we avoid remarking unproble-matically every representation of the penetrated male body as somehow feminized *because* penetrable. "Donne placing himself before God as a woman"; "To enter into Christ is to return to the womb"; "Christ's suffering flesh was 'woman' ": accounts that would hold forth the prospects of a female Jesus, or a male poet masquerading as a woman aching for ravishment, often do so at the cost of too quickly effacing the primary maleness of these bodies, a reflex appar-ently devolving from a perspective that fails to conceive of male/male relations that do not entail one man enacting the woman's part.[37]

Are male bodies impenetrable? Are they without their own holes? In Crashaw's poetry, as we have seen, Christ's male body is replete with them and for that reason fascinating and desirable. Here the longing for redemption is cor-porealized in terms of a thematics of bodily permeability and penetration. The portal for drawing near to Christ is a bodily orifice—one enters Christ or is en-tered by him, and then is engulfed in the salvific liquids that flow from his body. Moreover, such performances of spiritual rapture are seldom gender-bound. Male and female bodies alike can penetrate or be penetrated, can possess or be pos-sessed by the remarkably somatized devotional agents of Crashaw's febrile reli-gious imaginary. Thus his Saint Teresa, thrillingly entered by Christ's "sweet-killing DART" in "A Hymn," also wields her own, as a male angel learns in "The Flaming Heart": "Give her the DART for it is she / (Fair youth) shootes both thy shaft and THEE" (lines 47–48).

In Crashaw's poetry, then, as is the case in much seventeenth-century reli-gious expression, biological gender seldom poses the limit to what the devout body can enact or what can be enacted upon it. The positions of ravisher and ravished can variously and successively be taken on by the male, female, and un-decidably gendered bodies and souls that perform Christian devotion here. One can be a penetrated male body such as Christ's, or a penetrative female one like St. Teresa's. In Crashaw's "Ode to a Prayer-book," the gentlewoman to whom the poem is addressed is first laid open to "love's great artillery / which here con-tracts it self and comes to ly / Close couch't in your white bosom" (lines 15–17), and then she is herself afforded the cavalier lover's "power / To rifle and deflour" (lines 114–15). And if we allow a kind of gender transitivity to these devotional operations, we should also recognize that their attendant couplings of Christ and follower are sometimes framed in ways that are no less transitive across the bor-ders of what we now conceptualize as coherently distinctive sexualities. In so claiming, I am not so much looking to recast early modern literary expression according to our modern categories of identity, or to make these texts answer my own desires—though I also wouldn't be too quick to declare all such gestures critically illegitimate ones either. In opening the prayer closet of the metaphysicals, I am reacting against the unwarranted imposition on these texts of a normativizing metaphorics of heterosexuality—a historical formation which, as we conceive and experience it now, of course no more existed then than did its deviant twin, homosexuality. My argument here is thus that any mapping of an erotics of Christianity, whether early modern or modern, needs to consider as well the vagaries of homoerotic desire elicited in devotional expression. Stimulated by a spectacularized denuded male form—the ravished, the ravishing body of Jesus—the performances of the prayer closet, the site of a variety of homodevotional excitations to pleasure, desire, and devotion, require as much.

Notes

1. *Advocate Men*, for instance, named the tape its Best Feature Video of 1990 and honored Jerry Douglas as Best Director and Joey Stephano as Best Actor (May 1991, p. 90). The reviewer for *Adult Video News* finds *More of a Man* as "rais[ing] the adult feature into the realm of cinematic art without sacrificing the sexual intensity" and acclaimed its screenplay as "what may be the best . . . in the twenty year history of gay adult features" (November 1990, p. 72).

Not only has *More of a Man* been acclaimed within its own industry, it has also become the subject of a number of critical studies. In my discussion of *More of a Man*, I am much indebted to and follow in a number of ways the insightful treatment of the videotape's overlapping erotic, political, and redemptive trajectories in Mandy Merck's "*More of a Man*: Gay Porn Cruises Gay Politics," in *Perversions: Deviant Readings* (New York: Routledge, 1993), pp. 217–35. See pp. 220–21 for Merck's wry discussion of the opening scene as "the limit case in sacred submission." After I completed this essay, I became aware of Mark Simpson's provocative article, "A World of Penises: Gay Videoporn," which also considers how *More of a Man* "sets out not just to politicize gay porn but to eroticize gay politics" (pp. 138–39 in Simpson, *Male Impersonators: Men Performing Masculinity* [New York: Routledge, 1994]).

I am indebted to Jay Kutner for the Boswell epigraph, which is cited from the *London Journal 1762–1763*, ed. Frederick A. Pottle (New Haven: Yale University Press, 1950), p. 333.

2. For this contextualization, see Merck, "*More of a Man*," p. 224.

3. Eve Kosofsky Sedgwick, *Epistemology of the Closet* (Berkeley: University of California Press), p. 140.

4. Here I am adapting and somewhat retooling Merck's formulation: "In the eerie blue light of the float's plastic-lined interior (which itself suggests the inside of a giant condom) sex and religion finally come together. . . . [T]he couple consummate their romance and rejoin the march, leaving behind a used condom juxtaposed in a final freeze-frame with the abandoned rosary" ("*More of a Man*," p. 234). Unlike Merck, however, I do not see the rosary (and what it represents) as so much abandoned as erotically revalenced, in keeping with the videotape's array of homodevotional pleasures.

5. Although my discussion here is rather exclusively conceived in attending only to some

seventeenth-century male poets and the homoerotic circuits of desire in their religious "love poetry," this narrowing of focus is by no means intended to imply (as the received canons of Renaissance literature have done for years) that there are no important female religious poets worth considering in terms of the corporealities of devotional performance.

6. For all citations of Crashaw's poetry I use *The Complete Poetry of Richard Crashaw*, ed. George Walton Williams (Garden City: Anchor, 1970).

7. This is Williams's translation of Crashaw's Latin.

8. As particularly important examples, see Leo Steinberg, *The Sexuality of Christ in Renaissance Art and Modern Oblivion* (New York: Pantheon, 1983); Caroline Walker Bynum, *Holy Feast, and Holy Fast: The Religious Significance of Food to Medieval Women* (Berkeley: University of California Press, 1987); *Fragmentation and Redemption: Essays on Gender and the Human Body* (New York: Zone Books, MIT Press, 1991); and Peter Brown, *The Body and Society: Men, Women, and Sexual Renunciation in Early Christianity* (New York: Columbia University Press, 1988). See also selected essays in *Zone 3–5: Fragments for a History of the Human Body*, parts 1–3, ed. Michel Feher, Ramona Naddaff, and Nadia Tazi (New York: Urzone, 1989).

9. Bynum, *Holy Feast and Holy Fast*, p. 6.

10. See my "Pleasure and Devotion: The Body of Jesus in Seventeenth-Century Devotional Lyric," in Jonathan Goldberg, ed., *Queering the Renaissance* (Durham: Duke University Press, 1994), esp. pp. 264–69. Portions of my readings of Crashaw and Donne presented here reprise and rework materials from that essay.

11. For example, from Vaughan's "Cock-crowing": "If joyes, and hopes, and earnest throws [throes], / And hearts, whose Pulse beats still for light / Are given to birds; who, but thee, knows / A love-sick souls exalted flight?" (lines 31–34), in *The Complete Poetry of Henry Vaughan*, ed. French Fogle (New York: Norton, 1964). For another instance, see Vaughan's poem simply entitled "Love-Sick."

12. "Artillerie," lines 19, 25, in *George Herbert: The Complete English Poems*, ed. John Tobin (Harmondsworth: Penguin, 1991). All citations of Herbert are according to this edition.

13. Lines 17 and *passim*, in *Robert Herrick: Poetical Works*, ed. L. C. Martin (Oxford: Oxford University Press, 1956, rev. ed. 1965).

14. All citations of Donne's poetry are according to *Donne: Poetical Works*, ed. Sir Herbert Grierson (London: Oxford University Press, 1933).

15. Even George Walton Williams, Crashaw's usually rather reserved, Christian humanist modern editor, cannot restrain himself here. Taking his cues from the poet, Williams himself becomes punningly improprietous (consciously or unconsciously?) in commenting on these lines: " 'soft bowells . . . discharge,' however, by process of elimination, has quite a different meaning; it may be thought not in the best taste to introduce scatology into eschatology—the stanza has no Latin original" (*The Complete Poetry of Richard Crashaw*, p. 191).

16. For a strong account of pornography's "principle of maximum visibility" and its fetishizing drive to probe and bring into visibility the body's surfaces, inner spaces, and interior mechanisms, see Linda Williams, *Hard Core: Power, Pleasure, and the "Frenzy of the Visible"* (Berkeley: University of California Press, 1989), esp. pp. 48–57.

17. Robert Martin Adams, "Taste and Bad Taste in Metaphysical Poetry: Richard Crashaw and Dylan Thomas," *Hudson Review* 8 (1955): 67.

18. Once again, this is Williams's translation of Crashaw's Latin epigram.

19. See "*Vexilla Regis*, The Hymn of the Holy Crosse," stanza 2.

20. John Waters, *Shock Value: A Tasteful Book about Bad Taste* (New York: Delta, 1981), p. 65.

21. On the differences between modern and early modern regimes of sexuality, see in addition to Foucault's epochal *The History of Sexuality*, vol. 1, *An Introduction*, trans. Robert Hurley (New York: Pantheon, 1978), Alan Bray, *Homosexuality in Renaissance England* (London: Gay

Men's Press, 1982); David M. Halperin, *One Hundred Years of Homosexuality* (London: Routledge, 1990); Gregory Bredbeck, *Sodomy and Interpretation: From Marlowe to Milton* (Ithaca: Cornell University Press, 1991); Jonathan Goldberg, *Sodometries: Renaissance Texts, Modern Sexualities* (Stanford: Stanford University Press, 1992), as well as the essays gathered *in Queering the Renaissance*, also edited by Goldberg. Goldberg is particularly adept at parlaying the recognition, on one hand, that strictly speaking one cannot talk of sexuality in Renaissance texts (that is in terms of a hetero- or homosexuality to be found there), and, on the other hand, of how the "refusal of the term *sexuality* for these texts could all too easily suggest a desexualizing of them" *(Sodometries*, p. 22). Thus, while recognizing that the Renaissance does not differentiate (as we tend to do) between two types of sexual subjectivizations, Goldberg nonetheless seeks out (and finds) "sites of sexual possibility" outside those engaged in by the married or marriageable couple.

22. Samuel Johnson, "The Life of Cowley," in *Lives of the Poets*, cited from *Literary Criticism of 17th-Century England*, ed. Edward W. Tayler (New York: Knopf, 1967), pp. 420–21.

23. For example, C. S. Lewis, no great lover of Donne, terms his Elegy 19 ("To His Mistress Going to Bed") "a pornographic poem," in "Donne and Love Poetry in the Seventeenth Century," in *Seventeenth-Century Studies Presented to Sir Herbert Grierson* (Oxford: Clarendon Press, 1983), pp. 75–76. Indeed, the poem was one of those censored from the posthumous publication of Donne's verse in 1633.

24. T. S. Eliot, *For Lancelot Andrewes* (Garden City: Doubleday, 1929), pp. 134–35.

25. William Empson, *Seven Types of Ambiguity* (New York: New Directions, 1947), p. 222.

26. Adams, "Taste and Bad Taste," p. 66.

27. In addition to "Pleasure and Devotion," pp. 272–73, see my article "Christ's Ganymede," in *The Yale Journal of Law and the Humanities*, forthcoming 1995. This essay, which likewise begins with the opening scene of *More of a Man* in church, considers how both the pornographic videotape and Donne's sonnet explore ways in which religion can authorize transgressive possibilities that in other contexts remain taboo.

28. Stanley Fish, "Masculine Force: Donne and Verbal Power," in Elizabeth D. Harvey and Katherine Eisaman Maus, eds., *Soliciting Interpretation: Literary Theory and Seventeenth-Century English Poetry* (Chicago: University of Chicago Press, 1990), pp. 242, 241.

29. Debora Kuller Shuger, "Saints and Lovers: Mary Magdalene and the Ovidian Evangel," in Jonathan Crewe, ed., *Reconfiguring the Renaissance: Essays in Critical Materialism* (Lewisburg: Bucknell University Press, 1992), p. 167.

30. Ann Baynes Coiro, "New-found-land: Teaching Metaphysical Poetry from the Other Side," in Sidney Gottlieb, ed., *Approaches to Teaching the Metaphysical Poets* (New York: Modern Language Association of America, 1990), p. 86. Further citations of Coiro's essay will be supplied in the text.

31. Richard Dyer, "Coming to Terms: Gay Pornography," in *Only Entertainment* (London: Routledge, 1993), p. 121–34. Previously, this essay appeared in *Jump Cut* 30 (1985), and in *Out There: Marginalization and Contemporary Cultures*, ed. Russell Ferguson, et al. (Cambridge: MIT Press, 1990).

32. Dyer, "Coming to Terms," p. 128.

33. For this criticism of Dyer's discussion, see David Pendleton, "Obscence Allegories: Narrative, Representation, Pornography," in *Discourse* 15.1 (fall 1992): 154–68, esp. p. 157.

34. Simpson likewise discusses the tape in terms of anality and virility: "This remarkable video appears to offer a narrative in which the star not only gets fucked but learns that to be fucked is not shameful but rather a sign of 'strength'—hence the title" (p. 137). Simpson regards this a step in the right direction, away from what he finds, in accordance with Dyer's view, as the more usual overvaluation of the position of the "topman" (such as Jeff Stryker) in gay porn, one which functions to "de-gay" the medium: "what should be the most obviously,

unapologetically, *explicitly* gay images—that of men offering their penises to each other—becomes something not very gay at all, something that instead goes out of its way to distinguish its men from 'those damn queers': a position rather similar to straight male porn" (p. 134). However, it seems to me rather simplistic to assume that in the pornographic spectacle of fucking, the desire represented is always, as Simpson and Dyer insist, that "of the fucker" (ibid.). And even if this were indeed so, does it, as they further maintain, straighten the pleasures of queer porn, or instead "queer" the pleasures of heterosexual porn, which entices straight men to get off by focusing on the sight of the male body in action, fucking and cumming? From this perspective, my inclination would be to reverse the claims of Dyer and Simpson and argue that pornography, whether homo or hetero, starts off as a queer pleasure rather than a straight one, proffering to its consumers multiple points of pleasurable spectacularization and identification, necessarily including same-sex ones. Finally, I think Simpson is mistaken in suggesting that the stars of gay porn are always tops; for every "trade" figure like Jeff Stryker, there is a star bottom like Joey Stephano.

35. See Merck, *"More of a Man,"* p. 230.

36. Merck reads the presence of Belle in *More of a Man* rather differently as enacting a solidification of "traditional gender asymmetry." Referring to Belle's title song ("I'm more of a woman than you'll ever have, / And more of a man than you'll ever be"), Merck finds that "Women are still what men 'have'—the phallic complement which enables them to 'be.' . . . [Belle] functions to reassure—offering the phallic femininity of sexuality without lack ('the best of both worlds, yes siree') and a new political legitimacy to the revels that follow" (p. 233). But arguably *More of a Man* isn't at all about men "having" women; instead the diegesis of the videotape, true to its genre as gay porn, is about "having" men, and about the performance of masculinity in sexualized relations between men. Merck, however, collapses the narrative's project of fashioning gay male subjectivities into heterosexual models of a male subjectivity predicated upon the possession of a woman. In other words, Merck's dismissal misses the mark here inasmuch as it, like the Renaissance critics I have been discussing, assumes the heterosexual as a governing model even for erotic relations that are not heterosexual. Moreover, Merck doesn't account for complications attendant upon the fact that the narrative's voicing of hypermasculinity is accorded to a figure who chiefly performs in the narrative as "female."

37. Jonathan Goldberg extends a similar criticism widely across the terrains of Renaissance literary scholarship in *Sodometries* pp. 46–47, 106–12, for instance. The androgynizing formulations I cite are from: Coiro, "New-found-land," p. 86; Leah Marcus, *Childhood and Cultural Despair: A Theme and its Variations in Seventeenth-Century Literature* (Pittsburgh: University of Pittsburgh Press, 1978), p. 148; and Bynum, *Holy Feast and Holy Fast*, p. 261. An important exception to the practice of rerouting along heterosexual lines the homoerotic currents of devotion to Christ is offered in Walter Hughes's essay, " 'Meat Out of the Eater': Panic and Desire in American Puritan Poetry," in Joseph A. Boone and Michael Cadden, eds., *Engendering Men: The Question of Male Feminist Criticism* (New York: Routledge, 1990), pp. 102–21.

Inter-Nationalist Interventions

6

Deviance and Dissidence
Sexual Subjects of the Cold War

Katrin Sieg

A T THE END of his book *Woman and Socialism* (1879), August Bebel, head of the Social Democratic Party in Germany, sketched out a sexual politics based on the abolition of private property. "Free love," which in his time was practiced by the upper classes even though denounced as immoral by bourgeois standards, should be the right of everyone in a communist society. Quoting his contemporary, the aristocratic sex radical and socialist revolutionary George Sand, Bebel emphasized the right of any human being to satisfy her or his sexual appetites without state sanction or intervention and the need to revise bourgeois notions of morality privileging marriage, monogamy, and procreation (Bebel 87, 88).[1] Moreover, Bebel was willing to extend sexual freedoms to homosexuals as well and became a prominent advocate for the emerging homosexual emancipation movement.[2] Thirty years later, however, the German Communist Party (KPD) firmly linked homosexuality with fascism in a widely publicized pamphlet, denouncing sexual deviance as a "symptom of the degeneration of the fascist bourgeoisie" (Stümke 99). Applauding the re-criminalization of homosexuality in the Soviet Union one year after the burning of the Reichstag,[3] Maxim Gorky wrote in the party newspaper *Pravda*: "Homosexuality which corrupts the youth goes unchecked in the fascist countries. In the country where the proletariat has taken power in a bold and manly way it is declared a crime against society and is severely punished. In Germany a saying goes around: exterminate the homosexuals and you will eradicate fascism" (quoted in Stümke, 99). In response to Gorky, the openly gay Klaus Mann deplored this bitter historical irony in an article he never published. As a homosexual antifascist, Mann was caught between conflicting allegiances.[4] His quandary and the subsequent closeting of his work is paradigmatic for the situation and identity formation of homosexuals in the German Democratic Republic (GDR), a state that defined itself as antifascist.

My preliminary historical sketch is meant to indicate that discourses on sexuality in the GDR (1949–1990), which I wish to examine in this chapter, were shaped by the three interrelated discursive complexes dating back to the early part of this century on homosexuality, sex radicalism, and socialism. They were modified by two factors: on the one hand, the GDR's antifascism imprinted itself on its gender legislation and sexual politics. Theoretically, that implied a radical break with the Third Reich's misogynist and homophobic ideology and social practice, including that regime's persecution and eradication of sexual deviants. On the other hand, the socialist society's adversarial relationship to the capitalist Federal Republic of Germany (FRG) determined the configuration of a socialist subject as heterosexual, which I will elaborate later in the chapter. Briefly, the interpretation of sexual deviance as political dissidence harkened back to Weimar communists' strategy of using the accusation of homosexuality in order to discredit the political enemy. It also reflected the specific, androcentric structure of a centralist state that expected its citizens to duplicate patriarchal relations in the domestic sphere as a sign of political loyalty (see Dölling, 42). Although these two factors contradicted each other in regard to sexuality—one would have called for the rehabilitation of homosexuals as victims of the Nazi regime, the other designated them as "enemies of the state"—I summarize both under the term "Cold War," since the GDR's relation to its fascist history was instrumentalized in the competition for political legitimation. In the United States, the connection between Cold War discourses and the configuration of homosexuality has already been documented.[5] So far, however, such an account is missing in regard to the relation of socialism and sexuality.

As postwar discursive formations around sexuality reactivated and modified elements from earlier constellations, so were modes of articulation and performance informed by previous styles. I would like to very roughly map out two styles in particular, and sketch their relation to sex radicals, homosexual activists, and communists during the Weimar republic. With the flourishing coalition of leftist, feminist, and homosexual organizations during the 1920s, discourses on sexuality polarized: the sex reformers articulated their agenda in the documentary, scientific discourse used by sexologists like Hirschfeld, Adler, and Reich, and abandoned anti-bourgeois, poetic, and subjectivist modes of sexual expression.[6] The movement combated the dominant culture's perception of homosexuality as degenerate, pathological, and asocial—notions that had to some degree informed the bohemian reveling in perversion. Leftist artists, who, like the early Brecht, had expressed their anti-bourgeois politics through a rebellious, often violent sexuality, shifted their focus to the arena of class struggle, reinforcing the notion of the public as the primary site of political intervention. That shift reconstituted the private as secondary at a time when the regulation of sexuality became a concern of the state and its eugenics programs. The emotional, subjectivist language formerly deployed by anti-bourgeois radicals was appropriated by Nazi rhetoric on *Blut und Boden*. Thus a progressive sexual discourse of expression was vacated during the 1920s.

The work of Hedda Zinner, a communist who emigrated to the Soviet Union during the war and subsequently returned to the GDR, provides a kind of Urtext for the dominant configuration of socialist sexuality. Zinner is the most prolific and well-known woman playwright in GDR history, and one of the most visible female communist functionaries in the arts during the 1950s and '60s. Her drama *Der Teufelskreis* [*The Vicious Circle*] (1953), which made theatre history because it was the first post-war play written in the GDR which deployed the docudrama style to represent the recent past, in effect dramatized the *Braunbuch* [*Brown Book*] disseminated by the KPD in 1933, which blamed the Reichstag arson and the ensuing hounding of communist activists on Marinus von der Lubbe, allegedly the lover of SA-leader Ernst Röhm, and thus constructed the communist myth of a Nazi-homosexual conspiracy against the oppositional left (Stümke 97–99). The bulk of the play is set in the Nazi court where the accused communist arsonists were put on trial. By pitting a corrupt legal system against its innocent victims, the play staged the antagonism between the sexually degenerate Nazis on the one hand, and the morally superior communists on the other.[7] The drama's apparent aim was to anchor the historical roots of the GDR's identity in the communist opposition, and distance itself from fascist institutions and ideology which could thus neatly be attributed to West Germany as the proper heir of Nazi imperialism. At the same time, however, *The Vicious Circle* cemented the Weimar KPD's homophobia into the self-definition of the socialist state.

Eight years later, with the Cold War in full swing, Zinner provided theatre audiences with another example of communist purity threatened by Nazi perversion, this time offering a dramatic analysis of relationships between women. In *Ravensbrücker Ballade* [*The Ballad of Ravensbrück*] (1961),[8] the character of Frau Beier, the brutal, lesbian overseer in a Nazi concentration camp for women, exemplifies the depiction of the lesbian as a monstrous incarnation of the ideological Other. In the play, Frau Beier sets in motion a chain of events that lead to the death of the main character Maria, a political prisoner and communist resistance fighter. Whereas Maria is characterized as a nurturing woman who sublimates her maternal yearnings through her care for fellow-prisoners and her political work, Beier is drawn as a mannish sadist who enjoys abusing her authority over the incarcerated women. Bonds between inmates, especially between the political prisoners, are carefully portrayed as either maternal or sisterly, but in no way sexual. In that way, the "red triangle" prisoners are distinguished not only from their lesbian tormentor, but also from the criminal and so-called asocial women wearing the green and black triangles, respectively, who engage in (and enjoy) sexual relations with the Nazi guards. Communist identity is thus tied to asexuality, sexuality to asociality.

Zinner stressed the authenticity of her drama by referring to her research and her collaboration with Erika Buchmann, a longtime prisoner in the Ravensbrück concentration camp and later instrumental in transforming it into an antifascist museum. A letter by Buchmann is published in a recent anthology documenting the play's reception history, in which she uses the same rhetoric as Zinner when she describes the "asocials" as the political prisoners' worst adversaries, and characterized them as egotistical, perverse, primitive, loud, immoral, lewd, and murderous (Buchmann 32–36). She associated them with a "shameless, uninhibited" homosexuality (Buchmann 38, 39) contrasted with the compassion, solidarity, and, above all, the "quiet and discipline" of the communist prisoners (35).[9]

The antagonistic pair of Maria and Frau Beier, authenticated by Buchmann's testimonial, made its appearance a few months after the Berlin Wall was built, illustrating the way homophobia as well as a sexually repressive morality were woven into official socialist culture. *The Ballad of Ravensbrück* was recognized as a foundational text to state ideology by contemporary critics. The play even continued to signify socialism's historical and moral center even after the state that it legitimated had collapsed (see Jarmatz).

The opening scene of *The Ballad of Ravensbrück* is remarkable when compared to Zinner's otherwise less than experimental writing. A nightmare, expressionistically represented by flashing lights and disembodied voices calling from the dark, torments a former camp inmate. That prologue frames the realistic enactment of the past, deploying a discourse of truth and documentation embodied by the "selfless" Maria and her real-life counterpart Erika Buchmann.[10] The play invokes the incoherent and threatening eruptions of the nightmarish past in order to stage its repression. The individual subjectivity of communists then at odds with a hegemonic system is transformed into the unified chorus of the socialist society. *The Ballad of Ravensbrück* advocated and celebrated the erasure of a subjective space defined outside of, much less in disagreement with, state ideology. At the moment that the Wall demarcated a homogenous and literally closed national identity, the play staged the convergence of subjective expression and national history, and the subsumption of the former under the latter.

The effacement of sexuality and subjectivism from socialist identity occurred under pressure from the cold war. During the 1960s, the ruling party's general secretary Walter Ulbricht envisioned a *Sozialistische Menschengemeinschaft* [Socialist Brotherhood] held together by the "Ten Commandments of Socialist Morality" (1958). Among other things, he advocated thriftiness, a "socialist work discipline," cleanliness, decency, and respect for the family (Ulbricht 918). The concern of this vision with economic achievement and citizens' obedience and faith in the rules, bought at the expense of socio-political experimentation and individual self-realization, was a far cry from earlier socialist imaginations. GDR playwright Heiner Müller addressed precisely those contradictions in his play *Zement [Cement]* (1972). It brings on stage early Russian revolutionary Alexandra Kollontai, the only female member of the first Central Committee after the 1917 revolution and author of several theoretical works, novels, and short fiction on gender and sexuality. Her vision of a revolutionized communist culture in the areas of sexuality and daily life went far beyond the government's policies on women's equality with men and their integration into the work force. Kollontai explored alternative sexual relationships, collective living experiments, and promiscuity both in her writing and in her life. Sexuality is always placed in the context of revolutionary change and the abolishment of private property, which transforms notions of gender and sexuality on a social and on a psychological level in unforeseen and not at all untroubled ways. Kollontai's writings soon made her an embarrassment to the male members of the Central Committee, who advocated marriage and monogamy and decided to send her into "honorary exile" as a Soviet emissary in 1922 (see Rowbotham, 15).

Müller's *Cement* dramatizes competing notions of revolution in the two protagonists, Dasha (modelled after Kollontai) and her husband Chumalov, who becomes a functionary in the new Soviet bureaucracy. Dasha attempts to invent and practice a new, communist morality of loving according to her desire rather than moral conventions tied to property relations within marriage. Like Kollontai, she faces not only the contempt and condemnation of her contemporaries for her "whorish" behavior, but also the social constructedness of her own desire. In a confrontation with Chumalov, she tells him:

> Something inside me wants the master, Gleb
> Just as a dog wants the whip and it doesn't.
> I have to tear that out of me each time
> I go to bed with a man.
> [. . .]
> Maybe I have to tear love, or what is called love
> Out of me, and my lust, too, which sometimes
> Was one with it and sometimes not—just like a nail
> Grown into the flesh, so that finally
> The waltz of force and submission will end
> Which turns us back into the bourgeoisie
> As long as there are owners in this world. (Müller 43)

The Soviet government's adoption of the "New Economic Policy" in 1921, however, signaled a turning point from the idealistic radicalism embodied by Dasha to the growth of a bureaucratic hierarchy run by apparatchiks like Chumalov.[11]

Although the play for the most part stands in the tradition of the epic theatre, it contains an extraordinary passage entitled "Heracles 2 or the Hydra," whose form differs drastically from the rest of the drama. Written as an inner monologue of sorts, the text describes the Greek hero walking through a forest in search of the Hydra. He discovers in walking that the forest is identical with the monster, that there is no clear distinction between himself and it, and that both have turned into one giant machine. In this dense, breathless fiction which conveys the narrator's pain and horror at being the machine that dehumanizes him, Müller uses an imagistic, metaphorical language to show that the goal (Heracles' battle with the monster, as a metaphor for the proletariat's victory over capitalism) cannot be separated from the path toward it (the forest, or everyday habits and social practices). The passage also reveals the entanglement of revolutionary impulses with the bureaucratic social apparatus or machine which encompasses the individual consciousness, a subjectivity that had conceived itself as separate from society:

> [h]e learned to read the continually changing plans of the machine which he
> was ceased to be and again was different with each glance grip step, and he
> learned that he thought changed wrote it with the signature of his labors and
> deaths. (Müller 40)

In a commentary published together with the English translation of *Cement*, Helen Fehervary called attention to the breakdown of the objectivist model of the epic theatre as the productive moment of the play, which prefigures "a theater of confrontation and ritual, [and] the release of subjective human potential in modern societies dominated by categorical, historical truths" (Fehervary 5).

The imbrication of socialist state ideology and apparatuses with a puritanical heterosexuality, which Zinner had celebrated and Müller deplored, generated a number of contradictory effects in regard to the configuration of sexuality and dissidence in the former GDR. Sexuality became a central site for the articulation of a critique of "real existant" socialism, as in Müller's case, a site from which the gap between revolutionary theory and praxis became painfully visible.[12] Significantly, the refocusing of critical attention on personal relations, individual experience, and quotidian practices was not extended to homosexual constituencies fighting for recognition, but actually duplicated the dominant culture's homophobia. Homosexuality marked the limit of a radical critique of socialist subjectivity, a point which is illustrated particularly well by the sex-change stories written by GDR women.

In 1975, a collection of short stories appeared which was later re-edited and published under the title *Sex-Change*. It signaled the emergence of GDR feminist literature in the mid-1970s.[13] The sex-change stories, which proceed from the female protagonist's biological transformation, compound a twist in heterosexual relations with a critique of "real existing socialism." The most complex story in the volume is a piece called "Valeska's Good News in 73 Stanzas" by Irmtraud Morgner, one of the most prominent GDR feminist writers.[14] Valeska, the heroine of the story, decides to hide her changed state from her fiancé Robert and travels to Moscow in order to consult with her old friend Shenja who lives in a women's collective there. Valeska comes to appreciate her altered condition when she has sex with Shenja, an experience sweetened by the sensation that she can fuck her "like a man" without treating her "as a woman," because her newly-acquired penis operates as a sex-toy, not as signifier of patriarchal privileges. After a period of experimentation and various sexual encounters with women, Valeska returns to Robert. Their relationship has improved due to her male shape, because Robert is now willing to share equally in domestic tasks. Since homosexual sex is out of the question for him, she changes back into her female version for the duration of sex. The ostensible symmetry of pleasure (sex with penis with Shenja, without penis with Robert) hinges on the eroticized intertwining of social equality and biological difference, and manages to present a critique of patriarchal power structures from a position within socialism. Shenja's desire for a woman with a penis is as crucial to the story's political thrust as her nationality.[15] Although "Valeska's Good News" managed to denaturalize the compound of heterosexism and state ideology which inhibited dissent in the GDR, it left the heterosexual organization of desire unquestioned.

Sarah Kirsch's story "Blitz aus heiterm Himmel" [Out of the Blue] traces the impact of the protagonist's sex change on her relationship with her boyfriend Albert. Whereas before their heterosexual relationship is characterized by great sex, close friendship, and unequal division of labor, their relationship after the transformation is asexual, comradely, and based on an equal workload. "Now that I'm a guy I'm gettin' emancipated," Max, the former woman, says to herself in a thick Berlin accent. The third story in the anthology, written by Christa Wolf, describes the process of becoming male as the increasing inability to love, and the draining of eroticism from the protagonist's emotional life. Wolf is less optimistic than Kirsch that male bonding and friendship can compensate for sexuality.

All three authors use sex change as a metaphor to critically examine the GDR's gender politics, which turns women into men, offering them equality at the expense of "love," a term that begins to take center stage in the emerging feminist discourse.[16] I would argue that, like *Cement*, the sex change stories signal the re-emergence of an earlier sex-radical and socially-critical discourse, one that is at pains to locate itself within a socialist (even Soviet) tradition of thought. They attempt to invigorate the stalled socialist vision of a humane society through their (feminist) attention to gender relations, sexual expression, and everyday life. The either/or alternative of equality and eroticism which these stories set up in order to articulate a critique of "real existing" socialism, however, renders them problematic because of their refusal to think eroticism together with homosexuality. Valeska's episode with Shenja remains a warm-up for the "real" sex with Robert, just as feminism provides the foreplay to "real" communism.

The "queering" of the feminist subject in women's fiction unraveled the inscription of national allegiance encoded in heterosexism. The invocation of the transsexual in representation enabled and propelled a feminist critique of the patriarchal/socialist alliance. Within Morgner's narrative, lesbian sex became the site of ideological dissent, inhabiting a queer space of difference vis-à-vis a "repressively egalitarian" (Adorno) hegemonic discourse. "Real" lesbians had to suffer state surveillance and silencing precisely because of the symbolic overload which feminists capitalized on. In this way, the appearance of the queer in representation, as linchpin of a critical agenda, crossed out the material possibility of a terrain of sexual differences in the socialist state. In other words, and put somewhat simplistically, feminists and homosexuals in the GDR developed two strategies of intervention against dominant configurations: feminist writers purchased a critique of socialist ideology at the expense of sexual diversity, whereas gays and lesbians fought for an extension of sexual visibility to their communities while foregoing a fundamental critique of homophobia in conjunction with nationalist formulations.

As I have tried to show, the configuration of homosexuality in opposition to socialism, exemplified here by Hedda Zinner's work, was a remnant of the earlier (fascist and communist) condemnation of homosexuality as a symptom of asocial attitudes, behaviors, and beliefs. It was also informed by a repressive discourse codified by Ulbricht's "Ten Commandments," which configured sexuality (irrespective of orientation) as a symptom of bourgeois individualism and an anti-socialist morality, prompting the denunciation of expressive, subjectivist discourses. The socialist subject was articulated in the terms and styles of objectivism and documentation, mapping a subjectivity in complete accord with state apparatuses and ideology. The petrification of contradictions, the dwindling of "real alternatives," and the vanishing of "essential concerns" from the horizon of institutionalized thought which Christa Wolf noted for the 1970s prompted the resurgence of a sex-radical critique of "real existant" socialism deployed by socialist dissidents and feminists (see Wolf, "Culture" 93, 98). Unfortunately, homosexuality remained unthinkable within their literature as well.

The discursive compound of socialism and heterosexism served to police and persecute gay and lesbian constituencies. It also shaped the efforts at gay liberation during the 1970s and '80s by imposing on that enterprise the constant obligation to prove its ideological fidelity to a state that regarded homosexuals as asocial and untrustworthy by dint of their sexuality. Their efforts to claim an identity based on their sexuality were not only at odds with the socialist anthropological model according to which identity was solely determined by class. Gays and lesbians sat on the horns of a dilemma: defined as a community by virtue of their sexuality, they came to personify sexuality per se, and were thus subject to the anti-sexual mores governing the culture-at-large, which rested on the principle of deferred gratification and the subordination of individual happiness to economic-political exigencies.[17] Lesbians more than gay men were hard hit by

the instrumentation of sexuality in the planned economy of techno-scientific socialism, since it defined women primarily as mothers (see Fischer/Lux, 38), men
as workers. Their perceived violation of the puritanical, anti-sexual code of ethics
and morality which bolstered the "socialist personality" and the socialist state
prompted endless navigations around the issue of identity and the question of
naming. In the search for a "neutral" or positive term, some GDR homosexuals
rejected "lesbian" and "homosexual" because of the perceived emphasis on sexuality.[18]

Moreover, the attempts of gays and lesbians to organize as a marginalized
constituency called into question the paternalistic provider ideology in the
GDR, suggesting that some citizens were neglected by "Father State." Their
wish to establish meeting places was interpreted at best as an isolationist endeavor
within and against the socialist community. At worst, it was viewed as treason,
and gays and lesbians were frequently treated as the agents of the capitalist enemy.[19] Consequently, homosexual experiences were confined to the closet and
could neither be historicized nor politicized. Likewise, homophobia could not be
conceptualized as systemic to socialist ideology; it was experienced as instances
of individual suffering and victimization.

The GDR abolished the bourgeois private sphere by extending the organ-
izational principles of the public domain into the home, and thus positing a "socialist personality" in complete accord with the interests of the state (see Horn
103, and Dölling 42). During the 1980s, however, the state and its security agencies created (or at least condoned) certain pockets of social space that were designated "oppositional," "resistant," or "critical." Officially, they were outside its
purview, but nevertheless remained under surveillance. The church played an important role in this scenario, since much of the oppositional activity took place
under its aegis, including feminist, pacifist, environmentalist, and homosexual
organizations. At the same time, the state quelled the spontaneous, uncontrolled
performance of dissident subjects and practices. After this brief recapitulation,
let me turn to the performative acts through which gay men and lesbians in the
GDR constituted their identities.

One important discursive site for homosexual intervention were the annual
celebrations of antifascism, since they marked a crucial node of socialist morality
and Cold War ideology. That compound reproduced the homosexual as Other, a
notion based on the repression of aspects of Nazi history (contrary to official
accounts) and its continuation in the present. That injustice provided a point of
purchase for the movement's efforts at literally inscribing itself into socialism.
Although ostensibly honoring all victims and survivors of German fascism, the
festivities privileged the communist resistance fighters, illustrating the purpose
of these festivities as that of historical and ideological legitimation. When the
first gay and lesbian groups were founded in 1982/83, they began calling public
attention to their existence by visiting memorial services in Buchenwald, Ra-

vensbrück, and Sachsenhausen.[20] These public demonstrations did not go uncon-tested: repeatedly, wreaths disappeared and pages in the camps' visitor's book were torn out on which groups had recorded their presence and expressed their mourning for the homosexual victims of the Nazi regime (HOSI 116–18).[21]

GDR sociologist Ursula Sillge's book *Un-Sichtbare Frauen* [*In-Visible Women*] (1991) documents the attempt of a group of lesbians to participate in a memorial service for the inmates of Ravensbrück. They were harassed by police officers who prevented them from attending the event and laying down a wreath. The pressure of the apparatus that was brought to bear on this group of lesbians en-sured the heterosexist homogeneity of the German socialist subject which con-stituted itself around such public performances of antifascism.

The self-presentation of homosexuals as victims under the Nazi regime util-ized the state's proclaimed condemnation of the fascist past and its promise to citizens to rectify historical injustices. They challenged the denigration of ho-mosexuality as asocial, on which the model image of the morally pure and col-lective-minded socialist subject depended. That this strategy was in part effective is demonstrated by the state's decision not to air a televised version of Zinner's *Ballad of Ravensbrück* on the occasion of the 40th anniversary of the camp's lib-eration. Officials justified their refusal with the play's negative portrayal of the "asocials."[22]

GDR homosexuals' efforts to proclaim themselves antifascist and therefore socialist subjects challenged the state's homophobic policy of exclusion, but told little about the self-perception and experience of these constituencies. The so-called protocol filled this lacuna and developed a style of subjective expression in which individual instances of gay and lesbian lifestyles, oppression, liberation, and discrimination combined in a rich collage which challenged both the mono-lithic notion of a "socialist personality" or morality, and of sexual deviance as an a priori asocial and therefore anti-socialist identity.

The protocol genre consisted of biographical collages written and compiled by gay men and lesbians in the GDR, which were published right around reunifi-cation in 1989–1990. In some respects, these texts echo the objectivist discourse deployed by the homosexual emancipation movement in the Weimar period. That intention is signaled by the term "protocol," which commonly denotes the tran-script of a scientific experiment or the description of a natural phenomenon. The genre aimed at demonstrating the congruence of subjective and social dimen-sions by extending the boundaries of the latter. It functioned somewhat as a sub-terfuge, purporting to document what it was actually contesting: gender and sexuality in the GDR.[23]

Jürgen Lemke's *Ganz Normal Anders* (1989), published in English translation as *Gay Voices from East Germany*, and Kerstin Gutsche's *Ich Ahnungsloser Engel* [*Innocent Angel*] (1990) make possible an analysis of the way dominant formulations impacted the self-perception and political strategies of gay and lesbian citizens in the GDR.

The collection *Innocent Angel*, which records the verbal self-portraits of twelve lesbians, is remarkable in its lack of sexual references, underscored by the title. As a representation of lesbian life in the GDR, that telling omission pays tribute to a long-lasting taboo. The emphasis on couples and families in these accounts amounts to the collective appeal to be regarded as "different but normal," as Jürgen Lemke entitled his collection of gay voices from East Germany. Although his book presents a much wider range of social circumstances and sexual practices than does *Innocent Angel*, the implication is that the furtive, occasional or anonymous sex practiced by some men is merely a result of the closet into which socialism forced them. If left in peace, it is implied, gay men would lead perfectly "normal" lives by heterosexual standards.[24] Those who would call for a critique of homophobia and a deconstruction of the socialist patriarchy were marginalized within gay organizations.[25]

Closeted homosexuals were forced to choose between an "integrated" existence at the expense of their desire—Lemke's book yields numerous examples—or they paid for their lived sexuality with a record of short-term jobs or even unemployment. The twenty-six-year-old Martina in *Innocent Angel*, whose occupation is given as "occasional jobs," and who values her "lesbian family of choice" very highly, confesses: "In regard to work, I have great difficulties, i.e.: difficulty to adapt. When I hear 'collective,' it means little to me. So far, I have always experienced it as an obligation to integrate with a group of people I couldn't choose" (Gutsche 71). In a culture that viewed work as the primary category of identity and where self-employment was almost non-existent, women such as Martina came dangerously close to falling through the social net of the "provider state." Prolonged unemployment was deemed asocial and punished with prison sentences. In *Hohenecker Protokolle* [*Protocols from Hoheneck Prison*] (1984), we meet those lesbians who did not fulfill the minimum requirements of socialist citizenship—not in the role of narrator, which was restricted to the victims of political persecution, but as the petty thugs, hustlers, and mannish women who haunt the speaker's homophobic accounts, unworthy of their sympathy or solidarity.[26]

The protocol as a genre based on collective memory, and by virtue of its collage-like, fragmentary shape, proved congenial to a culture in transition, documenting for instance the end of the decade-long collaboration of lesbians and gay men. These "archeological texts" (Lemke), chronicling a system that has ceased to exist but continues to shape the lives of its former citizens, now enable a critical assessment of sexuality in the GDR, as acts performed in the interstices of official policies and individual possibilities.[27]

Together, the protocols are symptomatic of the mounting pressure of contradictions which could no longer be ignored as "merely personal." The intimate explorations of socialist subjectivity, while purporting to "speak privately," actually created a performative, quasi-dramatic genre built on dialogue, diversity, and collective enunciation. Its subjective and collective mode of communication carved out a cultural space that Wolf described earlier as "more spontaneous[ ], also more sociabl[e] than the structures of the novel or the drama" ("In Touch" 164). The protocols created an alternative performance site to the state theatre, not only in terms of content, but especially in terms of a communicative structure based on a multiplicity of voices, on contradiction during and across moments of enunciation, and the informal articulation of individual and collective utopias. Collections like Lemke's stimulated and participated in the informal but highly reliable networks of communication located in the private sphere. They attest to the transformation of the private sphere into a growing site of civic consciousness and responsibilities, which has prompted many East European feminists to recast the public/private split in terms of state and family as more appropriate to political culture in socialist societies. I would argue that these documents participated in the erosion of a repressive apparatus bent on the elision of all ideological dissonance. It is auspicious, I think, that the dramatized version of Lemke's gay voices, published in January of 1989, was also the last show to be produced at the ostentatious Theater im Palast in East Berlin, the showcase stage for socialist culture.

Lemke's book is particularly rich in its range of sexualities, ages, professions, and classes. The protocols collected in his volume revise a singular notion of "normality." The spectrum extends from a longterm, monogamous couple who live "like a married couple without children," a bisexual, closeted man living in a rural area, a seventy-year old artist and educator who has compartmentalized his life into carnal "sexus" and aesthetic "eros," to the flamboyant Lothar, a transvestite who came out in the 1920s and proclaims to be his "own woman."[28] The diversity of practices and meeting points—ranging from anonymous sex at the local railway station to monogamy and abstinence—throws into question the notion of a "gay identity." In a key passage, Bert, a young worker who is "out" to his colleagues and neighbors in Berlin, describes the weekly tenants' breakfast, to which all attending contribute (Lemke 58). A society's sexual composition is thus compared to a potluck; according to Bert, the harmony between all involved depends just as much on the cheerful attitude of the homosexuals as on the open-mindedness of the heterosexual majority. Bert's protocol is also instructive in that it explicitly links being out sexually to openly discussing political issues as well, creating an analogy between sexual diversity (he is critical of marriage, for instance) and political diversity, instead of the decreed party ideology.[29] Bert's enthusiasm and insistence on openness are put in perspective by the voices of those not living in the large gay communities of Berlin or Leipzig. In addition, the protocols by older men (Erich, Karl, Lothar, and J. A. W.) throw some light on the persecution of and discrimination against homosexuals not only under the

Nazi regime but also during the first decades of socialist rule. These texts in particular create a sense of historical progress, confirmed by the decriminalization of homosexuality in 1968.

In retrospect, after the Wall had come down in 1989, Lemke admitted in an interview that, contrary to the tenor of his book, gay identity in East Germany was defined by a cohesive stance of dissent vis-à-vis the socialist state: "One had more solidarity, because one knew that one was, as a rule, against the party. You didn't have to be a big resistance fighter, but we were more or less agreed that it couldn't continue that way" (Peck 146). His admission points to a convergence of "deviant" subjectivity and dissident politics which had previously been taboo. Moreover, this convergence occurred on the part of gays and lesbians who would admit to a political critique, as well as on the part of feminist dissidents who no longer felt compelled to omit homosexuality from their critical agenda. In 1990, two feminists published a collection of protocols entitled *You Cannot Make a State without Us*, which presented the intersection of political and sexual dissidence in the erstwhile GDR. The GDR Independent Women's Union (UFV) offered drafts for a new constitution of the unified Germany, the Party Law, the Unification Law, and the Electoral Law to the socialist interim government in 1990, which officially documented this convergence (Schenk 164). The months between the socialist ruling party's demise and the first free elections, in which opposition groups cherished hopes for a "third path" of a democratic socialism, saw the flourishing of feminist, gay, and lesbian organizations, who saw themselves as central to a new social order (see Schäfer, Grau).

In the unified Germany, sexual politics have entered a new phase and the first euphoria about the permissiveness of the West, which many GDR women and homosexuals first welcomed, has evaporated.[30] A new sobriety has set in on the part of lesbians in particular, having to do both with the gender relations prevailing in the West and with the power inequality between the two parts of the formerly divided Germany. The protocol of Martina, an s/m dyke from East Berlin, speaks to the sexual dynamics of reunification. She describes how she came out into a community that combined dissident politics with sexual experimentation and openness. It allowed her to engage in top-bottom role-playing but eschew the gendered sexuality she associates with butch-femme. She views her butch identity and desire for other butches as strictly separate from heterosexual patterns, which for her are tied up with property relations, jealousy, and competition. With the opening of the inter-German borders and her entrance into the West Berlin leather dyke scene, Martina became involved in an s/m relationship with a West German woman in which the fluidity of desire and exchangeability of positions, which she deems central to her sexuality, were locked into what she now experienced as oppression and sexual slavery. The "attraction to feel the strength of another woman, her physical forcefulness" became impossible in a relationship in which she felt herself to be cast as feminine (she was expected to do the housework, for instance) and as the object of the other woman's property (her lover proposed to lend her out to friends). An acknowledged factor in the western woman's erotic attraction to her partner was Martina's feminism. In view of the way in which the GDR has come to be identified with its women-friendly socio-political measures so that (somewhat ironically) "feminism" has come to stand for the GDR in public discourse,[31] I would argue that Martina's personal history registers the inscription of heterosexual power structures in inter-German relations, which I have discussed elsewhere (Sieg 1993). If, as Martina's story implies, domination and submission have become fixed positions between East and West Germany, the question is whether masochism can offer a way to reclaim pleasure within such a scenario, as many Western s/m practitioners are apt to argue.

Martina's own discourse on feelings and relationships reflects a new concern with investment and revenue when she declares, "When I fall in love, I assume, in a positive way, I invest part of my subjectivity." And anybody who claims to love her back must "invest the utmost" in order to warrant Martina's outlay of emotional capital (Gutsche 67). I do not want to romanticize an "equal," liberated, or non-alienated GDR sexuality that blossomed despite or because of a repressive sexual regime and thus escaped commodification. Her story provides the coda to my narrative of deviance and dissidence and illustrates my own suspicion of happy marriages. The convergence of these two terms in the brief moment of the "third path," the possibility of a sexually diverse society, had already become obsolete once it could be publicly represented. Nevertheless, the theorization of post-Wall sexualities does not begin at yet another "zero hour" of German history, but carries with it the baggage of Cold War subjects.

Notes

1. Like Sand, feminists and sex radicals in this century would see the interrelation of a social revolution and sexual freedom. In the Weimar Republic, when women's alleged frigidity was perceived as a national crisis and prompted a movement of Sexual Reform, some feminists insisted that neither the perfecting of sexual techniques nor the securing of reproductive rights could remedy the problem. What was at issue, they contended, was a rigidly heterosexist social structure of which frigidity was merely a symptom (Grossmann 168).

2. In 1897, Bebel signed the petition to the German parliament to decriminalize (male) homosexuality and took the issue in front of the Reichstag.

3. The burning of the Reichstag was a significant turning point in the relationship between communism and homosexuality, because the KPD denounced the arsonist, Marinus von der Lubbe, as a Nazi homosexual, offering something like a "homosexual conspiracy" theory.

To bolster this claim, Lubbe was characterized as SA-leader Röhm's "pleasure slave," a claim that turned out to be completely fictional. From a communist perspective, the etiology of the Third Reich was henceforth firmly connected to homosexuality.

At the same time that the Soviet Union re-criminalized homosexuality, abortion was made illegal and the divorce law was tightened, showing the interconnectedness of these issues as part of a repressive politics of sexuality. See Stümke, 99, 100.

4. This situation also explains why the opportunist protagonist of his novel *Mephisto*, modeled after Mann's gay brother-in-law, is portrayed in an interracial rather than a homosexual relationship. That displacement has been attributed to Mann's being a closet case. However, his work was closeted because of his political allies' homophobia. In 1936 when he published *Mephisto*, Mann merely saw the damaging implications of depicting a homosexual Nazi. Incidentally, Mann was closeted during his exile in the United States as well.

5. The relation between red-baiting and homophobia in the 1950s is addressed by, among others, Joan Nestle's collection *A Restricted Country*, Audre Lorde's autobiographical novel *Zami: A New Spelling of My Name*, and Gayle Rubin's theoretical essay "Thinking Sex."

6. The subjectivist discourse on sexuality was exemplified by Bertolt Brecht's early plays, the expressive dancer Anita Berber, and the utopian fiction by Russian revolutionary and writer Alexandra Kollontai. Brecht's anti-social heroes uttering an immoral, Rimbaudian discourse of "desire and derangement" gave way to the orderly dialectics of the Epic drama with its focus on class struggle. See Case, "Homosexuality and the Mother."

7. The interpretation of the Nazi state's *homosocial* (and homophobic) structures as fascism's alleged affinity with homosexuality was later refuted by Klaus Theweleit's groundbreaking study *Male Fantasies*, which hinges on that distinction.

8. According to Zinner, the Volksbühne in Berlin showed the play from 1961 to 1965. It also ran at other theatres in the GDR. See Jarmatz, 85.

9. See the recent study on lesbians in the Third Reich, especially the chapter on lesbians in concentration camps, by West German scholar Claudia Schoppmann. Her research confirms that the political (communist) prisoners stressed the non-sexual and "pure" nature of their relationships with other women, as a way to distinguish themselves from the "asocials." See Schoppmann, 236–44.

10. In her essay "Legitimer und legitimatorischer Antifaschismus" Zinner describes Buchmann and underscores her model behavior, her modesty, and her selflessness. "She always spoke of others, never of herself," Zinner stressed (181).

11. In 1922, Kollontai left the Soviet Union to go to Oslo, later to Mexico City. Her faction, the Workers' Opposition, was banned because they opposed the New Economic Policy introduced by the communist party in 1921.

12. In the mid-seventies, Müller was no longer alone in his recapturing of a radical subjectivity long suppressed and absorbed by state ideology, a subjectivity linking sexual expression with a critique of "real existant" socialism—a phrase that already points to the discrepancy between theory and praxis. A younger generation of writers like Ulrich Plenzdorf (*Die neuen Leiden des jungen W.*, 1971) and film makers like Heiner Carow (*Die Legende von Paul und Paula*, 1973) articulated the demand for individual happiness, including a sexuality not functionalized for the reproduction of the socialist state, and rejected Ulbricht's puritanism. The desire for bluejeans, rock music, western-style dancing, and extramarital sex were politicized, because to socialist functionaries they signified a longing for "Western" culture, rather than a contestation of the state's moral rigidity and expectation of individual sacrifices.

13. Wolfgang Emmerich, a West German literary scholar who wrote the afterword to the anthology when it was later re-published by a West German press, called the book "the first literary enterprise in the GDR that deliberately and exclusively addressed the topic of women's emancipation" (Kirsch et al., 111).

14. It should be noted that Morgner for a long time resisted the label "feminist," which may have been due to the term's Western baggage, and hence the suspicion that feminists in the GDR were conspiring with Western women against the socialist state.

15. It is perhaps not coincidental that this emancipated woman, who lives in a collective household in Moscow, is the namesake of Alexandra Kollontai's youngest protagonist in her novella "Three Generations," who is also characterized as the most advanced in her progress towards a liberated, socialist morality and sexual practice.

16. See Lennox, and Sieg, "Subjectivity and Socialism," on the politics of "love."

17. The representation of reunification in the Western media, with its exploding fireworks above the Brandenburg Gate and foam squirting out of innumerable champagne bottles, played on the orgasmic image of releasing the pent-up sexual energies of forty years. Finally, these televised pictures implied, our brothers and sisters "over there" can stop saving themselves for communism and enter the order of excessive expenditure.

18. See Sillge, "Nomen est Omen?" *Un-Sichtbare Frauen*, 71.

19. Sillge reports: " . . . those who got involved in issues not sanctioned by the Party, no matter what they were, became suspect. As late as the 1980s, men and women were asked who had incited them to organize lesbian and gay groups. The 'class enemy' was suspected to lurk behind every activity" (Sillge, 84). The German language uses the passive voice much more frequently than English; however, its use in these sentences conveys a sense of the ubiquitous and nebulous presence of state agencies, and the powerlessness of subjects under surveillance.

20. One of the first official organizations was the *Arbeitskreis Homosexualität* [Study Group on Homosexuality], founded under the auspices of the protestant church in Leipzig in 1982. In 1983 others followed suit in East Berlin. The church facilitated the organization of homosexuals through an open door policy. Under its auspices, a whole range of oppositional and dissident groups was able to gather. One of the main advantages of this arrangement was the use of the church's infrastructure. For the first time, networking on a national level became possible; documents and newsletters could circulate if they bore the phrase "Only for church use." This applied to the document reprinted in Sillge as well.

21. The editors of *Rosa Liebe unterm Roten Stern*, an Austrian collective that documented the situation of gays and lesbians in East bloc countries in 1984, point out that these incidents were highly publicized and gloatingly commented upon by Western media. They contend that on the whole the public "coming out" of gays and lesbians on these occasions was successful, and that state repression occurred less frequently than the Western press suggested.

22. In a discussion between the production team, television officials, and members of committees representing former concentration camp inmates, the latter criticized the depiction of the asocials: "One must consider that they [the asocials] too were imprisoned by the Nazis, they too were treated badly and in an inhumane way, they too were absolutely opposed to fascism. I don't see that [the script] depicts that conviction. One might be led to believe that the Nazis did right, Hitler did right in throwing the asocials into the camp" (Jarmatz, 84). The production team, including Zinner, interpreted the rejection of the script as censorship. Klaus Jarmatz, editor of the anthology *Ravensbrücker Ballade: oder Faschismus-Bewältigung in der DDR* (1992), argued that the state's refusal to produce or air a television version of Zinner's play illustrated the instrumentalization of antifascism. Officials no longer supported Zinner's "genuine" confrontation of the topic but preferred to give lip-service only.

23. I will not address the early protocol-collections published in and about the GDR here, the most important of which was Maxie Wander's book *"Guten Morgen, Du Schöne": Frauen in der DDR* (1978). For a detailed discussion of that volume, and later ones by GDR women, see Sieg, "Subjectivity and Socialism." Wander's book configures sexuality and socialism similarly to the sex-change stories, although lesbian sex is never thematized.

24. In 1989, Günter Amendt, a prominent West German sexologist, edited a book whose title signals this claim: *Natürlich anders. Zur Homosexualitätsdiskussion in der DDR* (Cologne: 1989). See also Jürgen Lemke's rejection of West German gays' "stridency," in Peck, 152.

25. See Brühl. He criticizes particularly the secular organizations, such as the Sonntags-Club, for their "tameness and their waving of the white flag in front of the stalinist power structures." He reports that those groups rejected his politics because of its basis in Western theory, and because of its "intellectualism." Brühl is the only GDR homosexual I have discovered so far who did not pursue an agenda of integration.

26. See esp. "Conversation with Helgard Krumm," Ulrich Schacht, ed., *Hohenecker Protokolle: Aussagen zur Geschichte der politischen Verfolgung von Frauen in der DDR* (Zurich: Amman, 1984): 236–67. Her testimony, although the least homophobic of all statements collected here, repeats the stereotype of the "mannish lesbian" that haunts this book: " 'You can take the bed next to mine, I'm *assi* . . . I'm also a lesbian.' That was Rappel . . . I would never have thought her to be a woman. Small, shapeless (flat-chested), short-haired, very deep voice. She's one of Hoheneck's originals. She's spent 17 years here. Almost half of her life. In little bits. For bad working habits [meaning "asocial life style," called "*assi*" in jargon] and petty theft" (241).

27. Social scientist Christine Eifler contends that "only the examination of the tension between the individual and societal interpretation of gender relations will yield an accurate picture of women's development during the forty years of the GDR's existence. Such an examination must not forget that women's self-realization and self-perception came up against limits set by themselves and by society, and thus their very individuality is of general significance." Christine Eifler, "Identitätsbruch als Orientierungschance: Zu den Nachwirkungen der (auf)= gelösten Frauenfrage in der DDR," *Wider das Schlichte Vergessen*, 37.

28. Lothar is the subject of West German filmmaker Rosa von Praunheim's latest movie which, like the protocol in Lemke's book, is called "I Am My Own Woman."

29. Maxie Wander had already stressed the analogy between sexual and political hypocrisy in her protocols of GDR women.

30. The protocols in the Lux/Fischer anthology convey the initial ambivalence between relief and rejection in response to the influx of pornography, the opening of Beate Uhse's sextoy chain stores in the former East Germany, and the rise of prostitution. A Berlin friend of mine reported that street vendors met visitors from the GDR at the newly opened crossing points while the Wall was still in place, making pornography one of the first mass export products inundating the East.

31. The conflation of the GDR with feminism became particularly pronounced in the debates around abortion rights during and after reunification. See Funk, introduction to *Gender Politics and Post-Communism*, and "Abortion and German Unification" in the same volume.

Works Cited

Baumgardt, Manfred. "Das Institut für Sexualwissenschaft und die Homosexuellen-Bewegung in der Weimarer Republik." *Eldorado: Homosexuelle Frauen und Männer in Berlin 1850–1950. Geschichte, Alltag und Kultur.* Berlin: Frölich und Kaufmann, 1984.

Bebel, August. "Die Frau in der Zukunft" [1879]. *Grundlagentexte zur Emanzipation der Frau.* Ed. Jutta Menschik. Cologne: Pahl-Rugenstein, 1976.

Brühl, Olaf. "Fünf Begegnungen mit 'homosexuellen BürgerInnen.' " *Lesben und Schwule—was nun? Frühjahr 1989 bis Frühjahr 1990.* Ed. Günter Grau. Berlin: Dietz, 1990. 53–61.

Buchmann, Erika. "Brief an eine Berliner Reporterin." *Ravensbrücker Ballade oder Faschismus-Bewältigung 1989 in der DDR.* Ed. Klaus Jarmatz. Berlin: Aufbau, 1992.

Case, Sue-Ellen. "Brecht and Women: Homosexuality and the Mother." *Brecht Yearbook: Women and Politics* 12 (1983), 65–78.

Dölling, Irene. "Frauenforschung mit Fragezeichen?: Perspektiven feministischer Wissenschaft." *Wir wollen mehr also ein 'Vaterland': DDR-Frauen im Aufbruch.* Ed. Gislinde Schwarz and Christine Zenner. Reinbek: Rowohlt, 1990.

Fehervary, Helen. "Heiner Müller and *Cement.*" *New German Critique,* special issue (1979).

Grau, Günter, ed. *Lesben und Schwule—was nun? Frühjahr 1989 bis Frühjahr 1990. Chronik-Dokumente-Analysen-Interviews.* Berlin: Dietz, 1990.

Grossmann, Atina. "The New Woman and the Rationalization of Sexuality in Weimar Germany." *Powers of Desire: The Politics of Sexuality.* Ed. Ann Snitow, Christine Stansell, and Sharon Thompson. New York: Monthly Review Press, 1983.

Gutsche, Kerstin. *Ich Ahnungsloser Engel: Lesbenprotokolle.* Berlin: Reiher, 1990.

Homosexuelle Initiative (HOSI) Wien, eds. *Rose Liebe unterm Roten Stern: Zur Lage der Lesben und Schwulen in Osteuropa.* Kiel: Frühlings Erwachen, 1984.

Horn, Erdmute. "Überlegungen zur staatlichen Gleichberechtigungspolitik in der Bundesrepublik Deutschland und in der Deutschen Demokratischen Republik." *Unterm neuen Kleid der Freiheit das Korsett der Einheit: Auswirkungen der deutschen Vereinigung für Frauen in Ost und West.* Ed. Christel Faber and Traute Meyer. Berlin: Rainer Bohn, 1992.

Jarmatz, Klaus, ed., *Ravensbrücker Ballade; oder, Faschismusbewältigung in der DDR.* Berlin: Aufbau, 1992.

Kirsch, Sarah, Irmtraud Morgner, and Christa Wolf. *Geschlechtertausch: Drei Geschichten über die Umwandlung der Verhältnisse.* Afterword by Wolfgang Emmerich. Darmstadt: Luchterhand, 1980.

Lemke, Jürgen. *Ganz Normal Anders.* Frankfurt a/M: Luchterhand, 1989. Translated as *Gay Voices from East Germany.* Ed. John Borneman. Bloomington: Indiana University Press, 1991.

Lennox, Sara. "'Nun ja! das nächste Leben geht aber heute an': Prosa von Frauen und Frauenbefreiung in der DDR." *Literatur der DDR in den siebziger Jahren.* Ed. P. U. Hohendahl and P. Herminghouse. Frankfurt a/M: Suhrkamp, 1983.

Lux, Petra, and Erica Fischer. *Ohne uns ist kein Staat zu machen: DDR-Frauen nach der Wende.* Cologne: Kiepenheuer und Witsch, 1990.

Mann, Klaus. "Homosexualität und Fascismus." *Heute und Morgen. Schriften zur Zeit.* Munich: Edition Spangenberg, 1969.

———. *Mephisto: Roman einer Karriere.* Munich: Spangenberg, 1981. Translated by Robin Smyth, *Mephisto.* New York: Random House, 1977.

Marshall, Stuart. "The Contemporary Political Use of Gay History: The Third Reich," *How Do I Look? Queer Film and Video.* Ed. Bad Object Choices. Seattle: Bay Press, 1991.

Merkel, Ina. "Another Kind of Woman." *German Politics and Society* (special issue on "Gender and Germany") 24, 25 (winter 1991–1992), 1–9.

Müller, Heiner. *Cement.* Trans. Helen Fehervary, Sue-Ellen Case, and Marc Silberman. *New German Critique* 16, supplement (winter 1979).

Peck, Jeffrey M. "Being Gay in Germany: An Interview with Jürgen Lemke." *New German Critique* 52 (winter 1991), 144–54.

Rowbotham, Sheila. Afterword (and Introduction) to *Love of Worker Bees,* by Alexandra Kollontai. Trans. Cathy Porter. Chicago: Cassandra Editions, 1978.

Schacht, Ulrich, ed. *Hohenecker Protokolle: Aussagen zur Geschichte der politischen Verfolgung von
Frauen in der DDR.* Zurich: Ammann, 1984.

Schäfer, Efa. "Die fröhliche Revolution der Frauen: Frauenbewegung in Ost und West." *Wir
wollen mehr als ein 'Vaterland': DDR-Frauen im Aufbruch.* Ed. Gislinde Schwarz and
Christine Zenner. Reinbek: Rowolht, 1990.

Schenk, Christina. "Lesbians and Their Emancipation in the Former German Democratic Re-
public: Past and Future." *Gender Politics and Post-Communism: Reflections from Eastern
Europe and the Former Soviet Union.* Ed. Nanette Funk and Magda Mueller. New York:
Routledge, 1993.

Schoppmann, Claudia. *Nationalsozialistische Sexualpolitik und weibliche Homosexualität.* Pfaffen-
weiler: Centaurus, 1991.

Sieg, Katrin. "Subjectivity and Socialism: Feminist Discourses in East Germany," in *Postcom-
munism and the Body Politic.* Ed. Ellen Berry. New York University Press, 1995.

———. "The Revolution Has Been Televised: Reconfiguring History and Identity in Post-
Wall Germany." *Theatre Journal* 45:1 (March 1993).

Sillge, Ursula. *Un-Sichtbare Frauen: Lesben und ihre Emanzipation in der DDR.* Berlin: Links
Druck, 1991.

Stümke, Hans-Georg. *Homosexuelle in Deutschland: Eine politische Geschichte.* Munich: C. H.
Beck, 1989.

Ulbricht, Walter. "Zehn Gebote der sozialistischen Moral." *DDR-Handbuch II.* 3rd ed. Ed.
Bundesministerium für innerdeutsche Beziehungen. Cologne: Wissenschaft und Politik,
1985.

Wolf, Christa. "Culture Is What You Experience—An Interview with Christa Wolf." *New
German Critique* 27 (fall 1982), 89–100.

———. "In Touch." *German Feminism: Readings in Literature and Politics.* Ed. Edith Altbach-
Hoshino. (161–69)

Zinner, Hedda. *Der Teufelskreis.* Berlin: Henschelverlag, 1953.

7

As the Master Saw Her

Parama Roy

THE TITLE OF my chapter repeats with a difference the title of a book Margaret Noble wrote in 1910, a book entitled *The Master as I Saw Him*. Margaret Noble, known in India and elsewhere as Sister Nivedita, came to the subcontinent in the last decade of the nineteenth century in order to serve as a disciple to the Hindu monk and religious leader Swami Vivekananda, and to serve, at his behest, as a model and guide to downtrodden Hindu womanhood. In this chapter I want to use the figure of Nivedita as a point of entry into questions of colonialism, nationness, and gendering, especially as they were mediated through religious discipleship in late nineteenth-century India. What I want to do is examine the ways in which a certain position (here, discipleship) within religion (here, upper-caste Hinduism) figures as the ground upon which traffic around gender identification and national identity can circulate. I would like in particular to contemplate the "Western woman" as "native," and to scrutinize the ways in which she is solicited as central to the project of imagining India/Hinduness[1] and Hindu masculinity and yet also constructed as a blank space, as the receptacle of the displacements of various religious, sexual, and nationalist imperatives.[2] But if the Western woman, here called Nivedita, is the name of a set of displacements, we cannot begin with her. In order to speak of her at all, we have to speak of a number of intersubjective relays, involving her, Ramakrishna, and Vivekananda. So we have to begin elsewhere; we have to begin with Ramakrishna.

Ramakrishna Paramhansa was the guru or religious mentor of Vivekananda (the latter translated the word "guru" as "Master," a translation Nivedita retained), who in turn was Nivedita's guru.[3] Ramakrishna features as an important figure in nineteenth-century Bengali culture, as does his better-known disciple, Narendranath Dutta, who assumed (in 1893) the monastic name of Swami Vivekananda. Ramakrishna was born in 1836 in Kamarpukur, in rural Bengal, and grew up barely literate in an orthodox Brahmin family. In his late teens he went to Calcutta to officiate as a priest at the temple of the goddess Kali at Dakshineshwar. By the 1870s he had established a reputation for himself as a mystic,

Sri Ramakrishna; photograph courtesy of the Vedanta Society of Northern California.

and had attracted a large number of devotees, most of them male and from the Bengali *bhadralok* (colonially educated, urban, and bourgeois) class.

Ramakrishna was well known as an idiosyncratic figure, who claimed to have tested through a ritualized and highly literal process of psychic identification the truth of the varied sects that were subsumed in the nineteenth century under the

Swami Vivekananda; photograph courtesy of the Vedanta Society of Northern California.

label Hindu, as well as of other religions like Buddhism, Islam, and Christianity. In his thirties, he was initiated into Islam by a supposedly Muslim "guru" (Govinda Ray, a convert to Sufism), and for three days thereafter he worshipped Allah, lived outside the temple precincts, and, in one version of the story (admittedly one that is not often repeated), even consumed beef, though he had to assume the form of a dog feeding on the carcass of a cow in order to do so.[4] As a result, the prophet Muhammad appeared to him in a vision and merged into his body. Several years later, in his "Christian" phase, the experience was repeated, though with greater intensity, when he achieved a comparable union with the body of Christ.

Analogous to this kind of mobility between varieties of religious identification is another, and more obviously, if differently gendered, transaction. Ramakrishna located in (what we will conditionally call) heterosexual masculine desire,[5] and in the greed of material possessions (a configuration he conflated and designated *kaminikanchan*, woman-as-seductress and gold) the greatest obstacle to religious truth. Of these two impulses the first was infinitely the more powerful and dangerous, and therefore to be guarded against by vulnerable and exploited males.[6] (Hetero)sexuality could not however be kept in check by mere abstinence; it could only be transcended by becoming the troubling object of desire. The only way to shun woman was to become woman. (I hardly need add that this assumption of corporeal femininity and feminine identification was quite compatible with and, indeed, grounded in, a marked gynophobia.)[7] This "transvestic" discipline was enjoined in a general way upon the male disciples (though, interestingly, it was not enjoined upon the best-loved disciple Vivekananda, who Ramakrishna identified at several points as fixed in a masculine identification). I quote here from an address by Ramakrishna to the disciples:

> A man can change his nature by imitating another's character. By transposing on to yourself the attributes of woman, you gradually destroy lust and the other sensual drives. You begin to behave like women. I have noticed that men who play female parts in the theatre speak like women or brush their teeth like women while bathing.[8]

At several points in his life, therefore, Ramakrishna literalized his transcendence of the body by assuming all the outward and inward signs of female identity (including bleeding; the best-known biography in Bengali of the sage of Dakshineshwar claimed that he had periods when he was a woman).[9] The transcendence of the body made the body itself its vehicle and was made manifest in a continuum of corporeal, gendered signs; it should be noted at the same time that in becoming woman, Ramakrishna became not *kamini* (woman-as-seductress) but the "handmaid of God":

> I spent many days as the handmaid of God. I dressed myself in women's clothes, put on ornaments, and covered the upper part of my body with a scarf, just like a woman. . . . Otherwise, how could I have kept my wife with me for eight months? Both of us behaved as if we were the handmaids of the Divine Mother. I cannot speak of myself as a man. (*Gospel*, 603)

Hinduism (in its upper-caste as well as its popular, demotic forms) does of course provide paradigms for shifting gender identifications or what may very contingently be designated "transvestic"[10] display for men (but not, as far as I know, for women). The hermaphrodite god/dess Ardhanarishwara (literally, "the god who is half woman") may perhaps be said to provide one such (decidedly patriarchal) paradigm, as might Tantric disciplines that prescribe the satiation and internalization of heterosexual desire as the means of transcending it.[11] Ramakrishna's practice then was not entirely eccentric within the norms provided by certain strains of Hinduism, and this obviously is not what I wish to argue. What I *would* like to argue is that becoming woman ("handmaid of God") is, for Ramakrishna, an entry into guruship; my interest is in the gendering of guruship and discipleship.

In most varieties of Hinduism, the guru is almost always male, and his disciples almost always male as well. And the master-disciple relationship is situated within a non-money economy, an economy that functions moreover outside relations of reciprocity; that is to say, the guru makes a gift of his knowledge to the disciple, who compensates the former in the currency of service, which can never, of course, be adequate to the gift.[12] In this respect the relationship between men in discipleship (which is situated within the economy of the "gift") is notably different from the relationship of men with women; as Ramakrishna saw it, the relationship with women was always mediated by money. So through most of his later life, Ramakrishna surrounded himself with young unmarried male devotees, to whom he was particularly attached. The intensity of this bond, though, did not pass without notice, even among the most devout. That this conspicuous attachment was perplexing and even embarrassing for some of his followers is evidenced by the remarks of some of the older male (and married) devotees, as well as by the discomfort voiced by the favorite young disciple, Vivekananda, who once castigated his guru for his "infatuated" pursuit of him.

What indeed is the nature of Vivekananda's investment in this gender traffic, especially when it is refracted by his colonial and nationalist concerns? To answer this question, we will have to make an apparent detour through Vivekananda's travels at "home" and in the "world." What is certain is that in almost every conceivable way this favorite disciple seemed to set himself against the example set by Ramakrishna after the latter's death in 1886; this is a turn that requires some consideration of the disciple's social and intellectual milieu during his youth and

early adulthood. Vivekananda was a *bhadralok* male, and an English-educated Cal-
cuttan, and he seems to have been challenged in obvious ways by colonialism,
Christianity, and by the Enlightenment intellectual heritage in its colonial and
specifically South Asian inflection. Clearly, I do not wish to assert that Ramakrishna was not hailed by colonialism.[13] I am suggesting, rather, that he probably
was hailed by colonialism-and-nationalism (I speak of this here as a single category)[14] in a way distinct from the ways his best-known disciple was hailed. At
this point I will simply be content to say that this category occupies a recessive
place in the *Ramakrishna Kathamrita* and in his life. This is what Vivekananda
seeks to address (and redress) in his own capacity as guru.

In Vivekananda, then, Hinduism becomes very specifically an address to colonialism (especially to the male colonizer) and the "West." In 1893, at the World
Parliament of Religions in Chicago, he vindicated Hinduism and Indianness—to
Vivekananda, as to so many other Hindu nationalists of his time (and ours), the
two were the same—and, indeed, proclaimed the moral and intellectual superiority of India and Hinduism before an apparently electrified North American
audience. He spent several years after this in North America and Europe (including England), lecturing, acquiring disciples (mostly Western [white] women)
and amassing a gigantic reputation (from a distance, of course) in India. That is
to say, Vivekananda discovered himself as the swami, as Indian, as Hindu, and as
male, and implicitly a heterosexual male, in the West, outside the Indian nation-
space. It is his placement in the United States and in England that allows
Vivekananda to conceive of a national horizon for the geographical and moral
space designated "India." And through his travels in the West, Vivekananda the
disciple becomes, additionally, Vivekananda the guru, and his disciple Margaret
Noble becomes crucial to his gendered conceptualization of Hindu psychic and
national identifications; Vivekananda, in other words, is made possible by
Nivedita.[15]

In distinction to Ramakrishna, Vivekananda insisted on a stabilization of
personal and national identity (and identification) in gender terms and, in light
of the gendered representation of the colonial encounter, this is hardly unex-
pected. As Partha Chatterjee says, paraphrasing Ashis Nandy's well-known argument, "The 'hyper-masculinity' of imperialist ideology made the figure of the
weak, irresolute, effeminate babu a special target of contempt and ridicule."[16]
Vivekananda's call for Hinduism and nationalism, like that of many of his West-
ern-educated and nationalist contemporaries like Bankim Chandra Chatterjee,
was therefore a call to Indian/Hindu men to reclaim a lost or forgotten masculinity. This call must also be seen as a phobic response to Ramakrishna's un-
seemly demands; that is to say, it is a phobic response not just to femininity, but
to its disturbing location in masculinity. Unlike his guru, Vivekananda could
neither become woman himself nor could he exhort Indian/Hindu men to be-

come woman in the interest of transcending (hetero)sexuality, since the problem with Indian men was that they were Indian women. So for him Hindu men were not, as for Ramakrishna, too manly for their own (spiritual) good, they were rather too womanly for their own (nationalist) good.

Vivekananda's message to his own (feminized) countrymen was to inculcate virility: "the older I grow, the more everything seems to me to lie in manliness."[17] It is not surprising, therefore, that if Vivekananda in his address to the East was emphatic about "man-making," in his address to the West he assumed the posture of a "Napoleon of religion."[18] His identification with and promotion of "manliness" was thus a two-fold project. It implied not only a repudiation of the feminine identification urged by Ramakrishna, but also a paradoxical embrace of colonial masculinism that could then be deployed against colonizing males. Spiritual mastery over the West was a reversal of the long conquest inaugurated by colonialism and, on home ground at least, the swami insisted on complete deference from his Western (women) disciples. Contemptuous of dietary and caste restrictions himself, he was insistent that the same freedom could not and should not be available to a Western woman in India. "You must give up all visiting, and live in strict seclusion. . . . You have to set yourself to Hinduize your thoughts, your needs, your conceptions, and your habits. Your life, internal and external, has to become all that an orthodox Hindu Brahmin Brahmacharini's ought to be. . . . *You have to forget your own past, and to cause it to be forgotten. You have to lose even its memory!*" he told Nivedita.[19] (There is no evidence of Vivekananda's having made similar demands on Western males.)

So while Ramakrishna mimed woman, Vivekananda had to mime masculinity and heterosexuality (though his miming has necessarily to be understood somewhat differently from Ramakrishna's experiences of possession). To most observers Vivekananda appeared the personification of the "manliness" that was so central to his message, and this manliness had a decided corporeal dimension. The various contemporary (and present-day) accounts, both American and Indian, of the swami speak almost obsessively of his "powerful," athletic body and his commanding good looks, which distinguished him from his fellow monks and devotees; his impact abroad is almost inevitably represented in biographies and Indian newspaper reports of the time in terms not just of his message or his personality but also of his appearance, including details of his clothing. It may be instructive to consider briefly the representation of the swami's body in photographs, especially in contrast to that of the other religious figure, Ramakrishna. Vivekananda is almost always photographed standing upright and fully clothed in a mixture, usually, of upper-class North Indian and Western costume. He is by Bengali standards a strongly built man; the poses seem calculatedly "masculine" and grave. I do not of course wish to imply that Ramakrishna was un-self-conscious about being photographed, or that there is a greater degree of premeditation or self-reflexiveness in Vivekananda's photographic representations. My assertion rather is that Vivekananda's photographs, as indeed the descriptions of his "personality" (a fairly transparent and habitual code for his body), undoubtedly had the effect of "masculinizing" and eroticizing him, first to a Western audience and then to an Indian one. The body of Vivekananda is thus made available—particularly after his return from the United States and Europe—as (erotic) spectacle through travels and addresses and photographs.

The young monk, whose "manly" body had been erotically solicited for discipleship by Ramakrishna, seeks, as guru, to sublimate and relocate that eroticism at least partially within a heterosexual imaginary. This is a simple enough explanation of his turn to heterosexual female disciples; but why is their (white) Westernness an essential component of their fitness for discipleship? We have to remember that Vivekananda assumed his status as guru in partial reaction against colonizing males; and for them as for him, "whiteness becomes most visible, takes form," as Mary Ann Doane says (in her discussion of the place of white women in a racist economy), "in relation to the figure of the white woman."[20] So in order to identify as a masculine, heterosexual Hindu male, he has to interpellate a fit female audience, but a female audience less intimate and less powerful than and, paradoxically, more mobile than, Indian/Hindu womanhood. Moreover, the nationalist dialectic of his mission—which demands a recognition of the colonized male as (heterosexual) male by the (male) colonizer—also makes Indian women incapable of supplying the swami with the satisfactions of guruhood. The proper audience, and the proper disciple, is Western woman.

Vivekananda's audience of admirers and disciples, however, is quite heterogeneously constructed, in ways that complicate his insistence on masculine heterosexuality. What about audiences not female and not necessarily constructed in discipleship? The swami remains, for instance, an important figure for Indian males (far less so for Western males); this audience poses a number of interesting questions. How does he hail them? How do they hail him? Steve Neale's reading of the problems of spectatorship and the spectacle of masculinity, albeit grounded in the codes of Hollywood cinema, nonetheless affords a fruitful point of theoretical entry into our colonial Indian situation.[21] Vivekananda's exorbitant masculinity was, it is clear, not without its own intellectual and libidinal complications. He had to construct himself as masculine and therefore heterosexual in response both to the emasculizing process of colonialism as well as to the erotic solicitations of Ramakrishna. But though Woman as concept-metaphor, in setting off his masculinity and heterosexuality, assumed a value for him that she had not for his guru, he could not sanction the presence of femininity in the male. Hence he was overtly contemptuous of Indian males who, like his guru, were "feminine" in their psychic identification and who conceivably directed their erotic attention to other, more "masculine" males. But it was clearly his "masculinity" that had attracted the guru; so, in consolidating this feature of his appeal, he could conceivably be making himself an even more attractive erotic object for men like Ramakrishna. In his hyperbolized masculinity, Vivekananda is available obviously as an identificatory figure, as an ego ideal. But equally obviously, and especially in light of his relation with his guru and other Indian males (characterized as a "nation of women"), one cannot rule out the solicitation of a fetishistic and masochistic contemplation from this audience.

How does this conceptualization of Indianness and Hinduness conceive of Ramakrishna's unruly (Indian) *kamini*? For Vivekananda, this Indian/Hindu masculinity can only be realized through a localization and circumscription of the "feminine" and its ultimate relocation outside a libidinal economy, in a place where Hindu/Indian woman will be neither subject nor object of desire. He deals with Hindu femininity—which Ramakrishna had consistently characterized as powerful, active, indeed predatory in its form as *kamini*—by rewriting Hindu womanhood in specifically bourgeois nationalist terms. The (Hindu/Indian) woman question for Vivekananda becomes abstracted, regulated, and desexualized in a suffering and idealized Mother India. It is a familiar pattern. What, however, is distinctive in Vivekananda's case is his remapping and elaboration of the contiguous and overlapping terrains of sexuality/matrimony and the religious life. His ideal of the devotee-disciple (given his belief in strict celibacy for both monks and nuns) was not so much the unmarried Hindu nun but the Hindu widow, whose life of enforced quasi-religious fidelity to a deceased husband he greatly admired. It is this model, in fact, of erotic feminine energy sublated as worship of the husband/male, in a non-reciprocal union, that he seems to have replicated in his model of the guru-disciple relationship. Nivedita, who appears to have faithfully reproduced in her writings Vivekananda's notion of Hindu femininity, provides the following description of the wife as devotee:

> [F]or the woman supreme love is . . . a duty. Only to the man his mother must always stand first. In some sense, therefore, the relation is not mutual. And this is in full accordance with the national sentiment, which stigmatises affection that asks for equal return as 'shopkeeping.' . . . As a disciple might, she prostrates herself before him, touching his feet with her head before receiving his blessing. It is not equality. No. But who talks of a vulgar equality, asks the Hindu wife, when she may have instead the unspeakable blessedness of offering worship?[22]

Woman (as concept-metaphor) thus remained central to Vivekananda's religious-nationalist schema (despite his discrepant, shifting, and imperfectly articulated postures on the position of women in India and the West). He never failed to declare to Nivedita and others that he was committed to the cause of "Woman and the People," whose oppression was the cause of Indian degradation. Nivedita in fact was recruited precisely for the purpose of uplifting Indian women. How this uplift was to be achieved, however, was a matter of some perplexity. He believed, in common with bourgeois nationalists of Partha Chatterjee's description, that "not only was it not desirable to imitate the West in anything other than the material aspects of life, it was not even necessary to do so" in the psychosocial sphere (represented by woman) because of Indian spiritual superiority over the West.[23] Yet he was significantly dependent upon the West, especially upon Western women, for validation as nationalist, masculine, heterosexual. He needed then to make a place for them in the Hindu polity. In what capacity, though? As saviors of Hindu women (who were in need of saving, *and* not in need of saving, according to his testimony)? Or as Hinduized, assimilated Western women? This is the point at which Vivekananda's program of the reconfiguration of Hindu masculinity through the figure of the Western woman reaches a point of impasse and finds itself unable to proceed. Vivekananda himself was unable to work through this impasse except to gesture—obviously inadequately and contradictorily—at the already available but unsatisfactory (because associated most obviously with both colonialism and indigenous but English-inspired social reform movements) model of Western women as teachers (though not religious gurus). His foremost disciple, Nivedita, lost little time after his death in downplaying the cause of women's uplift and female education.

The life of Nivedita itself illustrates some of the tensions of this position. Born into an Irish nationalist family, she was distinguished in early adulthood for her disquiet with traditional Christianity and her interest in women's issues. She was powerfully drawn to the swami's "personality" when she encountered him in London in 1897, and it was this, rather than any admiration for the originality of his thought, that led her to call him "Master" within a month of their first meeting. He on his part recognized in her the ideal disciple, who could also serve as a power in her own right: "I am now convinced that you have a great future in the work for India. What was wanted was not a man but a woman; a real lioness, to work for the Indians, women especially. India cannot yet produce great women, she must borrow them from other nations."[24]

Vivekananda's appeal was not novel; other reformist men had made similar appeals to Englishwomen. So his recruitment of Nivedita as the most proper teacher of Hindu/Indian women followed in some respects an already available trajectory. It is notable that the necessity for the Western woman disciple meant that Vivekananda had to remember to forget Indian women except as symbolic figures or as figures for rescue. He spoke of Indian (primarily Hindu) women as bereft of Indiana female leadership and, further, as incapable at the present moment of generating such figures; he was able to insist on this, moreover, despite his personal encounters with the associates of the redoubtable Pandita Ramabai,[25] despite his acquaintance with Ramakrishna's wife Sharada Devi,[26] and despite the abundant evidence of female education, professional activity, and feminist organization in several parts of India, including Bengal.[27]

What made this trajectory different in Nivedita's case was that it was necessary for Western woman to become Hindu woman in order to educate Hindu women. Of Indian males, Indian females, and Western females, it was only the last that could take up Ramakrishna's call to be Indian woman. Despite being unable to assume any of the assigned subject positions of mother, wife, or widow assigned to Hindu women—she settled finally for the position of Vivekananda's "daughter," perhaps the only position in the Hindu family romance she could assume—she lived a fairly orthodox life with regard to diet, worship, and the observance of caste taboos. Though she did not maintain *purdah* herself, and in fact traveled, lectured, and wrote copiously, she spoke and wrote with considerable ardor in favor of the orthodox Hindu ideals of femininity.

Nivedita obviously must function only as partial substitute (not quite / not white, or is it not quite notquite?) for Indian woman, since it is her very (racial) difference that guarantees Vivekananda's and, paradigmatically, the Indian male's Indianness and masculinity. But more importantly, Nivedita, like the figure of the Western woman in general, functions as a sign of subjective insubstantiality, or as the repository of the psychic displacements of dominant Hindu males like Vivekananda; she apparently acquiesces to being the object onto which or whom meanings are (dis)located. Of all the figures in the colonial scene— Western man, Indian man, straight Western woman, and Indian woman—it seems that it is only the Western woman whose identity is available—for the Indian man—as relatively open, mobile, malleable. She is distinct from the Indian woman, whose identity has to be in the nationalist context, fixed quite as much as the Indian male's is. We are all familiar with the mimic man that Macaulay seeks to interpellate through English education: "a class of persons, Indian in blood and colour, but English in taste, in opinions, in morals, and in intellect."[28] What we have here is the process performed in reverse, and for the Indian nationalist male; (Hindu) nationalism demands at this point its mimic wo/man. Ramakrishna's demand for ambulatory identifications in discipleship finds, for Vivekananda and the Hindu nationalist movement, its best prototype in the Western woman.

This identification, however, was not achieved without conflict, and Nivedita's account of her discipleship, *The Master as I Saw Him* (1910), was notably different from the usual biographies of the swami in touching upon the agonistic, conflictual nature of the guru-disciple relationship. The conflicts were not simply or inevitably "political"—though Vivekananda took her to task for her loyalty to Britain and the Empire—but also affective and libidinal. Commentators hint as much when they speak, typically, of her "passionate adoration" of the guru. Nivedita herself was to speak of this in a fairly circumspect way: "I was made to realise, as the days went by, that in this [discipleship] there would be no personal sweetness."[29] The emphasis in her narrative is on Vivekananda's demand for complete submission as his disciple (a demand quite different, by the way, from anything that his own guru had made of himself). He warned her about the absence of reciprocity in their relationship:

> I see persons giving me almost the whole of their love. But I must not give anyone the whole of mine in return, for that day the work would be ruined. Yet there are some who will look for such a return, not having the breadth of the impersonal view. It is absolutely necessary to the work that I should have the enthusiastic love of as many as possible, while I myself remain entirely impersonal. . . . A leader must be impersonal.[30]

This non-reciprocity, then, was to be the keynote of their relationship. She was to submit to him fully and exclusively in discipleship; when on a trip to Europe she became the temporary intellectual helpmeet of the sociologist Patrick Geddes, the swami construed it as an act of infidelity, and was conspicuously cold to her. One might speculate that Nivedita's fervent defence of Hindu gender orthodoxy is also a meditation on her own discipleship, as well as a reparation of the "failures" of that discipleship.

If Nivedita was to be Hindu woman in her worship of the guru, what precise form was her discipleship to take and what was its relation to Hindu women? The first form it took was the establishment of a school for girls in northern Calcutta. This school, catering to young unmarried girls and child-widows, was situated in Nivedita's own home in Bosepara Lane, for reasons of economy, no doubt, but also undoubtedly to ensure as little separation as possible between the "home" and the "world." Nivedita was careful to keep the education religious (that is, Hindu) and domestic in tone and free from "de-nationalising" influences. The school was supported by Nivedita's own savings as well as by contributors in the West; the swami's role in the school was quite minimal. In fact his interest in the project appeared at one time so small that Nivedita wondered if he had forgotten to what ends he had recruited her and invited her to India. His indifference to the pedagogical project may have ensured the school's early closure. It was revived again after Vivekananda's death, this time with the assistance of an American woman disciple, Sister Christine (Christine Greenstidel), as well as an Indian teacher, Sister Sudhira. Nivedita, however, became less and less involved in the running of the school, having immersed herself in a variety of nationalist projects; when her assistants abandoned the institution for the Brahmo Girls' School in 1911, she was unable, perhaps unwilling, to keep it going.

In this she was doing no more than emulating the Master. From all accounts, Nivedita's training in discipleship was a fundamentally "nationalist" rather than a "spiritual" one. Much of her apprenticeship consisted in accompanying Vivekananda in his travels to northern India, where he schooled her in the glories of Indian civilization and hammered away at her English partisanship. The lesson was so well learned that even before Vivekananda's death Nivedita began to betray some impatience with the "limited" project of women's education. In a letter she wrote about the proliferating and discrepant allegiances that were present before her: "I belong to Hinduism more than ever I did, but I see the *political* need [that of decolonization] so clearly, too!"[31]

It is not entirely clear how Vivekananda himself responded to this version of his disciple's nationalist politics. In the years before his death, he was known to assert that spirituality rather than politics was India's greatest strength, and the Ramakrishna Order that he established after his return from the West in 1897 was explicitly non-political in nature. This may, of course, have been both a way of forestalling the unwelcome attention of a colonial government as well as of placing himself above party politics. He remained, however, a nationalist, though unevenly so, and more actively so in relation to Western disciples than Indian ones. Nivedita's involvement in Indian nationalist politics, however, proved a somewhat complex matter. Some biographies of Nivedita maintain that the swami was too weary and close to death to elucidate a position about her (new) politics. Other accounts claim that the swami told her to choose between religion and politics.[32] In any event, what is noteworthy about the matter is Vivekananda's failure to endorse fully his disciple's new commitment to nationalist politics, given that his mission had been to Indianize her (that is, to make an Indian/Hindu nationalist of her). This failure, or this hesitancy, seems to me explicable in terms of his conception of the gendering of nationalism and political agency. The struggle was to be carried in the name of woman, and in a manner that allowed (Western) woman to serve as a counter in the nationalist engagement with colonialism. Nivedita's assumption of orthodox Hindu femininity and Hindu nationalism would have represented, for her guru, the triumph of Hindu nationalist masculinity. For her to become agent, however, rather than symbol or counter (as Indian women already were for bourgeois nationalists), fit very uneasily with his notion of a Mother India served by nationalist sons—who were adored by Western women.

If he had been ambivalent about Nivedita's actively nationalist politics, his brother-monks were not. Immediately after his death they compelled her to choose between "religion" and "politics," a somewhat difficult choice in an era antedating the hegemony of the bourgeois (and secular) nationalist politics of the Congress Party. She chose politics, detaching herself thereby from any formal association with the Ramakrishna Order. At this time she wrote to Josephine MacLeod, a friend of Vivekananda: "I think my task is to wake the nation, not to influence a few women."[33] Thereafter she was to associate primarily with Indian male political leaders like Gokhale and Aurobindo Ghosh, though she also continued her association with Ramakrishna's widow Sharada Devi and her companions. She had little to do with Bengali women's organizations,[34] nor did she associate with women nationalists, Indian or British. Nationalism and women's concerns intersected only occasionally and unsystematically for her, as when during the Swadeshi movement of 1905–1911 she took her students to patriotic lectures and included the song "Bande Mataram" (banned by the colonial government) in the daily prayers of the school as part of a specifically "feminine" training.[35]

In other words, the dynamic of the masquerade shifted decisively after the guru's death in 1902. After his death she became more emphatically a supporter of political and "public" (rather than primarily religious and women-centred) and "private" causes, though, as in the case of Vivekananda, her message was one of "manliness." She was often impatient with the Congress Party's demand for constitutional reforms, and probably came to believe that armed resistance to colonial rule was both inevitable and necessary.[36] Indeed, she played the role of the militant nationalist so well that a vast popular mythology about her mentorship of the Bengal anticolonial terrorists through figures like Aurobindo and Bhupendranath Dutta (the swami's younger brother) began to take shape during her lifetime.

The relay of discipleship (though not the process of displacement) was to come to a formal end with Nivedita. As a foreign-born woman, who had never formally "converted" to Hinduism (and for whom such an option may not even have been available), it is doubtful that she could herself have been acknowledged as a guru by Hindu subjects in India (or even by Western subjects), despite her eager Hindu doctrinal orthodoxy and nationalism.[37] To the end of her life, however, Nivedita remained an authoritative and active personality, publishing, lecturing, and advising on topics as diverse as education, national art, and the "woman question," and many Indians were to express their gratitude for her informal guidance and encouragement. Nivedita's biographers (particularly those associated directly or indirectly with the Ramakrishna Mission) speak rather uneasily of her political involvements, as they do of her allegedly uncompromising and decisive personality, and of her sustained attempts at mastery over her friends and acquaintances. It is almost as though she had violated the implicit taboo against assuming the role of the guru—albeit in a "secular-nationalist" sphere—instead of being the perpetual disciple she had been chosen to be. And it is evident that Nivedita herself felt some guilt about this deviation from proper (female) discipleship. The subject position that the swami had envisaged for her was occupied instead by another (Western) female disciple, Sister Christine, who was performing the reclusive, religious, female-oriented service for which she had been earmarked. "All the things Swami dreamt for me, *she* is fulfilling," she wrote to Josephine MacLeod,[38] yet this realization did not keep her from her activities or from expounding and miming the "manliness" of her own guru.

We do not know how Sister Christine conceived of and played Hindu womanhood, the performance of which had been displaced onto her; nor is much, if anything, known of the dynamics of her relationship with Nivedita (though it is implied that she was somewhat disapproving of the better-known disciple's unwomanly activities). The position of Hindu Woman in this easily nationalist movement could not, it turns out, be filled by those who would not be recognized as Hindu women; and for all other subjects it either was or became an ideologically untenable position. The production of the mimic (wo)man, envisaged variously and distinctly by Ramakrishna, Vivekananda, and Nivedita, was to remain a continually deferred and displaced, yet continually urgent, project.

Notes

I am grateful to Joe Childers, Lalitha Gopalan, Sandhya Shetty, and Carole-Anne Tyler for their reading of this chapter.

1. If it seems at several times in my chapter that Indianness and Hinduness are being conflated, this is because they usually (though not invariably) functioned as a single term for Vivekananda, Nivedita, and other Hindu revivalists of this period. In the present time, the Hindu revivalist Bharatiya Janata Party continually inscribes national geography as sacred geography. For an astute and historically rigorous critique of Hindutva's production of an ancient, singular, and recognizable Hinduism, see Romila Thapar's "Imagined Religious Communities? Ancient History and the Modern Search for a Hindu Identity," *Modern Asian Studies* 23, no. 2 (1989).

At the point in Indian history when Vivekananda and Nivedita became public figures, bourgeois and Hindu nationalisms—the first represented for instance by "moderates" in the Congress Party calling for secular and constitutional reforms, the latter by Tilak, Bankim, Vivekananda, and others—had assumed the status of two distinct categories (though quite often they functioned as one). It is useful to bear in mind Sudipta Kaviraj's important caveat against the conflation of distinct nationalisms (his own concern is with "early" and "mature" nationalisms), which must be seen as often disjunctive rather than articulated phenomena in Indian history; see "The Imaginary Institution of India," *Subaltern Studies* VII, ed. Partha Chatterjee and Gyanendra Pandey (New Delhi: Oxford University Press, 1991).

2. I do not wish to imply that Indian women did not or could not participate in Indian nationalism. They too were solicited in large numbers by various nationalisms; the Swadeshi movement of the early twentieth century and the Congress/Gandhian nationalism of a later period both made an appeal to women. But that involves a somewhat different problematic from the one under consideration here.

3. "M's" (Mahendranath Gupta's) *Sri Ramakrishna Kathamrita*, published in several volumes at the turn of the century, is a highly unusual "diary" of one disciple's encounters with his guru and with other disciples over the last four years (1882–86) of Ramakrishna's life. In this Bengali text, Ramakrishna is referred to as *thakur*, which is both a common way of designating a brahmin as well as a word meaning god; M, who was a schoolteacher, is called "master" in this work. In the English translation of 1942 by Swami Nikhilananda, *The Gospel of Sri Ramakrishna*, "the Master" is the standard appellation for Ramakrishna; this usage may have been popularized by Vivekananda.

4. Brian K. Smith, "How Not to Be a Hindu: The Case of the Ramakrishna Mission," in *Religion and Law in Independent India*, ed. Robert D. Baird (New Delhi: Manohar, 1993).

5. The term heterosexuality is here used catachrestically, since Ramakrishna seems to be largely outside the formations within which we would situate "modern" Indian subjects, including Vivekananda.

6. It is interesting to note that the disciples of Ramakrishna, notably Vivekananda, preferred the term *kamkanchan*, "lust-and-gold," over the Master's *kaminikanchan*, and went to great lengths to explain that the sage's "symbolic" use of the term did not imply any misogyny. (Colonial) modernity and nationalism appear to have persuaded them in ways that would probably have been inconceivable for their guru.

7. This insight derives in a general way from Carole-Anne Tyler's reading of the ambivalent politics of gay drag ("Boys Will Be Girls," in *Inside/Out: Lesbian Theories, Gay Theories*, ed. Diana Fuss [London: Routledge, 1991]) as well as from Kaja Silverman's account of the mastery permitted by T. E. Lawrence's reflexive masochism ("White Skin, Brown Masks: The Double Mimesis, or With Lawrence in Arabia," *differences* 1.3 [fall 1989]).

8. *The Gospel of Sri Ramakrishna*, trans. Swami Nikhilananda (New York: Ramakrishna-Vivekananda Center, 1942, 1973), 176. All subsequent references will be incorporated parenthetically into the text.

9. Cited in Sumit Sarkar, "The Kathamrita as Text: Towards an Understanding of Ramakrishna Paramhamsa," Occasional Paper 22, Nehru Memorial Museum and Library (New Delhi, 1985), 33. Sarkar cites Swami Saradananda's *Sri Sri Ramakrishna Leelaprasanga*. In the English version of this hagiography, there is, however, no *explicit* reference to menstruation; see *Sri Ramakrishna the Great Master*, 2 vols., trans. Swami Jagadananda (Madras: Sri Ramakrishna Math, 1952, 1978).

10. I put this term within quotes advisedly, since one cannot assume that transvestism was inflected in the same way for a nineteenth-century (straight?) Hindu male as it might be for, say, a contemporary straight U.S. male. One has to concede that his masculinity might have been constituted differently, and in a different relationship to femininity than might be the case for a U.S. male.

11. Wendy Doniger, *Women, Androgynes, and Other Mythical Beasts* (Chicago: University of Chicago Press, 1980), 319.

12. Women could, on occasion, function as gurus; the Bhairavi Brahmani, for instance, was one of the earliest of Ramakrishna's gurus. Sharada Devi (Ramakrishna's wife) herself had a number of (female and male) disciples. I do not think, however, that this militates against my understanding of the guru-disciple relationship as functioning for the most part for and among males, nor against my reading of its gendered significance in turn-of-the-century nationalism.

13. Sumit Sarkar has pointed to the ways in which Ramakrishna distanced himself, once he had assumed guru status over his *bhadralok* disciples, from the folk Hinduism of his early youth ("The Kathamrita as Text," 79–81). And Partha Chatterjee has persuasively described Ramakrishna's teaching and life as offering an ideal of weakness, detachment, and non-striving particularly attractive to a male Bengali bourgeoisie assaulted by colonialism's mandate to accumulate and to assert an aggressive masculine heterosexuality ("A Religion of Urban Domesticity," 60–61).

14. Nationalism's dependence on colonialism has been extensively documented. See Ashis Nandy, *The Intimate Enemy: Loss and Recovery of Self under Colonialism*, 1983, and, more importantly, Partha Chatterjee, *Nationalist Thought and the Colonial World* (Zed Books, 1986; University of Minnesota Press, 1993). Certainly nationalism-and-colonialism seems to function as one category for Vivekananda.

15. Nivedita functions here as a type of Western female disciple.

16. Partha Chatterjee, "A Religion of Urban Domesticity: Sri Ramakrishna and the Calcutta Middle Class," *Subaltern Studies* VII, ed. Partha Chatterjee and Gyanendra Pandey (Delhi: Oxford University Press, 1991), 61.

17. Swami Nikhilananda, ed. *Vivekananda: The Yogas and Other Works* (New York: Rama-krishna-Vivekananda Center, 1953), 151. The Rashtriya Swayamsevak Sangh's cult of physical fitness and martial arts training has a great deal in common with Vivekananda's endorsement of "beef, biceps, and Bhagavad-Gita."

18. *Reminiscences of Swami Vivekananda, by His Eastern and Western Admirers* (Calcutta: Advaita Ashrama, 1961, 1964), 347.

19. Nivedita, *The Master as I Saw Him* (Calcutta: Udbodhan Office, 1910), 388 (original emphasis).

20. Mary Ann Doane, "Dark Continents: Epistemologies of Racial and Sexual Difference in Psychoanalysis and the Cinema," in *Femmes Fatales: Feminism, Film Theory, Psychoanalysis* (New York: Routledge, 1991), 244.

21. Steve Neale, "Masculinity as Spectacle," in *The Sexual Subject: A* Screen *Reader in Sexuality* (London: Routledge, 1992), 277–87. Neale outlines and distinguishes between the three psychic functions and processes—identification, voyeurism, and fetishism—that come into play in a consideration of the male as object of the look, arguing that all of these work to conceal or deflect homoeroticism.

22. Sister Nivedita, *The Web of Indian Life* (London: William Heinemann, 1904), 32–45.

23. Partha Chatterjee. "The Nationalist Resolution of the Women's Question," in *Recasting Women: Essays in Indian Colonial History*, ed. Kumkum Sangari and Sudesh Vaid (New Brunswick: Rutgers University Press, 1990), 237–38.

24. Cited in Barbara Foxe, *Long Journey Home: A Biography of Margaret Noble (Nivedita)* (London: Rider, 1975), 32–33.

25. Pandita Ramabai Saraswati (1858–1922), a notable sanskrit scholar and a reformer, was a Hindu widow who converted to Christianity on a visit to England; she dedicated her life to the uplift of other young Hindu widows. Her book, *The High Caste Hindu Woman*, and her travels in England and the United States, won her the sympathy of feminists as well as Christian missionaries in the West and the censure of Hindu conservatives in India. Her shelter for widows, the Sharda Sadan in Pune, was supported in large part by funds raised by the Ramabai Circles in the United States and England. Her travels in the United States in the 1880s received extensive coverage in the U.S. press.

26. Sharadamoni Devi was married, at the age of five, to Ramakrishna. At eighteen, she moved to Dakshineshwar, and looked after him for most of the remaining decade and a half of his life; she is said to have acceded to his request that the marriage remain unconsummated. After his death, she returned to her natal village, and spent the rest of her life initiating several people into discipleship, and helping to take care of her relatives.

27. See, for instance, Meredith Borthwick, *The Changing Role of Women in Bengal, 1849–1905* (Princeton: Princeton University Press, 1984), especially chapters 8 and 9; Ghulam Murshid, *Reluctant Debutante: Response of Bengali Women to Modernization, 1849–1905* (Rajshahi, Bangladesh: Sahitya Samsad, 1983); and Radha Kumar, *The History of Doing: An Illustrated Account of Movements for Women's Rights and Feminism in India, 1800–1990* (London: Verso, 1993), especially chapters 2 and 3.

28. Thomas B. Macaulay, "Minute on Indian Education" (1835), in *Selected Prose*, ed. G. M. Young.

29. *The Master as I Saw Him*, 136–37.

30. Quoted in Pravrajika Atmaprana, *Sister Nivedita of Ramakrishna-Vivekananda* (Calcutta: Sister Nivedita Girls' School, 1961), 30.

31. Foxe, 128.

32. Foxe, 136.

33. Foxe, 150–51.

34. Barbara N. Ramusack, "Cultural Missionaries, Maternal Imperialists, Feminist Al-

lies: British Women Activists in India, 1865–1945," in *Western Women and Imperialism: Complicity and Resistance*, ed. Nupur Chaudhuri and Margaret Strobel (Bloomington: Indiana University Press, 1992), 130.

35. S. B. Mookherjee, "Nivedita and Indian Womanhood," in *Nivedita Commemoration Volume*, ed. Amiya Kumar Majumdar (Calcutta: Dhiraj Basu, 1968), 244.

36. She met Gandhi briefly in Calcutta, in the early years of the century. He admired her Hindu partisanship, but was unable to agree with her on nationalist politics. The Congress Party under Gandhi had a profoundly uneasy relationship with militant and nationalist women like Nivedita and the Rani of Jhansi.

37. Women could, in rare cases, function as gurus; the Bhairavi Brahmani, for instance, was Ramakrishna's first guru.

38. Foxe, 205.

8

Tango and the Postmodern Uses of Passion

Marta E. Savigliano

I wish to slip into your thoughts,[1] into the music of your untameable reflections, with the broken noise of my tango: a repetitive, syncopated, wet lamentation over postmodernism's absurd wound. You see, "I come from a country / turned permanently gray by forgetfulness," where "small pieces of memory and displeasure / drip into a lazy, slow [but insidious] grumble" and where tears turn into curses, there, in the "deep underground / where the mud subverts."[2] In this tango-mood I offer some choreographed contours of postmodernism as perceived by *una Otra*—female *latina* Other from the South of the world. *El Sur también existe.*[3]

This chapter is a twisted ethnography of postmodernism, in which postmodernism stands for the culture of late, post-industrial capitalism and for the paradigmatic philosophy of influential intellectual inhabitants of the First World.[4] The bold anthropologist who performs this dizzy analysis attempts to resist, through her interpretation of postmodernism, the imperialist shadow of postcoloniality. Eager to subvert postmodern teachings that attempt to naturalize and universalize the hectic despair and desperation of capitalism's most recent crisis, I invoke my tangos. The result is a challenging moan over postmodernism, a melodramatic attack in which I appropriate postmodernist strategies (post-structuralism, deconstruction, Lacanian psychoanalysis, and postfeminist writings) in order to trick back rather than to unmask postmodernism. Since it responds to a provocation, this is a strongly prejudiced interpretation, a move to join in what Antonin Artaud has called "the right to lie" (Artaud quoted in Escobar 1988: 133)—i.e., to accept the risk of exaggerating.[5] Tangoing a passionate counter-spell I intend to reverse postmodernism's curse.[6]

Through these pages I (*una Otra*) depict "postmodernism" as a culture of Desire: a desire obsessed with passion. This obsession leads "postmodernists" to pursue consumption passionately and to consume passion conspicuously. Unlike natural resources, passion, when it is subjected to conspicuous consumption, is not necessarily exhausted or depleted. Desire is fueled by passion, but it also generates more of it, provoking an oozing fermentation and scooping out of the most precious part, right at the bottom. Exotic others laboriously cultivate passionate-ness in order to be desired, consumed, and thus recognized in a world increas-ingly ruled by postmodern standards. Auto-exoticism plays an essential part in this regenerative process of identification, performing that value that exudes a surplus without which there is no survival.[7]

Tango is a dramatic expression (dance, music, lyrics, and performance) origi-nated in the Río de la Plata region (Argentina/Uruguay) toward the end of the nineteenth century. The worldwide popularity of the tango has been associated with that of a scandal: the public display of passion performed by a heterosexual couple, the symbol of which is a tight embrace and suggestive, intricate foot-work. As a powerful representation of male/female courtship, stressing the ten-sion involved in the process of seduction, the tango performance has gone through successive adjustments as it was adopted and legitimized by higher classes and by Western hegemonic cultures. Tango was "polished" and accepted by the wealthy and powerful as it made its way from the slums and brothels of the South American harbors to the cabarets and ballrooms of Paris, London, and New York. By the 1920s it had become clear that the sin of tango was related to its racial/class origins rather than to its erotic content. When appropriated by "high society," especially that of Europe, dancing the scandalous tango became an enjoyable, spicy entertainment. As a performance of exotic passion, like many other exotic products, tango was promptly packaged and distributed by the show business industry: records, dance handbooks, films, fashion, stars. . . . Tango in its new bourgeois version was readdressed to the world market including, ironi-cally, those Third World nations where it originated.

Tango emerged as a symbolic expression and ended up as a sign of status. Tango became an "exotic" good in the Political Economy of Passion:[8] appropria-tion, accumulation, marketing, packaging, commercialization, distribution, and consumption of the wealth of exotic feelings, that is, the passion of the Other/ *Otra*.

Autoexotically I return to the tango because it is my only solid resource. As the stereotype of the culture to which I belong, I have had no choice. If I reject my stereotype I fall, caught in nowhere. Caught in endless explanations of what I am not and justifications of what I am; caught in comparisons with the post-colonizer. By assuming a tango attitude and taking it seriously, I can work at ex-panding its meaning and its power. My power, actively tango.

Tango is my strategic language, a way of talking about, understanding, and responding to postmodernism from an absurd position. Tango is a strategy with multiple faces: music, dance, lyrics, performance, philosophy. . . . None of these aspects exactly reproduces or reinforces the others. The dance stops when the music pulls; the lyrics challenge the dance; the male and female couple follow and resist each other's movements; the music, syncopated, surprisingly halts. Starts again. Tango is recognizable in these contrasts and the tension that they generate. And the tension itself is dramatized in a melodramatic way, a melodrama of stereotypes on the move, unstable stereotypes, stereotypes of the unpredictable.

Tango is a practice already ready for struggle. It knows about taking sides and risks. And it knows about accusing and whining, about making intimate confessions in public. Tango knows how to make a spectacle of its cruel destiny: improvise, hide away, run after them, stay still, move at an astonishing speed, shut up, scream in a murmur, turn around, go back without returning, upside down, let your feet do the thinking, be comfortable in your restlessness. Tango. Pragmatically, tango.

Through the tango I have dealt with my own questionings as an *argentina* living transitorily abroad, exposed to an intellectual training that urged me into reshaping my own identity. Tangoing to myself, I have tried to resist intellectual colonialism. Following tango's negotiations between us and the First-Worlders, I recognized my own dealings. Reflecting on the disciplining/promotion to which I was subjecting myself in academia, I saw tango polished and promoted in the hands of dance masters and spectacle entrepreneurs. Looking at tango's endless search for origins and authenticity, I came to understand the colonized nature of this attempt. Amazed at the colonizing appropriation of tango through exoticism, I found myself transformed into an exotic object and colonized. Even more stunned by tango's achievements at home as a result of playing the exotic game, I put into question my own auto-exoticism. So here I am, with a tango on postmodernism.

This tango, like most tangos, stages a first person,[9] a possessive account in a highly personalized voice of an "I" struggling to stand on her feet, untrustfully relying on the strength of intimacy. Rather than representing or standing for, tangos' "I" attempts to move, to create in its audience of readers, musicians, and dancers a co-motion, an empathy that will permit overcoming the grotesque nature of the "I"—that pretentious "I" claiming to be something or someone. In tango lyrics the "I" dangerously curves around ridicule as it exposes the need to be interpreted. So that it can actually speak, the tango language needs to constitute an equally imperfect and human, personalized receptor/interpreter. Tangos' "I" is dialogical and "sings nostalgically the loss of itself as it becomes an other" (Panesi 1990: 22). To write tangos, then, is to write in a first person that will be inhabited by others. Those who listen, sing, dance, read, and play tangos are expected to introject their identities into them, in a dialogue that curiously retains the tango "I" (Kamenszain 1990).

This tango, like most tangos, should be murmured, restrained between the lips with precise difficulty, neither active nor passive (García 1990). In tangos, the (active) subject denounces impotence and the (passive) object reveals the vital powers of fate. Tangos perform an almost perfect exhaustion in their sentimental accusations of betrayal, skirting banality—tango's closest foe.

This tango, like most tangos, asks to be heard in a state of ironic distance. Tangos tell impossible truths (Panesi 1990) and repeat them up to that point at which truth becomes a farce. Tango-voices display gendered parodies of disgrace: these voices are feminized in falsettos and broken by sobs and alcohol when sung by run-down men; masculinized by deep, sarcastic, streetwise nuances when sung by fallen women. Tango-voices create a space for disbelief alongside the earnest words of tango lyrics. Tango-voices seem to mock what they are saying and to place a scornful doubt on the identity of those who are saying it. Who is this "I," this *Otra*, seriously yet ironically claiming alterity?[10]

> *Don Beto was a cheap womanizer ("chinitero," as they used to say) and, eventually, my paternal grandfather. He taught me how to dance the tango. Twenty five years later, twenty after his death, I came to realize what those gazes and complicitist smiles dazzled across the festive livingroom meant. The women of my family shared a secret. Don Beto, now "el abuelo Alberto" to his grandchildren, was once "un arrabalero": an expert in the Buenos Aires underworld. The tango as he danced it could only have been learnt through systematic nightlong practicing at brothels and cabarets. I was benefiting from a skill my grandfather had acquired embracing prostitutes and "milonguitas" (cabaret tango dancers). "El abuelo Alberto" did not participate in the chuckling ambiance; when we danced tango, he was serious. So was I. Only now I understand that through our tango I was being initiated into the spectacle of sex, class, and power of everyday life.*

Postmodernism asks us to dance, intensely, a fantastic choreography rendered in the genre of horror-fiction. I read challenge in the postmodern attitude: a passionless invitation to perform Otherness passionately. Like a *milonguita*, I follow the steps of my postmodern partner, and I resist.

> *Don Beto, my "abuelo Alberto," was a trespasser, not a transgressor. Like many Argentinean men of his generation, his nomadic steps were drawn to the crossing of boundaries. He wandered from the protected walls of his family life to the excitement of the cabaret underworld.[11] The signal for his moves was natural: sunrise, sunset. He never questioned the boundaries themselves; household and cabaret were as natural as the paths of the sun. So was the existence of the women confined in both places. Mothers and wives were to be found over here, prostitutes and "milonguitas" over there. Two worlds inhabited by different social classes. He never needed to ask why. It was a fact.[12] Don Beto "tangueaba" (tangoed) in and out, crossing over, never overtly challenging territories, indirect, tense, comfortably uptight in his irony, like the tango. He had power. A viscous power nurtured by two races of women. A solid bridge of eroticism tailored to his desire. My grandmother, here, washing and perfuming the shirts he wore to the cabaret. Mireya or Margot, there, sending him back home, invigorated by skillful pleasures. For him all women alike were blank pages, on which to write his story. He wrote his story on those feminine bodies: immobilized, restricted in space like pages, equally confined in a household or a cabaret.[13] Honorably privatized or publicly*

blamed, they were all owned by someone: the same men they were devoted to, the men they loved. The "tangueros" like Don Beto were invested with this viscous power: a power produced of simmered erotic passion. So what was he so serious about?

Si soy así, que voy a hacer	If I'm like this, what am I to do
nací buen mozo y embalao para el querer.	I was born good-looking and wound up for love.
Si soy así, que voy a hacer,	If I'm like this, what am I to do,
con las mujeres no me puedo contener.	with women I can't restrain myself.
[. . .]	[. . .]
Si soy así, que voy a hacer,	If I'm like this, what am I to do,
es el destino que me lleva a serte infiel.	it is destiny that makes me be unfaithful to you.

Si Soy Así (If I'm Like This), 1931
Lyrics: Antonio Botta; Music: Francisco Lomuto.

One of postmodernism's most elaborated stratagems is that of intellectual seduction. This "fatal stratagem," to put it in Jean Baudrillard's words, seems to be the rule and the limit of the postmodern game. Passion is the necessary thrust of intellectual play. Illusory and embodied participants become interchangeable players. In the guts of a postmodern, outbursts of committed passion are futile; what counts is the tension involved in seducing.

Postmodernism is the delirious political enterprise of meticulous actors, both thinkers and unthinkers: busy burrowers attempting to reveal the simultaneity of all mysteries only to leave them half bitten, exposed to erosion. First, its members think of themselves as endangered, as survivors of the modern world driven into a chaotic vertigo provoked by their own intellectual arrogance. Second, postmoderns reproduce the cult of instrumentality and efficiency, indefatigably obsessed with the discovery-and-development of "strategies" even though they disbelieve in human agency and its outcomes faced with the powers of chance. Third, the inhabitants of postmodernism question the possibility of a true self and worship an Other within a fragmented oneness, establishing the fragmentation of that which *does not* exist. Fourth, in the eyes of a postmodernist, life is a perpetual homesickness in a disharmonious world where we happen to miss experiences that actually never occurred and where desire for that which is impossible maintains the tension necessary for us to keep on living. Fifth, the postmodern world is ruled by Discourse, a powerful divinity—although not supernatural—that controls and normalizes humans by exerting untraceable bureaucratic violence on their/our bodies; the subjects of Discourse are accomplices in this process by way of practicing techniques of self-formation or "subjectification". Sixth, postmodernists are prone to look at the world as a text, to rewrite what has been written, practicing a meticulous unwriting process named deconstruction, and are haunted by an unwritten volume that nevertheless has a well-known title and author: *The History of Bodies* by Michel Foucault. Seventh, postmodern intellectuals apply a strenuous genealogical and archaeological method in order to make sense of their own history based on exploring silences, repetitions, and difference, but they mistrust their own interpretation of past events just as much as they disbelieve traditional narratives and story-telling.

Needless to say, the list could be expanded. But my intention is to point out the proliferation of unsettling paradoxes present in the postmodern "ethos." Paradoxes are dramatized through images and scenarios of black mysticism. Think of Georges Bataille's exhibition of curses, sacrifice, and the ecstasied vertigos of mysticism and eroticism (Bataille 1988, 1979, 1954); Jean Baudrillard's panicked explorations of the seductive power of obscenely exuberant signs (Baudrillard 1984, 1981); Jacques Derrida's frenzy for erosion, chasing difference and crypts (Derrida 1976, 1986, 1982); Michel Foucault's invitations to ritualized transgressions and to the contemplation of bodily horrors (Foucault 1977a, 1984a, 1987); Jacques Lacan's impossible discoveries of cosmic terror such as the constitutive wound/split of the self, the impossibility of communication and the nonexistence of women (Lacan 1977a, 1977b, 1981, 1982; see also Butler 1987: 186–204); Jean-François Lyotard's inflammatory callings to accept, beyond rejection, that domination and exploitation are desired, enjoyed by the libidinal bodies of its victims, a phenomenon that his libidinal economists should not subject to interpretation but rather witness, read, and keep in writing (Lyotard 1990). How to survive these occultist postmodern enterprises and their persuasive findings? Could it be through passion and by trusting the power of passion?

Don Beto's tango was pure tension, cyclic struggle in its steps, frozen conflict at the moment of the resolution. He led, I followed. My eyes on the floor, attentive to the intricacy of the footwork. Tight embrace, straight torsos, never leaning on each other. Our gazes never met, nor should they. A slow run, walking in between each others' feet, facing directly towards one angle of the room, stop. Abruptly. This was the moment of the fancy figures with no displacement: the "eight," "double eight," the "hooks," the "backwards crossings" . . . a sharp turn. A tense stillness. A new diagonal runaway, another bundling of legs. Every movement was contrasting in itself and with the next. Carefully entangled and incommunicatively connected from the first to the last musical time. Suddenly the singer was louder.[14]

Quién sos, que no puedo salvarme,	Who are you, that I can't protect myself,
muñeca maldita castigo de Dios.[. . .]	damned doll, curse of God [. . .]
Por vos se ha cambiado mi vida [. . .]	Because of you my life has turned [. . .]
en un bárbaro horror de problemas	into a barbarous horror of problems

que atora mis venas y enturbia mi honor.	that clogs my veins and blemishes my honor.
[. . .]	[. . .]
No puedo reaccionar,	I can't react,
ni puedo comprender,	nor can I understand,
perdido en la tormenta	lost in the storm
de tu voz que me embrujó . . .	of your voice that bewitches me . . .
la seda de tu piel que me estremece	the silkiness of your skin that makes me shiver
y al latir florece, con mi perdición . . .	and that flourishes thanks to my throbbing, and my ruin . . .

Excerpt from "*Secreto*" (Secret), 1932
Lyrics and Music: Enrique S. Discépolo.

Passion is one of those feelings of impossible conceptual definition, but also strong experiential presence. Passion is a performance, more of an "enacting" than an "acting-out," in which both actors and spectators are staged spectacularizing each other as entangled objects/subjects. According to Baudrillard, passion is a "desperate and beautiful *movement*" of which everything could be said and yet, we know not what to say (Baudrillard 1984a: 105, 119). It seems an impossible task to engage passion discursively, without performing passionateness, without folding into a tense, polarized, rhythmic movement involving some kind of excess.[15] What constitutes "passion" varies, of course, sociogeographically, socioeconomically, sociopolitically, and sociohistorically, and the particular configuration of a passional universe, to a certain extent, allows one to define cultural specificities. An emotion, a statement or behavior regarded as passionate in one context can be interpreted as "normal" in another, and these judgments often depend on how and where the threshold demarcating surplus or excess is established within a specific scale of "sensitivity"—a moral and political reading of physiology. Eugenio Trías, in his recently published *Tratado de la Pasión*, provides an example of this mimesis. After allegedly resisting to define passion for more than one hundred pages (a fact he calls attention to), he finally succumbs (in his own words), laying out "a sextuple, although hypothetical statement" (thereby delivering an excess in a defensive state of full awareness):

(1) Passion is something that the soul suffers. [. . .]
(2) Passion is something that takes possession of the soul/subject [. . .]
(3) Passion is something that insists on the pure repetition of itself beyond the resistances and obstacles that it builds for itself. This dialectic of insistence and resistance is the foundation of what we here call the passional subject.
(4) Passion is habit, *habitus*, in the literal sense of the term [. . .]: it is the memory that the subject has of itself [. . .]
(5) Passion is that excess at the core that commits the subject to the sources of

its being, alienating and foundational at the same time. It is the *essence* of the subject (unconscious alterity that lays the basis for the subject's identity and sameness, the root of its strength and of its nontransferable power).
(6) Passion is that which can carry the subject to its ruin, the condition that enables its rescue and redemption: it is that which creates and recreates subjectivity through its own immolation and sacrifice. Hence, its trying places are those of death, madness, crime, and transgression. (1991: 126–27, my translation)

Western ethics and epistemologies from the Greeks to the stoics, to Descartes, Spinoza, Kant, and German Idealism, to cite but a few moments of stardom, have produced variations on the sole theme of establishing *logos* or reason as a premise for a free, potent, and lucid subjectivity by conquering the always-threatening passions (Trías 1991, Rouanet 1987, Lebrun 1987). The differences within and among these schools and authors are very important, but my wicked tango only pays attention to points of repetition. Body politics have been at stake all along, and more precisely, gendered body politics: the feminine passions seductively luring the masculine *qua* human *Ethos*, Reason or Desire (the focus changed with the times), provoking the necessary conquest. Theories of passions, whether philosophical or psychological, adopt the form of taxonomies—classifying and hierarchizing passions—and operate through paradigmatic oppositional categories, linking passions not only to reason but also to actions, again of an active or passive, sacred or profane, moral or amoral, social or antisocial, life- or death-driven nature. The creation and conceptualization of the universe of passions and their dynamics, moralized by stoics and Christians, economized by the theoreticians of value and interest, or medicalized by scientific psychology, always engage in politics of exclusion and inclusion, contention and some kind of social world Order(ing). The confrontation of "legitimate versus illegitimate passions," at some obscure point between romanticism[16] and postmodernism, becomes a globalized fluid dance partnering Desire and Passion, each keeping the other alive. The question of who has the right to revolt now returns, repressed, as "Is it possible to revolt?" At some point, Western civilization's discontents have shifted from problematizing passions to apathy, and from discussing domestication to questioning mobilization, where virulence is the everlasting symptom.

Passion and its lack, containment and its shadow-mirrors of propagation and intensification run in circles, chasing the minds of traditional philosophical foes up to the point of creating unthinkable alliances. Hegel and Nietzsche, for example, shared a profound admiration for passion's capacity to actualize/actorialize excess.

Here we use the term *pathos* at a higher level, without any hint of censorship or selfishness. Antigone's sacred love for her brother, for example, is such that it consists of a *pathos* in the greek sense of the word [. . .]. Orestes kills his mother not under the dominion of one of those internal compulsions of the soul that we would call passion; the *pathos* that leads him to this action is well thought out and reflected upon [. . .]. *Pathos* should be limited to those kinds of human actions and it must be thought of as the essential rational content present in the human "I," which takes hold of and penetrates the whole soul. Nothing truly great could be accomplished without passion. (Hegel 1953: 314–15, my translation)

[Passion . . .] is the condition in which one is the least capable of being just; narrow-minded, ungrateful to the past, blind to dangers, deaf to warnings, one is a little vortex of life in a dead sea of darkness and oblivion: and yet this condition is the womb not only of the unjust but of every just deed too [. . .]. The greatest deeds take place in such a superabundance of love. (Nietzsche 1983: 64)

"Greatness" bridges, somehow, the pits of violence (Hegel's hero's murder; Nietzsche's hero's injustice) when passion is equated with that "compulsion that takes hold of the soul" or to that "vortex of life" that makes humans human. What constitutes this greatness," however, is not passion itself but rather who the hero/heroine was and on whose side was the one telling the story.

Agnes Heller, in her *Theory of Feelings*, states that the need for a "unified evaluation of passions [. . .] belongs to the realm of problems of bourgeois society" and that every passion comprises, at the same time, a "grandeur"—something significant—and a problematic aspect. The greatness dwells in the intensity of the involvement—commitment—provoked by passions; the danger, in pushing aside or extinguishing other emotions—the "wealth of feelings" (Heller 1979: 109–10). To which I would add the danger of pushing aside the emotions of diverse intensity of all those people whose passions have no space in the realms of either greatness or wealth.

Interestingly, rather than exploring these vast uncertainties postmodern authors have chosen to scrutinize the wound of "nothingness": that state of exhaustion and perplexity in between one outburst of passion and the next, the indifferent soft stone out of which events are carved. The melancholic longing of Sartre has finally been resolved in the stubborn lack of Lacan.[17] Passion and excess are there, only to flush humans—whether in a state of ecstasy or bored to death—down the flowing abyss. This unavoidable postmodern drive is called Desire.

Having said this, I risk giving a name to the unnameable mythical postmodern object of Desire—the ungraspable desire that circulates, unqualified, like the breath of a phantom, through every postmodern text, speech and life . . . desire for the desiring Other, desire for other's Desire.[18] This longing, this lack, this vacuum that keeps the world stumbling rather than illusively flowing is the fearful desire for passion.[19]

Translated into tango-tongue, the postmodern desire would be something like a fearful passion, and the postmodern attitude, a "sentimental education" in cultivating a passion for fear.[20]

> Fear of soft talk from the enemy, but even much more fear of the unexpected dagger jumping into the recently befriended hand, piercing our open breast or annihilating us from the back. And then, who knows, in that "fear that sterilizes embraces" we might discover that it is neither this nor that, something or someone that we fear, not even fear of our own shadow, only fear of fearfulness. Scare, dread, fright. Anguish, metaphysical fear without object, everything and nothing serves it to self-consummation until it reaches the apex: fear of fear. [...] The saddest among the sad passions. [...] Anyone who has felt it, knows. (Chaui 1987: 39, my translation)

But the postmodern version of fear is anxiety.[21] Destruction, death, and betrayal are no surprise and pain is expected. God and Man are dead, but Evil is still alive and kicking.[22] Its doings are no longer the doings of a blasphemous creature but are human doings; the doings of Others, but the Other is now also within the self.[23] "The anonymous other that is always 'within' splits the subject, leaving it a bit 'cracked' " (M. Taylor 1987: 81, paraphrasing Maurice Merleau-Ponty). The paranoid delirium of the postmodern soul is nourished by this anxiety. How long will it take until the next stroke of panic occurs? Who will I be after my next transgression? From where will the next blow come? Postmodern words of wisdom respond: "It is all on the surface; watch the play of surfaces." Moreover, Bataille recommends adopting the laughter of the idiot and Foucault's advice is to cultivate stupidity (Foucault 1977a: 107–109). Irony and cynicism are *passé* since they retain the conceit of a certain wisdom. The stupid either enjoys or gets in trouble without knowing it; the idiot commits cruelties and heroic deeds irresponsibly. Postmodern wisdom prescribes unawareness before and after the event/catastrophe: the outburst of passion.

> *No smiles. Tangos are male confessions of failure and defeat, a recognition that men's sources of empowerment are also the causes of their misery. Women, mysteriously, have the capacity to use the same things that imprison them—including men—to fight back.[24] Tangos report repeated female attempts at evasion, the permanent danger of betrayal. The strategy consists basically in seducing men, making them feel powerful and safe by acting as loyal subordinates, and in the midst of their enchantment of total control the tamed female escapes. The viscous power crystallizes. The "tanguero" witnesses, horrified, how the blank inert pages where he was writing his story grow an irregular thickness of their own. Female bodies are, actually, docile bodies in rebellion.[25] This is the tension of the tango, the struggle condensed in the dance. Don Beto doesn't talk about it. If you are doing the tango properly, conversations are sacrilegious.[26] The lyrics say everything that needs to be said. So listen.*

No te dejes engañar,	Heart,
corazón,	don't let yourself be fooled,

por su querer,	by her caring,
por su mentir.	by her lies.
No te vayas a olvidar	Don't you go and forget
que es mujer,	that she is a woman,
y que al nacer	and that from birth
del engaño hizo un sentir	it was her nature to deceive
[. . .]	[. . .]
Falsa pasión,	False passion,
¡No te engañes! . . . Corazón.	Heart . . . don't fool yourself!

"*No Te Engañes Corazón*" (Heart, Don't Fool Yourself), 1926
Lyrics and Music: Rodolfo Sciamarella.

The lyrics keep on repeating the same story; plagiarizing again and again the same plot.[27]

¡Decí, por Dios, que me has dao	Tell me, by God, what you've given me
que estoy tan cambiao . . .	that I'm so changed! . . .
no sé más quien soy! . . .	I don't know anymore who I am! . . .
El malevaje extrañao	The puzzled gang
me mira sin comprender.	looks at me without understanding.
[. . .]	[. . .]
Te vi pasar tangueando altanera,	I saw you pass by, tangoing arrogantly
con un compás tan hondo y sensual,	with a beat so deep and sensual,
que no fue más que verte y perder	that just one look at you and I lost
la fe, el coraje, el ansia e'guaperar . . .	my faith, courage and the eagerness to fight . . .
No me has dejao ni el pucho en la oreja	You haven't left me even the cigarette behind my ear
de aquel pasao malevo y feroz.	from that rough and ferocious past.
Ya no me falta pa' completar	Now I don't lack anything to complete the picture
mas que ir a misa e hincarme a rezar.	but to go to church and get down on my knees and pray.

"*Malevaje*" (Gang of Ruffians), 1928
Lyrics: Enrique S. Discépolo; Music: Juan D. D. Filiberto.

The dance continues. No harmony between the bodies, the rhythm holding us together; the rhythm of fate. He leads, I follow. Tight embrace; no leaning on each other. Don Beto prepares the stand; we are at the critical angle. Torsos stiff, feet in vertigo. My legs cut the air in all directions. He leads, although no one follows him now.

Postmodernism is neither an epoch nor an attitude.[28] It is a historically specific skill. Fear has become a passion; the anticipation of fear, an obsession; the domestication of fear, passionlessness. In Todd Gitlin's words, postmodernism is the passionate pursuit of passionlessness (Gitlin 1989: 347). Apathy does not mean insensitivity; it is rather a biopsy of passion. But the postmodern version of asceticism is a perverse skill: On the one hand, it is an intensified awareness of the dangerousness of passion; on the other, it is the desperate amplification of the search for passionate experiences. In short, postmoderns attempt to master passion—to develop apathy—both through panic and obscenity: They engage in the multiplication of passion to the limit of the impossible, and the sacrifice, the annihilation of that which was purposefully multiplied.

The trick by which the postmodern "ascete" piles up the passionate material to be burnt in sacrifice consists in another skill: the proliferation of Otherness. "Passion is always provoked by the presence or image of something that leads us to react, in general unexpectedly. It is a sign of one's permanent dependency on the Other. An autocratic being would not have passions" (Lebrun 1987: 18, my translation). The postmodernist nurtures his or her passion by the presence or image of Others—others who define the self, reassuring identity. However, the postmodern identity does not rely on sameness, it is unstable, permanently reshaped by the proliferation of *Otras*/Others, an Other/*Otra* even within the self. "A passion. And, as in 'jouissance,' where the object of desire, known as object 'a,' bursts with the shattered mirror where the ego gives up its image in order to contemplate itself in the Other, there is nothing either objective or objectal to the abject. It is simply a frontier, a repulsive gift that the Other [. . .] drops so that 'I' does not disappear in it but finds, in that sublime alienation, a forfeited existence" (Kristeva 1982: 9). *La Otra*/Other is a provocateur of the floating Self and a provider of passion. *La Otra*/Other must provide the necessary excitement for the postmodern playing with the Self.

La Otra's voice is my mother tongue, a tángo-tongue. I quote Elizam Escobar, a postmodern artist, to explain what this means:

> For the so-called First World the art and culture of the so-called Third World is the art and culture of the exotic (in Nietzsche's words, not only those who are on the outside but, contrary to the esoterics, those who look from "down-up") and in the best cases, it is the object of the true fascination with the unknown and the Other. The Tango is one of such art forms, in it there is aggression and seduction, drama and form, passion and control. An image that may have seduced [. . .] as a symbolic link between the European predominantly logocentric mentality and the 'natural' surreality of Latin America. (Escobar 1988: 125)

Tangueros (Tango dancers, singers, composers, musicians, poets, and fans) are invited to perform on the postmodern stage on these terms: as passionate "exotic" spectacles of themselves.

The passion of the Other is being permanently recycled: sacrificed and recreated through new, real or imagined, Others. The postmodernist, a critic of

Enlightenment colonialism, who cannot help but pursue further colonialist rationalization, is an incorrigible "voyeur," an untamed predator and a skillful ascete. Colonialists and postmodernists write the history of humankind and reserve for themselves the leading role, be it as winners or losers.

Postmodernism is a corroding skill, like that of a circus freak who learns to chew on blades, to swallow fire, and to sleep on beds of nails; an exploration in the realm of pain carried out by those who see pain from a distance, who find it uninteresting to admit the experience of pain as an unavoidable stroke on their lives. For postmodernists both pain and feeling, in the sense of "getting involved in something,"[29] is a choice—a question of strategy, a spectacle.

A "true" postmodernist is a strategist; her/his passion is to feel above or below, beyond or before the miseries of the world (in postmodernistic jargon, the world is a text; imperialist strategists assume the world is a map; in the courts of Louis XIV, the world was a *ballet opera*; in Disneyland, the world is a bunch of singing dolls . . .), fueled by the passion for passionlessness: the sacrifice of imported passion. *Las Otras*/Others—any *Otra* detected as a potential provider of the "real" passion still available in the planet—are invoked and invited to participate in the postmodern duel. Fiesta, women, tango, tortures, lotus blossoms, guerrillas, palm trees and tropical beaches, desaparecidos, *vírgenes*, flamenco, more women, blacks, Noriega, more violence, Colombia, Oriental veils, more dictators, drugs, colored women, and so on.

Others provide the passion of the "one [who], full of hopes, seeks / the road that dreams / promised in response to his [or her] yearnings [. . .]"

Pero un frío cruel	But a cruel coldness
que es peor que el odio,	that is worse than hatred,
punto muerto de las almas,	dead end of the souls,
tumba horrenda de mi amor,	horrendous tomb for my love,
maldijo para siempre y me robó	cursed me forever and robbed me
toda ilusión.	of all illusion.

"Uno" (One), 1943
Lyrics: Enrique S. Discépolo; Music: Mariano Mores.

To which postmoderns respond, transposing existential terms:

But there is something stronger than passion: illusion. Stronger than sex or happiness: the passion for illusion. Seducing, always seducing. Breaking the erotic power with the furious strength of gambling and stratagem—building some traps into the same vertigo, and continuing to endure mastery of the ironic paths of hell in the seventh heaven—this is seduction, the shape of the illusion, the malign genius of passion. (Baudrillard 1984a: 119, my translation)

While *las Otras* face the precariousness of passion, postmoderns playfully thicken every wound. Postmodernism enters into politics unexpectedly, making a spectacular use of Others' passion. Cultivating apathy, postmoderns join the power game by coming out of the trap-door. But tango taught me that in this dance of life (whether colonial, neo-colonial, imperialist, or post-colonial) there are no winners; only final musical times with a couple, incommunicatively connected, exhibiting frozen conflict at the moment of the resolution. And there is always another tango: new, dangerous embraces and infinite rebellions.

> *The voices of my brothers around the dinner table are suddenly audible; so are the kitchen noises. The family party is at its peak. Don Beto starts muttering "Yira, yira", the tango philosophy treatise. He picks up his hat and leaves.*

Cuando la suerte que es grela,	When lady luck,
fayando y fayando	failing and failing
te largue parao. [. . .]	stands you up. [. . .]
¡La indiferencia del mundo	The indifference of the world
—que es sordo y es mudo—	—that is deaf and mute—
recién sentiras!	only then will you feel!
Verás que todo es mentira	You'll see that everything is a lie,
verás que nada es amor,	you'll see that nothing is love,
que al mundo nada le importa. . . .	that to the world nothing is important. . . .
¡Yira! . . . ¡Yira!	It turns! . . . It turns!

"Yira . . . Yira . . . " (It Turns . . . It Turns . . .), 1930
Lyrics and Music: Enrique S. Discépolo.

> *Don Beto is not worried. He knows this is what life is all about. Sooner or later, I would be caught in another tango. New embraces and infinite rebellions. He had done his job.* Foucault does his, tangoing:

We should not imagine that the world presents us with a legible face, leaving us merely to decipher it; it does not work hand in glove with what we already know; there is no prediscursive fate disposing the world in our favor.[30]

Notes

1. Here I am playing with the opening words of Foucault's Inaugural Lecture at the College of France, 2 December 1970 (Foucault 1971).
2. Excerpts from "La Ultima Curda" (The Last Bender), a tango written by Cátulo Castillo in 1956. All lyrics cited are translated by Marta Savigliano and Jeff Tobin.
3. "The South also exists."
4. When I first drafted this essay in 1989, the polemic over "postmodernism" and "post-

modern" positions was already well underway. Since then much more has been written from the Left and from the Right. I refer readers only to a few now-classic texts that I found especially helpful: Jameson (1984), Lyotard (1988), and the collections of essays edited by Arac (1986) and Ross (1989).

5. For a more equitable analysis of postmodernism that proposes a distinction in contemporary cultural politics between a "postmodernism of resistance" and a "postmodernism of reaction," see Hal Foster's preface to *The Anti-Aesthetic: Essays on Postmodern Culture* (Foster 1983).

6. I thank Farideh Farhi for encouraging me to engage in melodramatic politics of exaggeration.

7. I thank Randy Martin for his comments on the generation of surplus in the context of the political economy of passion.

8. I share with Lyotard the intention of "tracing passion in economics and economics in passion" (1990), but not his understanding of the dynamics of power that intervene in the economy of the libidinal. See my forthcoming *Tango and the Political Economy of Passion* (Savigliano n.d.).

9. I thank Sue-Ellen Case for urging me to explain my obstinate use of the first person.

10. I am paraphrasing the opening question in Spivak (1989).

11. Horacio Ferrer (1980), Blas Matamoro (1971), Noemí Ulla (1982), Ernesto Sábato (1964), and practically every other author who has written on tango has established, sooner or later, the connection between the origins of the tango and the brothels and cabarets of the Río de la Plata region.

12. In reference to this point, Blas Matamoro writes: "The social world of the tango was static: there are rich and poor, but nobody knows why" (1971: 89, my translation).

13. I borrow these images from Jean Franco's insightful discussion of women's confinement and the uses of women by male authors in *hispanoamericana* literature (see Franco 1984). I have benefited much from her contribution.

14. Tango choreographies are improvised on a combination of traditionally set figures. This description is based on the dance style of Gloria and Eduardo, one of the few professional tango dance couples that have been recorded on video. I appreciate the crucial help of Judy Van Zile in the analysis of the dance movements.

15. For a sophisticated, methodical proposal aimed at analyzing the passional universe as it appears in discourse see Greimas and Fontanille (1993).

16. While passional taxonomies were disappearing, a concept of passion akin to a life principle, indivisible and unclassifiable, was developing, although it would not become important until the so-called age of Romanticism. Nietzsche (1968, 1974) and Freud (1955, 1961), for example, reinstalled passion at the center of all things human and at the origin of culture as the moving force of both collective and individual history (Greimas and Fontanille 1993; Lebrun 1987; Rouanet 1987; Kehl 1987).

17. See Sartre (1966) and Lacan (1977a and b). As an outstanding alternative view see Deleuze and Guattari's emancipatory interpretation of desire in *Anti-Oedipus* (1983).

18. For a comprehensive analysis of contemporary interpretations of desire see Butler (1987: 175–238). On the triangulation of desire and mimetic desire see Girard (1978).

19. For a contemporary philosophical elaboration on the ontological differences between passion and desire see Trías (1991: 135ff.).

20. The term "sentimental education" is borrowed from the title of Gustave Flaubert's famous volume.

21. Gitlin (1989) mentions anxiety as a feature of postmodernism.

22. The death of God and Man have been repeatedly addressed by Nietzsche, Heidegger,

Foucault, and others. My point here is that the Devil has been resurrected by postmodern thinkers, although rather than in supernatural proportions—like in premodernism—this time on a human scale.

23. On the interjection of the Other in the self as part of identity constitution see Lacan (1977a; 1977b; 1981).

24. In Jean Franco's words I am talking here about the sexual politics of sadomasochism (1984).

25. At this point my interpretation of sexual politics in tango departs from the Foucauldian account of "docile bodies" (1984a) as well as from Franco's conclusions (1984), which are influenced by Lacan.

26. Julie Taylor synthesized the question of the isolation of the tango dancers in the following sentence: "They dance together in order to relive their disillusion alone" (1976: 290).

27. On the uses of plagiarism in tango see Arnold Hauser's poem in *Ulla* (1982: 15).

28. In "What is Enlightenment?" Foucault suggests analyzing "modernism" as an attitude rather than as an epoch (1984b: 39). I play with his words.

29. Heller repeatedly uses this definition of feeling in *A Theory of Feelings* (1979).

30. Foucault (1971). I thank Jeff Tobin for calling my attention to the parallel between Discépolo's "Yira . . . Yira . . . " and Foucault's repeatedly cited paragraph from "Orders of Discourse."

Works Cited

Arac, Jonathan, ed.
    1986   *Postmodernism and Politics*. Minneapolis: University of Minnesota Press.

Bataille, Georges
    1954   *L'Expérience Intérieure*. Paris: Galimard.
    1979   *El Erotismo*, trans. Toni Vicens. Barcelona: Tusquets Editores.
    1988   *The Accursed Share: An Essay on General Economy*, volume I: *Consumption*, trans. Robert Hurley. New York: Zone Books.

Baudrillard, Jean
    1981   *For a Critique of the Political Economy of the Sign*. St. Louis: Telos Press.
    1984   *Las Estrategias Fatales*, trans. Joaquín Jorda. Barcelona: Editorial Anagrama.

Butler, Judith
    1987   *Subjects of Desire: Hegelian Reflections in Twentieth-Century France*. New York: Columbia University Press.

Chaui, Marilena
    1987   Sobre o medo. In *Os Sentidos da Paixão*, pp. 35–76. São Paulo: Funarte.

Deleuze, Gilles, and Felix Guattari
    1983   *Anti-Oedipus: Capitalism and Schizophrenia*, trans. Robert Hurley, Mark Seem, and Helen R. Lane. Minneapolis: University of Minnesota Press.

Derrida, Jacques
  1976 *Of Grammatology*, trans. Gayatri Spivak. Baltimore: Johns Hopkins University Press.
  1982 Différance, trans. A. Bass. In *Margins of Philosophy*, pp. 1–27. Chicago: University of Chicago Press.
  1986 *Glas*, trans. John P. Leavey Jr. and Richard Rand. Lincoln: University of Nebraska Press.

Escobar, Elizam
  1988 The fear and tremor of being understood. *Third Text* 3/4: 119–41.

Ferrer, Horacio
  1980 *El Libro del Tango: Arte Popular de Buenos Aires*. Barcelona: Antonio Tersol.

Foster, Hal
  1983 Postmodernism: A Preface. In *The Anti-Aesthetic. Essays on Postmodern Culture*, ed. Hal Foster, pp. 3–15. Seattle: Bay Press.

Foucault, Michel
  1971 Orders of discourse, trans. Rupert Swyer. *Social Science Information* 10 (2): 7–30.
  1977a Fantasia of the library. In *Language, Counter-Memory, Practice: Selected Essays and Interviews*, trans. Donald F. Bouchard and Sherry Simon, pp. 87–111. Ithaca: Cornell University Press.
  1977b A preface to transgression. In *Language, Counter-Memory, Practice: Selected Essays and Interviews*, trans. Donald F. Bouchard and Sherry Simon, pp. 29–52. Ithaca: Cornell University Press.
  1984a Docile Bodies. In *The Foucault Reader*, ed. Paul Rabinow, pp. 179–87. New York: Pantheon.
  1984b What is Enlightenment? In *The Foucault Reader*, ed. Paul Rabinow, pp. 32–50. New York: Pantheon.
  1987 Nietzsche, genealogy, history. In *Interpreting Politics*, eds. Donald F. Bouchard and Sherry Simon, pp. 221–40. New York: New York University Press.

Franco, Jean
  1984 Self-destructing heroines. *The Minnesota Review* 22: 105–15.

Freud, Sigmund
  1955 Beyond the pleasure principle. *Standard Edition of Complete Psychological Works*, trans. J. Strachey. Volume 18, pp. 1–64. London: Hogarth Press.
  1961 Civilization and discontents. *Standard Edition of Complete Psychological Works*, trans. J. Strachey. Volume 21, pp. 57–145. London: Hogarth Press.

García, Germán L.
  1990 El tango, ese murmullo. In *Dossier: Tango, el Himno Pasional Argentino, Babel* 3, 21: 23–24.

Girard, René
  1978 *Des Choses Cachées depuis la Foundation du Monde*. Paris: Bernard Grasset.

Gitlin, Todd
  1989 Postmodernism: roots and politics. In *Cultural Politics in Contemporary America*, ed. Ian Angus and Sut Jhally, pp. 347–60. New York: Routledge.

Greimas, Algirdas J., and Jacques Fontanille
  1993   *The Semiotics of Passions. From States of Affairs to States of Feelings*, trans. Paul Perron
          and Frank Collins. Minneapolis: University of Minnesota Press.

Hegel, Georg W. F.
  1953   Vorleßungen über die Aesthetik I. In *Hegel Sämtliche Werke*, vol. 12, ed. H. Glök-
          ner. Stuttgart: Fr. Fromanns.

Heller, Agnes
  1979   *A Theory of Feelings*. Assen, The Netherlands: Van Gorcum.

Jameson, Frederic
  1984   Postmodernism, or the cultural logic of late capitalism. *New Left Review* 146: 53–
          92.

Kamenszain, Tamara
  1990   Personas del Tango. In *Dossier: Tango, el Himno Pasional Argentino, Babel* 3, 21: 23.

Kehl, Maria Rita
  1987   A Psicanálise e o domínio das paixões. In *Os Sentidos da Paixão*, pp. 469–96. São
          Paulo: Funarte. Editora Schwarcz.

Kristeva, Julia
  1982   *Powers of Horror: An Essay in Abjection*, trans. Leon S. Roudiez. New York: Colum-
          bia University Press.

Lacan, Jacques
  1977a   The subversion of the subject and the dialectic of desire in the Freudian uncon-
          scious. In *Ecrits: A Selection*, trans. A. Sheridan, pp. 292–325. New York: W. W.
          Norton.
  1977b   The mirror stage as formative of the function of the I as revealed in psychoanalytic
          experience. In *Ecrits: A Selection*, trans. A. Sheridan, pp. 1–17. New York: W. W.
          Norton.
  1981   *The Four Fundamental Concepts of Psycho-Analysis*, ed. J. A. Miller, trans. A. Sheri-
          dan. New York: W. W. Norton.
  1982   A Love Letter. In *Feminine Sexuality: Jacques Lacan and the Ecole Freudienne*, ed. J.
          Mitchell and J. Rose, trans. J. Rose, pp. 149–61. New York: W. W. Norton.

Lebrun, Gerard
  1987   O conceito de paixão. In *Os Sentidos da Paixão*, pp. 17–34. São Paulo: Funarte. Edi-
          tora Schwarcz.

Lyotard, Jean-François
  1988   *The Postmodern Condition: A Report on Knowledge*, trans. Geoff Bennington and
          Brian Massumi. Minneapolis: University of Minnesota Press.
  1990   *Economía Libidinal*. Buenos Aires: Fondo de Cultura Económica.

Matamoro, Blas
  1971   Historia del Tango. In *La Historia Popular*, vol. 16. Buenos Aires: Centro Editor
          de América Latina.

Nietzsche, Friedrich
  1968   *The Will to Power*, trans. W. Kaufmann and R. Hollingdale. New York: Vintage.
  1974   *The Gay Science*, trans. W. Kaufmann. New York: Vintage.

1983   *Untimely Meditations*, trans. R. J. Hollingdale. Cambridge: Cambridge University Press.

Panesi, Jorge
1990   La Garúa de la Ausencia. In *Dossier: Tango, el Himno Pasional Argentino, Babel* 3, 21: 22, 23.

Ross, Andrew, ed.
1989   *Universal Abandon? The Politics of Postmodernism*. Minneapolis: University of Minnesota Press.

Rouanet, Sergio
1987   Razão e Paixão. In *Os Sentidos da Paixão*, pp. 437–67. São Paulo: Funarte. Editora Schwarcz.

Sábato, Ernesto
1964   *Tango: Canción de Buenos Aires*. Buenos Aires: Ediciones Centro Arte.

Sartre, Jean-Paul
1966   *Being and Nothingness: A Phenomenological Essay on Ontology*, trans. H. F. Barnes. New York: Washington Square Press.

Savigliano, Marta E.
1994   Tango and the Political Economy of Passion. Boulder: Westview Press.

Spivak, Gayatri Chakravorty
1989   Who claims alterity? In *Remaking History*, ed. Barbara Kruger and Phil Mariani, pp. 269–92. *Dia Art Foundation Discussions in Contemporary Culture*, No. 4. Seattle: Bay Press.

Taylor, Julie M.
1976   Tango: theme of class and nation. *Ethnomusicology* 20 (2): 273–91.

Taylor, Mark C.
1987   *Altarity*. Chicago: University of Chicago Press.

Trías, Eugenio.
1991   *Tratado de la Pasión*. Mexico D. F.: Editorial Grijalbo.

Ulla, Noemí
1982   *Tango, Rebelión y Nostalgia*. Buenos Aires: Centro Editor de América Latina.

9

Hyphen-Nations

Jennifer DeVere Brody

> No two writers . . . would agree as to the hyphenization
> of any fifty words taken at random.
>
> —*Philadelphia Sunday Times*, 1894

THIS CHAPTER EXAMINES the shifting roles in which "postmodern" discussions of multiculturalism and American national identity cast the hyphen. There are many ways to read the role of the hyphen; however, all those who think critically about this punctuation mark agree that the hyphen *performs*—it is never neutral or natural. Indeed, by performing the mid-point between often conflicting categories, hyphens occupy "impossible" positions. Hyphens may link or divide, move away from things or toward them; but they always *act*. Hyphens are problematic because they cannot stand alone: in fact, they do not "stand" at all,; rather, they mark a de-centered if central position that perpetually presents readers with a neither/nor proposition. Hyphens locate intermediate, often invisible, and always shifting spaces between supposedly oppositional binary structures. Thus, although hyphens are central, they are not individual (indivisible or unified) entities.

At the level of grammar, the hyphen marks the ever-emergent space between two distinct terms and negotiates a space of (distantly) connected difference.[1] It is a sign that both compels and repels: it is not a fixed point; but rather, a shifting positionality—a continually collapsing structure. As the joint, it is the site of intersection and therefore the weakest link of any construction. The hyphen can be used as a transitive verb that suggests the term's tendency to connote travel. It is in transit, the object of transformation, and subject to translation.[2]

Evolutionary Unions: The Race for One

Many U.S. narratives cast the hyphen as the tension between assimilation and difference. This section explores the etymology of the hyphen in the context of debates about cultural pluralism. The classic manual of "proper" American grammar, *The Elements of Style*, presents the normative view of hyphenates by asserting that, "The steady evolution of the language seems to favor union: two words become one, usually after a period of hyphenation."[3] This statement privileges "evolutionary unions" over merely temporary terms represented by the hyphen. Here, Strunk and White place the hyphen within a linear narrative that strives toward unity.

Similarly, the authors of the United States Government Printing Manual note that:

> Word forms constantly undergo modification. Two-word forms first acquire the hyphen, later are printed as one word, and not infrequently the transition is *from the two- to the one-word form, bypassing the hyphen stage.* . . . The rules laid down cannot be applied inflexibly. Exceptions must necessarily be allowed, so that general good form will not be offended. However, current language trends point definitely to *closing up words* which, through frequent use, have become associated in the reader's mind as units of thought. The tendency to amalgamate words . . . *assures easier continuity*, and is a *natural* progression from the older and less flexible treatment of words. (my italics)[4]

The official (as in authorized by the nation) authors of this tome, which contains a thirty-page section called "Guide to Compounding," naturalize the process of amalgamation and assimilation. They suggest that proper solidification secures and "assures easier continuity." "Older and less flexible" terms give way to the "natural progression" of properly amalgamated words. The guide to compounding mimics dominant strategies of the nation that cover over connections that are complicated. Like American anti-miscegenation laws, this guide regulates reproduction. The emphasis on "solid compounds," occludes the viscous and asymmetrical workings of power. The guide recommends bypassing the hyphen in favor of reducing two to *one*.

This drive toward unity has been prominent in United States discourse—appearing in rhetoric about the Civil War as well as debates about the melting pot (to name but two examples that illustrate Strunk and White's idea that evolution favors union). Such readings denounce broken, hyphenated forms and praise whole, wholesome or holy unions. The valuing of unbroken forms suggests that power resides only with the "pure" or "solidified."[5] The idea of bringing together supposedly opposite forms (e.g., Platonic souls, the Biblical one flesh) continues to influence everyday actions. As Timothy Brennan states, "the nation is not only a political plea, but a formal binding together of disparate elements."[6]

Werner Sollers has delineated two main strategies through which this "formal binding together" works in American cultural narratives. Sollers represents the tension between consent and descent in American discourse as:

The opposition between the artificial and the organic, between the organization of one's choice and the organism of one's essence. . . . In America, we may
feel "filiopietism," but we pledge "allegiance" to the country. To say it plainly,
American identity is often imagined as volitional consent, as love and marriage,
ethnicity as seemingly immutable ancestry and descent.[7]

Thus, in the United States citizens *pledge* allegiance—they recite a symbolic oath
in order to become naturalized. This tradition of consensual allegiance began at
the Columbia Exhibition in 1893 and has been a regular and regulating practice
throughout the twentieth century.[8] Of course, the quest to secure "American"
national identity is impossible since "Nationalism, like culture, is a moving base
. . . of differences, as dangerous as it is powerful, always ahead or deferred by
definitions, pro or contra, upon which it relies.[9] Still many chroniclers of American civilization, even or especially those who praise America's ethnic diversity
and pluralism, tend to dismiss issues of power and ignore the historical and political dimensions that created specific subjectivities.[10]

For example, the early focus on *distance* from England as *difference* from the
English, anchored the *New* Englanders in a new generation that excluded both
Native Americans and "Africans-becom[ing]-Americans" (to modify a phrase
from Hortense Spillers).[11] These racialized others were *imagined* and treated in
the juridical realm as being(s) from a different space and time. In short, some
volitional immigrants were permitted to create a new "American" identity; others were forced to adjust to accept an identity legislated for them.

Xenophobic critics who see themselves as "solid/solidified" Americans worry
that "their" nation is beginning to favor those whom they think were and by
definition should remain un-American (often people of color, the lower classes).[12]
Americans of different ideological positions register fear about the "browning of
America," as *Time* magazine called the phenomenon of America's changing
demographics. Historian Daniel J. Boorstin, author of the Pulitzer Prize-
winning trilogy *The Americans*, and the nation's only emeritus Librarian of
Congress, has claimed that " . . . the notion of a hyphenated American—whether
Polish-American, Italian-American, or African-American—is *un-American*"[13]
(italics mine). Boorstin, like Strunk and White, presents the hyphen as the
marker of emergent entities that should evolve by dissolving into a dominant,
unified "whole." He believes that unified formations must forget or rather actively efface their hyphenated origins and complicated histories.

Boorstin consciously ignores the constantly contested constructing of national character by arguing that evolutionary unions are naturally progressive
and that hyphen-nations are unnaturally regressive. He reveals his contempt for
hyphenated Americans by stating: "Some of us who have believed the glory of
our nation has been our ability to encompass all comers as Americans are shocked

to see any of our fellow-citizens demand to be known as *nothing* but hyphenated Americans" (p. 15, italics mine). Boorstin's statement labels the act of qualifying one's "heredity" heretical. He conceptualizes America as an absorbing and homogenizing nation in which there is no place for marked differences.

In his reading, contestation from hyphenated groups threatens the fertile future of America. If such fracturing continues to be overt and visible, America will become "balkanized." (Of course the covert and largely invisible dependence on and expansion of global capital need not complicate this vision of American hegemony.) The fact that the nation has always already been "undone" gets elided in Boorstin's focus on mythic and monolithic nationalism. He cannot conceive of the fundamental impurity of purportedly "pure" identities and thus, he misses the fact that pure forms are always already troubled by their own hyphenated/hybrid origins.

Not only does Boorstin ignore the problem of global capitalism, he disregards the material history of Native Americans (a term he despises) when he attributes the success of American assimilation to the fact that Americans, unlike Europeans, are " . . . people . . . at a great distance from their old burial grounds, it's harder for them to keep their old name and insist on respect because of their grandfather" (p. 5). Boorstin wants to cover over the *process* of unification in favor of presenting the *product* of a discrete, perfectly homogeneous American identity. The grand*father* appears as the marker of heritage—to be either re-membered or dis-membered in these opposing strategies. Unfortunately, Boorstin fails to discuss the reactionary "Grandfather Clause" that privileged white Southern voters during Reconstruction by actively excluding black men, who had recently been given the right to vote, from exercising this constitutional right.[14] So too, he never addresses maternal genealogy and, therefore, people whose religious and/or racial coding is determined by their mother's social inscription are marginalized (this includes slaves whose "condition followed that of the mother").[15]

Boorstin bemoans the loss of the "perfectly respectable Negro," as a label for the now "shocking" African-American.[16] His response presumes that he possesses the power, like Adam, to name those over whom he has dominion. His argument displaces those who were explicitly *not* Americans. Again, many people of African descent began as chattel personal, then became second-class citizens denied rights and equal access. This legacy of *de jure* and *de facto* discrimination necessarily constitutes and qualifies our Americanness. Attention to the historical shifts of power are crucial to understanding national identities. As Joseph Roach explains,

> The marginal condition of life between powerful categories, the condition that postmodern ethnographers find so rich . . . renders the persons actually trying to live between them extremely vulnerable to the punitive consequences of their undecidability. If they choose not to take a path of straight forward as-

similation . . . or if they are forbidden this path by some uncorrectable accident of their births, [what Spivak calls an enabling violation] they live, . . . in a double-culture invested in two worlds, yet faced with powerful laws and customs favoring unitary identities. American society has a tendency to collapse culture into categories of race and then to enforce those categories as absolutes.[17]

Boorstin's linear narratives of development consistently deny these "other" more complicated narratives that posit repetition with (a) difference. The difficulty with Boorstin's perspective is that it ignores figures who have not followed his own assimilationist narrative or those who have been prevented from doing so, even when they desired to assimilate and achieve the "American Dream." When he argues that "We are in danger of becoming a nation of 'minorities' rather than 'majorities,' " (p. 24) he speaks from an uncritical, or assumed, position of centrality in which his "we" is not qualified. He casts the hyphen as the breaking point—the point not of passage, but of partition. Rather than read the hyphen as a productive site of contestation which provides agency to subjects who wish to mark their difference, Boorstin mandates American correctness.

In such scenarios, all the ingredients in the pot can melt until blended into an uncomplicated "pure" form. As E. San Juan states,

> Every time the identity of "the American people" is celebrated as a uniquely composite blend of European immigrants who settled in the Atlantic colonies or passed through Ellis Island, a political decision and historical judgment is being made. A decision is made to represent Others—as missing, absent, or supplemental.[18]

In the normative narratives discussed previously, the hyphen may move horizontally between two points. The proper role requires the hyphen to horizontally *merge into* the center. There is also concern, however, about belated hyphenates that *emerge from* the center. Both readings stage "the American" as the dominant and originary center. This reading contrasts with those who more comfortably straddle the hyphen. Unlike Boorstin's infertile hyphenated Americans that are destined to disappear, hyphenates who incarnate the margin disturb binaries by throwing such straight-forward narratives into disarray.[19]

Still, more often than not, the hyphenate is destined to become a portmanteau—a carrying-case that folds in the middle of a word that combines two things into one. William Safire, the vigilant grammarian who writes the *New York Times* editorial "On Language," disdainfully notes the new use of "portmanteau" names by legally married couples. He claims that "in olden times when a woman wished to keep her maiden name [identity] separate from her husband's, she hyphenated it as did Charlene Hunter-Gault." He observes a new trend that literalizes the merger between "equals" by combining two different names into one new name (again proving Strunk and White's prediction).[20] Safire dislikes this trend in part because the husband dissolves into the wife's genealogy. The heterosexual couple becomes a model for the proper perpetuation of a unified nation.

Jeffrey McQuain, a guest writer for Safire's column, also chose Carroll's "portmanteau" as an apropos term for describing these movements in contemporary culture. McQuain's piece, "Blending In," begins with praise for Sister Souljah's self-coined moniker, "raptivist," which combines rapper and activist and is "a deft double play on rapt."[21] He admits that, "Blends are a colorful, interesting category, *but not a particularly productive one until recently.* Their numbers are low and studies suggest that many blends are *infrequent in use or even a single writer's fixation*" (my italics; p. 12). These phrases are completely in line with the largely negative history of hyphenated hybrids. McQuain calls authors Lewis Carroll and James Joyce men "obsessed" with these blends, thereby implying that only a "pathological" person would be attracted to these miscegenated, grossly hybrid terms that are destined to die out. McQuain concludes by asking, "Will these faddish phrasings last?" and predicts that "heavy-handed blends like infotainment . . . probably won't [survive]."[22] McQuain's emphasis on survival and uncomplicated descent is perfectly in line with the other authors who participate in promoting the race for ONE.

Zero Identity: The Race of None

I'm a hyphenate, which is the '90s equivalent of a Renaissance man.

—Micky Dolenz, member of pop group The Monkees

Like rocker Micky Dolenz, performance artist Papo Colo presents his own hyphenated identity as "the wave of the future."[23] When asked to answer queries about his identity, "Is he black or white? Puerto Rican or American? Colonial or Post-Colonial? Arab or Greek?" Colo concludes that he may be none of the above or all of them. He disowns any notion of fixed identity, believing that "he is the antidote to the essentialism of Leonard Jeffries on the left and David Duke on the right. Where they trumpet racial purity, he advocates miscegenation. . . . He calls himself the man of "Zero Identity" (p. 68). Colo's "Zero Identity" that is everything and nothing, everywhere and nowhere, omnipresent and unreadable—cancels itself out. His philosophy exposes the fact that the active process of proclaiming one's identity requires (false) separation: one must draw a line between self and other and artificially mark an impossible boundary. Colo adds that " . . . in reality we are all so mixed up, not only Latinos, Blacks but Russians, Italians, and Irish, that to have an identity is like having a fake passport" (ibid).[24] Technically, he is right; however, one is still required to carry such identification, even as one strives to deconstruct it by paying attention to the historicity of such "identities."[25]

Barbara Ehrenreich's essay "Cultural Baggage" contributes to the debate by stating:

> Throughout the 1960's and 1970's, I watched one group after another—African-Americans, Latinos, Native Americans—stand up and proudly reclaim their roots while I just sank back ever deeper into my seat. All this excitement over ethnicity stemmed, I uneasily sensed, from a past in which *their* ancestors had been trampled upon by *my* ancestors, or at least by people who looked very much like them. In addition, it had begun to seem almost un-American not to have some sort of hyphen at hand, linking one to more venerable times and locales.[26]

Ehrenreich's pronouncement about American ethnicity in which she notes the transference of the un-American (now a white minority) and the American (once hyphenated others) reveals the difficulty inherent in unifying differences under a national sign. She valorizes the other side of the binary set up by Boorstin.[27] For Ehrenreich, to be un-American is "not to have a hyphen at hand"; but despite this difference, both Boorstin and Ehrenreich choose to leave the binary in place. Ehrenreich's articulation contradicts Boorstin's naming of the un-American; yet, each author assumes his or her own authority in naming what is and what is not American. By declaring herself and her children as proud members of the "race of none," she displays the desire to erase (erace?) a past already in place. She reproduces those narratives of the nation that in the evolutionary struggle to survive have violently excised and/or condensed disparate origins and aberrant histories. Perhaps unwittingly, she proves that proper form requires the hyphen to enact its supposed "will-to-self-erasure." While Ehrenreich has "no race," others are "raced." She "e-races" whiteness as an identity so that it becomes the (un)masked universal. What Ehrenreich misses is her own complicity in keeping the category of her "race of none" discrete. She sets it up in opposition to the other hyphenated categories; indeed, she has the luxury of doing so. Thus, both Ehrenreich and Boorstin present themselves as the only "just" Americans [pun intended].

Other evidence for the increasing trend toward the normative race of none or the "average(d) American" comes from the opposite end of the spectrum—the white-power movement in the United States. Racist groups such as the KKK and the Aryan Resistance Movement also concern themselves with hyphenations. In her piece "Long Day's Journey into White" journalist Kathy Dobie writes:

> If ethnic identity and ethnic suffering are valued now, what's a mongrel white kid to do? (Most of the skins are some hodge-podge of Western European ancestry that ceased to mean anything a long time ago.) What about *our* history?

they yell. They don't seem to see themselves as part of the big white backdrop that people of color have charged against for ages, making a mark here and there.[28]

This is an amazing configuration of the minuscule latecomer ceaselessly beating against the pure and solidified original. The statement delineates clearly the "original" members of the nation, whose ancestry no longer signifies. They are "hodge-podge" "mongrels" who are de-valued in an era in which "ethnic identity and ethnic suffering" are over-valued. Thus, they proclaim their own (false) purity and reclaim "whiteness" as a new endangered racial species.

Dobie continues:

They're just blanks. Because of their white skin they've escaped hyphenation. They're just American kids; not African-American or Asian-American or Mexican-American.

Of course, no one *escapes* hyphenation. These youths, who are part of various pro-Aryan movements, feel rootless. They want an ethnic community, a flag to defend: "But what is it? What can it be for a mongrel white person in an America" increasingly troubled by new multi-colored hyphenated Americans?

Strunk and White are again useful. They warn that "The hyphen can play tricks on the unwary . . . obviously, we ask too much of the hyphen when we ask it to cast its spell over words it does not adjoin" (p. 81). But what words are "impossible to adjoin"? This statement alludes to unbreachable chasms and uncrossable divides. It might refer to race in America where African-Americans and many "others" must perpetually perform a "permanent" hyphenated identity. As Toni Morrison argues:

To identify someone as South African is to say very little; we need the adjective "white" or "black" or "colored" to make our meaning clear. In this country it is quite the reverse. American means white, and Africanist people struggle to make the term applicable to themselves with ethnicity and hyphen after hyphen after hyphen.[29]

In the United States, African-Americans too often function as "the most othered" coloreds—sometimes at the expense of other embattled "races," classes, and/or ethnicities. Constructed as the anchoring side of a continually repeated black-white binary, African-Americans can be seen as the impossible to adjoin, the unassimilatible "other" precisely because, to paraphrase Fanon, we are comparison. We are perpetually confronted by the hyphen that simultaneously joins and separates us. African-Americans and other others perpetually perform a permanently hyphenated identity. We are staged as the limit text that no alchemy of rights can erase. We make ourselves and are made distinct with hyphen, after hyphen, after hyphen. . . .

Holding On-To the Hyphen

Self-proclaimed nineties hyphenated Americans include people of color, immigrants, and/or sexual "minorities" who threaten to disrupt "traditional" (assimilated) American identity, which their own discourse unwittingly reproduces. Many of these resistant or "othered" Americans seek to play on the hyphenated divide rather than into it, to paraphrase lesbian theorist Sue-Ellen Case. Such persons seek to fundamentally re-figure "minority" discourses.[30] In her influential article "Toward a Butch-Femme Aesthetic," Case provides a paradigmatic example of counterhegemonic hyphenation. She reads the butch-femme couple " . . . not as split subjects, suffering the torment of dominant ideology . . . [but as] coupled ones that do not impale themselves on the poles of sexual difference or metaphysical values, but constantly seduce the sign system . . . replacing the Lacanian slash with a lesbian bar.[31] Case's oxymoronic "coupled-*ones*," that exhibit a "terror of wedding" work against the *evolutionary* unions previously posited.[32]

Similarly, Diane Gifford-Gonzalez, an anthropologist at the University of California, Santa Cruz, whose hyphenated last name follows "the archaic Spanish usage [that] combines patronymic and matronymic" presents another resistant reading. When reviewers of Gifford-Gonzalez's latest book translated her last name literally, thereby implying that she had "undergone some mitotic division," and other reviewers assumed that she had co-authored the book, she retorted with a letter published in *American Anthropologist*. She criticizes the "postmodern tendency toward deconstruction and ironical collage . . . as well as the Anglo-American misperception of the Hispanic binomial . . . [that has questioned her] integrity as a hyphenated individual.[33] She ends her statement by paradoxically "urging reviewers and editors to *respect the integrity of hyphenated individuals*, regardless of their origins" (p. 703). Gifford-Gonzalez thus shifts the debate to respect for difference and like Case makes a claim for the importance of resisting the pull towards normative integration. In so doing, she powerfully retains the subversive and inclusive aspects of the hyphen.

The link between nation formation and its corollary, the legitimation and creation of subjectivities, becomes clear when we notice the increasing trend to utilize the hyphen to denote differences. For example, on July 25, 1993 the New York *Times* ran a front page story entitled "Immigrants Forgoing Citizenship While Pursuing the American Dream." The article chronicles "new" refugees who refuse to become full-fledged citizens of the United States. The article notes that these immigrants are "not healthy for democracy" because they choose to live in their own "subculture" and are content to have taxation without representation.[34] These immigrants from other times and more venerable locales represent a new class of trans- or inter-nationals who live in a liminal state as resident aliens. They are reluctant to embrace "America" fully and often are dissuaded from assimilating into the land of asylum.

In her 1989 novel *Jasmine*, Bharati Mukherjee compares Jasmine, who immigrates from India, with Jasmine's adopted son Du, who immigrates from Vietnam. Jasmine proclaims:

> My transformation has been genetic; Du's was hyphenated. We were so full of wonder at how fast he became American, but he's a hybrid, like the fantasy appliances he wants to build. His high-school paper did a story on him titled: "Du (Yogi) Ripplemeyer, a Vietnamese-American. . . . "[35]

The difference between Jasmine and Du is the difference between assimilation and hyphenation. Du, a "resistant" hyphenate, retains his hyphenation. In contrast, Jasmine struggles to ignore her past. Jasmine admits that she " . . . was afraid to test the delicate thread of [Du's] hyphenation. Vietnamese-American: don't question either half too hard" (p. 200). Du's resistant reading re-writes the hyphen. Like many "marginalized" people, Du proves that it is possible (and even desirable) to maintain one's hyphenated roots—to resist the eventual pull toward the vanishing point. Gayatri Spivak has called this phenomenon "riding the hyphen."[36]

These readers reverse and revise the debate about hyphens by insisting upon the respect for difference. They foster hyphenation in order to resist uncomplicated integration. So too, they imagine the hyphen as an everpresent entity that acts to de-essentialize and re-member difference. As Homi Bhabha says in his discussion of performance artist Guillermo Gomez-Peña:

> Hybrid hyphenations emphasize the incommensurable elements—the stubborn chunks—as the basis of cultural identifications. What is at issue is the performative nature of differential identities: the regulation and negotiation of those spaces that are continually, contingently, 'opening out,' remaking boundaries, exposing limits of any claim to a singular or autonomous sign of difference—be it class, gender, or race. Such assignations of social differences—*where difference is neither One nor the Other but something else besides, in-between*—find their agency in a form of the 'future' where the past is not originary, where the present is not simply transitory. It is . . . an interstitial future, that emerges *in-between* the claims of the past and the needs of the present. (emphasis in original)[37]

The question remains, how are we to evaluate the eruption of ever-emergent hyphenates? Is this shifting space actually a liberatory one? Can it function as a site of resistance, as many claim? The difficulty with determining the efficacy of the suspended hyphen lies largely in the subject who reads. Although the hyphen attempts to mark more accurately the discontinuity of specific subjects, it too is highly reductive. Here, we should remember that,

All human subjects . . . are continuous. Identities continue across and exceed the political and discursive boundaries of sexual preference, racial markings, age, physical abilities, economic class, and so on. It serves certain interests, however, to insist that selves are distinguishable from others. . . . (Phelan, p. 170)

What I have been interested in here is how certain "marginalized" figures cling to the hyphen as a means of resisting dominant strategies of erasure and marginalization.

I would like to thank Ann Cubilie, Michael Harris, Nicole King, Ting-Yao Luo, Amy Robinson, Carole-Anne Tyler, and the organizers and participants of the Unnatural Acts Conference and the 1992 Women and Theatre Pre-Conference for providing me with invaluable resources and incomparable advice.

Notes

1. The *Oxford English Dictionary* defines the hyphen as: "a short dash of line (-) used to connect two words together as a compound; also to join the separate syllables of a word, as at the end of a line; or to divide a word into parts for etymological or other purposes." This definition points to the versatility of the hyphen and reveals its flexibility as a term that serves many, often contradictory purposes.

2. In this it may share something of the hymen as discussed by Jacques Derrida. See Jacques Derrida, "The Double Session," *Disseminations*, trans. Barbara Johnson (Chicago: University of Chicago Press, 1981), pp. 174–226.

3. William Strunk and E. B. White, *The Elements of Style* (New York: Macmillan, 1979), p. 35. In 1959 when E. B. White revised William Strunk's text, he became the nation's expert on grammar. White won a Pulitzer Prize and a Presidential Medal of Freedom for his contributions to American literary culture.

4. United States Government Printing Office Board, *United States Government Printing Office Style Manual* (Washington, D.C.: U.S. Government Printing Office, 1967), p. 73.

5. Much "Afrocentric" discourse focuses on the need to strengthen the "traditional" family in which women are to be revered as bearers of future generations. For more on this topic see Paul Gilroy, "It's a Family Affair," in Gina Dent, ed., *Black Popular Culture* (Seattle: Bay Press, 1992).

6. Timothy Brennan, "The National Longing for Form," in Homi K. Bhabha, ed., *Nation and Narration* (London: Routledge, 1990), p. 62.

7. Werner Sollers, *Beyond Ethnicity: Consent and Descent in American Culture* (New York: Oxford University Press, 1986), p. 151.

8. Many African-American children and arguably other disenfranchised groups creatively deformed the pledge; rather than repeating the proper closing, "With liberty and justice for all," these everyday subverters (my mother among them) would state, "With liberty and justice for *some*."

9. Gayatri Chakravorty Spivak, "More on Power/Knowledge," *Outside in the Teaching Machine* (New York: Routledge, 1993), p. 35.

10. Here I am thinking of Arthur M. Schlesinger, Jr., whose popular tract *The Disuniting of America* ends by heralding an America in which "individuals are melted into a new race of men [sic]." See his *The Disuniting of America* (Knoxville: Whittle Direct, 1991), p. 138. April Schultz makes a similar critique of Lawrence Fuchs's *The American Kaleidoscope: Race, Ethnicity and the Civic Culture* (Middletown: Wesleyan Press, 1990). In her review, "Searching for a Unified America," she says, "It is the pain of history that, to our peril, gets lost in the search for an exceptional, unified America." *American Quarterly* 45, no. 4 (1994): 647.

11. See Hortense Spillers, "Neither/Nor: Notes on an Alternative Model," in Meese and Parker, eds., *The Difference Within: Feminism and Critical Theory* (Philadelphia: John Benjamin, 1989), p. 183.

12. Of course, until the recent break-up of the Soviet Union and the end of the Cold War, communists were also tried for their un-American activities.

13. Daniel J. Boorstin, "A Conscience-Wracked Nation," *The Economist* (September 11–17, 1993), p. 24. Subsequent references to this edition shall be noted in the text. According to the *OED* the hyphenated term "un-American" entered the language in 1818 in a protest against the importation of "foreign" Italian marble. Thus, from its first usage the phrase un-American has been concerned with the importation of distant others.

14. See C. Vann Woodward, *Origins of the New South: 1877–1913* (Baton Rouge: Louisiana State University Press, 1971), pp. 334–35.

15. For a discussion of the slave "mother," see Hortense Spillers, "Mama's Baby, Papa's Maybe: An American Grammar Book," *Diacritics* (summer 1987).

16. At a press conference in 1987, Jesse Jackson announced his preference for this moniker. See Ben L. Martin, "From Negro to Black to African American: The Power of Names and Naming," *Political Science Quarterly* 106, no. 1 (1991): 83–107; Sterling Stuckey, *Slave Culture* (New York: Oxford University Press, 1987) and Kimberly W. Benston, "I Yam What I Yam: The Topos of (Un)Naming in Afro-American Literature," Henry Louis Gates, Jr., ed., *Black Literature and Literary Theory* (New York: Methuen, 1984), pp. 151–72. It should not be presumed that only Boorstin is critical of this nomenclature. Indeed, many so-called African Americans use other signifiers or alternate between identificatory labels.

17. Joseph Roach, "Mardi Gras Indians and Others: Genealogies of American Performance," *Theatre Journal* 44 (1992): 467–68.

18. E. San Juan, *Racial Formations/Critical Transformations: Articulations of Power in Ethnic and Racial Studies in the United States* (New Jersey: Humanities, 1992), p. 131.

19. In a discussion of white supremacy and anti-abortion activism, Peggy Phelan notes that, "The visibly pregnant woman embodies the literal swelling of [the] proliferating hyphen. This is why she is . . . an unresolved figure which Law continually recalculates. . . . Is she a double subject or a half-subject? (Who controls her other half?)" In Peggy Phelan, *Unmarked: The Politics of Performance*. (New York: Routledge, 1993), p. 171.

20. We should not lose the analogy with the other nineties "merger" phenomenon occurring in the "other" private sector, namely, companies in the capitalist system. Both merger practices reflect the survivor's necessity to become one, and consistently drop ungainly/ unprofitable parts that threaten the whole.

21. Jeffrey McQuain, "Blending In," *New York Times Magazine*, August, 1992, p. 11. In keeping with the conventional vocabulary and construction of the hyphenated hybrid, McQuain notes that many of these blended terms enter the standard language from the world of advertising, which is starved for new products.

22. I am sure that the students at my alma mater who recently formed a bi-racial support group called "Blend" will be disappointed to hear this.

23. Anemona Hartocollis, "Zero Identity: The End of Ethnicity," *New York Newsday* (December 12, 1991), p. 68. I thank Ellen Gruber Garvey for sending me this article.

24. Colo's catalogue includes the category "black" along with other ethnic/national groups, some of whose citizens are "black." This elision helps to expose the largely sociological or cultural (as opposed to biological) construction of race as well as the paradigmatic paradox that continues to confuse race and national origin. For more on this subject see Graziella Parati, "Strangers in Paradise: Foreigners and Shadows in Italian Literature," which looks at African-Italian literature produced in Italy since 1990, and Jack D. Forbes, *Black Africans and Native Americans: Color, Race and Caste in the Evolution of Red-Black Peoples* (Oxford: Blackwell, 1988).

25. See Peggy Phelan, *Unmarked: The Politics of Performance* (New York: Routledge, 1993).

26. *New York Times Magazine*, April 14, 1992, p. 16.

27. For more on scientific definitions of race, see Marvin Zuckerman, "Some Dubious Premises in Research and Theory on Racial Differences: Social, Scientific, and Ethical Issues," *American Psychologist* (December 1990): 1297–1303.

28. Kathy Dobie, "Long Day's Journey into White," *The Village Voice* (April 28, 1992), p. 29.

29. Toni Morrison, *Playing in the Dark: Whiteness and the Literary Imagination* (Cambridge: Harvard University Press, 1992), p. 47.

30. See the special issue of *October*, "The Identity in Question," 61 (summer 1992) for a superb critique of a "multiculturalism" that homogenizes differences within minority communities.

31. Sue-Ellen Case, "Toward a Butch-Femme Aesthetic," in Lynda Hart, ed., *Making a Spectacle: Feminist Essays on Contemporary Women's Theatre* (Ann Arbor: University of Michigan Press, 1989), p. 283.

32. *The Terror of Wedding* (1987) is a play by Amy Robinson that juxtaposes Florence Nightingale's decision not to marry with discussions about conflicts during the Intifada.

33. Gifford-Gonzales, "We Are Not amused," *American Anthropologist* 94, no. 3 (Sept. 1992): 703. I am grateful to Jeff Tobin for bringing this article to my attention.

34. Deborah Sontag, "Immigrants Forgoing Citizenship While Pursuing the American Dream," *New York Times*, July 25, 1993.

35. Bharati Mukherjee, *Jasmine* (New York: Ballantine, 1989), p. 198.

36. Sneja Gunew and Gayatri Spivak, "Questions of Multiculturalism," in Mary Lynn Bruce and Angela Ingram, eds., *Women's Writing in Exile* (Chapel Hill: University of North Carolina Press, 1989).

37. Homi K. Bhabha, "How Newness Enters the World: Postmodern Space, Postcolonial Times and the Trials of Cultural Translations," in *The Location of Culture* (New York: Routledge, 1994), p. 219.

Works Cited

Benston, Kimberly W. "I Yam What I Yam: The Topos of (Un)Naming in Afro-American Literature," in Henry Louis Gates, Jr., ed., *Black Literature and Literary Theory*. New York: Methuen, 1984.

Bhabha, Homi K. "How Newness Enters the World: Postmodern Space, Postcolonial Times and the Trials of Cultural Translation," in *The Location of Culture*. New York: Routledge, 1994.

Boorstin, Daniel J. "A Conscience-Wracked Nation," *The Economist*, September 11–17, 1993: 24–26.

Brennan, Timothy. "The National Longing for Form," in Homi K. Bhabha, ed., *Nation and Narration*. London: Routledge, 1990.

Case, Sue-Ellen. "Toward a Butch-Femme Aesthetic," in Lynda Hart, ed., *Making a Spectacle: Feminist Essays on Contemporary Women's Theatre*. Ann Arbor: University of Michigan Press, 1989.

Derrida, Jacques. "The Double Session," in *Disseminations*, trans. Barbara Johnson. Chicago: University of Chicago Press, 1981.

Dobie, Kathy. "Long Day's Journey into White." *The Village Voice*, April 28, 1992.

Ehrenreich, Barbara. "Cultural Baggage," *New York Times Magazine*, April 14, 1992: 16–17.

Gifford-Gonzales, Diane. "We Are Not amused," *American Anthropologist* 94, no. 3 (Sept. 1992): 703.

Gunew, Sneja and Gayatri Spivak. "Questions of Multiculturalism," ed. Mary Lynn Bruce and Angela Ingram, *Women's Writing in Exile*. Chapel Hill: University of North Carolina Press, 1989.

Hartocollis, Anemona. "Zero Identity: The End of Ethnicity," *New York Newsday*, December 12, 1991: 65–69.

Martin, Ben L. "From Negro to Black to African American: The Power of Names and Naming." *Political Science Quarterly* 106, no. 1 (1991).

McQuain, Jeffrey. "Blending In," *New York Times Magazine*, August, 1992: 11–12.

Morrison, Toni. *Playing in the Dark: Whiteness and the Literary Imagination*. Cambridge: Harvard University Press, 1992.

Mukherjee, Bharati. *Jasmine*. New York: Ballantine, 1989.

Phelan, Peggy. *Unmarked: The Politics of Performance*. New York: Routledge, 1993.

Roach, Joseph. "Mardi Gras Indians and Others: Genealogies of American Performance," *Theatre Journal* 44 (1992): 461–83.

Safire, William. "On Language," *New York Times Magazine*, 1992.

San Juan, E. *Racial Formations/Critical Transformations: Articulations of Power in Ethnic and Racial Studies in the United States*. New Jersey: Humanities, 1992.

Sollers, Werner. *Beyond Ethnicity: Consent and Descent in American Culture*. New York: Oxford University Press, 1986.

Sontag, Deborah. "Immigrants Forgoing Citizenship While Pursuing the American Dream." *New York Times*, July 25, 1993.

Spillers, Hortense. "Neither/Nor: Notes on an Alternative Model," Meese and Parker, eds., *The Difference Within: Feminism and Critical Theory*. Philadelphia: John Benjamin, 1989.

———. "Mama's Baby, Papa's Maybe: An American Grammar Book." *Diacritics*, summer 1987.

Spivak, Gayatri Chakravorty. *Outside in the Teaching Machine*. New York: Routledge, 1993.

Strunk, William and E. B. White. *The Elements of Style*. New York: Macmillan, 1979.

Stuckey, Sterling. *Slave Culture*. New York: Oxford University Press, 1987.

Szulc, Ted. "The Greatest Danger We Face: An Interview with Daniel J. Boorstin," *Parade Magazine*, July 25, 1993: 4–7.

United States Government Printing Office Board. *United States Government Printing Office Style Manual*. Washington, D.C.: U.S. Government Printing Office, 1967.

Woodward, C. Vann. *Origins of the New South: 1877–1913*. Baton Rouge: Louisiana State University Press, 1971.

Community Cruises

10

"We Are Family"

House Music and Queer Performativity

Brian Currid

Dysfunctional Family, or Dys(sing) Functional Families

"WE ARE FAMILY." Undoubtedly recognized as something of a queer national anthem, Sister Sledge's affirmation of the sisterhood has served and continues to serve as an important site for the performance of gay and lesbian/queer community identity. Anyone familiar with recent urban gay/lesbian communities and their politics is probably also familiar with the occupation of this site as a mobilization of national or commercial forms of publicity to make intelligible forms of local queer performativity. In Chicago, a recent IMPACT fundraiser invoked the rhetorical power of the anthem by calling itself after the song title; on a recent Maria-Shriver-explains-it-all-to-you about the "Gay Nineties," one lesbian couple announced firmly to Maria that yes, we ARE family. As queers, gays, lesbians "do their thing" to this disco anthem, it becomes a ground to perform, debate, and refashion queer identity and community politics. Important in this regard are the contradictions inherent in this simple opening line; these words and the style(s) in which they are sung mobilize alternatively queer-national and assimilationist sentiment. In the former, the interest of the song lies precisely in its imprecision (who are "we," and what is family?) while the latter assimilationist version performs (lip-synchs) a yes, "we are family, too," where both we and family reflexively enforce a stability within each category. Further, one can map recent work in gay and lesbian studies and queer theory onto these two very different mobilizations. Here, family stands metonymically for community; while Gilbert Herdt continues to argue "we are authentically community, too," adopting a notion of community which remains firmly rooted in a hetero-logic of genital reproduction performed as "history"; work like that of Sue-Ellen Case and Judith Butler places the community and identity performances of the queer in a critical relation to the presumed stable reproduction of community through historical progression.[1]

House music, a genre of dance music popular internationally in gay urban clubs, continues to embody the power of these contradictions, both arguing for the continuity of community in sound, and reveling in a celebration of the provisional, in the performativity of family and community as wider categories. Community and family in House music appear in drag, and in so doing, to misquote Judith Butler, "constitute the mundane way in which [community] is . . . theatricalized, worn, and done; it implies that all [community] performance is a kind of impersonation and approximation."[2] House argues that communities should not be distinguished by their falsity/genuineness, but rather by the style in which they are imagined.[3] More importantly, however, "we are family" says that the style in which "we" imagine "our" community is oh-so-much-more-fabulously stylish than imaginings made possible through the uncritical repetition of stodgy national anthems. In being labeled a "disco anthem," the disco classic implicitly serves to invoke and critique conventional configurations of national belonging, in that a disco anthem is never something that is repeated and "sung" together in community gatherings, but rather serves as a tool to channel disembodied diva-nity and fierceness through the embodied, eroticized practices of dance and lip-synching. A national anthem is to be sung solemnly and slowly;[4] a disco anthem is to be lip-synched on the dance floor, feet stomping and hands in the air. But, at the same time, it *is* an anthem; the imitation of national belonging that seems to be ironically invoked is often invoked in sincerity as well. The community that lip-synchs itself into existence in the dance club lies between these two contradictory pulls of queer sex and community/"family" values, as the ghostly voice of the disco diva is reassembled and rearticulated for consumption on the dance floor. The sacrificial dismemberment of past articulations of community, heard in the beat of the aging disco classic twisted into a new form by the manipulations of DJ and dancer in the club, reveals this history as not something that is rooted in notions of heteronormative generational time, but rather a necrophiliac, queer operation, which performs its history across fragmented, perverse chronologies of commodities. This reading of House and its critical potential seems especially important in light of the implicit heteronormativity and homophobia that inhere within recent articulations of a generationally produced black identity which disallow the very ontological possibility of the black queer, and certainly of a black queer history. The operations of this heteronormativity are especially clear in recent work done on black popular musics.

Rap and House are ostensibly of the same "age." While rap has enjoyed a certain vogue in the academy, little work has been done that addresses House or dance music more generally in any substantive way. When it does appear, it is often described as derivative of "real" innovation in rap—or, alternatively, House is read as simply yet another "po-mo" pastiche. These acts of omission and erasure are indicative of a not-so-latent distaste for homo-culture. Houston Baker, Jr., has written, in his article "Hybridity, the Rap Race, and Pedagogy for the 1990s":

There are gender coded reasons for the refusal of disco. Disco's club DJs were often gay, and the culture of Eurodisco was populously gay. Hence, a rejection of disco carried more than judgments of exclusively musical taste. A certain homophobia can be inferred. . . . But it is also important to note the high marketplace maneuvering that brought disco onto the pop scene with full force. . . . What was displaced by disco, ultimately . . . were a number of black, male, classical R&B artists. Hey, some resentment of disco culture and a reassertion of black manhood rights (rites)—no matter who populated the discotheques— was a natural thing.[5]

Baker's almost parenthetical remarks about a homophobia that "can be inferred" from the anti-disco "movement" is immediately followed by what reads as a denial of the very blackness of disco/dance music. Gay here operates as the opposed category to "black, male," as "gay" disco DJs "displaced" these "black, male, classical R&B artists." Indeed Baker's authorial interjection, "Hey," serves to code his own identity performance as part of that "reassertion of black manhood," remarking that his identifications are "a natural thing," as opposed to the artificial, commodified world of the discotheque. Even in the use of the word "discotheque," Baker's text serves to mark the otherness of these musical practices— "disco" has long been the word of choice on the "street"; the use of the archaic, more stylized (French, effeminate?) term is explicitly in opposition to Baker's natural "hey" reaction. Finally, if it isn't important who was in the discotheque, it is indeed curious that Baker makes that "who" so explicit. Baker seems to want to naturalize homo-hatred as a typical black, masculine response, and in so doing, inevitably allies his strategy with the "homosexual panic" defense of queer bashing. But perhaps more importatntly, Baker's analysis sacrifices the very existence and ontological possibility of the black queer to the so called "rites" of black manhood.[6]

Baker and other critics have refused to take the music and the culture in which disco and House was and is embedded with the same seriousness that they read rap, and dismiss these forms of dance music as "derivative" of real innovation in straight "culture." Public Enemy's Chuck D. makes Baker's point in a much less back-handed way:

My thing is I don't like house music. I first heard it as a DJ, when I was doing radio shows, and I said then that I thought the beats lacked soul. . . . And I dislike the scene that's based around house—it's sophisticated, anti-black, anti-culture, anti-feel, the most ARTIFICIAL shit I ever heard. It represents the gay scene, it's separating blacks from their past and their culture, it's upwardly mobile.[7]

The continued celebration of a musical genre that has been so consistently denigrated, within the academy and without, as somehow expressive of an "unreal"

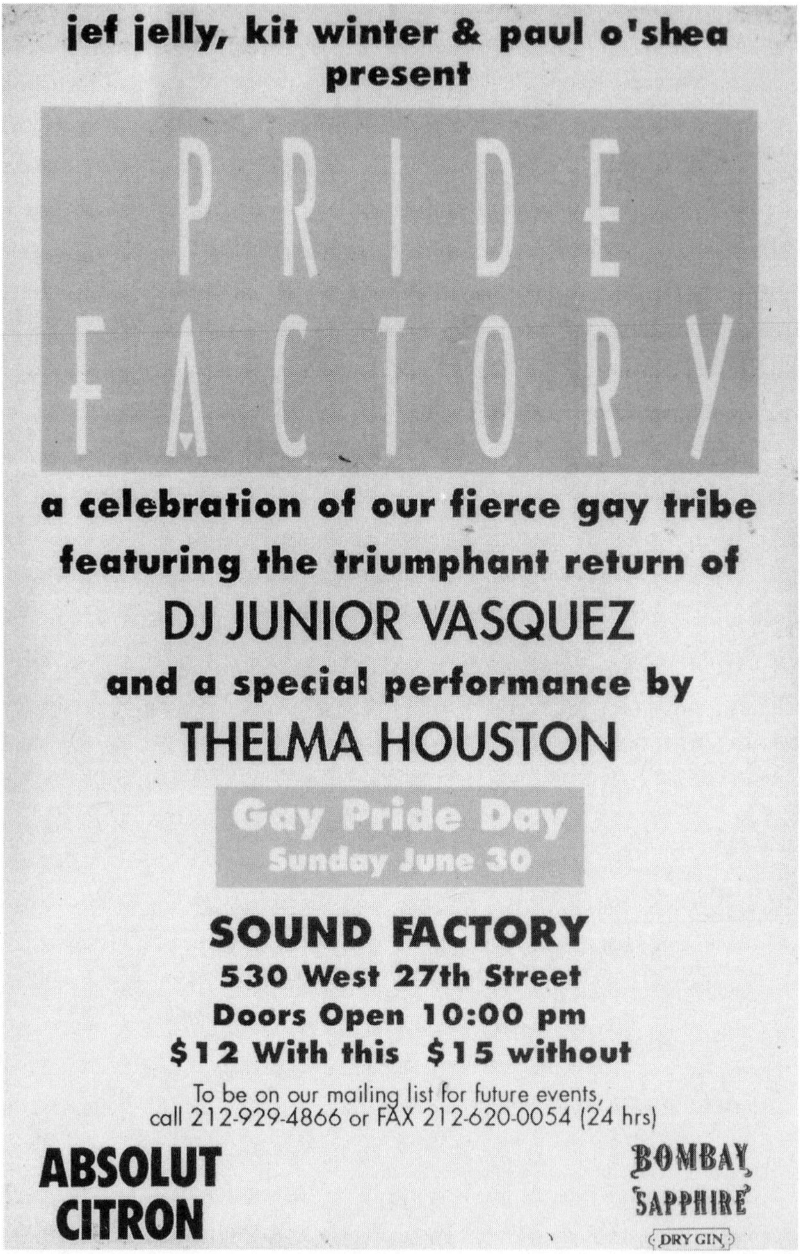

Invite to Sound Factory. Pride Day, 1991.

performance of community or, as "the music of a decadent, alienated culture,"[8] resists the heteronormative force of this denigration, and performs a critique of the insistence on the "authentic" and the "real" in communal musical production. House becomes a terrain for the "manufacture" of community: witness this Sound Factory invite from Pride Day, 1991: in featuring the performance of Thelma Houston, disco diva *par excellence*, this invite marks the resistant continuation of disco, against both the voices of the critics as well as the perceived destruction of disco culture due to the AIDS crisis. This invite beckons one to join the manufacture of pride, the factory production of "fierceness." Community here *is* commodity. Rather than attempting to reproduce a notion of community grounded as "authentic" and real, this invite argues that what is fabulous about queer culture is precisely its ability to critique traditional notions of community reproduction, celebrating our fierce gay tribe as a tenuous performance on the unstable ground of commodity capitalism. It refashions Baker's "high market maneuvering" into "a celebration of our fierce gay tribe."

This chapter consists of three parts: the first, a brief introduction to give a "feel" for House abstractly conceived as a "genre" of pop music; the second, an examination of House and disco used as historical narrative; and finally, a discussion of queer identity in House/disco negotiated through a terrain simultaneously crafted by the operations of race and gender as performed through the ambivalent positioning of the black queer and the disco diva in club space. What is crucial to remember in reading (and writing) this chapter is that it cannot explain what House is, rather it seeks to be a "remix" of various discursive productions and personal memories, and as such an invitation to further appropriation and "remixing," rather than an affirmative explanation of any particular musical phenomenon.

"So Many Questions Have Been Raised about This New Dance Craze . . . "[9]

In this discussion of the discursive strategies that have defined House as a particular "genre" of popular dance music, I will present what I understand as the canon of House and its "familial relations." This "history" has been compiled from both the gay and music press, and interviews within the "House community." Histories of House are produced all the time; House is a genre which is intensely focused on a sense of its own history, of its roots. To understand what House is one cannot rely on a straightforward "present tense" description; one must rather discuss the production of "origins" behind and through a present day pop music phenomenon.

This amalgamation of popular styles known collectively as House music is described by performers and audience alike as "born" in Chicago. Characterized

Musical Example 1
Kim Syms, "Too Blind to See it"
mm. 1–2   122 bpm

1. Two-measure keyboard line. "Too Blind to See It," Kim Syms; produced and mixed by Steve "Silk" Hurley for ID Productions; executive producers Steve Hurley, Frank Rodrigo; mixed and additional production Maurice Joshua for ID Productions; 1991, Atlantic Recording Corp., 12″ single.

"musically," House music is recognized by its strong 4/4 drum machine kick, usually at a tempo of 120–135 beats per minute. On this rhythmic basis the producer overlays treble keyboard riffs, often composed of simple triads, or major or minor seventh chords. This keyboard riff is often designed in two-bar segments, where the beginning of the two bars starts on the beat, followed by an increasing move toward syncopation. Exemplifying this strategy is "Too Blind to See It," a particularly melodic, heavily disco influenced track, which was a hit in 1989. Sung by Kim Syms, and remixed by Steve "Silk" Hurley, who is regarded as one of the "founding fathers" of the House community and one of the lead remixers of pop/dance music,[10] the basic two-measure building block of this anthem might be characterized musically as it is presented in the first musical example.[11] Over this basis is layered "the song," as it was recognized in its radio version, with verses and refrains. It is important to note that in the twelve-inch mix, which is the mix more likely to be used on the dance floor, the body of the song itself is subordinated to this basic two-bar block in its various permutations—without bass, with bass, without keyboard, without high treble keyboard line, or "complete." This twelve-inch is then often further manipulated and re-mixed on the dance floor itself. In this context, the record loses its import as a song in and of itself, and becomes a tool used to play on the response of the crowd. Dancers leave the floor when things on the turntable do not continue to be exciting or provocative; the DJ must respond to this demand to avoid the perils of the dead dance floor.

While this musical structure is very common, particularly in present day forms of House music, the styles of House are highly varied, holding in common the strong 4/4 bass drum beat. This rhythmic anchor was first pioneered in disco in the late '70s and provides a way to continue a firm tempo through multiple record changes, and even through abrupt changes in idiom. For example, in the now-antiquated style known as Acid House, the presence of a voice was not necessary to generic conventions. Here, the style was marked by the warbling sound

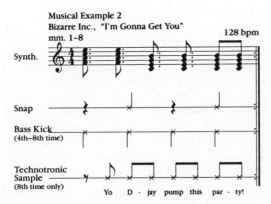

Musical Example 2
Bizarre Inc., "I'm Gonna Get You"
mm. 1–8
128 bpm

Synth.

Snap

Bass Kick
(4th–8th time)

Technotronic
Sample
(8th time only)

Yo D · jay pump this par · ty!

2. One-measure unit. "I'm Gonna Get You," Bizarre Inc. (featuring Angie Brown); Original Flavour Mix; mixed by Alan Scott and Bizarre Inc.; produced by Alan Scott and Bizarre Inc.; 1992, Vinyl Solution, 12″ single.

of the Acid Box, a MIDI instrument which was used to constantly alter the timbre—and sometimes the pitch as well—of a consistent melodic line. The now wildly popular Techno or Rave, which in many ways has lost its association with "real" House because of its very popularity, became dominated by angular chordal progressions in the treble line and a generally more rapid tempo, which would produce a feeling of high drama, more perhaps like the feel of Carl Orff's *Carmina Burana*, a piece which has actually served as the basis for a Techno classic.[12] Often in Techno, Acid, and "Deep" House, this two-bar structure is replaced by a one-bar unit, where the drive toward increased syncopation is heard within the space of one bar, rather than as in the above example. Exemplifying this construction is the song "I'm Gonna Get You," by Bizarre Inc. The musical illustration represents the first eight bars of the "Original Flavour Mix."

Despite the preceding attempts at stylistic description, House cannot be easily delineated by any specific questions of "style." What marks a track as a House track is its use on the dance floor, where all songs are mixed smoothly, one into the other at body-vibrating volume, and its associations with a "history" of House rather than specific questions of chordal structure, rhythm, and timbre. House is a coherent style only when considered in opposition to other styles, here disco and rap, the first delineated by its association with '70s disco culture, and the second marked in relation to House by a long history of explicit opposition.

That said, it becomes important to review the basic narrative that circulates as "the" history of House music. Described by performers and audience alike as "born" in Chicago, the date of birth varies from as early as 1977 to as late as 1984. In 1977 Frankie Knuckles, a New York DJ, began spinning records at a club in Chicago known as the Warehouse. The Warehouse had an "economically democratic" admissions policy,[13] unlike similar venues at the height of the disco era. The Warehouse was indeed a gay black club by all accounts: "a haven of jack for only the most fabulous black fags."[14] In a personal interview with a House production team, they described The Warehouse as having been at least 80 percent gay in its clientele.[15] Anthony Thomas, in his essay "The House the Kids Built," has vividly described the "scene":

> A mixed crowd (predominantly gay—male and female) in various stages of undress (with athletic wear and bare flesh predominating) was packed into the dance space, wall to wall. Many actually danced hanging from the water pipes that extended on a diagonal from the walls to the ceiling. The heat generated by the dancers would rise to greet you as you descended, confirming your initial impression that you were going down into something very funky and "low."[16]

House was music constructed, in this history, to appeal to a certain audience, i.e., lower-income gay African Americans. Depending on one's account or musical understanding of House, Knuckles mixed together the sounds of club music[17] and older soul-dance records or, alternatively, the sounds of European techno-pop and disco to create a new sound. This musical style was in this narrativization originally one which appropriated the commodities of the music industry to create a new sonic world, one which responded to the needs of a particular community. As the popularity of House grew, its style became more defined, and the first specifically House records began to be released, at first only on small independent labels, most notably DJ International and Trax in Chicago, to be followed later by major label pressings.

As these records gained in popularity, the localized aspect of House consumption was retained in that the real art of House music remained in the hands of the DJ, who often released records of his own at the same time. Localized styles of House music grew up in various communities, in Detroit, London, and New York. Both Acid House and Detroit Techno were successfully imported by often unscrupulous record distributors in the British market, where they began to take on a life of their own, culminating in the former Acid and now Techno raves which became so prominent in the European dance music scene. But the deeper inflections of "soulful" Chicago-based House have retained their popularity in the queer clubs: many more recent House tracks combine the innovations of Techno and Acid with the "soulful," gospel-inflected feel which made the Chicago sound famous.

"Nothing but a String of Songs"

House music has served and continues to serve in two ways as a means of fashioning queer past(s), present(s) and future(s). As the predominant form of dance music in gay-marked social space, House is a celebration of a continuous history of gay community identity, "helping to unite the present with both past and future in an intelligible way."[18] Built around the reconfiguration of the sounds and styles of disco, House serves as a site where queers create historical narratives of continuity across time and space, centered around the continuous production and consumption of meaning in these musical signifiers. At the same time, the construction of these narratives in such a dynamic and contested realm of signification as music, no less as a music that is explicitly identified as African American, provides an alternative to unilinear white middle class understandings of queer history. House thus powerfully accesses the primary contradictions of "we are family," as it is used simultaneously to mobilize a notion of community which performs the ontological stability of the "we" across time and space, and to defer that very stability, critically problematizing who and what this "we" is.[19]

Andrew Holleran, in his novel *Dancer from the Dance*, an exploration of the world of '70s disco and New York's gay underground, describes the relation of pop songs to his historical understanding of gay community solidarity; indeed, for Holleran, any understanding of that history is rooted in song or the memory of song:

> There was a moment when their faces blossomed into the sweetest happiness . . . when everyone came together in a single lovely communion that was the reason they did all they did; and that occurred about six-thirty in the morning, when they took off their sweat soaked T-shirts and screamed because Patty Joe had begun to sing, "Make me believe in you, show me that love can be true. . . ."
> (Or because the discaire had gone from Barrabas's "Woman" to Zulema's "Giving Up," or the Temptations' "Law of the Land." Any memory of those days is nothing but a string of songs.)[20]

More than a decade later, we continue to hear disco songs sampled within House texts, disco songs played in their entirety, House songs that "sound like" disco classics, remakes of disco hits, and finally, when played by a good DJ, the smooth unnoticeable transitions between each song. It is through the construction of these uninterrupted sound texts of musical cross-references that House becomes the site for an embodied performance of historical continuity which is felt as memory.

But rather than serving merely as a tool of nostalgia, House also critiques and metaphorically reorders the dominant styles of the performance of gay identity, serving as a force of pluralization, multiplying and re-mixing the pasts, presents, and futures of gay community. House insists on its "anti-whiteness," as well as its dominance, its "control" of the dance floor (e.g., "Let the Music Take Control," "Pump Up New York," commanding titles such as "Jack Your Body," etc.). House thus re-figures the operations of race and class within constructions of gay identity, providing an alternative narrative in which gay black men are not marginalized, but central to the history of gay community and identity.

By the end of the seventies, disco had been popularized, homogenized, heterosexualized, and perhaps bleached. In contrast to this trend towards homogenization and popularization, House insists on a plurality of styles and a multiplicity of local sites of production. House texts often use an explicit rhetoric of ownership. One striking example of this claiming of House music is in Phortune's (DJ Pierre's) "House Rights (Fight for It)." DJ Pierre goes under a number of different names, Phuture, Pierre's Phantasy Club, and Phortune. In this track, Phortune actually creates a canon of House producers, Mickey, Mario, Phortune, Pierre, Phantasy (he lists all three of his names at some point in this record), all of whom are recognized as producers on the Chicago scene; each name is attributed with "owning" House, e.g., "this is Phortune's House." He also recites various sites of local production, placing the ownership of House not only in Chicago but in Detroit, New York, and London as well. House then becomes a music created and owned by various local producers and communities, rather than an object devoid of local specificities and designed for universal consumption. "Don't mess with my House, leave my House alone." This focus on local production and "ownership" consciously breaks from the slick, universalistic packaging of generalized pop production, reclaiming popular music as local property. This House text cannot be "universalized," in that it is based on a local form of knowledge, a specific local canon of House producers and "artists."

Aside from explicit textual and narrative constructions of locality, the style of House also allows for a critique of "mainstream" pop consumption. Sounds that have their roots in late '70s universal pop production have been re-styled and re-configured to be expressive of local exigencies. LNR, two Chicago-based House producers from the mid-'80s, put it this way: "I think most of the DJs in this city [Chicago] . . . wanted the beat to be harder . . . whenever they would do . . . a disco record they would have . . . a real jammin' part in the middle of the record, a break in the middle of the record, and that's where . . . House came from, the real good parts."[21]

To explain this understanding of House's relation to disco, I compare a song from the canon of high Eurodisco to one of the first House records to be released. Donna Summer's "No More Tears (Enough is Enough)," a duet with Barbra Streisand produced by Gary Klein, is a fairly typical example of high Eurodisco, and contains a clear "disco break." After a slow introduction, we go from verse to refrain twice (ABAB), followed by an up-tempo re-arrangement of some of the slow introduction. Following this "bridge," we return to the refrain. After this third refrain, all the instrumentation is pared down to a basic beat and a simple motive derived from the refrain. This motive is elaborated upon, after four measures of "pure" rhythm, for an additional thirty-two measures, when we return to the bridge. The narrative structure of the song is interrupted, the climax delayed, by this extensive focus on the "pure" rhythmic characteristics of the refrain material. The voices are consigned here to a non-narrative back-

Musical Example 3
Donna Summer/Barbara Streisand, "Enough is Enough (No More Tears)"

3. The logogenesis of the disco break. "No More Tears (Enough Is Enough)," Donna Summer and Barbra Streisand; produced by Gary Klein; from the LP *On the Radio: Greatest Hits Volumes I & II*; 1979, Casablanca Record and Film Works, LP.

ground role, the words become unimportant, subordinate to the rhythm, and have the character of "free" improvisation. The break here serves to reinforce the unity of the song as a whole, bringing the listener toward climax at the moment of return to the song text.

Comparing this disco classic to an early House track, one finds that the House track is the disco break writ large. The focus is on rhythmic and motivic developments, and narrative structure is secondary. Loleatta Holloway's "So Sweet," produced by Farley "Jackmaster" Funk, formerly one of Chicago's Hot Mix 5, clearly exemplifies this "deconstruction" of disco narrative in early House productions. Not organized by any straightforward song text, the structure of the song focuses attention on a repeating bass line. The song begins with sixteen measures of rhythm without bass, accompanied by Loleatta Holloway. Loleatta's singing consists largely of short phrases and is not organized by any straightforward song text. The entrance of the bass line is delayed and it becomes clear that all that has preceded has served to introduce this bass-motivic material. Otherwise the song is basically an exploration of various electronically produced rhythmic patterns over a hard 4/4 beat. If "So Sweet" were to be heard on the dance floor, this track would then be heard as part of an unending stream of sound, and Lolleata's voice would only be a briefly recognized part of the overall soundscape (undoubtedly accompanied by screaming queens), swept up by the rhythmic elaborations within this song and within the other songs that the DJ has chosen. "Enough is enough" is, in contrast, clearly focused around song text. The disco break is based on a logogenic motif, derived from the refrain. All of the Farley song is "break"; the voice merely becomes yet another sound that is manipulated within a dance-music frame. As song structure is replaced by a focus on rhythmic elaborations and DJ performance, House replaces the stability of the uncontested pop text, a metaphoric stand-in for an uncontested narrative of community solidarity, with "deconstructive" readings of those texts in the art of mixing and re-mixing, reclamation and reparticularization, and serves as a forum for the negotiation of historicized locality against those forms of "gay identity" which masquerade as universal.

"Miss Thing, there is no guest list tonight."[22]

While House and disco offer many opportunities for readings which celebrate the potential in popular culture for the oppositional performance of queer identities, communities, and histories, the practices of consumption and production around House and disco exhibit a form of queer performativity with a constituent dependence on other cultural operations whose political force must be "vigilantly critiqued."[23] The reconfiguration of queer cultural forms as centered around specifically black gay musical histories holds potential for the resistant staging of black queer identities, and is successfully mobilized in the space of the club against hegemonic configurations of gayness. Those configurations of gay identity which insist that gay identity is outside the realm of racial difference(s), where gay whiteness masquerades as racially unmarked, and can be partially contested by a music that re-narrates the history of gay "liberation" as sited in the sounds of a black gay underground, rather than in the growing political and economic clout of an assimilationist guppie clique, and further, by the consumption of a music that insists on the importance of racial difference in the understanding of black queer history. But at the same time, the mere fact of the popularity of House within gay social space says little about the real power relations which continue to structure the ways in which "gay community" is experienced; ironically, as black-identified musical styles dominate the dance floor, the racist practices of clubs and bar owners who insist on asking the black queen for two forms of identification—as it were, a black and a queer ID—continue with a frightening consistency.[24]

The prior analytic strategies of this chapter have focused on House music as a set of musical practices whose meanings circulate within doubled performances of queer/gay identities and communities. House, I have argued, can be read as much as a narrative of "gay community solidarity" through time and place as a political practice resistant to that very imagination of community. Further, I have argued that the very models of family and community circulate in House in two forms of drag: the first form being an attempt to pass as "real," and the second a drag which destabilizes the meanings of realness when applied to the production of community and identity. In this final section I will argue that the production of a liberatory narrative about the centrality of blackness in queer musical history is only liberatory insofar as it simultaneously functions within a regime of identity policing. There is no way to read the positive aspects of House music outside of this fundamental ambivalence. More precisely, I hope here to begin to look at the ways in which the gay eroticism heard and felt in both disco and House is an eroticism produced through the matrices of race and gender, through the consumption and fetishization of blackness and black femininity as sites of excess and transgression. By setting Kobena Mercer's analysis of ambivalence in Mapplethorpe's photography in counterpoint to Barthes's triangular conception of the production of photographic subjectivities, I hope to begin to examine the ways in which subjectivization happens in House music, in order to critically examine the racial structuration that is made possible by and makes possible the phenomenological and ontological configuration of "bodies" in the dance club. This structuration, I will argue, is the *sine qua non* for modern urban practices of queer performativity, and as such needs to be carefully examined in critiques of both the politics of race and the politics of sexual identity.

To begin this discussion, however, it is important to outline a model through which "experience" in the club might be understood.[25] The model I propose here is one of triangulation, whereby the practices that produce identity and community in the club oscillate between three nodes of subjectivization from which contradictory strategies are adopted. These three nodes might be described as authorial, spectatorial, and spectacular. The dancer in the club finds herself not as consistently engaged in one strategy of embodiment, but rather is constituted through a sort of oscillation between these three points, and it is through their interrelationship that the erotics and politics of House are made possible.

These three sets of practices might be compared to Barthes's description of the experience of photography and its relation to the erotics of the photograph. Barthes outlines three ways of relating to photography in *Camera Lucida*: that of the Operator, that of the Spectator, and that of the Spectrum. Barthes does not analyze photographic practice as an experiential totality, but rather a constellation of practices through which a fragmented subjectivity is produced. Coyly announcing that his need for immediate pleasure refuses him any opportunity to understand photographic authoriality, "I am not a photographer, not even an amateur photographer: too impatient for that," he goes on to hypothesize the pleasures of the Operator: "I might suppose that the Operator's emotion (and consequently the essence of Photography-according-to the Photographer) had some relation to the 'little hole' through which he looks, limits, frames, and perspectivizes what he wants to take."[26] The practices of the Spectator, on the other hand, are in this formulation dialectically opposed to those of the Operator, linked to the "chemical revelation of the object," rather than the "keyhole of the camera obscura."[27] Representing the relation through which photography becomes a meaningful visual economy, Barthes imagines these two nodes to be triangulated by a third, that of the Spectrum, that which is photographed, which serves as the ghostly materiality of the pleasures of both the Operator and the Spectator.

The pleasures fashioned around House music might be more productively understood and described by adapting Barthes's threefold analysis of photography to a description of the subjectivization that occurs within what I will provisionally term the club text. The profoundly visual experience of club-going lends itself to such an analytic tool, and, perhaps more importantly, Barthes's language allows us to consider the subjective experience of club-going as a plurality of forms of subjection/subjectivization, whereby each form implies a different sort of political relation. Homi Bhabha has argued that rather than focusing the point of intervention on the "identification of images as positive or negative," critical practice might more productively shift "to an understanding of the processes of subjectivization made possible (and plausible) through stereotypical discourse."[28] This model of triangulation will allow such a critical practice, one whose intervention does not stop at the point of identifying images and their political meanings, but rather goes on to explore the complicities and complications of House's imaging of blackness and queerness, the very contradictions and complicities that have made it such an important site for modern, urban queer performativity.[29]

The pleasures of the Barthesian Operator, those of authorship, are defined as those practices which assemble the spectacular illusion of authorial intentionality, the feeling of self control and personal enjoyment. I have outlined the ways in which the experience of disco and House is about the fabrication of communal histories. These histories are created partially in the string of memories and associations that are grounded within the thoughts and actions of the dancer on the dance floor; as s/he dances, s/he participates in a new narrativization of that history in response to the musical, visual, and aural stimuli that surround. In an article in *Dance Music Report*, published in 1982, we read about the "artistic" school of DJing:

> Graduates of this school manipulate the moods and memories of their crowd through careful selection of music. Their first concern is what they play not how they play it. They use themes, nostalgia, and other variables to stimulate the crowd, taking them on a trip. Energy levels are dictated not by bpm, but by emotional responses. The artistic school requires a high degree of aesthetics, a thorough knowledge of dance music through the years, and a sensitivity to people's need for experiences.[30]

Here however, in parallel to the fictionalized authorial control of the DJ, I am arguing that the listening practices and strategies of embodiment of the club-goer herself, gestures in the dance, participation in the music through screaming and whistling, the pleasures constituted are those of creation, inscribing an alternative narrative of community and identity history, written on the space of the body and traced through the available spaces on the dance floor. The themes and nostalgia that are said to be motivated by the DJ's spinning of particular records can also be seen as produced by the club-goers themselves. How the club-

goer chooses to dance, when she chooses to scream, generates particular interpretations of queer history in the space of the club, by marking certain songs,
certain gestures, as rooted within a mythical past of queer community belonging. The queer "decides" in this form of subjectivization what will be made visible
in the metaphorical photograph that is queer identity/history, and the pleasures
of these practices are those, like Barthes's Operator, of looking, limiting, framing, and perspectivizing.

It should be already clear that this set of interpretive, authorial practices only
makes sense as response to another set of practices that might be simply defined
as spectatorial. In other words, the authorial subject is here constantly in oscillation with that of the spectator. These narratives of self and community production are only made possible through the consumption of spectacle, be that
spectacle the sounds from the DJ booth, the dancing of other dancers, or the
eyes of the gorgeous man across the room: that is to say, the pleasures of looking
are not those of Barthes's Operator, but rather of his Spectator, whereby the club-
goer's practice is that of reception—receiving the "chemical revelation of the object,"[31] the object being localized embodied queer performativity. It must be
made clear that the authorial practices which mark the scene as community, like
those which produce Barthes's photographic pleasures, are then not authorial in
essence, but rather the authoriality is an *effect produced by the very act of spectatorship*, in a dialectically formed "intersection of two quite distinct procedures."[32]

The embodied practices of history and community that have been located
between the poles of spectatorship and authoriality are only possible when spectatorship and authoriality are themselves consumed as spectacle. The subjectivization of the queer is then only legible as simultaneously a subjection to the "perspectivizing," the cruising of the other in the space of the dance floor. The
spectatorship that marks the voice of the disco diva as divine is only achieved
through the very *spectacle* of that spectatorship. The spectacle of spectatorship
takes a number of forms in the scene of the club. First, here I would include a
particular musical practice of many House records, the fantasy production of
"audience" within the sonic text itself. The simulated enjoyment of the erotics
of diva-nity, revealed through the whistles and screams that appear on the record
itself becomes part of the spectacle of diva-nity. Secondly, and perhaps more interestingly, one might think about the practices that constitute authoriality and
spectatorship on the dance floor themselves as spectacle. One of the pleasures of
club-going is to see and hear histories as they are spontaneously assembled in the
embodied strategies of memory and memorialization. This spectatorship is only
made possible by an immersion in the spectacle of the dance club itself: the darkness, the lights, the throbbing rhythms, and the cinematic fantasy of communal
belonging. This interpelation into the *scene* of community and identity production, whereby the identifications which engender subjectivity lie not with the
Operator or the Spectator, but rather with Barthes's Spectrum, with the object

of spectatorial consumption, is an interpelation of queer performativity into the erotics and politics of "posing." The agencies of authorship and spectatorship are here reinterpreted as the scene of the club becomes precisely that: a "scene." In-as-much as House is about performing imagined histories of community belonging and the spectatorial enjoyment of the enactment of that performance, the club is also, like the photograph, the "advent of myself as other,"[33] by which the posing of the dancer is consumed as *posed*, and subjectivity is objectified, mortified, in the uncontrollable circulation of the pose. Identity thus becomes not an authorial production, but a "disinternalized countenance,"[34] subjected by the authorial and spectatorial practices of others to the position of object. This is in itself another form of pleasure: perhaps exhibitionistic, but an exhibitionism which is divorced from any firm grounding in embodied agency. This exhibitionism on the dance floor, when we identify with the disco diva or with the movements of other dancers on the floor, when we realize that we are part of the "scene" and not its directors, is a masochistic pleasure, controlled by the voyeur and a director who resides somewhere behind a mythical camera. As spectacle, the dancer is herself consumed on the dance floor and "put at the mercy" of a representation outside our control, as it circulates in the photographic evidence of the club rag, or in the diary-like features which describe the "scene" in the club.

The concept of "ambivalence," as elaborated by (among others) Homi Bhabha and Kobena Mercer, offers a critical tool which can clarify the political ramifications of this form of triangulated experience. Mercer has defined ambivalence not "as something that occurs inside the text [here, the "texts" of House music and the club scene], but as something that is experienced across the relations between authors, texts [spectacle] and readers [spectatorship], relations that are always contingent, context-bound, and historically specific."[35] Mercer's "Skin Head Sex Thing: Racial Difference and the Homoerotic Imaginary" itself reads as an exercise in autobiographical ambivalence and the instability that constitutes the practices of stereotype and spectatorship. Structured as a revision of an earlier reading of Mapplethorpe's photographic representations of black masculinity, Mercer seeks to replay his own ambivalent reactions to both the photographs themselves and to the contexts in which they are situated. Mercer's prior analytic strategy was to read the Mapplethorpe photographs as an inscription of "a process of objectification in which individual black male bodies are aestheticized and eroticized as objects of the gaze."[36] Here, the work of the photographs was one of fetishization, whereby a black-white duality is signified within the symbolic economy of the gaze. In this argument, black is marked by Mapplethorpe's photographic practices as object, as being-seen; white, like masculinity in the work of Laura Mulvey, is imagined as an omnipotent, all-seeing, disembodied positionality, as subject. Mercer has argued that the decontextualized skin of the black body allowed for a "scopic fixation on black skin,"[37] a fixation which implies

Photo collage. Taken from *Babble*, week #40. October 6–12, 1993.
Reproduced with permission.

a " 'negrophilia,' an aesthetic idealization and eroticized investment in the racial other that inverts and reverses the binary axis of the fears and the anxieties invested in or projected onto the other in 'negrophobia.' "[38]

Mercer's second, revisionary interpretation revolves around what he terms the "homosexual specificity" of Mapplethorpe's work. Mercer argues that the lack of specificity in his earlier critical intervention belied the very specific pleasures that he as black queer experienced in consuming the photographs, photographs that became an "illicit object of desire."[39] The black queer spectator was in his earlier analysis inevitably interpellated into the "empty, anonymous, and impersonal ideological category I described as 'the white male subject.' "[40] The argument that Mercer then lays out positions the black queer spectator ambivalently between the spaces of authorship, spectatorship, and spectacularity, whereby identification is split between the "seen" and the "unseen" aspects of Mapplethorpe's photographic work. As Mercer's rereading continues, he situates Mapplethorpe's work in relation to questions of genre and subculture, specifically gay male porn, and argues that it is precisely the visibility of the black body as queer in Mapplethorpe's work, when set upon a pedestal usually reserved for the white nude, that allows for a deconstruction of the ideologically produced apositionality of whiteness. The negrophobic and the negrophiliac are exposed as opposite sides of the same coin, and in so doing a structural split in white subjectivity is actually brought into full view.[41]

House music should also be read within such a structure of ambivalence, along two axes of identification/fetishization, the first being the spectacle of black-queerness which is produced in histories of House, and the second being the "fierceness" of the voice of the black disco diva.

The "blackness" of House might first be described as an authorial production of the black queer, as she claims House as somehow expressive of her own sense of subculture. In this narrative, House is "my House," and is traced in a genealogy with other Black musics—of course disco, but older soul and, crucially, gospel as well. Not only is the music then part of this identity performance, but the narrativization of the "history" of House also becomes crucial to this performance of identity. The almost mythical status of clubs like the Warehouse or Paradise Garage is one example. Here, the term "underground" takes on an almost concrete meaning, as the Warehouse is remembered as "underground," i.e., alternative to dominant clubs at the time, and indeed literally as "underground," in the basement.

House becomes in this view explicitly "African" in its sensibilities, and claims a space for the black queer as both queer and black. The success of House in the white gay community is described as "crossover." House, as a music contrived to express the needs of the "kids" and "unique to the character of gay black Chicago,"[42] was later adopted and popularized by mainstream clubs and record companies precisely because of its specific gay black sensibility. Its blackness and its gayness, in this reevaluation, were precisely what made House, in all its fabulousness, popular:

> What's also continued to emerge from the underground is the music of gay black America. More energetic and polyrhythmic than the sensibility of straight African-Americans, and simply more African than the sensibility of white gays, the musical sensibility of today's House music—like that of disco and club music before it—has spread beyond the gay black subculture to influence broader musical tastes.[43]

The music invoked a certain "freedom," runs this narrative, "a freedom that permitted total improvisation."[44] As Thomas (and others) argue that House is properly "experienced in a gay black club,"[45] the rhetorical force of the popularity of this music becomes a resistant insistence on the difference and particularity of gay black subcultures and their musical and dancing styles, indeed reconfiguring subculture as the (fierce) point of origin for a more widely dispersed (and therefore diluted) national popularity.

When this narrative is read as a resistant declaration of queer black pride, a description of the authorial and spectatorial practice by which "black gay" becomes a unified subcultural referent with a positive valence, it is clear that House serves an important function as a performance of resistant community and identity. But "black gay subculture" is not a hermetically sealed phenomenon, and hence the authoriality of the black queer behind House music is simultaneously interpellated as spectacle to the gaze of the white queer, and as such takes on a very different political valence. Insomuch as the insistence on the blackness of House music functions to claim a space of difference for the identity performance of the black queer, this performance is mortified by the spectatorial gaze of the white queer boy. The "strategic essentialism" of Thomas's analysis becomes something quite different, still essentialist and still strategic, yet operating in a very different political register.[46]

The implications of the "negrophilia" evidenced in the spectacularization of the "black gay underground" or the "black gay subculture" as they are "posed" by the white queer as part of his/her authorial construction of "gayness" are twofold. First, it might be argued that the embrace of an "authentically" black gay cultural form in the "wider gay community" can be used to erase the political significance of the racial difference that the music can signify. Here, the "blackness" of the music, and indeed of the black queer, are integrated into a history again of "gay community solidarity," where the steady 4/4 beat resonates as a timeless, global simultaneity that effectively reconstitutes the illusory "we" and re-invokes the indexicality of that "we" to "family," providing a naturalized mythos of effortless cohesion or "familiarity" rather than generating an ironic effect. In the photographic collages of club rags, we see a piecing together of that fantasy "familiarity," where individualized photographs of dancers and club-go-ers isolate and dehistoricize the practices that revolve around dance musics. In this production of familiarity, those subversions of more dominant constructions of gay identity and community which I have atttributed to House as a musical style and a discursive formation are hidden from view, the club serving instead as a fantasy space for the projection of a more generally current liberal pluralist model of "cultural diversity" onto the microcosm "the gay community," as it appears in its minoritizing formulation.[47] The effects of raced power as they op-erate "within" this community are erased, as all the dancers of the club, dancing (coincidentally) to a black musical form, enact their "togetherness," without any consciousness of race, class, or gender difference; in the darkness of the club, the social significances of skin color disappear. Door policies, ID checking, all the practices of racial policing that operate outside the club are blissfully forgotten, or perhaps ignored. When House is seen through these lenses, Simon Reynolds's critique of the a-political nature of the "scene" becomes meaningful:

> [T]he magical dissolution of origins of class, race, and sexual differences is what the dance floor is all about. House constructs its ideal consumer as a bi-racial lost in a swirl of polymorphous sensuality and fantasy glamour, lost for words and lost to the world. Immediately outside the club, the world and all its differences impinge: people kill each other on the doorsteps of (the) Paradise Garage.[48]

Second, and perhaps more powerfully, the "strategic essentialism" of the re-sistant adoption of House as symbolic of a specifically black queer identity is spectacularized in yet another way, as the dynamic production of that identity is "mortified" in the metaphorically photographic practices of the (post)colonial stereotype.[49] The authorial production of black queer identity is here consumed in the practices of white queer spectatorship as the disrobed black models in Mer-cer's temporally prior analysis of Mapplethorpe's photography. The specificity of "whiteness" is here erased, ironically even as it becomes more visible, in the dark-ness of the dance club.[50]

In *Without You I'm Nothing*, Sandra Bernhard enacts a monologue of queer self discovery. She begins: "Pretend for a moment its 1978. And you're straight."[51] As the narrative continues, a "straight (white) boy" is taken to a disco by his "buddy," only to slowly realize that the place to which he has been taken is in fact a gay disco.

> Somebody hands you a tambourine.
> Suddenly, in the corner of the disco, you see a big black man with a gold lamé capped head looming above the crowd. He has a blonde Afro, red lipstick smeared across his face. He's a black angel. There to take you higher. You feel

like Columbus crossing the Atlantic. You discover the new world. You feel free. Thank God Almighty, Free . . . at last. Do it Sylvester, do it girl.[52]

The metaphor of discovery here is vital: the self-discovery of the white queer is only made possible through the simultaneous discovery of an ahistoricized, essentialized black queer body, the black angel. The white queer is here a Robinson Crusoe character, who (accidentally, like Columbus) lands on a desert island of strange practices and bizarre "tribalisms" . . . or perhaps the hapless ethnomusicologist, learning to play a typical native instrument—the tambourine. The black queer is located in "the corner of the disco," firmly rooted in that New World, as if s/he had always been there, deep in the jungle of the black queer underground, and almost seeming to somehow belong there, permanently in "the corner of the disco," while the white boy enters this fantasy space from somewhere without, a land where there is no disco, and certainly no gold lamé capped black men with blonde Afros. "There to take you higher." Ms. Sandra sings those words, invoking a soul classic, and continues to sample bits from an identity constellation clearly marked as that of the African American queer. The use of the Martin Luther King quote, and the final "Do it Sylvester, do it girl!" marks his transition from awkward white boy to a proto-glamorous snap queen, as the Sylvester song in the background of this narrative, "You Make Me Feel (Mighty Real)," grows continuously in volume, until the white boy subsumes himself in the pleasures of this dark continent that this music seems to represent. Bernhard's queer changes from Columbus to Conrad's Kurtz: as he is mythically freed from his unmarked whiteness, she takes up her tambourine and becomes "one" with the wild and decadent pleasures of the "new world." But it is clear that this transformation is unidirectional, that the black queer is somehow ontologically prior to his discursive production as other, as decadent, as "underground."

Holleran's novel, discussed earlier as an example of the use of disco/dance music as a historical narrative, shines a particularly bright spotlight on the articulation of race and the formulation of (white) queer identities. While not often referencing African Americans, Holleran focuses on the world of the disco as populated by various "racially marked" categories constituted in opposition to the authorial and agentive subjectivity of the upper middle class white male—the (anti?) hero Malone, college educated, white boy from Ohio, who descends into an underworld of darkness, disco, and despair, and finds himself unable to leave. As such, it is strikingly similar in form to Bernhard's brief narrative, in that a "new world" of queer sensibility is discovered through erotic contacts with racially marked Others. Blackness in *Dancer from the Dance* most often circulates as implied, as the end point of a color continuum, populated as well by Puerto Ricans and Italians, rather than being said. But at one point Sutherland, the ruling queen of the novel, makes clear the operation of that color continuum, as he defines "dinge" for a young initiate into the "underworld":

"Blacks, darling. Schwartzers, negroes, whatever you like. Why are they the better dancers? For they are. They get away with things that no white boy could in a million years. And why do they get to wear white hats? And all the outrageous clothes? When gloves come back," he said, pulling at his own long black ones, "and I'm sorry they ever went away, you can be sure they'll be the ones to wear them first."[53]

Both narratives, Bernhard's and Holleran's, focus around the imaginary dissolution of a white, stable, *unmarked* subjectivity through the spectacular consumption of a "foreign" sensuality, be that the "black angel" with the gold lamé hat, or Sutherland's black queens donning white hats and gloves.

In an interview with Bill Coleman, a prominent manager/record producer in the House community, I asked him about the use of the term "underground" to describe House as a set of musical styles. His answer was provocative; he stated that the term as applied to House and the House community serves at least as much to "imprison" House and its producers and consumers in that imaginary cellar, as it does to describe any particular stylistic unit.[54] One might also think here about the reception of "Paris is Burning": Livingston's attempt to define the terms of "the black gay subculture" of houses in New York arguably remade the practices of vogueing and the glamorous balls into the stuff of consumption for white queer ethnographic fantasy.[55] The "hip" that Andrew Ross has analyzed in the histories of black music and the culture of white appreciation/appropriation is here comparable to the fierceness of the black queen, be she wearing a gold lamé hat, vogueing on the ball runway, or re-donning her gloves and her "outrageous clothes." Taking "hip" and "fierce" for a moment as in some way historically parallel trajectories, if not congruent formations, the problematic that Ross outlines for the former becomes vital to any clear understanding of the latter. Ross argues that the romantic consumption of hip by white intellectuals in the vanguardist cult of milieu of the 1950s placed the "a-sociality" of a particular historically situated black music with an imagined ahistorical black male body, and thus made "hip," as a category of "advanced knowledge about the illegitimate," limited in its capacity for effective contestation.[56] Similarly, the fierceness of the black queen vogueing on the dance floor or within Livingston's diegesis, while serving in one interpretation as a resistant site of black queer memory and memorialization, also functions, in so far as it serves as spectacle in the "corner of the disco" with gloves on, as a mechanism to allow the white authorial production of queer identity to imprison the black queer within that fantasy spectacular body.

The voice of the black diva is essential to any generic definition of House music. The pleasures that are produced around her disembodied voice on the dance floor can be described as identificatory—a channeling if you will of the

4. The violin passage—orchestrating Diva-nity. "I Will Survive," Gloria Gaynor; produced by Dino Fekaris; Grand Slam Productions; from the LP *Love Tracks*; 1978, Polydor, LP.

fierceness and soulfulness of her gospel-inflected singing style. From Gloria Gaynor to Ultra Naté, black women have long provided the vocal material of House and disco records. As opposed to the styles of House music that have become movements on their own, Acid and Techno, House has insistently retained the black diva as its focal point. Often singing about themes common in popular music but with a seemingly special appeal to queer performativity, unrequited love, survival, and desire,[57] she serves as the focus of "energy" and the site from which a queer erotics of dance is expressed and understood. In order to focus this description, it might be helpful to think through the musical structuring of that voice in a particular "anthem," this one taken from the disco canon, but an anthem that lends itself particularly well to re-appropriation in House, owing to its concise unity as a tribute to diva-nity.

Gloria Gaynor's "I Will Survive" is really impossible to describe. Its status as classic is guaranteed by a number of characteristics. The overdone drama of Gloria's words, reinforced by the portrayal of survival in her vocal technique, is entwined with the luscious string backups, by which the song is immediately recognizable: "At first I was afraid; I was petrified. . . . But then I spent so many nights thinking how you did me wrong, and I grew strong, I learned how to get along." This slow introduction is followed by the body of the song, with its strong rejection of the attempts of the jilting lover to get back into "Gloria's" life. "I Will Survive." The melodic structure of the verses reenacts this chain of events, beginning at a high point, dropping into the depths of despair, and ending each verse back on a high note: "You'd think I'd crumble, You'd think I'd lay down and die, oh no not I." The power of the song revolves around both the portrayal of despair and its rejection. "Then I spent oh so many nights just feeling sorry for myself. I used to cry, but now I hold my head up high. You'll see me with somebody new. . . . " The blackness of her voice is reinforced (signified, when interpreted through the apparatus by which genres of popular music are understood by the industry and the consumer) by the word choice, which portrays the "natural" anger of the powerful black (singing) woman, familiar from blues lyrics: "How you did me wrong." Perhaps more important are her sexualized moments of interjection: at one point the song breaks, and we hear a despairing "Oh," but then Ms. Gaynor refuses to be down, and picks up the angry tone of rejection. The violins which respond to the verse structure of the song reinforce Gloria's rejection of despair and turn to anger with their decisive bow strokes, exuberant runs, and anticipatory trills. Through these methods, the song becomes a coherent anthem for the jilted lover—a point of fantasy that seems key both to the imagining of black femininity and the configuration of queer boy desire.

The centrality of the black woman's voice presents a number of issues, not all of which I can begin to discuss here. But it seems crucial to show how the critical methods I have so far employed might affect an interpretation of the pleasures that are produced by the House/club texts through the disembodied voice of the diva. Again, I shall approach this issue with a doubled reading strategy. The diva is not a coherent phenomenon whose meanings circulate controllably within an economy of identification or spectacle, but rather, the triangulations of subjectivity that have produced queer performativity in House music are fields again of an unstable oscillation, whereby the diva becomes spectacle to the queer boy spectator, but simultaneously the very spectatorship of the queer boy can be reinterpreted as spectacular.

Kaja Silverman has argued that dominant Hollywood film practice works "to identify even the *embodied* male voice with the attributes of the cinematic apparatus, but always situating the female voice within a hyberbolically diegetic context."[58] In Silverman's analysis, the structuring of the Hollywood soundtrack can be seen as motivated by a system of displacements. The male voice is sutured to the unseen point of "apparent textual origin," while the female voice, qua female, has only been produced as firmly rooted to the visual spectacle of the diegetic image which serves as the signifier for a female signified. Synchronization, the production of an ideologically understood congruence between image track and sound track, maps out the spectacular female body as the site of a natural "speech," while seeking through the techniques of voice-over to remove the staging of masculinity from the risks to coherence that cinematic representation can produce. In this narrative the female voice can only be understood as spectacular and "exagerratedly diagetic" insomuch as the male authorial voice remains bodiless: outside the diegetic.

Taking it as axiomatic that recorded sound is always understood in relation to other forms of mass mediation, i.e., cinema and video,[59] it is crucial to think about the "presentness" and interiority of the diva's voice, her "soulfulness," in relation to Silverman's analysis. In this light, the black diva in House and disco is indeed excessively diegetic within, as it were, an imaginary film space, which serves to project a colonial fantasy of black feminine embodiment and "natural" sexuality. Rather than seeing the sound of the diva as a technological artifact, the historically located technological procedures used to generate diva-nity (echo effects, simulated crowds, simulated orgasm, the extension of high notes, and disco orchestration) are identified as *natural* emanations from the fantasy body of the "powerful" black woman. This diva-text operates by producing "the" black woman or indeed, black femininity, as spectacle to the dance-floor spectator. Further, as House music became popularized, the House diva circulated not only as an aural "image" but within videos, album covers, advertising, and club-dates. That is, the disembodied voice of the diva was continuously produced in relation to a visual image of the black woman. As these images are consumed within the largely heterosexualized contexts of MTV and "straight" bars the installation of the diva voice within the present bodily spectacle occurred within the racialized and gendered conventions of musical visual presentation.[60] The scandals that resulted from the fronting of various House singers by glamorous models in the late '80s, Black Box most prominently, illustrate that the visualization of the "actual" singing black woman became crucial to the popularity of House.[61] The discovery that a "voiceless" model was fronting for the "real" diva was unacceptable, because it failed to locate the divine voice within a specific star body, a body *at least in part* to be made available for the visual pleasures of an ostensibly straight male audience. In a promotion for the Diana Ross album "The force behind the power," Ross stands in a somewhat strangely contorted pose to express the origins of that force in a "naturally" sexualized display of her body. While this advertisement is not about "House music," the conventions of the portrayal of Diana as Diva here seem to condense the problematics of the visualization of the diva body in advertising, that same body which is fantastically situated as "the force behind the power" of House music.

But if one stops for a moment to think about the terms of this analytic strategy, it begins to seem tautological; like many other representationally founded critiques, its starting point masquerades as its conclusion. The argument sketched above only becomes plausible if the technologically produced effects in the space of the club are always already understood as the spectacularization of a "real" existing black female body, that of the black diva, and reproduces that identity category as ahistorically constituted prior to its phantasmatic recreation through the acts of consumption on the dance floor. Alternatively, the embodied/ disembodied contradiction of the divine voice, whereby her metaphorically hyper-diegetic presence is only assured by her visual absence, might be read as a "heteronomous" site where the presumed ontological stability of "her" femininity and blackness is instead revealed as an ideological production in the oscillation between identity and identification, "between the [represented] discursive space of the positions made available by hegemonic discourse and the space-off, the elsewhere of those discourses."[62] In this reinterpretation, the terms of diva-nity itself are read not as pre-given, but unstable: How is spectacle generated in diva-nity, and where is it si(gh)ted? What the club shows is that the spectacle in House is not always the missing "black woman's body." The very "interiorization" of black femininity that I argued in my first reading, where the diva as the force *behind* the power is naturalized in the consumption of black diva as spectacle, is simultaneously revealed as ideologically unstable when the club-goer herself/himself is interpellated into the scene of the club as spectacular. The burden of embodiment is then not borne by a diegetically confined femininity, but rather by a hyper-diegetic queerness within the club space, in which the lip-synching of the dancing queen is performed. The earlier reading is tautological in that it assumes that the diva is somehow about a *missing* "black woman's body," and leaves no space to think about the ways in which that concatenation of adjectives is socially and historically constructed, instead assuming the presence of an already complete, embodied subjectivity behind the technologically mediated divine voice. If we alter the terms of the argument, and think about the club as a space where the interiority of the recorded voice is embodied by the identificatory practices of the dancing queen, which do not "follow gender,"[63] the contours of diva-nity become very different, as do the operations of political power across its surface. When the burden of embodiment is seen as glamorously worn by the lip-synching drag queen, the phantasmatic missing diva-body is enacted ironically in the identity performance of the dancing queen. The club and its sonic drag are then a site for the display of the always present incongruity between the recorded voice and the seen body; and through the performance of this incongruity, the further incompleteness and failure of all performances of gendered identity.[64] The very portrayal of interiority in this critically misgendered space is a chance to destabilize the normative assignation of that interiority to the spectacle of the absent "black woman's body," and in so doing allow the deconstruction of the supposed unitary signified that is represented by the metaphorically diegetic production of black femininity in the diva voice.[65]

But it is important to keep these two interpretations in tension with one another. If the earlier reading I offered of the diva as representational appratus can be seen as tautological, it should also be remembered that tautological is, within its own logic, trivially true: insofar as ideology can be understood as a discursive mechanism for the production of trivial truth, it rests in some sense on a social logic that is tautological. Further, if analytical practice does not make any pretense to being outside that social logic, it becomes clear that the goal of any intervention should not be to label the tautological "false," as certain forms of apparatus theory tend to do, but rather to explain its terms as they are understood as true in order to grasp their operation. In other words, the spectacularization of the queer body in the club does not in any way replace the ideological construction of the black female body and her voice, and remains only a partial intervention in the subversion of essentialized identity categories even while depending on their logic. White queers in particular can enjoy the sensation of being "part" of a spectacle of a de-essentialized diva-nity, as long as that spectacularity is limited to the space of the dance club. As a white queer, as I leave the dance club, as I turn off the music, I can, in some sense, leave behind that performance of queer identity, re-occupying the closet on a moment's request by refusing identification, while the black queer and the black woman enter into new realms of objectification, are "identified." The white gay man can take on a positionality of "negative difference," and enjoy the stereotypes of licentiousness and "perversion," stereotypes he inevitably has a role in creating and maintaining. In this mode of inter-identity identification, the white queer "perpetuates the historic burden black women in representational practices have borne to represent embodiment, desire, and the dignity of suffering" on behalf of those white queens, unable and unwilling "to strip themselves of [all] the privileges of white heterospectacle."[66] At the same time (s)he can indeed use those stereotypes to subvert the very operations of power that created them, by confusing the "realness" of the identity assignations that are produced under their hegemony. But honestly, ultimately, *she* can always return to *his* closet, turn off those Donna Summer records, and pass invisibly, his "consigned" or "self-identified" marginality hidden in a masquerade which can perform the stability of a subjectivity which seems congruent to his normatively gendered white body.

The final "real" to which the white queer has the option to flee, be it the subject effected by Bernhard's monologue or the more abstract blandness and blankness of Holleran's narrator, serves to confine the mobilizations of irony to a naturalized place in the "underground" or subculture. It is this and the parodic for the white queer that sustains the "timeless" characterizations of the black diva and the black queen, incarcerated in a fantasy disco. Race, simply put, inevitably structures where and how white queerness "takes place," both on an abstract map of the social and a metaphorically richer map of urban space. A closer look at something like House music provides a way of examining that structuration as one achieved not primarily through some abstract notion of representation, but rather through a more dynamic conception of production in everyday practice, in the pleasures of the club and the various forms of subjectivization it engenders.

Category: Embodied Realness

"The cover of *Thing* magazine proclaims that 'She Knows Who She Is,' . . . [mobilizing] the common gay use of the feminine pronoun in the ventriloquized voice of the woman's magazine to categorize 'insiders' by attitude rather than by gender or sexual identity."[67] Sampling and remixing that fierce metaphor, House music serves as a sort of second order ventriloquization; screaming with "Miss Thing," as she works that runway, the queer children voice an identity performance from within the space of her fantastic/phantasmatic body, saying "we know who we are," reveling in and revealing the historical and local contingency of their performances of community on other productions of embodied identity. The preceding pages then only represent a preliminary examination of the multiple and contested uses of musical sounds as a site of queer performativity. Making "us" *feel* mighty real, House music and the complicated play of identifications that circulate around the dance floor reveal that all identity and community performances are contingent on how real they feel, not how real they are.

Notes

1. For the first form of analysis, where "gay culture" is imagined as a distinct cultural unit, see Gilbert Herdt, "Introduction," and " 'Coming Out' as a Rite of Passage: A Chicago Study," in *Gay Culture in America*, ed. Herdt (Boston, 1992). In contrast, see Judith Butler, "Imitation and Gender Insubordination," in *Inside/Out*, ed. Diana Fuss (New York, 1991) and especially on the subject of queer identity and its displacement of the generational production of history, Sue-Ellen Case, "Tracking the Vampire," in *differences* 3 (summer, 1991):1–20. A shorter version of this chapter was presented at the Family Values Graduate Studies Conference at the Chicago Humanities Institute in April 1993, and I'd like to thank the organizers of that conference and the participants for their helpful comments. This chapter has been helped along the rocky road to completion by many people and I would like to acknowledge the help and support of the following motley crew: Daud Ali, Philip V. Bohlman, Brad Borevitz, George Chauncey, Bill Coleman, the Chicago Recorded Music Reading Group, Greg Downey, Elizabeth Freeman, Carolyn Johnson, LNR, Robert Massa, Nayan Shah, and Wilhelm von Werthern. Finally, I would like to thank the editors of this volume for their patience and support.

2. Butler, "Imitation and Gender Insubordination":21 [brackets mine].

3. Benedict Anderson, *Imagined Communities* (London, 1983):15.

4. Anderson's comments on the national anthem inform these comments: "Take national

anthems, for example, sung on national holidays. No matter how banal the words and mediocre the tunes, there is in this singing an experience of simultaneity. At precisely such moments, people wholly unknown to each other utter the same verses to the same melody. The image: unisonance. Singing the Marsellaise, Waltzing Matilda, and Indonesia Raya provide occasions for unisonality, for the echoed physical realization of the imagined community" (Anderson:132). House seems to "echo" the structure of national anthems while throwing their mythologized ontological ground very much into question, not only by stomping on that ground but also by lip-synching it away.

5. Houston Baker, Jr., "Hybridity, the Rap Race, and Pedagogy for the 1990s," in *Technoculture*, ed. Constance Penley and Andrew Ross (Minneapolis, 1991):198.

6. For a critique of Baker that focuses on the problematic gender politics of his analytic strategy, see Tricia Rose, *Black Noise: Rap Music and Black Culture in Contemporary America* (Hanover, 1994):151. Rose reads this same passage in Baker's article, focusing on the ways it not only portrays male straightness and masculinity, but also how it "renders sustained and substantial female pleasure and participation in hip hop invisible or impossible."

7. Quoted in Simon Reynolds, *Blissed Out: The Raptures of Rock* (London, 1990):154.

8. See Katherine Hazzard-Gordon, *Jookin': The Rise of Social Dance Formations in African American Culture* (Philadelphia, 1990). Hazzard-Gordon describes modern urban dance music in the following passage, exhibiting fairly clearly the ease of speaking this homophobically inflected dialect of criticism in the academic sphere. "What is left? Private house parties, discos, show bars, and nonentertainment bars dominate the contemporary urban scene. As *sophisticated and glittering* as it may *appear*, black core culture is deteriorating. . . . Disco, the glittering dance arena of the 1970s, was highly commercial and youth oriented. Not all blacks were *seduced by its lure*, but some were. . . . For blacks who see dance as more than *mere entertainment*, disco proved *distasteful*. Aside from encouraging the most insensitive uses of African American dance movement, the acrobatics reflect a decadent, alienated culture" (Hazzard-Gordon:174 [italics mine]). Here, disco is characterized as associated with a "deteriorating" culture, in echo of the "family values" rhetoric produced by right-wing ideologues.

9. Maurice Joshua, "This Is Acid," *House Hallucinates*.

10. Many pop songs today are produced both in 7" mixes for radio play as well as 12" dance versions for club consumption. The producers responsible for this translation are often those who are attributed with "inventing" House, e.g., the Hot Mix 5 and Frankie Knuckles.

11. A brief note about my use of musical examples: these are intended to assist those with no familiarity with the "sound" of House music, but are not in any way intended to distill what the "music" is. They appear here as marginally descriptive, not as definitive.

12. Apotheosis, "O Fortuna." 12" single. Radikal Records, 1992.

13. Anthony Thomas, "The House the Kids Built: Dance Music's Gay Black Roots," *Outlook: National Lesbian and Gay Quarterly* 5 (summer, 1989):28.

14. *Thing* 5 (fall, 1991):39.

15. Interview with LNR at Mirage Entertainment, Chicago, 22 February 1992.

16. Thomas:28.

17. "Club music" is usually placed somewhere between high disco and House music in the usual style history. Like all of these sub-groups of dance music, its stylistic characteristics are notoriously difficult to pinpoint. For a general description, see Thomas.

18. Anthony Seeger, "When Music Makes History," in *Ethnomusicology and Modern Music History*, ed. Stephen Blum, Philip V. Bohlman, and Daniel M. Neuman (Chicago, 1991):34.

19. On music serving to produce and contest histories, see Christopher Alan Waterman, *"Jùjú History: Toward a Theory of Sociomusical Practice,"* in Blum, Bohlman, and Neuman, eds. (Urbana, 1991).

20. Andrew Holleran, *Dancer from the Dance* (New York, 1978):39.

21. Interview, LNR.

22. From "Club Lonely (I'm On the Guest List Mix)," Lil' Louis and the World. 12" single. SONY, 1992. Even before its release, this quote became a "staple" sample in queer clubs across the country.

23. See John Corbett, "Free, Single, and Disengaged: Listening Pleasure and the Popular Music Object," *October* 55 (fall, 1990):79–101.

24. This notion of gayness as being un-raced or "white," is policed not only within hegemonic configurations of gay identity, but also within what might be termed reverse discourses of racial identity. See Houston Baker's article critiqued above, where "gay" and black male are utilized in explicit opposition.

25. I hope not to engage "experience" as a new foundation for social critique, but rather, like Joan Scott, begin to think about ways in which to describe the "experience" of House music as something historically produced in contingent situations. "*Experience* is not a word we can do without. . . . Given the ubiquity of the term, it seems to me more useful to work with it, to analyze its operations and to redefine its meaning. This entails focusing on the politics of identity production, insisting on the discursive nature of 'experience' and on the politics of its construction. Experience is at once always already an interpretation *and* something that needs to be interpreted." Joan Scott, "The Evidence of Experience," in *The Lesbian and Gay Studies Reader*, ed. Henry Abelove, Michèle Aina Barale, and David M. Halperin (New York, 1993):397–415.

26. Roland Barthes, *Camera Lucida* (New York, 1981):10.

27. Ibid.

28. Homi K. Bhabha, "The Other Question: Difference, Discrimination, and the Discourse of Colonialism," in *Out There: Marginalization and Contemporary Cultures*, Russell Ferguson, Martha Gever, Trinh T. Minh-ha, and Cornel West, eds.:71.

29. In his analysis on disco, Richard Dyer argues that the way that queer "culture" and popular articulate with one another is not about "resistance" and domination simply put, but rather the location and expression of contradiction. Richard Dyer, "In Defence of Disco," *Only Entertainment* (New York, 1992):148–58.

30. Tom Silverman, "Dance Biz," *Dance Music Report* 5:5 (March 20–April 2, 1982).

31. Barthes:10.

32. Ibid.

33. Ibid.:12.

34. Ibid.:15.

35. Kobena Mercer, "Skin Head Sex Thing: Racial Difference and the Homoerotic Imaginary," in *How Do I Look?: Queer Film and Video*. Bad Object Choices, ed. (Seattle, 1991):170.

36. Ibid.:171.

37. Ibid.:175.

38. Ibid.:175.

39, Ibid.:169.

40. Ibid.:179.

41. Additionally, as his reading is contextualized and historicized, Mercer argues that the circulation of Mapplethorpe's work as a powerful symbol of urban queer resistance in the late 1980s must also be taken into account. In this argument, readings that do not take into account ambivalences and specificities in the practices that constitute that which is read can often become "assimilated into a politics of homophobia." See Mercer:192.

42. Thomas:30.

43. Thomas:25.

44. Ibid.:30.

45. Ibid.:33.

46. On this concept see Gayatri Chakravorty Spivak, "Subaltern Studies: Deconstructing Historiography," in *In Other Worlds: Essays in Cultural Politics* (New York, 1987).

47. On "minoritizing" and "universalizing" as two epistemologies of sexual identity, see Eve Kosofsky Sedgwick, "Introduction: Axiomatic," in *Epistemology of the Closet* (Berkeley, 1990).

48. Reynolds:154.

49. Barthes:10.

50. See Richard Dyer, "White," *Screen* 29 (autumn, 1988):44–64.

51. *Without You I'm Nothing.*

52. Ibid.

53. Holleran:48.

54. Personal interview with Bill Coleman (New York, December, 1991).

55. For a reevaluation of the relationship of "subculture" to mass cultural formations and the logic of "appropriation," see Cindy Patton, "Embodying Subaltern Memory: Kinesthesia and the Problematics of Gender and Race," in *The Madonna Connection: Representational Politics, Subcultural Identities, and Cultural Theory.* Cathy Schwichtenberg, ed. (San Francisco, 1993):81– 106. For a specific discussion of *Paris is Burning,* see bell hooks, "Is Paris Burning?" in *Black Looks: Race and Representation* (Boston, 1992):145–56. Also see Judith Butler, "Gender is Burning: Questions of Appropriation and Subversion," in *Bodies That Matter: On the Discursive Limits of "Sex"* (New York, 1993):121–40.

56. Andrew Ross, "Hip and the Long Front of Color," in *No Respect: Intellectuals and Popular Culture* (New York, 1989):101.

57. For a description of the queer pleasures of disco, pleasures that are similar to those produced in House, see Dyer (1992) on disco.

58. Kaja Silverman, *The Acoustic Mirror: The Female Voice in Psychoanalysis and Cinema* (Bloomington, 1988):45.

59. See Simon Frith, "Hearing Secret Harmonies,"in *Music for Pleasure* (London, 1988): 128–37. Frith suggests that cinematic signification and meaning in popular music are intertwined and mutually inextricable. From this suggestive point of departure, my reading of House as "having" a metaphorical diegesis is intended to suggest that it might be useful for critics to adapt the strategies of film criticism to the study of popular music, to see what they illuminate about the structuring of pleasure in popular music practices.

60. A brief note about the use of videos in club space: they aren't used in large clubs where the music is "real" House, mixed by a DJ, since videos are centered around pop songs as units, and would obviously not coincide with the virtuosic practices of urban DJs. At the same time, the videos often play in smaller bars, gay or straight. The historical development of the figure of black House diva-nity in the 80s cannot be thought about without at least some thought of video practice; but the power of the diva in the club, her "exaggeratedly diegetic" nature, is not to be taken literally, as produced only through videos, but rather to be understood as the projection of a fantasy diegetic space: it is only through the embodied sound of a disembodied voice that the figure of the diva in club space is achieved.

61. On this subject see Barbara Bradby, "Sampling Sexuality: gender, technology, and the body in dance music," *Popular Music* 12.2 (spring, 1993):155–76.

62. Teresa de Lauretis, "Technology of Gender," in *Technologies of Gender* (Bloomington, 1988):26.

63. "I will endeavor to show that classic cinema has the potential to reactivate the trauma of symbolic castration within the viewer, and that it puts sexual difference in place as a partial defense against that trauma. I say 'partial' both because no system of defense is impregnable, and because this one serves to protect only the male viewer. It has very different consequences for the female viewer, at least assuming that identification in any way follows gender . . . " [Silverman:1]. If Silverman's analysis depends on this first-page assumption that identification "in

some way follows gender" and a description of her argument which takes the "female viewer" and the "male viewer" as her starting point for criticism, is it possible to use her work to produce a theory of queer listening pleasures? Silverman's argument becomes an argument with which the queer critic (the critically queer?) needs to play cat and mouse—that is to say, her argument in *The Acoustic Mirror* offers all this space to think about listening pleasure and its politics that is in some sense radically new, while forcing us to think about those pleasures along a frame which makes queerness itself illegible. I hope my argument here has been a step toward "re-tooling" Silverman's useful analysis, in order to make legible a queer listening (spectatorial) engagement that "follows gender" in another sense—haunts, stalks—to become a primary subject of concern in the discussion of how identification works in sound theory.

64. "The parodic repetition of gender exposes . . . the illusion of gender identity as an intractable depth and inner substance. As the effects of a subtle and politically enforced performativity, gender is an 'act,' as it were, that is open to splittings, self-parody, self-criticism, and those hyperbolic exhibitions of 'the natural' that, in their very exaggeration, reveal its fundamentally phantasmatic status." Judith Butler, *Gender Trouble: Feminism and the Subversion of Identity*. (New York, 1990):147–48.

65. Particularly interesting in this light is the work of RuPaul and other drag queen House stars, or perhaps, more provocatively, the work of Jamie Principle. Principle takes on the traditional trappings of diva-nity in his singing style, including the hyper-sexualized orgasmic sounds common to late 80s House music, but inserts them into an obviously queer "diegesis" in the song narrative. Of parallel interest on the academic plane is Carolyn Abbate's critical reappraisal of approaches to various forms of the cultural critique of opera. Insofar as Abbate re-examines the relationship between authoriality and performance, her discussion of the woman's voice in opera dovetails quite neatly with the situation of the diva-voice on the dance floor. See her "Opera; or, The Envoicing of Women," in *Musicology and Difference: Gender and Sexuality in Music Scholarship*, Ruth A. Solie, ed. (Berkeley, 1993):225–58.

66. Lauren Berlant and Elizabeth Freeman. "Queer Nationality," *Fear of a Queer Planet: Queer Politics and Social Theory*. Michael Warner, ed. (Minneapolis, 1993):218.

67. Ibid.:178.

11

Compulsory Homosociality

Charles Olson, Jack Spicer, and the
Gender of Poetics

Michael Davidson

to be tumescent I

The affairs of men remain a chief concern

—Charles Olson, "The K"

I

MY TITLE CONFLATES two influential revisions of feminist theory. The first
is Adrienne Rich's diagnosis of the compulsory character of heterosexuality in marking gender divisions; the second is Eve Sedgwick's use of the term
"homosocial" to refer to forms of same-sex bonding in which male interests are
reinforced. Both works represent a second or third stage of feminist theory based
on the recognition that patriarchy sediments its authority not only by excluding
women from its orders but by basing its exclusions upon a heterosexual norm.
When heterosexuality is regarded as the (untheorized) standard for evaluating
gender differences, then the possibility of describing all forms of gender relations
becomes moot. Such structural marginalization of others has political implications for a society in which certain types of homosocial bonding (boardroom
politics, corporate networking, lockerroom badinage) are essential to the perpetuation of capitalist hegemony.

I have linked Rich's and Sedgwick's terms in order to suggest that in certain
communities—literary circles or artistic movements, for instance—obligatory
heterosexuality is reinforced even when those communities contain a large number of homosexual males. It is often assumed that because underground literary
movements are marginal to the dominant culture, they are therefore more toler-
ant and progressive. Such assumptions need to be historicized by asking *for whom*

progress is being claimed and *by what* aesthetic and social standards. The structure of homosocial relations, genitalized or not, often undergirds the producton of new art forms and practices, even though that structure is often at odds with the liberatory sexual ethos that articulates those practices. One might, therefore, reverse Nancy K. Miller's question, "does gender have a poetics" (xi) and ask "does poetics have gender," and if so, how do homosocial relationships participate in constructing both terms?

Such questions become extremely pertinent when studying the formations of literary postmodernism where the attempt to go beyond the artisinal poetics of high modernism often replicates phallic ideals of power, energy, and virtuosity that it would seem to contest. Most commentators regard the shift in literary periods as one in which a model of literary performance regarded as realized totality—what John Crowe Ransom called "miraculist fusion"—is displaced by speech act. While never alluding to Austin's theory of the performative, poets of the late 1950s nevertheless thought of their work as capable of effecting change—of "doing" rather than "representing"—by the sheer authority vested in the speaker. This authority is purchased not by establishing ironic distance or by invoking institutional or cultural precedents. Rather, authority derives from an ability to instantiate physiological and psychological states through highly gestural lineation and by the treatment of the page as a "field" for action. In the rhetoric of Black Mountain poetics, the poet "scores" the voice—and by extension the body—through lines that monitor moment-to-moment attentions. The poem's authenticity resides not so much in what the poem says as paraphrasable content but in the ways the poem displays its own processes of discovery. Many of the terms for such performance (gesture, field, action) derive from abstract expressionist painting, for which the heroic ideal of physicality serves as aesthetic as well as communal precedent.

I would like to study two literary circles of the 1950s in which homosocial relations were compulsory, even though each group consisted of numerous homosexual males. The groups in question are the North Beach bar scene surrounding Jack Spicer, who was openly gay, and the Black Mountain milieu surrounding Charles Olson, who was not.[1] Both poets wrote foundational documents in poetics that have become the basis for much discussion of postwar, non-traditional verse. Both poets developed their poetics within a group ethos of male solidarity and sodality that often betrayed homophobic qualities. Although women were sometimes associated with each group (Helen Adam and Joanne Kyger with Spicer, Denise Levertov with Olson), they were seldom acknowledged as literary innovators. While women were often absent from the centers of artistic and intellectual life in general during the 1950s, their absence in these groups was a structural necessity for the liberation of a new, male subject.[2]

Before focusing on particular cases, it is necessary to emphasize that com-

pulsory homosociality was hardly limited to the Black Mountain or Spicer circles. One could say the same for Beat writers like Jack Kerouac and Allen
Ginsberg, who developed their ethos of cultural disaffiliation by rejecting
"momism" and other vestiges of female authority (marriage, commitment, sexual
fidelity). In his novels Kerouac fetishized the (hetero) sexual prowess of Neal
Cassady and celebrated the rough camaraderie of men "on the road." Ginsberg,
in his most famous poem, elegizes those "who let themselves be fucked in the ass
by saintly motorcyclists" while, at the same time, despairing over those who "lost
their loveboys to the three old shrews of fate the one eyed shrew of the heterosexual dollar the one eyed shrew that winks out of the womb and the one eyed
shrew that does nothing but sit on her ass and snip the intellectual golden threads
of the craftsman's loom . . . " (128). And in his most infamous confession of misogyny, "This Form of Life Needs Sex," Ginsberg despairs of woman, the "living
meat-phantom, / . . . scary as my fanged god" (284), who stands between him and
"Futurity."

The same could be said for poets of the Deep Image movement like Robert
Bly and James Wright who developed their theories of the ecstatic, "leaping" image out of Jungian archetypalism and Bultmanian theories of matriarchal cultures. For Robert Bly, the presence of the Great Mother sensitizes the male poet
to his natural or childlike potential, but when She appears in her more medusan
form as the Teeth Mother, her icon is the vagina dentata and her function is to
destroy the male's psychic life (Bly, 41). In both Beat and Deep Image movements, greater sensitivity or vision is purchased at the expense of women, even
when her gender (as in more recent Men's Movement rhetoric) is invoked as a
positive value. And even where homosexuality is openly celebrated, as it is in
Ginsberg, it is often in opposition not only to heterosexuality but to women in
general:

> Woman
>   herself, why have I feared
>   to be joined true
>   embraced beneath the Panties of Forever
>   in with the one hole that repelled me 1937 on? (285)

II

The date is important here beyond what it means for Ginsberg's sexuality. It
marks a specific moment in the development of homosociality that coincides with
a shift into what we now recognize as postmodernism. If Ginsberg was "repelled"
by female genitalia, he could say so within a range of same-sex associations
brought about by World War II. As John D'Emilio and Lillian Faderman have

pointed out, the war expanded possibilities for homosocial—and specifically gay and lesbian—interaction. The sudden removal of men and women from small towns into "sex-segregated, nonfamilial environments" (D'Emilio, 458) such as the armed services or defense industries provided new possibilities for same-sex contacts. Networks of gays and lesbians continued after the war as service personnel were demobilized in San Francisco, Los Angeles, or New York where the presence of bars and social services provided a hospitable environment. The inquisitorial climate of the Cold War—from the House Un-American Activities Committee hearings of the late 1940s through the McCarthy committee—often linked political and sexual deviance, thus creating a greater sense of alliance among various "subversive" cultures. Many federal and state employees were fired for "sexual misconduct" and many more were subjected to surveillance. Gay community was challenged by increased police crackdowns on gay bars which, far from diminishing homosexual or lesbian activity, heightened awareness. Literary communities in Greenwich Village and North Beach were particularly affected by these developments since many of them evolved in the same bars that were the targets of police raids. And while regulars of those bars may have made distinctions between homosexual and straight patrons, the outside world and the mass media tended to link literary bohemia with sexual deviancy and dismiss both accordingly.

The expansion of gay and lesbian community during the 1950s was accompanied by the evolution of new, non-traditional masculine identities within the popular imagination: the *Playboy* swinging bachelor, the motorcycle renegade, the Hollywood cowboy, the pelvis-gyrating rock star and, of course, the Beatnik. As Barbara Ehrenreich notes, many of these roles were explicitly misogynist in nature, treating women as little more than sex toys or castrating viragos. At the same time, these new masculine roles offered alternatives to the usual domestic scenario with its breadwinning male and housekeeping wife. Advertising saw the possibilities of the new male consumer and adjusted its agenda to accomodate the single, discerning—even avant garde—purchaser of Marlboros, Hathaway Shirts and hi-fi components. Within the "triumphant" middle class lay pockets of male resistance, whether in the white-collar executive who becomes a connoisseur of jazz or the truck driver who dons a leather jacket on weekends. These alternative masculinities were commodities to be purchased, even by those cultural producers who excoriated Madison Avenue techniques. Jack Kerouac writing about beat hipsters "taking drugs, digging bop, having flashes of insight" in the glossy pages of *Esquire* or *Playboy* seemed somehow appropriate to the times. The change of Allen Ginsberg, market researcher, to Allen Ginsberg, poet, may not have been such a transition after all.

I make this point about the 1950s because theories of homosocial literary culture have often focused on its development in earlier periods. The most significant treatment of the phenomenon, Eve Sedgwick's *Between Men*, is devoted to " . . . a new range of male homosocial bonds . . . connected to new configurations of male homosexuality" (207) that emerged in the nineteenth century and helped to articulate stratifications within the new middle class. The amorphous character of new class relations during this period necessitated the reassertion of gender roles to give "an apparent ideological distinctness" (207) to an unstable social and economic context. That distinctness was—and remains—reinforced by an asymmetry between same-sex groupings among women and men. For the former, same-sex bonding carries little of the social opprobrium that it does for the latter. This asymmetry not only differentiates two kinds of homosocial groupings but ensures male domination of women, since whereas male-bonding often leads to material enrichment the same experience among women has no such material base.

Obviously by the mid-twentieth century the unstable class relations Sedgwick describes had become stabilized, and the asymmetries of gender relations sedimented into institutional and bureaucratic structures of great complexity. Furthermore, the British class relations Sedgwick studies are a great deal more stratified than those in the U.S. (e.g., there is no American equivalent to the aristocratic Oxbridge homosexual culture of the sort depicted in novels like *Brideshead Revisited*), and thus any use of homosociality as a general concept of same-sex bonding must be defined within its specific cultural formations. The question of what it meant to be masculine in the 1950s must be set against those very bureaucratic structures—giant, anonymous corporations, a new class of technical and intellectual expertise, a concensus ideology in institutional life— by which mid-century America is known. The development of aesthetic models based on the body and gesture, on voice and orality, represent a response to the increasing alienation of individuals within these social forms. What inheres between mid-nineteenth and mid-twentieth century same-sex relations is the asymmetry between male and female homosocialities and between their access to the same material conditions. What is unique to the movements that I will study here is the degree to which literary communities reinforced this asymmetry through gender-marked models of performance and action.

III

The best place to begin studying such models is in Charles Olson's "Projective Verse" (1950) which advocates a theory of "open field" composition where the poet composes by attending to the physiology, breath, and breathing "of the man who writes as well as of his listenings" (*Selected Writings*, 15). Even allowing for the gender inflections of the day, Olson's use of the masculine pronoun throughout the essay seems extreme. Speaking of the advantages of Pound's musical phrase, Olson advises "go by it, boys, rather than by, the metronome" (16); of the unity of form and content, "There it is, brothers, sitting there for USE"

(16); of the advantages of using the syllable, "if a man is in there, will be, spontaneously, the obedience of his ear to the syllables" (18). The syllable is "king" and when used properly, it is close to the mind, "the brother to this sister [the ear]" (18). Finally, out of this "incest" of male mind and female ear comes the line

> from the breath, from the breathing of the man who writes, at the moment
> that he writes, and thus is, it is here that, the daily work, the WORK, gets in,
> for only he, the man who writes, can declare at every moment, the line its met-
> ric and its ending—where its breathing shall come to, termination. (25)

The highly subordinated and punctuated syntax of Olson's prose is as much a demonstration of projectivist poetics as it is a description. The prose is literally breathless with intensity as Olson maps the "breathing of the man who writes."[3] The work-ethic implied by this impatience is reinforced by a productionist vision of poetry's effect on the social world, its "stance toward reality outside a poem" (24). It is here, in Olson's more utopian claims for projective verse, that his geni-talization of performance most limits its practitioners:

> It comes to this: the use of a man, by himself and thus by others, lies in how
> he conceives his relation to nature, that force to which he owes his somewhat
> small existence. . . . For a man's problem, the moment he takes speech up in all
> its fullness, is to give his work his seriousness. . . . But breath is man's special
> qualification as animal. Sound is a dimension he has extended. Language is one
> of his proudest acts. And when a poet rests in these as they are in himself . . .
> then he, if he chooses to speak from these roots, works in that area where na-
> ture has given him size, projective size. (25)

It is clear that the body from which poetry is projective is a heterosexual one whose alternating pattern of tumescence and detumescence, penetration and pro-jection, dissemination and impregnation, structures more than the poem's linea-tion. Despite his repudiation of traditional figuration (the "suck of symbol") Olson uses a familiar metaphor of the male as generative principle operating on a passive female nature, "that force to which he owes his somewhat small exist-ence" (25). Such sustained masculinization of poetry gives the first syllable of "Manifesto" new meaning.

Were "Projective Verse" the work of a single individual it could be seen as the product of an isolated sensibility in revolt against the New Critical strictures of his day. But the essay is, in fact, a collaborative work, constructed out of letters between Olson and Robert Creeley in the late 1940s. Portions of Creeley's letters are embedded in Olson's prose as are quotations and paraphrases of other authors (Pound, Williams, Fenollosa) that, as Marjorie Perloff has pointed out, make this less an original work than a collage enterprise. The document has become the centerpiece for Black Mountain poetics, a movement composed largely of men, and although it involves several bisexual or gay males (Robert Duncan, John Wieners, Michael Rumaker, Jonathan Williams, Fielding Dawson), its cultivation of heroic expressivism betrays a strongly heterosexual bias.[4] Finally, "Projective Verse" is a pedagogical instrument, written at the beginning of Olson's teaching career and designed to educate a certain kind of student. Since, as we shall see, that student is gendered male we may assume that this collaborative project is not extended to female readers.

Olson's belief that projective verse extends the private into the social body is demonstrated in *The Maximus Poems*, which claims to restore "that which is familiar" to an estranged polis. In his epic design, Olson sustains homologies between individual and community whereby the recovery of physiology and orality in one translates into the recovery of place and geography in the other. The capitalist entrepreneurs who threaten to dissolve the local fishing economy of Gloucester, Massachusetts, can be counteracted by the citizen who "[takes] the way of / the lowest," and learns thereby that "there are no hierarchies, no infinite, no such many as mass, there are only / eyes in all heads / to be looked out of" (33). However egalitarian, such passages are contradicted by Olson's epic stance as an "Isolated person in Gloucester, Masachusetts" who addresses "you islands / of men and girls" (16). Where men are men and women are girls, the possibilities for equal access to polis are limited. For in Olson's imagination of social change, man is active ("The waist of a lion / for a man to move properly") whereas a woman is passive ("And for a woman, / who should move lazily / the weight of breasts" [39]). Thus the dynamic possibilities of a historical poetics based on local action are sustained by a myth of gender inequality.

In the early *Maximus* series, Gloucester serves as a microcosmic example of lost American plenitude. Sites of resistance can be found in small enclaves of male community, from the Dorchester Company who first settled Cape Ann in 1624, to contemporary sailors in whom Olson sees limited possibilities for heroic action. In later books, Olson expands his field of interest to include archaic history and myth as performing on a cosmological scale what Gloucester performs on the local level. A central figure of the late *Maximus* series is the Cretan war god Enyalion whom Olson venerates as an ideal of male virtue (arete). His heroism is embodied in the fact that he "goes to war with a picture," a phrase that appears several times in the series as a statement of male rectitude:

> The only interesting thing
> is if one can be
> an image
> of man. "The nobleness, and the arete." (473)

Enyalion's ability to imagine himself as man, able to act "with a picture" rather than a weapon, means that he becomes redeemed potentiality rather than limited nature. And it is precisely this opposition between the male, reflected in his self-image, and feminine nature, as ground or material, that structures Olson's vision. The picture that Enyalion carries with him is quite literally of himself, "the law of possibility," and as such controls what he sees. Woman is left out of the picture, serving as " 'Earth' mass mother milk cow body / demonstrably, suddenly, MORE / primitive and universal" (333). Woman cannot hold an image of herself since she is the primordial condition out of which images are made.

Olson's Jungian perspective in the late *Maximus* series represents not so much a departure from his earlier historical concerns as a universalizing of qualities first discerned in America's colonial past. The self-reliant homosociality of New England fishermen continues in Enyalion, an archetypal hero out of whom a new city, a *civitas dei*, might be constructed. Olson had no less of an aspiration for Black Mountain College, "the largest city I'll ever know" ("On Black Mountain," 68) which in its last days consisted of fourteen people, the same number as made up the original Dorchester Company. Such parallels were not lost on Olson, who often regarded Black Mountain as a "City on a Hill" and who linked it with earlier American social experiments. At each level of polis, from the small town to the redeemed Jerusalem, community exists to reflect the aspirations of man, not simply as a generic category for humanity but as a gendered principle of power. In a late *Maximus* poem, Olson admits that there is a price to pay for visionary struggle: "I've sacrificed every thing, including sex and woman / —or lost them—to this attempt to acquire complete concentration" (473). If this is a confession of vulnerability and limit on Olson's part, it is no less a statement of personal resistance by which "sex and woman" are kept out of a city they had yet to occupy.

Female students who attended Black Mountain were not exactly "kept out" of Olson's classes, but they had a difficult time learning under his autocratic pedagogy. Francine Du Plessix Gray, who came to the college in 1951, acknowledges Olson's importance but describes the difficulties that she and other female students had in dealing with Olson's Ahab-like authority. "You're still writing conservative junk!" she reports Olson as saying to her in class; "AND ABOVE ALL DON'T TRY TO PUBLISH ANYTHING FOR TEN YEARS!" (348). Gray proved to be a "dutiful daughter" and waited a decade before publishing her first story—in *The New Yorker*, of all places. Another Black Mountain student, Mary Fiore, reported that "in both [Olson's] classes and his private circle of followers he tended to perpetuate the standard Black Mountain 'straight' male view of women as alluring but largely vacuous creatures—'Me Tarzan heap big intellect, you Jane full of mysteries' " (Clark, 210). When feminist scholar Nancy Armstrong showed up for the first day of Olson's modern poetry seminar at SUNY, Buffalo, she was told that the course was going to be about "Men's Poetry," and any women who wanted to attend would have to watch from the hallway.[5] Such dismissive treatment imposes a phallic test on learning that must be seen as a dimension of projectivism—an attempt to literalize the power of male speech by refusing women any interlocutory relationship within it. By relegating women to literal and figurative hallways, Olson could perfect the *civitas dei* after his own fashion (and image) and sediment his Socratic authority.

If female students were relegated to the hallways, the male students who remained became acolytes in complex rituals of filial obligation that were not without their erotic charge. Fielding Dawson's memoir of his student years at the college describes both Olson and the painter Franz Kline as surrogate fathers who offered a measure of manhood based less on affection than upon competition and daring. "Measuring up" as student and son also meant negotiating challenges to traditional sexual roles. Dawson's ambivalence about his own sexuality begins the first day he enters the college:

> ... when I ... walked up that gutted dirt road towards the Dininghall, a feminine building (it held a lot), I walked into a different world; (2)

This feminized space of difference permits him homosexual as well as heterosexual relationships, although his anxiety about the former leads him to self-recriminatory reflections as he seeks to conform his relationships with men to heterosexual terms. "Hell no . . . I'm married," he says in response to the renewal of contact with a former male lover: "Very well, I say bitterly to hurt yourself and pretend that game, remember the night in the shadows under the tree by the place where you saw the bee? Kitty was furious at you: '*Cut this faggot game out, Fee Dawson, you're not queer.*' I was ashamed" (36). The complex pronominal interplay of this passage embodies Dawson's confusion as he seeks to differentiate himself from both lover, interlocutor, and that version of himself that *does* remember the "night in the shadows." Is he ashamed at his previous actions or at his continuing homosexual desires or at his (current) heterosexual ménage?

The way that Dawson compensates for such fears is by adopting a competitive attitude toward his teachers, especially Olson. The crowning expression of this is the moment when he strikes out the 6'7" rector in a game of baseball. Olson "threw his bat in the bushes, cursed me, and stormed off the field" (18). Physical competitiveness extends to intellectual aggressiveness as the student apes the teacher's confrontational mode. When a new faculty member comes to campus, he is subjected to a withering attack from the students:

> Every now and again a Liberal showed up to teach. That poor social anthropologist and his pretty wife left fast, went down the road in shock. They had sat before the student body, some of the faculty stood around, we were a savage bunch, and the social anthropologist tried to answer our questions; it was probably because the guy had never heard of Frobenius that we wiped him out. His weak theories, limited possession of source material, lack of fieldwork and almost total lack of feeling for literature and the plastic arts, was the end of him. We sat silently, coldly staring at him. (41–42)

This description is a summary of Olsonian values: hatred of liberal intellectuals, the necessity for arts education, unquestioning faith in Poundian sources like Frobenius, cynicism about the social sciences, fetishization of "source materials," fieldwork as basis for scholarship. Olson's stance, articulated through Dawson, reflects a particular anxiety of many during the 1950s about the status of intellectuals in general. For many artists and writers of Olson's generation, disenchanted with New Deal or socialist politics, the professionalization of knowledge resulted in a "new class" of academically trained specialists. Ex-New-Dealer Olson, while hardly a neoconservative, nevertheless embodies a kind of populist intellectualism that betrays many of the same suspicions of Cold War liberalism of his more right-wing colleagues.[6]

Such suspicions of official intellectual culture are not without their gendered component. In *The Black Mountain Book* the "bad" liberal intellectual turns out to be Paul Goodman, who taught for brief periods at the college and who had been considered for a permanent teaching position. As Dawson sees him, Goodman comes to the college armed "with psycho-therapy (his own), literature, history, community planning and sex, as weapons" (133). For Dawson, the openly-homosexual Goodman is a tempter with whom the students must do battle, using weapons of verbal clarity and concision:

> Most of the things Paul said were right but he often told them badly, deliberately; he, characteristic of Liberal Intellectuals, used his brilliance as a whip. . . .

> That guy was loaded with guns, and when he fired it didn't altogether work, because we knew the words he used better than he did—which surprised him, calling a snake "You're a SNAKE!"
> "Yeah, I'm a snake. Watch out." (133–34)

Dawson distinguishes between figures like Goodman, who continue to live within the orbit of the university, and artists like Franz Kline or Olson, whose intellectual accomplishments are embodied in physical acts of painting and writing. The latter are "real guys," in Dawson's hagiographic memory, and their art is a direct expression of that reality.[7]

Dawson was describing more than his own homosexual panic in discussing Goodman's effect on the college. Olson also experienced Goodman as a sexual threat and said so in a poem written after that visit. In "Black Mt. College Has a Few Words for a Visitor" Olson plays upon the allegorical character of Goodman's name, transposing good-man into every-man in order to display how ultimately banal his influence at the college has been:

> Names names, Paul Goodman
> or else your own
> will be the Everyman of sugar sweet, the ginger cookie

> to scare the Witch with you, poor boy—if we must have
> such classes
> as "equals," the young, your lads, the fearful lasses
> (*Collected Poems*, 268)

What Dawson describes as Black Mountain's positive leveling of distinctions between pedagogue and ephebe here becomes a dangerous mixing of instructions. When classes transform lads into lasses, then Olson's more hierarchical, masculinist approach to learning is destroyed; pedagogy becomes pederasty. In Olson's mind it is a short distance between the Platonic grove to anonymous cruising in Central Park. In Goodman's "ginger cookie," Olson discerns "a rougher thought . . . he could corrupt an army" (269). At the same time, Olson recognizes his own complicity in Goodman's sexual and literary intentions:

> Look: us equals, that is, also sons of witches, are
> covered now with cookies
> dipped in same from your fell poem. It fell, all right,
> four footed
> with one foot short where five were called for—five,
> sd the Sphinx,
> confronted with senescence and with you, still running
> running running
> from her hot breath who bore you, Hansel Paul,
> to bore us—all. (269)

These cryptic lines say a great deal about how Olson configures homophobia through misogyny, identifying with Goodman as "sons of witches" and subject to Circe-like powers of transformation. But Goodman's poem (he had written verses critical of Black Mountain after his sojourn at the college [Clark, 224]) falls short; his "four foot" line is inadequate to the occasion. Olson's considerably longer iambic lines are, presumably, the proper (phallic) form for this kind of male challenge. In the allegory of Hansel and Gretel that Olson employs here, sons are vulnerable to witches who may transform them into ginger cookies and emasculate their poetry. Goodman's solution is to become the "Everyman of sugar sweet" and thus evade battle with the Sphinx. Olson, as author of "a Few Words for a Visitor" adopts an oedipal stance, refusing to run "from her hot breath" and answer her riddle.[8]

Black Mountain, as this example indicates, was both a place and an ideology, a community and a poetics. As a poetics, it was never far from a vision of social totality, and while this vision was often progressive in its resistance to commercialism and conformism, it was often limited in its incorporation of others. Olson's belief that the projective act in poetry will lead "to dimensions larger than the man" (*Selected Writings*, 25) was not hyperbole; it produced a generation of poets that shaped literary history in the 1960s and 1970s. If projectivism enlarged "the man" it also reinforced his position as Subject looking out on a feminized universe of passive objects. This specular position was by no means stable in the 1950s, as Dawson's memoir makes clear, necessitating an almost parodic reassertion of masculine self-sufficiency. This may have been a Cold War ritual that many individuals had to undergo at this time, even when they declared themselves "Isolatos" from outposts in North Carolina or Gloucester.

IV

Or San Francisco. Jack Spicer's poetics of dictation, like Olson's "Projective Verse," was never formulated in any systematic way but through a kind of occasional workshop conducted in various North Beach bars. It receives its most famous articulation in the Vancouver lectures of 1963 where Spicer describes poetry as being received from the "outside" rather than generated from within. The poet is a medium or channel into which the poem comes from an endistanced source. In formulating his poetics of dictation, Spicer often alludes to Cocteau's movie, *Orphee*, in which the poet receives his poetry via his car radio, and to Yeats's later experiments with mediumistic writing. This theory of poetic dictation thwarts intentionality by demanding that the poet remain open to the Martians, ghosts, and spooks who are constantly blabbering at the margins of discourse.

Such spirited metaphors for poetic reception have obvious precedents in romantic poetics, but they also have practical implications for the bohemian culture in which Spicer lived. At bars like Gino Carlos and The Place, the Spicer circle lived out certain rites of exclusion, acceptance, and initiation in relation to a potentially hostile "outside" world. In the homophobic 1950s the group had every reason to fear that world where beatings, arrests, and incarceration of homosexuals were regular features of North Beach life. If the poetry/bar world was insular, it was also necessary, in a pre-Stonewall era, for developing gay community. I have discussed the significance of this sense of community in *The San Francisco Renaissance* but would add that such insularity of the Spicer circle did not prevent the development of its own forms of exclusion and homophobia.

The origins of Spicer's group ethos can be traced back to his college years at the University of California at Berkeley during the late 1940s. As students of medieval literature and history Spicer, Robert Duncan, and Robin Blaser were fascinated by the lore of Arthurian knights, crusades and secret societies. Contributing significantly to the Berkeley poets' sense of insular community was the influence of the medieval historian Ernst Kantorowicz who was teaching at Berkeley during the late 1940s and with whom the three poets took classes. He had been a member of the circle of homosexual artists surrounding Stefan George in Germany that included Kantorowicz's own teacher, Friederich Gundolf. During the famous loyalty oath controversy at Berkeley, Kantorowicz courageously refused to sign and went, instead, to Princeton's Institute for Advanced Study. In Kantorowicz, the young poets found a model for homosocial community upon which their own Pre-Raphaelite Berkeley Renaissance was based.[9]

This cultishness of the Berkeley period continued into the 1950s when Spicer developed another male fraternity in North Beach bars. The poets in Spicer's circle, like those at Black Mountain, preferred a kind of hard-drinking, macho ethos, supplemented by sports, pinball, and verbal fisticuffs. Group magazines like *Open Space*, *J*, and *Capitalist Bloodsucker*, along with publishing poetry by members of the circle, also printed satires and imitations of other poets and movements. Retaining one's marginal status meant maintaining a vigilant stand against the forces of co-option: "Tell everyone to have guts," Spicer urges; "Come through the margins / Clear and pure / Like love is" (*Collected Books*, 63). And in his later poems, Spicer extends his metaphor of poetic reception to include baseball and boxing:

> The poet is a radio. The poet is a liar. The poet is a
>   counterpunching radio.
> And those messages (God would not damn them) do not
>   even know they are champions. (218)

The inability to spar within this circle meant that one lacked will, that, to adapt one of Spicer's favorite metaphors, Orpheus had lost direction by turning back to find Eurydice.

Spicer's tough-guy stance configured homosexuality within an almost Calvinist sense of moral imperatives. The battle for poetry had to be waged against the twin evils of femininity and assimilation. Effete or effeminate forms of gay behavior were not permitted. When asked about Spicer's relation to the New York School, Landis Everson said that "he didn't like them. He disliked John Ashbery intensely. He called him 'a faggot poet.'" John's first book was called *Some Trees* and Jack always made it a point of pronouncing it "Some Twees" (Ellingham, 62). Nor was homosexuality to be contained within institutional structures. Its revolutionary potential was not in solidarity but in solitude: "Homosexuality is essentially being alone. Which is a fight against the capitalist bosses who do not want us to be alone" ("Homosexuality and Marxism"). Although Spicer participated in a limited way with older, more established homosexual institutions like the Log Cabin and the Mattachine Society, at least one poem in *Language* warns of the dangers of too much assimilation:

> Which explains poetry. Distances
> Impossible to be measured or walked over. A band of
>   faggots (fasces) cannot be built into a log-cabin
>   in which all Western Civilization can cower. And

> look at stars, and books, and other people's magic
> diligently. (*Collected Books*, 227)

Spicer equates "faggots" with fascists ("fasces") when their outsider status is accomodated within the rest of "Western Civilization."[10]

Against feminized or assimilated versions of gay identity, Spicer mounted a group offensive among faithful followers. The enemy was official verse culture with its publishing center in New York, its magazines and academic venues, but the enemy was no less the heterosexual outside world, especially that which nightly invaded "his" North Beach in tour buses searching for Beatniks. Part of the group offensive involved creating a frontal, unadorned image of gay reality that excluded not only a heterosexual viewer but a certain kind of homosexual as well:

> For Joe
>
> People who don't like the smell of faggot vomit
> Will never understand why men don't like women
> Won't see why those never to be forgotten thighs
> Of Helen (say) will move us into screams of laughter.
> Parody (what we don't want) is the whole thing.
> Don't deliver us any mail today, mailman.
> Send us no letters. The female genital organ is hideous. We
> Do not want to be moved.
> Forgive us. Give us
> A single example of the fact that nature is imperfect.
> Men ought to love men
> (And do)
> As the man said
> It's
> Rosemary for remembrance. (62)

This poem is based on a vertiginous logic that mixes homosexual desire, homophobia, and misogyny. Spicer seems to be saying that in a society where one's homosexual nature is defined as "imperfect" he has no choice but to love "faggot vomit" and feel that "The female genital organ is hideous."[11] Moreover the authority of this logic demands that he refuse any ameliorating position; he will not be "moved," ideologically or emotionally. Once he accepts this logic, misogyny becomes a structural prerequisite by which difference can be constructed. Whether or not the "female genital organ is hideous" is a moot point; it is a position required within the heterosexist continuum by which homosexuality is marked as other. The proposition that "Men ought to love men" contains both the hope that there might be a world where men *can* love men but also the realization that in a world where men *do* love men, men ought *not* to love women.

As I have recounted elsewhere, "For Joe" was written on the occasion of

Denise Levertov's visit to the San Francisco Bay area and was designed to provoke the visitor as much as test the loyalty of the audience. The poem is also dedicated to another poet, Joe Dunn, and as such introduces a second level of address into the confrontation. Many of Spicer's poems speak directly to specific individuals, often in the form of letters, and thus demand a highly specific act of decoding. Each letter "is a mirror, dedicated to the person that I particularly want to look into it" (55), Spicer declares in *After Lorca*, thus removing the poem from its identity as discrete lyric and placing it in a dialogic relationship to the reader. Single poems are "one-night stands . . . as meaningless as sex in a Turkish bath" (61). Against the isolated lyric stands what Spicer called the "serial poem," a suite or book of single lyrics, often incomprehensible by themselves but linked when read as a group. The serial poem becomes the literary analogue of sexual community, each separate lyric given identity by its combative relationship to the whole: "Poems should echo and reecho against each other. They should create resonances. They cannot live alone any more than we can" (61).

Spicer thematized the communal implications of the serial poem by developing each of his books around one or more models of male fraternity: cowboy mythology in *Billy the Kid*, Gnostic theology and Orphic legend in *Heads of the Town Up to the Aether*, Arthurian knights in *The Holy Grail*, baseball teams in *Language* and *Book of Magazine Verse*. Unlike modernist uses of myth, in which cultural decay is offset by the salvific presence of prior narratives, Spicer rewrites classical and popular stories to enforce solidarity among a small group of adepts. It is precisely because the larger culture has become fragmented that the marginal culture, with its rules and local deities, becomes necessary. The social role of poetry lies not in the author's political views but in the degree to which he can create a linguistic alternative to the instrumentalized language elsewhere in society.

It is in *After Lorca* (1957) that we see the most obvious blend of poetics, correspondence and homosociality. The book consists of a series of translations and mistranslations of García Lorca's poetry, interlaced with letters written to and from the Spanish poet. It is in these letters that Spicer makes his most direct equation between correspondence regarded as epistolarity and correspondence as metaphor: "Things do not connect; they correspond. That is what makes it possible for a poet to translate real objects, to bring them across language as easily as he can bring them across time" (34). By addressing the dead García Lorca, Spicer attempts to bring the dead poet "across time" so that he may "correspond" with him. By writing his own poems and calling them translations, Spicer suggests that Lorca's poetry lives on in the poetics he created for subsequent poets to appropriate.

Most commentary on *After Lorca* has noted the parallels between Spicer's theory of correspondence and Symbolist or other modernist forms of literary non sequitur. What must be added is the level of homosocial male desire that animates every level of this work. The object of the series, García Lorca, was himself a gay male, whose ambivalence about his sexuality is a central theme in *Poeta en Nueva York*.[12] Two of the poems Spicer "adds" to that volume are based on the Narcissus legend as a central tale of homoeroticism. Since most of the translations are dedicated to other homosexual males, Spicer is also "corresponding" to and within a closed world of male friendship. Finally, the terms for Spicer's correspondence theory are written in the rhetoric of homosexual desire:

> How easy it is in erotic musing or in the truer imagination of a dream to invent a beautiful boy. How difficult to take a boy in a blue bathing suit that I have watched as casually as a tree and to make him visible in a poem as a tree is visible, not as an image or a picture but as something alive—caught forever in the structure of words. Live moons, live lemons, live boys in bathing suits. The poem is a collage of the real. (34)

This passage would seem to be a classic statement of modernist aesthetics—a merging of Thomas Mann's "Death in Venice" with Russian Formalist *ostranenie*. Yet far from textualizing desire by creating an aesthetic monad as displacement for lost beauty, Spicer recreates it again and again in the complex deixis of his poem. To make the beautiful boy visible means creating a network of references to dead poets (Lorca, Whitman, Rimbaud) and living (dedicatees include many of Spicer's friends) that blurs the distinctions between "original" and "belated" texts. The boy Spicer desires is brought into the poem as something "caught forever in the structure of words," not in their power to fix him in an image.

Oddly enough, Spicer signals his own homosexual anxiety most fervently in the one poem that is most faithful to the original. In his version of Lorca's "Oda a Walt Whitman," Spicer recreates Lorca's conflicted view of New York, a city that embodies both Whitman's healthy "adhesive" comrades as well as those *maricas* or "perverts" who "Sprout out along the beach of your dreams" (29). Although most of the poem is faithful to the original, Spicer displays a degree of linguistic license in those passages involving forms of homosexuality that are uncontainable within Whitman's masculine comradeship. Lorca's poem excoriates

> vosotros, maricas de la ciudades,
> de carne tumefacta y pensamiento immundo,
> madres delodo, arpias, enemigos sin sueno
> del Amor que reparte coronas de alegria. (Lorca, 124)

which in Ben Belitt's translation reads:

> But you! against all of you, perverts of the cities,
> immodest of thought and tumescent of flesh,
> mothers of filthiness, harpies, sleeplessly thwarting

the Love that apportions us garlands of pleasure.
(Lorca, 125)

Spicer's version is a great deal more frontal in its attack:

But against the rest of you, cocksuckers of cities.
Hard-up and dirty-brained,
Mothers of mud, harpies, dreamless enemies
Of the Love that distributes crowns of gladness. (31)

And where Belitt translates Lorca's "Esclavos de la mujer, perras de sus tocadores, / abiertos en las plazas confiebre de abanico" as "Toadies of women, dressing-room bitches, / brazen in squares in a fever of fans" Spicer is more direct: "Slaves of women, lapdogs of their dressing tables, / Opening their flys in parks with a fever of fans . . . " (31). Clearly Spicer wants to force Lorca's language into more extreme statement ("abiertos in las plazas" is demonstrably not the same as "Opening their flys in parks") to display not only the Spanish poet's fears of homosexuality but his own.

Spicer's radical rewriting of Lorca, like his attack on female genitalia in "For Joe," represents his view that poetry must be a forum where exclusions and seductions in the bar-world of San Francisco can be played-out in a textual form. Poetry must not merely depict such conflict but must perform, through its language, the unbridgeable gaps between subject and object. Traditional poetics has no adequate terms to describe this merging of the aesthetic and quotidean, and thus Spicer resorted to baseball, comics, magic, and pinball as metaphors for poetry. Such ludic pleasures insist on their own entertainment value and imply a fruitful tension between skill and chance. But linguistic performativity is enabled through a more complex performance of masculinity within the Spicer circle that, in order to allow the "outside" into the poem, had to recreate the "inside" as a bunch of guys, "heads of the town up to the aether."

V

One of the key terms in both Olson's and Spicer's poetics is objectivism (or what Olson called "objectism"): the attempt to escape the "lyrical interference of the individual as ego," by regarding the poem as a form of materiality within the world. This attempt to separate "inside" from "outside" should be seen not only as a restatement of Keats's negative capability but as a form of what Judith Butler calls "gender border control" whereby the integrity of the Subject is discursively maintained "for the purposes of the regulation of sexuality within the obligatory frame of reproductive heterosexuality" (136). The discursive means by which both poets sought to differentiate realms involves the development of a poetics of gesture within which the poet could escape reflection and "act" on the moment. But what "was" reflection if not a feminized space of interiority and psychic boundlessness? What "was" lyrical interference if not the intrusion of seductive reason and beautiful rhetoric? Language-as-gesture was a defense against such feminization. It could reinforce the integrity of the male body by regarding its nonreflective acts as significant, even heroic, at a moment when the possibilities for heroism were in short supply. But in projecting the poet as object and the poem as unmediated gesture, both heterosexual and homosexual poets feared a reciprocal objectification—and feminization—against which only male community could serve as protection.

By studying compulsory homosociality as a structure of subject production rather than a "value system" or form of "sexual preference" I am arguing that even within the most progressive communities—whether homosexual or heterosexual—forms of misogyny and homophobia are often necessary to their continuation. By applying this analysis to the Black Mountain and San Francisco literary communities, I do not mean to diminish the subversive and oppositional possibilities that these groups represented. In fact, it is because these movements mounted such a significant challenge to traditional models of American social identity during the 1950s that we need to understand what ideological closures continue to speak through a verse so often characterized as "open."

Olson's poetics of the body and breath led to a participatory, historically critical poetry that has been influential for gay as well as straight poets. Likewise, Spicer's foregrounding of the linguistic basis of identity, his recognition that "where we are is in a sentence," anticipates many recent theories of identity construction. By linking poetics to ideas of community and social resistance, Olson and Spicer provided an important corrective to modernist narratives of artisanal authority and objectivity. But in their postmodern attempts to turn, as Spicer said, Logos into Low-ghost, discourse into performance, these poets and their followers often spoke less as prophets than as ventriloquists. As belated readers of this highly mediated speech, we must be sensitive both to the possibilities of community it projected and those it could not yet pronounce.

Notes

1. Although Olson led a heterosexual life, he often worried over the "troubles of Androgyne" in relation to his male students. Tom Clark reports that "He dreamed of ambiguous sexual encounters involving male students" (224), one dream of which may have been that described in "The Librarian" (1957). In this poem, the author of *Maximus* discovers a "young musician" and librarian of Gloucester "in my parent's bedroom where I / found him intimate

with my former wife" (*Collected Poems*, 413). The replacement of young musician for husband, son for parents, librarian for poet, suggests a complex substitution of speaker and male other. Within this substitution set, every term of the poet's life—his patrimony, poetry, marriage—is met by a younger surrogate male. It would not be hard, then, to assume that the violation of the marriage bed is also a violation of the terms of heterosexual marriage as well, in which access to the female partner is blocked by the male.

2. I have discussed the relationship between literary communities and gender during the 1950s in *The San Francisco Renaissance*. Some of the discussion in this chapter repeats that in my book, but I now see some of the inadequacies of that earlier treatment and want to redress them here. I am encouraged to return to this material by recent developments in Queer theory and gender studies that have provided me with terms I lacked in my book.

3. It is no little irony that the poet who staked so much on the unfettered breath was himself a chronic sufferer from emphysema, worsened by a lifetime of heavy smoking.

4. On homosexuality at Black Mountain, see Duberman, 225–27, 330–33.

5. Interview with Nancy Armstrong, Aug. 27, 1993.

6. On intellectuals and the "new class" see Andrew Ross, *No Respect* and Barbara Ehrenreich, *Fear of Falling*.

7. On Goodman at Black Mountain, see Duberman, 329–33.

8. For an excellent overview of Goodman's relationship to Black Mountain and Olson see Steven P. Horowitz, "An Investigation of Paul Goodman and Black Mountain."

9. On Kantorowicz and the Berkeley Renaissance, see Ellingham.

10. The reference to looking at "other people's magic" seems to refer to Robert Duncan, who had been accused by Olson of dabbling in mysticism as a sectarian practice rather than as received truth. Olson's criticism appeared in an essay, "Against Wisdom as Such," which is mentioned in the previous poem where Spicer aligns himself with Olson against Duncan's "gleeful, crass, and unworshiping [*sic*] / Wisdom . . . " (226). Thus Spicer's attack on institutionalized homosexuality combines with his rejection of Duncan's "crass" wisdom in a complex form of male-bonding with Olson.

11. This line inspired Denise Levertov to write her own critical response, "Hypocrite Women," which counters Spicer's rather outrageous claim as part of her own feminist response. I have discussed both poems in *The San Francisco Renaissance*, 172–73.

12. Lorca is a central figure in the poetics of the New American poetry. His "Theory and Function of the *Duende*" is often quoted in manifestos and essays of the 1950s and serves as a precursor to Spicer's theories of literary image. His poetry was translated extensively by poets, especially those among the Deep Image poets searching for non-French versions of Symbolism and Surrealism.

Works Cited

Bly, Robert. "I Came Out of the Mother Naked." *Sleepers Joining Hands*. New York: Harper, 1973. 29–50.

Butler, Judith. *Gender Trouble: Feminism and the Subversion of Identity*. New York: Routledge, 1990.

Clark, Tom. *Charles Olson: The Allegory of a Poet's Life*. New York: Norton, 1991.

Davidson, Michael. *The San Francisco Renaissance: Poetics and Community at Mid-Century*. Cambridge, Eng.: Cambridge University Press, 1989.

Dawson, Fielding. *The Black Mountain Book*. New York: Croton, 1970.

D'Emilio, John. "Gay Politics and Community in San Francisco Since World War II." *Hidden from History: Reclaiming the Gay and Lesbian Past*. Ed. Martin Duberman, Martha Vicinus, and George Chauncy, Jr. New York: Meridian, 1990.

Duberman, Martin. *Black Mountain: An Exploration in Community*. New York: Dutton, 1972.

Ehrenreich, Barbara. *Fear of Falling: The Inner Life of the Middle Class*. New York: Harper, 1989.

———. *The Hearts of Men: American Dreams and the Flight from Commitment*. New York: Anchor, 1983.

Ellingham, Lewis. "The King's Two Heads: from 'The Jack Spicer Circle.' " *Line* 7/8 (spring/fall, 1986). 57–89.

Faderman, Lillian. *Odd Girls and Twilight Lovers: A History of Lesbian Life in Twentieth-Century America*. New York: Penguin, 1991.

Ginsberg, Allen. *Collected Poems 1947–1980*. New York: Harper and Row, 1984.

Gray, Francine Du Plessix. "Charles Olson and an American Place." *Yale Review* 76:3 (June 1987). 341–52.

Horowitz, Steven P. "An Investigation of Paul Goodman and Black Mountain," *American Poetry* 7:1 (fall 1989). 2–30.

Kerouac, Jack. "The Philosophy of the Beat Generation." *Esquire* XLIX:3 (March 1958). 24–25.

Lorca, Federico García. *Poet in New York*. Trans. Ben Belitt. New York: Grove, 1955.

———. "Theory and Function of the *Duende*." Trans. J. L. Gili. *Poetics of the New American Poetry*. Ed. Donald Allen and Warren Tallman. New York: Grove, 1973. 91–103.

Miller, Nancy K., ed. *The Poetics of Gender*. New York: Columbia University Press, 1986.

Olson, Charles. "Against Wisdom as Such." *Human Universe and Other Essays*. Ed. Donald Allen. New York: Grove, 1967. 67–71.

———. "On Black Mountain." *Muthologos: The Collected Lectures and Interviews*, vol. II. Ed. George Butterick. Bolinas, CA: Four Seasons Foundation, 1979.

———. *Selected Writings*. Ed. Robert Creeley. New York: New Directions, 1966.

———. *The Maximus Poems*. Ed. George Butterick. Berkeley: University of California Press, 1983.

Perloff, Marjorie G. "Charles Olson and the 'Inferior Predecessors': 'Projective Verse' Revisited," *ELH* 40:2 (summer 1973). 285–306.

Rich, Adrienne. "Compulsory Heterosexuality and Lesbian Existence." *Powers of Desire: The Politics of Sexuality*. Ed. Ann Snitow, Christine Stansell, and Sharon Thompson. New York: Monthly Review Press, 1983.

Ross, Andrew. *No Respect: Intellectuals and Popular Culture*. New York: Routledge, 1989.

Sedgwick, Eve Kosofsky. *Between Men: English Literature and Male Homosocial Desire*. New York: Columbia University Press, 1985.

Spicer, Jack. "Homosexuality and Marxism." *Capitalist Bloodsucker* NP (1962).

———. *The Collected Books of Jack Spicer*. Ed. Robin Blaser. Los Angeles: Black Sparrow, 1975.

———. "Vancouver Lecture #1." *Caterpillar* 12 (July, 1970). 175–212.

12

Performing "Nature"

Shamu at Sea World

Jane C. Desmond

WHAT MICKEY MOUSE is to Disneyland, Shamu is to Sea World. The most celebrated orca whale of all time, Shamu is the synecdoche of Sea World. She is the nodal point around which the ideological work of Sea World revolves as it constructs a problematic of the natural based on the trope of family. By uniting the idea of family with that of nature, both sides of the equation are reconfigured. Families as specific social organizations are naturalized as paradigmatic of all relations, whether on a global scale or between humans and animals. Obversely, nature becomes part of the human family, completely culturalized and incorporated during the utopian moments of the shows. Complex tensions pull at the edges of these formulations and are revealed in the structure of the performances at Sea World. The lines between the "natural" and the "cultural" are continually asserted and erased, drawn and redrawn throughout the shows, revealing the elasticity of this boundary as well as its power, durability, and marketability.

Selling "nature" is big business, and Sea World's growth is part of a nationwide trend in entertainment and recreation involving animals. A 1990 survey reported that more than one hundred million visitors a year are attracted to wildlife facilities, including zoos and animal theme parks (Nelson 34). Industries based on looking at animals, what I refer to as animal tourism, sell an experience of the natural through exposure to "wild" animals, whether or not the particular animals have ever lived in or even seen the mythical "wilderness" they are tied to in our imaginations. Despite these contradictions, the animals both stand in for the rest of "the natural" as that outside of human cultivation (one of the word's earliest meanings), and they are seen as "natural" themselves, subject to "natural" forces or laws.

These multiple connotations represent some of the historical roots of the concept in European and American discourse. As Raymond Williams has noted, the word "nature is perhaps the most complex word in the [English] language" (1983: 184). It is so central that multiple, even contradictory meanings emerge

within the same utterance as we shift back and forth among residual traces to
more contemporary ones. "Nature" and "civilization" play a dialectical tune of
critique and redemption with one or the other in ascendancy at particular historical moments. This fluidity of discourses about the "natural," about its relation to a "cultural" realm, and about the positioning of humans relative to both,
is one of the hallmarks of sites like Sea World.

The intensity of public discourses of the natural rises and falls at different
historical junctures. The last twenty years have seen an intensification of this
concern with the rapid popularization of the concept of ecology, and its designa-
tion as something that we must save. But the beginnings of this conservation
paradigm are much earlier. Raymond Williams has argued that the opposite and
yet double of conservation is exploitation (1980: 81). With the intensification of
our separation from the natural world, in the turn from an agrarian-based economy to an industrialized, urbanized one, we can trace a concomitant idealization of nature. Bits of it are cordoned off and set aside as public parks and nature
preserves (private parks and nature preserves predate these). This is apparent especially from the nineteenth century on in Europe and the United States, and
can be seen in the commitment to city parks, to the emphasis on rejuvenating
travel to unindustrialized parts of the country, and on the establishment of federal park systems. In these cases, nature was what was left over, saved, or left
empty. This double ideological move simultaneously commodifies nature while
positing it as outside of commodification.

Animal theme parks, ecotourism sites, and zoos and aquariums are contemporary extensions of this commodification. They meld commerce with the sal-
vage paradigm of a vanishing wilderness. They are, in fact, huge industries based
on the idea of "nature" as one of the last bastions of idealized authenticity in the
postmodern era and on animals as exemplars of wildness. And within these industries, mammals are supreme. They are presented as our interlocutors, living
on the border between the categories of humans and nature. They are the medium through which a nostalgia for families as ideal social units is united with
a nostalgia for a simpler past associated with idealized concepts of "nature."

While zoo mammals still garner the largest audiences, it is the marine facilities that are experiencing the fastest growth. Marine mammals are rapidly
becoming the most bankable stars in this entertainment industry. Sea World's
corporate history reflects this growth. Founded in 1964 by four graduates of
UCLA, the park opened on twenty-two acres of land in San Diego. Thirty years
later, it occupies 150 acres on San Diego's Mission Bay and has spawned three
other Sea Worlds in Ohio, Texas, and Florida. Purchased in 1976 by Harcourt
Brace Jovanovich, Inc., ownership of all four Sea Worlds transferred to the Anheuser-Busch Companies, Inc., in 1989 for a price of $1.1 billion.[1]

As a sign at the entrance reminds us, Sea World is "not just another park,
it's another world." This world is extensive, comprising dolphin shows, walrus

and seal shows, five aquariums full of sea creatures, a dolphin petting pool, the world's largest display of sharks, a penguin "encounter" area featuring 400 penguins, as well as a musical show (by water-skiing humans).

There are many additional services and products. There are nautical gift shops, places to have your picture taken with Shamu (in the form of a fifteen-foot statue or of a person dressed in a Shamu suit), restaurants, a space needle ride, a play area called Cap'n Kids World, and the Busch pavillion, where visitors can sample a wide variety of Busch products. Souvenir shops are plentiful and feature stuffed versions of Shamu, commodifications of the personification of the natural.

All of this is set in a beautiful park, carefully groomed, squeaky clean, wholesome, and full of carefully tended plants and animals. "Family entertainment at its best," is what the brochure for the theme parks promises. The same threats of violence that are banished from the human/animal interactions in the shows are also absent here. A small-town sense of safety, scale, and simplicity governs the physical design. Sidewalks wend gracefully from exhibit to exhibit, trash is immediately whisked away. The city of San Diego, set off from the park by a very long access drive, is not even visible from the complex. Urban components like crime, dirt, pollution, noise, and different groups of people with competing needs are not found here. Park-goers represent a relatively homogeneous population in terms of class background, although there is some variation. More important to this homogeneity, perhaps, is the shared sense of a community goal among all of the visitors—to play, to have fun, to escape from daily routine. A day at Sea World is a vacation day, a day of animal tourism. A nostalgia for a simpler, safer, small-town past is transmuted into a nostalgia for an Edenic community of animals and people that co-exist in harmony.

The guarantee of education underlying all the fun allows guilt-free pleasure and a justification for the steep entrance prices. Adults enter for $23.95, children under twelve for $17.95, while toddlers are free. This brings the price for a day's entertainment for a "typical" family of four to $83.80, plus the cost of lunch, snacks, and the requisite souvenirs. All attractions and exhibits in the park, with the exception of the two rides, are free once the entrance fee is paid. Even so, taking the mythical family of four to Sea World for the day is easily a $100 proposition.

The corporate structure of the Sea World empire is further emphasized by the presence of various major corporations who "sponsor" particular shows or exhibitions. For example, the Penguin Encounter is "presented by ARCO." Public relations information notes that Sea World's relationship with these firms involves participation in national and regional consumer promotions, and mutual institutional advertising programs. Other sponsors include Southwest Airlines, Adohr Farms, Pepsi, and Kodak. In these mutually beneficial institutional advertising programs, the affiliates garner good will for their support of conservational programs, but even more importantly they get to be associated with the very positive and powerful image of Shamu.

The Nature of Culture

The Shamu show constructs a notion of family which binds all animals and all humans together in a vision of harmony. The diversity of shows and exhibits at Sea World, which include penguins, walruses, seals, porpoises, dolphins, and reef-dwelling animals emphasizes this idea of a family of diverse species coexisting in the ocean world. This represents a sort of horizontal unity. A vertical unity between animals and humans is complementary, and leaves us on top, just like parents are in positions of control within a family. The specific values associated with the family paradigm and promoted during the show include trust, affection, mutual respect, and a high degree of individuation. What is not allowed is a visible show of force, aggression, competition, or violence of any kind. However, the lines of command remain clear even though unarticulated or covered over by assertions of mutuality and equality. Humans must control the nature that they display.

In the invisible assertion of this control and in the aesthetic design of the shows, the shifting boundary of the natural and the cultural is continually redrawn to accommodate the conflicts inherent in such a familial paradigm. The result is a complex overlay of discourses of the natural and the cultural that are at times mutually exclusive, but always mutually dependent. The mode of display aestheticizes the animals in two senses, producing the natural both as a cultural artifact and as the complementary concept to the cultural. In the first sense the careful design of movement in terms of symmetry, gracefulness, and geometrical patterns aestheticizes the whales as "art," the most historically recent sense of the term "culture" as Raymond Williams noted (1980, 1983). But at the same time, the earliest etymological sense of culture as "to cultivate" is also invoked.

At Sea World that which is cultivated is "nature" itself, designed through the choreography of the whales into pleasing shapes and forms just as the plants are designed into formal gardens. One key difference is that plants exceeding the bounds of cultivation do not pose a deadly risk to the gardener. With the whales, the other sense of nature as a set of primal forces that organize life and must be either obeyed or contained (depending on the particular philosophical juncture) is ever-present. Wayward whales on a rampage are uncontainable; such forces of "nature" unleashed against humans would be terrorizing.

Unlike the early Roman spectacles of human/animal combat, which depended upon an antagonistic construction of the human and natural worlds, such aggression (or the spectacle of its containment that structures the traditional lion tamer act, for instance) is deemed neither morally supportable nor economically viable. Instead, this constant threat is submerged, providing the shadowy base from which the utopian unity is constructed, and indeed, the basis which makes such unity utopian in design. The utopian aspects of the family vision depend on a simultaneous assertion and denial of the distinction between the natural world and the cultural world, between animals (standing for that which is "wild," "natural," and "free") and humans. If this division is not asserted, it cannot then be overcome in the discourse of transcendent familialism. In the transcendent moments of the shows (like the whale ballet, audience interactions, and the most spectacular acrobatic moves), these wild animals are fully incorporated into the family of humans. The culturalization of nature is complete. The product is a controllable sublime, and it is best marketed through the figure of a giant, smiling, dangerous but cuddly killer whale—Shamu. The huge scale of the park represents both the enormous capital investment in this animal and in her display, as well as the profitability of such ideological work.

Celebrating *Shamu*

"I Love Shamu" reads the bumper sticker I bought as a souvenir. Note that it doesn't say: "I Love Sea World." Shamu, like a movie star or any well-known public figure, is a character, a personality, a locus onto which we can project our fantasies. She is the only animal at the park to be so personified, blazoned on T-shirts and mugs, reproduced in cuddly form in Shamu stuffed whales (available in gradated sizes and costs, from three inches to four feet long). Although other animals at Sea World have names, only Shamu has been accorded emblematic status. Her picture dominates every piece of literature coming out of sea world, the sleek black and white torpedo form lending itself well to abstraction and to graphic reproducibility on everything from brochures to shopping bags to corporate stationery.

Of course, like "Lassie" who was played by a series of collies, Shamu isn't really just one whale. There is a "Shamu" at each of the four Sea Worlds.[2] Her presence is not only necessary, it is constitutive of Sea World sites. Physical form, personality, and physical presence are all condensed and compacted into the idea of "Shamu." The whale's physical body and its actions come to represent the complex of feelings, ideas, and fantasy that represent the ideological subtext of the park.

Constructing *"Shamu"*

Star personas are built over a period of time, and through numerous representations. Shamu has emerged as a megastar over the past quarter century, and through several modes of representation. These include the live shows; the entire rhetorical, ideological, and material structure of the Sea World parks which support and depend upon the Shamu signifier, and the numerous representations of Shamu in newspaper articles, publicity reports, and souvenir memorabilia. In this section, I want to concentrate specifically on the construction of the centerpiece of Sea World San Diego, the Shamu show in Shamu Stadium.[3]

As the signature show, this peformance is clearly the most important event of our day at Sea World. To miss it would be unthinkable. The importance is underlined by the size of the stadium, the largest of the three marine mammal show areas (the others are for the whale and dolphin show, and the sea lion and otter show, in order of decreasing stadium size). This outdoor stadium, built in 1987 at a cost of fifteen million dollars, is the largest marine mammal complex ever constructed, as a fact sheet from the public relations office notes. It holds five million gallons of gorgeous blue water, and seats 6,500 people per show. There are several shows a day during the peak season, so up to 20,000 people a day can watch Shamu perform.

The pools are stunning. Acres of azure water spread out in a huge horseshoe shape, with the viewing stands rising in a semicircle around the front curve of the pool. Only a chest-high clear acrylic wall separates this raised lake of water from us, and we can see right through the sides, the water brimming full to the top. The lip of the wall curves in slightly at the top giving the sense that the liquid is barely contained, a slice of the sea somehow magically misplaced on land. And this is travel poster water—sparkling clean, clear, aquamarine, and tipped with white from splashing waves as the orcas jump and breach.

From the whales' point of view, the stadium stands are always visible, blocking the horizon and the world outside of Sea World. We look "in" at the whales during the show, visually placing them and ourselves within the "world" of Sea World, our backs to the ocean and to San Diego. Like other theme parks, Sea World operates by creating a world within the larger world, a world that is nearly completely self-referential, a world literally looking in on itself and masking the boundaries which separate it from outside. Physically set off from San Diego by acres of parking, a long winding access route, and an undeveloped belt of greenery, Sea World is similarly psychologically set apart. As audience we join the whales in a shared nautical world for the duration of the show. This overarching theme of a nautical world is reinforced throughout the park in every show, exhibit, and even in most of the restaurants and the vast majority of souvenirs. We are joined with Shamu in a world apart from our modern urban one, but simultaneously, Shamu moves into our world. She crosses the watery divide literally at special moments in the choreography of the show, and metaphorically by surrounding us with her images and simulacra which abound in the park.

The Show: "Baby Shamu Celebration"

Each performance of the Shamu show is slightly different, depending on which whales and which trainers are working, and what their performance abilities are. But there is a strict formula that is followed for each show, so that the proportion of information, aestheticization, athleticism, and celebration remains the same. The formula consists of six segments done in the following order: (1) introduction, (2) meet an audience member, (3) whale ballet, (4) educational segment, (5) training segment, and (6) high energy finale. I'll sketch each briefly, but want to concentrate on the whale ballet since it is the heart of the show.

The performance begins as music from the pre-show tape fades down with the words "to touch eternity," cuing us to the utopian dimensions that will be brought out throughout the show. Soaring electronic notes fill the stadium, and two huge black and white orcas enter the performance pool, zooming around its circumference. A male voice-over announces: "Perhaps the most awe-inspiring, mighty, and majestic of all animals, the killer whale. . . . " On cue the two animals arc into the air, revealing the massive dimensions of their bodies, up to twenty-five feet long. Four trainers (male and female), clad in glistening red and black wet suits, run onto the cement platform and wave to us as the orcas exit through metal underwater gates. Immediately two more orcas enter. Their breaching leaps into the air elicit loud "oohs" and "aahhs" from the crowd of several thousand. The triumphal sounds of brass underscore the introduction "masters of their world: Shamu and Namu!"

At the end of this opening segment the music softens and the trainers introduce themselves, the facility, and the whales, including Baby Shamu, for whom the current show "Baby Shamu Celebration" is named. "This is the world's largest and most advanced breeding facility for whales. Baby Shamu is a milestone in marine science, the sixth calf born at a Sea World." Eight-and-a-half feet long and weighing in at 800 pounds, the baby will be present throughout the show, at times actively mimicking the behavior of the older whales, at times flubbing a routine. At less than a year old, her training so far is minimal, but her presence in this show is key. She not only points out the gigantic size of the adult whales (which can reach weights of five tons and above) through her (relatively) diminutive counterpoint, but provides the "evidence" of family that the rhetorical structure of the show is built around.

The refrain of the Shamu song spells it out: "We all share the sky, we all breathe the air. Water means life, and we're part of the sea. Just like a family." The family of man is here expanded to include sea animals, especially those who are mammals like us. Although the song says "we're part of the sea," the reality at Sea World is that the sea is represented by the giant holding tanks. This simulacrum is literally imported into our world while the "real" sea rests just outside the park, unnoticed. Still, in a secular, ecological cosmology, we are linked to these marine mammals who bear, nurse, and raise young as we do, and breathe the same air as we do, their warm-blooded bodies covered with a smooth sensitive skin just like ours. The "babiness" of Baby Shamu evokes these physical similarities as well as the social similarity ("family-ness," kinship system) between "us" and "them."

Press releases attest to the popularity of Baby Shamu: "A few times every week letters arrive at Sea World without an address . . . just the words 'Baby Shamu' scrawled carefully in crayon across the front of an envelope. There is little question the young whale has captured the hearts of children and adults nearly everywhere. Her daily appearances at Shamu Stadium are marked with eager and enthusiastic cheers. Baby Shamu's progress has been watched with affection since a summer afternoon in 1991 when 1,500 people witnessed her birth at Sea World." In this publicity statement we are positioned as doting parents and our own kids become trans-species penpals.

During the next part of the show someone from the audience, as our surrogate, meets one of the whales. Today it is an adult, but children often participate in this segment as well. "Mike" from Ventura, California, is led out to a small platform at the side of the pool. One of the trainers tells him what actions to perform to instruct the whale. Today Nikina is performing this segment, and as Mike marches in place, she mimics his walk with a series of tail flaps. Next, Mike meets Nikina "up close." Blindly following instructions, he throws both hands up, and jumps back surprised when, responding to his command, she squirts a stream of water toward him. Laughter ripples through the audience, the hapless human having brought the joke upon himself. Nikina here is the straightman. Finally, Mike rewards Nikina by giving her sensitive skin a rubdown. As he leaves, she ducks her head underwater and waves her upright tail "goodbye."

Audience participation segments like this are included in every whale show and in the dolphin show as well. They function to establish an individual link between each audience member and the individual whales via the identificatory mechanism of the participant. The trainers also function as avenues of identification, especially during the segments of the show when they are in the water with the animals. But their specialty training, their professionalism, sets them apart from us in a way that the audience volunteer is not.

By this point in the show, we have been exposed to the size and power of the whales in a preliminary way, seeing them jump and swim at top speed around the tank. We have seen them individuated and personified to some extent through their naming, and their interaction with specific trainers on a one-to-one basis. We have seen them respond to visual instructions from hand or body signals, even when these are given by a stranger, i.e., the audience member standing in for us. And we have seen evidence of their safety and trustworthiness when even a child can touch them on the nose, giving a rubdown reward. We have also associated the physical mass and power of the whales with humor, laughter, playfulness, and affection.

Next comes the most spectacular and most moving part of the show, dubbed by the producers as the "whale ballet." It represents the fantasy of cross-species melding, of the vanishing of the natural/cultural divide. An elite artistic form, ballet, is used as a frame for our perceptions in the segment, and facilitates the absorption of the human into the whale's aqueous world. The whale is aestheticized while the human is transformed into a marine mammal partner, equally at home in the water as the whale. The natural is culturalized while the cultural is naturalized, and this transformative process is framed as art.

The "Whale Ballet"

The opening lines of this segment's narration emphasize the close relationship between the trainers and the whales. "We create an environment for killer whales comfortable enough for them to breed." Breeding is a measure of success in recreating enough of the natural habitat for them to successfully participate in this most "natural" of natural (family linked) behaviors. "We care for them twenty-four hours a day. We have a special relationship with them. . . . *We enter their world. . . .* " With this, one of the trainers slips into the water with the whales for the first time. Throughout this segment, trainers and whales will work together in human-whale duets.

Like a ship's bowsprit, the trainer arches out in front of the orca, his feet balanced on the nose of the animal, arms extended to the side and behind him, like a nautical Nike. In this position, the whale pushes him all around the tank of water at a rapid speed, white foam flying from the trainer's chest. A second orca enters, and another trainer joins him. He stands on the whale's back, riding him like a surf board, and then does a series of jumps off his back as the whale keeps moving apace beside him. The whale swims to the side for a big reward of fish, then they start again. This time the trainer pushes on the whale's face, wrapping his legs around the huge neck and balancing each foot on a flipper. Together they rocket up out of the water, the trainer clinging like a gnat onto the giant body. They change to a barrel roll, the trainer walking rapidly in place as the swimming orca rotates under him like a living log in a lumberjack contest. Then the orca rolls to his side, one flipper in the air, and swims slowly around the pool in a display of control and precision of position like a ballet adagio. The trainer rides like a statue atop. Lots of fish are consumed as a reward.

In this ballet so far, we have already seen adagio partnering, movement in unison, supported display (like a ballerina who holds an impossible arabesque while pivoted by her partner), and lifts. Importantly, this centerpiece of the show is the only extended period when the trainers and whales are in the water together. The whole structure of the choreography and the theatrical aspects of its staging in terms of timing, visual focus, and sound score underline the concept of loving partners that frames the traditional heterosexual ballet duet. Just as a ballerina subtly cues her partner when she is ready to balance, the trainers give the cues to the whales through a series of nearly invisible presses, taps, and foot signals which are integrated into the continuous flow of the movement. There is no voice-over during the whale ballet, no verbal interference to distract from the visual display of man (or woman) and animal dancing together. The emphasis on sound rather than words helps construct the abstract qualities of this segment, heightening the artistic discourse. The literalness of movement mimicry is gone, replaced by expressive partnering. The synthesized music is melodious, sustained, full of soaring violin sounds, emotive.

Throughout the show, the musical score is very important, but nowhere more so than during the ballet. During this segment there are twenty-four behaviors that are possible, such as "anthropomorphic," "athletic," "slow activity," and "relational," and each has its own special sound. The taped score for the ballet has eight different tracks, and each can be activated separately or in combination with any other. The calliope sound can be used for "fun" endeavors, for example. Within a prespecified range of ballet behaviors, the trainer decides exactly which actions to do that day and in what order, and the sound technician follows. This sense of improvisatory flow comes through during this segment of the show as the whale and trainer come together and separate and unite again in a series of actions of varying length and energy.

The necessity for structured improvisation is not just to keep the trainers interested. If the whales become accustomed to pre-set routines which are then interrupted for any reason, they become belligerent. Also, the chaining of behaviors seems to have a limit of about four or five different actions. These require intermittent reinforcement, with a big reward at the end. The whales will not perform more extensive phrases of movement without reinforcement. These technical and psychological requirements thus have a direct effect on the aesthetic structure of the show.

To the uninitiated viewer, the physical cues given during the whale ballet section are nearly invisible. They meld seamlessly with the relational flow of action and interaction between the whale and trainer. For instance, the trainer may seem to be hugging the whale in an affectionate or playful embrace, but that hug is really a press on the whale's rostrum, which is the cue for "dive down." Similarly, a slap on the water, which may read as a playful splash at the whale, is a signal for the whale to return to the central staging area.

The invisibility of these cues enhances the playful relational discourse that the ballet segment (and its very name) presents. This is quite different from the more mechanical demonstration of broad cues that is highlighted in the "meet the audience" part of the show. There the emphasis is on the directive, instrumental aspects of communication. Here it is on the interspecies relationship. In this way the whale ballet sits at the heart of the show, representing an idealized relational state between human and animal, a relationship of equals where the lines of power and their communication are washed over in the continuous aqueous flow of partnering. We never see a command given, rather the coordinated behaviors seem to be the result of intuitive mutual understanding and desire.

Without warning, Shamu bursts out of the water in the center of the pool

Shamu soars during the "Baby Shamu Celebration" show at Sea World, San Diego, in 1992. Photo: Jane Desmond.

and rockets towards the sky. Sitting perched atop her nose is a trainer. The whale shoots straight up, thrusting its body nearly thirty feet in the air, the whole mass nearly exposed before the peak of the jump is reached. The trainer jumps off and the whale lands with a huge splash. We are stunned at the acrobatic quality of this feat, its grand scale of body mass displacement, its suddenness, and the remarkable coordination between animal and trainer that it represents, for the maneuver requires that the animal go straight up, not slanting or the human would fall off before the peak of the jump. It is the suspended moment at the top of the jump that emphasizes its height, thrust, and momentum as the whale hovers weightless for a split second before gravity accelerates the crashing return to the water.

"Get your cameras ready!" shouts the trainer through his portable microphone. And we do, for this moment is the highlight of the show, its punctum, the condensation of power, beauty, control, interspecies communication, and acrobatic aestheticization that the whole show is built upon. This time we are ready when the "spyhop" is repeated. Positioned right in the center of the pool, Shamu explodes twenty feet into the air once again, and this time it is even more spectacular, because the trainer, who had to dive thirty-six feet to the bottom of the pool with Shamu to prepare for the leap, is now *standing upright*, balanced firmly but delicately on the tip of Shamu's nose, the only point of contact being the soles of his feet. Arms outstretched above him, the trainer doesn't just fall off this time, rather he dives off in a graceful arc, pushing off from the nose at the height of the jump, extending it, using it as a springboard for another movement in the ballet. Together, the trainer and Shamu enter the water to thunderous applause.

The first time this action is performed, the element of surprise is fully utilized. Both the invisibility of the cue and of the preparation create a sort of visual silence which heightens the explosion of the action. When it is repeated, the voice-over directs us to the pyrotechnical aspects of the feat. Our attention is drawn to the unison dive thirty feet below the water, before unnoticed, now marked as preparation, and our cameras are positioned to catch the leap at its height. This way we can enjoy the drama and aestheticism of the suspended leap the first time through, and its technical achievement during the repetition. Like a musical encore at a concert, the repeat reactivates the emotional charge that attended the first viewing, but (like an instant video replay) also technologizes it. We are distanced from the act in two senses. First, by the attention to the technology of the action ("How'd they do that!!??"), and secondly through the camera eye. In taking the picture we produce a static representation of the consummation of the event, the peak of the jump as the visual, aesthetic, and dramatic apex of the ballet, indeed of the whole show. We also memorialize our experience for later consumption as a souvenir. We are already remembering the event (as the second leap is a reenactment of the first) as we reproduce it.

The spyhop is the punctum of the show, the moment most prominently featured in the publicity brochure. Our applause indicates a combination of awe at the physical force, mass, and power so dramatically displayed, and approval for the human control that has harnessed it into an aesthetic display. Most of all it acknowledges the visualization of the meeting of the cultural and natural spheres (their division based on essential bodily difference) and the interactive bridging of that divide. Animal and human are one in this moment. Underneath it all, we celebrate diversity, mutual love, understanding, and trust through the union of opposites, here elevated to the status of art. In this liberal, enlightenment philosophy of universalism lies the paradox of power and domination invisibly applied to achieve the fiction of a world living together in familial harmony modeled on a Christian notion of Edenic paradise.

The educational segment of the show comes next. It highlights notions of respect for the animals' intelligence and of an exchange between equals. Although it would appear that the people are educating the whales, in fact one of the trainers tells us that it is we humans who have the most to learn. This educational segment focuses on new research on the whales' ability to interpret audio systems of communication. While the trainers stand silent and still, sliding sounds like a loud penny-whistle slice through the air. Two orcas swim to the center of the pool and jump together on cue. More sounds, and the whales "vocalize" loudly, in "aarh, aarh" sounds. This is mildly interesting, but the tones are boring after the music of the first half, and the pacing is slow. Taking away the interaction of the trainers with the whales also lowers the emotional impact. It makes clear how much the power of this show depends upon and features the one-on-one interaction of each whale with each trainer.

The music cranks up again for the ending portion of the show. The synthesized sounds are bright and bouncy. "It's playtime!" announces one of the trainers. "We're going to get you guys wet!" Requisite education accomplished, it's time for fun again. One of the orcas swims slowly around the edge of the tank wall by the seats. He is turned sideways and makes huge splashes with his tail, purposely pushing the water over the rim and into the stands. Screams of delight move in a wave around the stadium as those seated in the "wet zone" get what they came for. The wildly spraying water marks the physical power of the whale as well as his ability to interact directly with us, the drenching bridging temporarily his wet world with our dry one.

The finale begins. Like a Fourth of July fireworks explosion, they have saved the biggest booms for last. Now the three adult whales swim in unison for the first time during the show. Side by side like a chorus line they jump and land. Then IN UNISON, they jet into the air and execute perfect back flips, rotating one and a half times in the air like giant pinwheels whipping around. It is stunning to see that much strength and speed harnessed into precision, and also to see the full bodies spinning in the air, suspended tonnage in motion with the perfect control of gymnasts. Once again we applaud not only the feat itself, but the invisible control and domination that is able to cultivate such "wildness."

Then two whales swim toward us once again, this time continuing right out onto the platform jutting into the stands. They slide out and arch their heads and tails upward, like a giant smile in black and white, taking a "bow." They have been on the border before, but this time they cross directly into our world, a place where their physical survival is ultimately impossible. The move represents a denaturalization of the natural. The music slows down, becomes more mellow, dreamy. "Here she is—Shamu," says the trainer. She picks up a small child who is waiting and places him on the broad back of the whale. "New life is the most precious thing that there is," she reminds us, at once invoking a linkage of Baby Shamu and this child, all children, and the ecological cosmology that opened the program with the Baby Shamu soft-rock song which plays again now.

The audience claps its approval, the child is removed, and the whales can finally relax their bowing pose and slip backwards into the water. "We build the future" sings the Shamu song as the crowd slowly begins to exit.

Borders and Border Crossings

These ending moments encapsulate two of the predominant themes of the show: the mobility of or crossing of the species (hence, nature/culture) border, and the emphasis on family as the paradigm for all relationships. The final image of the child safely astride a gigantic bowing Shamu on dry land symbolizes both of these themes at once.

Vision, animals and humans all cross this divide throughout the show. The architecture of the Shamu stadium with its tall, clear, acrylic wall surrounding the edge of the pool (like a thrust stage) allows us to see the animals not only as they glide on the surface of the water, but also for a portion of the way under the water as well, a position we could never take viewing these animals in the wild. We also have privileged views during the spectacular leaping segments where an unimpeded view of the complete whale body is afforded at the moment of suspension in the air. Rarely do leaps in the wild exhibit such verticality. The completely visible whale body is also reproduced in the stuffed Shamu souvenirs which allow us to hold the whale in our arms, or gaze at the whole body as it might be seen out of the water. Both such simulacra and the show's leaping choreography extract the whale body from its natural watery environment.

There are other moments too during the show that emphasize these border crossings. Signals and perceptions can cross the border as they do in the audience-participation segments. People can cross the border by slipping into the sea, as the trainers do during the whale ballet. And whales can move into our environment as they do metaphorically during the "get the audience wet" segment, which confuses the boundary between the land and sea, wet and dry, and as they do literally in the slide-out maneuver at the end of the show. In all of these ways both the trainers as our surrogates and the whales become hybrids, mediating between the two worlds of water and air. In these border crossings the amphitheater is constructed as a frontier of exchange.

But ultimately this is not a true exchange, although it is presented as such. The whales are literally imported into our world, placed in a huge (beautiful) container, completely out-of-situ. The conditions of possibility for the show are that wild whales are captured, transported thousands of miles, confined, trained, and forced to work for a living. They make money for the Busch corporation. To mask this reality, they are presented as willing partners, as part of our family, as equals from whom we have so much to learn, and their display is coded as art, as education, and as conservation.

Ironically, this emphasis on conservation has backfired. Some animal-rights groups protest against the capture, training, and display of animals for profit. Theme parks like Sea World have had to turn increasingly to captive breeding programs so they can reproduce the raw material, i.e., whale bodies, from which their shows are built. Sea World's emphasis on breeding as evidence of the park's sufficient reproduction of the natural habitat and of animal happiness covers over the monetary necessity of such breeding programs. The celebration of Baby Shamu in this show and of the other calves born at Sea World since 1985 presents breeding as a natural family discourse, or a discourse of naturalized familiarity, and structures the show around this baldest of financial necessities while completely hiding them.

This discourse of the familial is also carried out in the park's exhibits through animal/human analogues. A new promotion during the summer of 1991, for instance, had kids use special maps to travel the park in search of all sorts of animal babies. The unstated assumption of course is that the animal kids and human kids have much in common. This notion of similarity is emphasized throughout the show at the bodily level as well when mimicry posits animal body parts as parallel to human ones as flippers wave and whale "faces" nod "yes" or "no."

The oscillation between physical and social similarity and difference, between "the natural" and "the cultural," can be traced right through the formulaic construction of the show. First we see the whales without verbal framing (with the exception of the "all friends in the sea" overture). Our visual perception of them, their size and speed, is emphasized. Then these behemoths are named, personalized (in the introduction phase). Next, they are shown as obedient and safe, and possibly humorous (meet the audience). They are idealized as equal partners during the ballet, where their size and strength is harnessed into a duet with the trainer, culminating in the spyhop in which they perform together the most spectacular move of the day. The education segment emphasizes their cognitive abilities rather than their expressive or physical ones. But size and power take over again in playtime, where the whales splash us with gigantic sweeps of their tails. And finally, acrobatic ability, trainability, cooperativeness, precision, and body mass are all emphasized together in the huge unison somersaults at the end.

The "body-ness" of the orcas is at times highlighted, at times downplayed, but ultimately underwritten by the intelligence and trainability of these animals. Our consumption of radical bodily difference, of nature, played upon in the opening speed runs without narration and highlighted throughout the show, is ultimately a safe consumption tempered by similarity. Orca bodies may be different, indeed must be spectacularly different as their feats demonstrate. But they still hunger for hugs as well as fish, for fun as well as food, and for companionship rather than freedom, or so it seems.

Like huge pets, they embody the difference between human and other, between wild and tame, and between danger and safety. But ultimately, their mental capacity, their mammalness, and their tractability render their difference easily consumable. The orca "mind" makes the orca "body" safe and knowable. The mind/body binary that underlies the culture/nature division is overcome again in this framing as the whales are "given" the attributes of reason and emotion. The most powerful predator in the ocean is simultaneously the cute and cuddly Shamu. The simultaneity is what sells so well at Sea World because it demonstrates the drawing of borders and at the same time their transcendence. This simultaneity operates through a discourse of natural behaviors and their extensions.

Training, "Naturalism," and Performance

Everything we see in Sea World is presented as "extensions of natural behaviors." "Natural" can refer to behaviors occurring in a natural vs. manmade setting, i.e., in "the wild," or it can refer to behaviors occurring in manmade settings but without instruction from humans, such as leaping, swimming, etc. Some of these behaviors are marked as "bad," like fighting, and are prohibited. Other behaviors are deemed "good," but in need of tight control, like breeding.

The term "natural" can also refer to behaviors that are directly contradictory to "instinct," but which still involve an action that occurs in the wild. For example, the tiger can be taught to leap ("natural") through a burning ring of fire (the "natural" instinct would be to move away from fire, not toward it). Using this range of conceptual flexibility which emerges in the show's discourse of "natural" behavior, it is difficult to think of anything that an animal could possibly do that could *not* in some sense be considered, and presented as, "natural." If Shamu could be taught to speak English, that would be "unnatural," since orcas don't speak English to each other, but even that could be framed as an extension of a "natural" vocalizing ability, an "inborn" ability that would be necessary for any sound making at all.

Ideological and Physical "Extensions"

The "natural" is both cultivated and disciplined in the training process. Animals are trained through operant conditioning. Behaviors are isolated, shaped, and linked into sequences with rewards, tactile or food, given for proper performance. Punishment for incorrect behavior or for noncooperation is the withdrawal of the trainer from the interaction. Shaping, as the word implies, involves the gradual refinement of a behavior, like the development of height in a jump, or making the pathway of a body rotation in the air perfectly round. For example, teaching an animal to jump over a rope suspended above the water requires first training him to swim over, not under the rope in the pool, then over the rope floating on the water's surface, then over the rope as it is gradually raised higher and higher into the air.

The notion of "extending" natural behaviors codes several processes in constructing a performative style. First, it involves performing something on cue, and for the purpose of receiving a reward rather than for any other instrumental purpose, such as hunting. Second, it takes generic activities, like breaching, or flipping in the air, and makes them more aesthetically pleasing and links them in series. This can be done by codifying a specific pathway through space (a perfect circle in the air rather than an oblong one or a repeating sequence of leaps done in a certain part of the pool), and/or by setting a timing that is in unison with the movements of another animal or with a human. Space and time are regulated and codified with respect to the animal's body, so that his usage of space and time is not only "correct" but predictable. Movement is disciplined as is nature.

It is not so much an *extension* of behaviors that is going on, as it is the choreographing of complex and precisely articulated movements which the animal is *capable* of performing because the biomechanics of the movements are within the realm of possibility for that body. The movements of a highly skilled ballet dancer, for example, could be said to be based on the "natural" movements of the human skeleton—walking, jumping, and extending limbs. But few people would consider the 180-degree leg-split of a Balanchine dancer's arabesque to be "natural." Take the fact that the whale rolls over in the water. This movement then becomes choreographed so that its meaning is entirely rewritten. The rolling is repeated in a sequence in the whale ballet with the trainer riding the spiraling whale around the pool like a spinning log. The biomechanics of the rolling may be roughly the same, although repeated and performed at a regularized pace. But the meaning of the roll in the Shamu stadium with a trainer running on top bears no relation to the meaning of the roll in the open sea. "Extension" is as much a reference to the ideological content of the act as it is to any notion of "natural behavior."

Within the industry, however, the rationale for new behaviors is presented not only in terms of developing new performance material for the shows, but in terms of satisfying the whales' psychological needs for stimulation. The familial discourse emerges here too, with the whales positioned as children and the trainers as parents or teachers. The familial discourse of playful stimulation smooths over the fact that ultimately the "extending" of behaviors is done to benefit Sea World both by providing new performance material and by cultivating whale tractability.

Another way the meaning of "natural" actions is extended or reframed is through anthropomorphism and mimicry choreographed into the show. Although the amount of this material has declined as the shows have moved away from narrative/character entertainment shows to the educational format, it still figures prominently. The most obvious examples are those behaviors named after human actions, like moving a flipper back and forth upon the command to "wave good-bye." Like the caption of a photograph, these linguistic frames anchor the meaning of the visual display and guide the audience's reading of the polysemic movements and postures.

The animals also mimic human behavior in a follow-the-leader style. For example, during the ballet duet, the trainer might duck down shooting her legs straight up in the air and wiggle them. The whale will imitate by diving and waving his or her tail back and forth above the water too. In these mimicking actions the analogous nature of the bodies is highlighted, head, "arms," middle body, and "legs" can function in similar ways.

But ultimately the meaning of the action ("look, he's waving to us") and its fascination for the audience depends on the dissimilarity between the animal and ourselves. Part of the pleasure of this type of activity is, I think, generated precisely by the acknowledgment of the difference between the whales and ourselves, in terms of body construction and dimension, and the simultaneous closing of that gap momentarily through the performance of anthropomorphically framed behaviors. The whale doesn't have legs, but uses its tail as if it were "legs." The "as if" of the construction is the linkage that gives the action its specific intelligibility within the show and also produces the specific pleasure, the laugh of recognition for example, that the action evokes. The "as if-ness" also puts the actions into a performance category that separates "natural" behavior from its "extensions," in this case an extension of the meaning of the behavior.

This is balanced by an opposing emphasis on the whales' non-anthropomorphic behaviors, the spectacular display of their strength and mass which far exceeds our own, yet which appears harnessed to our uses and pleasures via their apparently willing cooperation as performers. However, there have been telling moments of disruption in this willing partner discourse. A few years ago a couple of bad accidents tarnished Sea World's image, endangered its staff and animals, and caused a whole revamping of training style and attitude at Sea World.

In 1988, serious injuries resulted when whales turned on two trainers,[4] and in the following year two performing whales collided and began fighting. One bled to death after the fight.[5] The incidents received not only regional but national press attention. These two incidents blow the willing partner and familial discourses wide open and reveal the hierarchies of force and domination that such ideologies naturalize. The whales exhibited "natural behavior" in fighting after an accidental collision which bore hallmarks of aggression. However, this was forbidden natural behavior as it threatened the economic stability of the park. The investment in the two animals was huge, as was their earning power. The aggression also contravened the familial discourse of peaceful unity among animals and particularly between humans and animals.

When directed against the trainer this aggression exposed the crux of the shows: absolute obedience to trainer commands, presented as pleasurable for the whales. This loss of control was obscene, as obscene as the site of pristine azure pools polluted with blood. The problematic of the natural as that which is ultimately subordinate to human cultural practice became insupportable in those moments. They threatened the stability of the Sea World conglomerate built on such a problematic, and required a great deal of "spin control" from the public relations office which isolated these events as accidents not symptoms.

Ultimately this subtext of danger, of nature as "wildness," is necessary to the successful functioning of Sea World, but it must not be allowed to erupt into visibility. Awesome strength, power, and mass must be coded as acrobatic ability, kinesthetic thrills, or grace and beauty, then tempered with "intelligence," and redirected through a relational discourse of emotional attachment to the trainers. The choreography constructs and presents this ideological process, staging bodily actions as symbolic practice. Combining awe, potential terror, beauty, grace, and power with massive scale, Sea World packages a controllable sublime.

The commodification of these intangibles, their production, performance, and marketing, depends on their attatchment to the physical specificity of the killer whale and its personification. It also demands a complex and continual reworking of the dialogic relationship between concepts of the natural and the cultural, at times opposed, at times united in transcendent familial unity, but always dependent on each other for their articulation. The complementary culturalization of the natural and the naturalization of the cultural is what Sea World sells so well.

Notes

My thanks to Bryan Wolf, Jennifer Wicke, and Virginia Dominguez for their comments on an earlier draft of this paper.

1. Chris Kraul, "Anheuser-Busch to Buy Sea Worlds for $1.1 Billion," *Los Angeles Times*, v. 108, sec. I (Friday, Sept. 29, 1989), p. 1. col. 1.

2. So noted in the Busch brochure describing all of their entertainment parks.

3. My viewing of the "Baby Shamu Celebration" show took place in March 1992.

4. See article by Robert Reinhold, "At Sea World, Stress Tests Whale and Man," in the *New York Times*, v. 137 (Monday, April 4, 1988), p. 13 (N), A 19 (L), col. 3; and in the *Los Angeles Times*, v. 107, sec. I (Saturday, June 11, 1988), p. 24, col. 1, "Trainers Allowed Back in Water with Sea World's Killer Whales" (no author given).

5. See H. G. Reza, "Whales Collide, 1 is Fatally Injured in Sea World Tank," *Los Angeles Times*, v. 108, sec. I (Tuesday, August 22, 1989), p. 3, col. 1, and the follow-up article by H. G. Reza and Greg Johnson, "Killer Whale Bled to Death after Breaking Jaw in Fight," *Los Angeles Times*, v. 108, sec. I (Wednesday, August 23, 1989), p. 3, col. 4. This was considered of national, not merely regional, importance, and the *New York Times* also covered the story. See "Perform-

ing Whale Dies in Collision with Another," *New York Times*, v. 138 (Wednesday, August 23, 1989), A 12 (L), col. 3.

Works Cited

Kraul, Chris. "Anheuser-Busch to Buy Sea Worlds for $1.1 billion." *Los Angeles Times*, v. 108, sec. I, Friday, Sept., 29,1989: p. 1, col. 1.

Nelson, Andrew J. "Going Wild." *American Demographics* 12.2 (Feb. 1990): 34–39.

Williams, Raymond. "Ideas of Nature." *Problems in Materialism and Culture*. London: Verso, 1980. 67–85.

———. *Keywords: A Vocabulary of Culture and Society, Revised Edition*. New York: Oxford University Press, 1983. 87–93.

13

"If We Could Talk with the Animals"

Elephants and Musical Performance during the French Revolution

Michael E. McClellan

O N 29 MAY 1798 a small orchestra of prominent musicians performed a concert of operatic excerpts and popular songs in the Jardin des Plantes in Paris. The performance of music at a park was not in itself an unusual event. Pleasure gardens such as the Tivoli and the Jardin Marboeuf frequently offered musical concerts to the general public. Parisians who relaxed in the botanical garden that day, however, remained unaware of this performance.[1] Scientists from the neighboring Muséum National d'Histoire Naturelle had arranged this concert for a select audience of two, Hans and Marguerite, a pair of Indian elephants living in the Jardin's recently established menagerie.[2] The museum naturalists carefully monitored the elephants' reactions to the musical program, detailing each response in order to measure precisely the power of music over these animals. As an indication of the serious nature of their endeavor, the organizers employed some of the finest performers in Paris for the concert. Indeed, almost all the performers held a position either with the Paris Opéra, the city's most prestigious musical theater, or with the Conservatoire National de Musique, a state-sponsored school of musical education.[3] The expertise of these musicians assured Hans and Marguerite an entertainment with an unusually high level of performance.

The presence of Indian elephants at the Jardin des Plantes represented something of a novelty for Parisian society, even though they were not the first pachyderms to find their way to Paris.[4] The French government had acquired the elephants in 1795 from a private menagerie in Holland shortly after the French army had overrun the Netherlands.[5] The two animals roused the curiosity of the public as soon as they arrived in Paris on 24 March 1798.[6] For the remainder of their lives Marguerite and Hans remained a highly popular attraction of the Jardin des Plantes.[7]

The first printed reports of this concert were written by the librarian of the Muséum National d'Histoire Naturelle, Georges Toscan, and appeared in the *Décade philosophique, littéraire et politique*, a journal that appealed to a general readership with wide-ranging interests in the arts and sciences.[8] In these articles Toscan not only recorded the details of the concert, but he also revealed certain cultural assumptions that informed the performance. He and fellow naturalists from the Muséum, who managed both the Jardin and its menagerie, showed a tendency to anthropomorphize the animals in their charge. They interpreted the reactions of animals to music and other stimuli in terms of human emotion.[9] Indeed, the supposed similarities between human sensibilities and those of animals formed a basic premise on which the zoo had been founded in 1794. In an essay that demanded the establishment of a national zoological garden in Paris, Bernardin de Saint-Pierre, naturalist and author of the enormously popular *Paul et Virginie*, repeatedly pointed to parallels between the passions of animals and humans.[10] The study of the habits of animals, Bernardin argued, advanced scientific knowledge of human passions and instincts.[11] The results of this musical experiment with elephants, accordingly, offered insight into the human response to music as well. The reaction of the elephants would differ in degree and subtlety but not in kind from that of men and women.

In addition to the presumed equivalence of human emotions and those of animals, the scientists also assumed that music in and of itself would produce a measurable influence on the emotions of animals.[12] Although vocal music was performed for the elephants, Toscan did not expect the animals to understand the text. On the contrary, the music's meaning was conveyed to the elephants through melody, harmony, rhythm, color, and other purely musical parameters.[13] By arranging this concert, the organizers stripped away the semantic content of the songs and revealed the expressive significance of music.

The concert demonstrated to Toscan and his fellow scientists that music possessed the power to address the emotional faculties without intellectual mediation. This expectation reflected a progressive aesthetic stance on the part of the concert organizers, and it related the concert to an on-going debate over the nature of music that had emerged in the second half of the eighteenth century around the writings of Michel Chabanon. Both a performer and composer, Chabanon argued in an essay published in 1785 that music did not imitate Nature and differed significantly from both the visual and verbal arts in its direct appeal to the senses.[14] Painting, sculpture, and literature, according to Chabanon, depended on imitative description in order to succeed as art. Composers, by way of contrast, simply organized sound in a fashion immediately pleasing to the senses.[15] With this argument, Chabanon broke with the established aesthetic tradition in France, which relied heavily on Jean-Jacques Rousseau's theories and employed a linguistic model to explain music as an imitative art.[16] This essay pointed the way toward an independent musical aesthetic that would ultimately privilege instrumental over vocal music.

Although Chabanon influenced contemporary French music theorists during the Revolutionary period, none of those authors developed his proposal for an autonomous aesthetic of music any further. Throughout the 1790s vocal music retained its central position within most discussions of music aesthetics.[17] Nevertheless, the idea that music possessed the unique power to express emotional content independently of an accompanying text survived and grew more widespread over the ensuing decades. The Concert for the Elephants provided suitably scientific evidence for this assertion.[18]

At about the same time, a number of essayists and critics argued that the future of the French Republic depended upon the state's control of its cultural products.[19] These authors maintained that the arts offered the Republic the most effective means to educate its citizens in revolutionary ideals and mores.[20] To this end the politician Jean-Baptiste Leclerc forcefully advanced the cause of governmental support for the performing arts, especially music. Leclerc, a member of the legislative Council of Five Hundred, based his aesthetic outlook on a tacit link between the political sphere and the world of music:

> Music perfected or corrupted nations in accordance with that which governments proposed for their liberty or debasement. Under the rule of tyrants [music] enervated and made them slaves. Under moral authority, it permeated the soul and strengthened the people's love of virtue and patriotism.[21]

This essay presented the history of music as a history of the political use and abuse of music. The enormous emotional power that Leclerc attributed to music provided any government that intelligently manipulated the rhetorical force of musical performance with invaluable influence over listeners. Most governments, in Leclerc's opinion, used music in order to amuse their subjects and thereby distract them from seeking political power. What had freed France from the servile mentality that afflicted the subjects of other European states was the introduction and enthusiastic reception of Gluck's operas at the end of the eighteenth century:

> It is not at all a mistake to say that the revolution carried out by Gluck in music ought to have made the government tremble. His vigorous harmonies reawakened the generosity of the French; their souls were renewed and were made to see an energy which was acclaimed soon after. The throne was shaken.[22]

Leclerc theorized a surprisingly direct connection between music and the political sphere; he argued that a musical event, Gluck's operatic debut in Paris, triggered the events of 1789. Although Leclerc did not claim that music itself caused the Revolution, his essay described music, potentially, as an agent of political power. To realize revolutionary political change, he asserted, the force inherent within music had to be controlled by the revolutionaries.[23]

Music, in Leclerc's view, did not merely reflect the spirit of the day, but rather it informed that spirit. Musical styles and forms influenced the political disposition of listeners. Therefore, all successful political ideologies entailed a coherent system of aesthetics; revolutionary music would therefore create revolutionary audiences. In contrast, if the state ignored the necessity of this aesthetic support, music and other arts could develop in a manner that would be detrimental to the future of the Republic.[24]

Toscan expressed a similar view of music in his second article on the concert experiment. There he characterized music as an instrument by which human society could "civilize itself and regulate its mores."[25] In this context the Concert for the Elephants represented an initial effort to determine the strength of this musical force and to measure its effects systematically. Toscan's observations would advance knowledge of music's power and possibly suggest the means to control it. In this way, the naturalists from the Muséum participated in the government's attempt to manipulate public opinion through music and to develop an appropriately republican culture.[26] Let us now examine the concert and the reaction of the elephants to this singular event in closer detail.

The concert organizers left nothing to chance; even the physical arrangement of the concert reflected their scientific intent. For the concert's first half, the orchestra performed in a gallery above the elephants' compound, concealed from view.[27] A trap door in this gallery, when opened, allowed the sound of the instruments to penetrate the enclosure. During the second part of the performance the orchestra moved down to the same level as the elephants and within the view of the animals. By hiding the musicians for the first part, the organizers hoped to keep the elephants' attention squarely focused on the music.[28]

The works performed at the concert are listed in the program notes below. The pieces were all well known and could easily have appeared on any contemporary concert program. What distinguished the programming for this event was the substantial amount of repetition. The musicians played "Ça ira," a popular patriotic tune, no less than four times, and the sentimental romance "O ma tendre musette" received two performances. Whenever the orchestra repeated a piece, however, they played it in a different key or with different instruments. By doing so, the organizers intended to explore the effect of various tonal centers and instrumental timbres on the elephants, using a simple melody as the constant.

At the sounds of the string trio that opened the concert, the elephants stopped eating and, in Toscan's opinion, appeared disconcerted. Immediately locating the source of the music, the pair approached the trap door, but after a cursory examination of the opening, they moved back toward their keeper, who patted and comforted them. Slowly they became accustomed to the sounds of the strings and appeared to relax. Their level of comfort increased gradually, and when the orchestra performed a dance from *Iphigénie en Tauride*, the pair began to pace in time to Gluck's rhythms.

To this point both animals had exhibited the same reactions, but as the orchestra played the first arrangement of "O ma tendre musette," Toscan recorded different responses for each animal. The male seemed more circumspect and in control of his actions, while the female became, in Toscan's view, inflamed with passion, stroking Hans's back and rump with her trunk in an overtly sexual manner. During the next piece, "Ça ira," Marguerite became increasingly agitated: "her caresses were more demonstrative, her gestures more provocative. She would quickly withdraw from the male and [then] return, backing into him, giving him light kicks from behind in order to let him know she was there."[29]

The first sound of a human voice, in a slow duet from the opera *Dardanus*, immediately calmed Marguerite, and both she and Hans responded in a more seemly manner to the next three pieces. Only when the orchestra repeated "Ça ira" for a third time and in the original key, D major, did Marguerite exhibit additional signs of sexual arousal. During this song, the music so overwhelmed Marguerite that she "fell down on her rump, threw her forelegs in the air and leaned back against the bars of the compound [. . .] emitting cries of desire."[30] Marguerite did not maintain this position for long. According to Toscan, "one moment later, as if she was ashamed to have behaved so in front of so many observers, she got up and resumed her pacing."[31]

During the second half of the concert, a Haydn symphony, which Toscan described as "très brillante," failed to impress either elephant. Perhaps exhausted from her exertion during the first part of the concert, Marguerite remained unmoved throughout the next piece as well. In contrast, the sound of a clarinet performing a melody from Dalayrac's *Nina* captured the attention of Hans, as did the repetition of "O ma tendre musette" using the same instrument. In Toscan's words, "[Hans] listened, attentive and immobile. Nevertheless, the fires of love crept within his veins, betrayed by external signs."[32] These external signs of love did not last long and Hans's musically induced sexual arousal appeared much less extreme than Marguerite's. At the end of the clarinet solo, he lost interest and took no further notice of the remaining music on the program.

Although the concert ended without further incident, Toscan also reported an event that occurred much later in his discussions of the elephant's reaction to the music. One evening, several days after the concert, the elephants' keeper awakened to unusual noises coming from the animals' compound. He got up and quietly made his way to the enclosure. Once there he observed "the female [elephant] lying on the ground, turned over on her back. The male stood over her, his legs spread, self-absorbed in his own movement."[33] The keeper had never witnessed the elephants behave in this fashion prior to the concert. Toscan argued that the sexual behavior of Hans and Marguerite resulted from the restlessness and excitement released by the music of the concert. To study the connection between music and the sexual behavior more thoroughly, Toscan felt that similar experiments ought to be performed. In order to enhance the effect of music during the next concert, however, he suggested that the performance should take place on a warm clear evening, under moonlight, with good food for the elephants, and all observers safely concealed from Hans and Marguerite's view. He also proposed that the two animals be separated for a period of time prior to this concert in order to intensify their ardor.[34] Toscan's fascination with the sexual behavior of the elephants emerged from a long-standing debate over this matter that involved the well-known biologist Georges Louis Leclerc de Buffon.[35] Through his observations, Toscan revealed his conviction that music caused, or at least elicited, a physiological response in animals, but the response, like the implausible missionary position Toscan ascribes to copulating elephants, represents an all too human norm.

Following his description of the elephant's reaction to music, Toscan surveyed the rest of the animal kingdom for signs of innate musicality. He created a hierarchy in which those animals that exhibited appropriate responses to music received privileged positions. Birds, not surprisingly, earned high marks, as did domesticated mammals such as horses, oxen, and dogs, since these creatures answered to musical calls or signals. Because fish live submerged in water, Toscan felt they possessed a limited capacity for experiencing music. Nonetheless, the naturalist did not dispute Michel Chabanon's evidence that certain fish exhibited a primitive curiosity when confronted with a music stimulus. Toscan even quoted a section of *De La Musique considérée en elle-même* in which Chabanon insisted that some fish he kept in a vase would ascend to the water's surface and "listen" to him whenever he played his violin.[36] Similarly, Toscan repeated a story found in the memoirs of the composer Grétry which demonstrated the power of music over insects. There Grétry described a spider that would descend from its web above the musician's harpsichord whenever the composer sat down to perform.[37] For Toscan this was proof positive of the spider's exceptional musical taste. In this context, music such as that composed by Grétry existed independently of cultural constraints. Indeed, the stylistic conventions and traditions that informed French music could now be seen as consistent with a natural order that was intuited by certain animals. What distinguished human beings was both the ability to control other species through musical means and the capacity to overcome the emotionally persuasive power of music by means of superior intellect.

Of course even within the same species, distinctions could be made based on different reactions to musical stimulus. The example of Hans and Marguerite responding independently to the same musical performance was not lost on Toscan's contemporaries. Indeed, an early nineteenth-century dictionary of medicine cited the Concert for the Elephants as an example of music's influence over the emotions of animals and less "civilized" humans.[38] The dictionary's entry on music argued that Europeans, although not free from music's coercive power, were less susceptible to its force than were "the most barbaric or the least civilized peoples" (*peuples les plus barbares ou les moins civilisés*).[39] The example used to support this statement described a group of "barbaric and ferocious" (*barbare et féroce*) Caribbean natives who, not unlike Grétry's spider, were pacified at the sound of a harpsichord.[40]

Using musical responses to distinguish civilized Europeans from primitive Caribbean natives was only one application of the cultural assumptions reinforced by this concert. The sexual response Toscan had observed in the elephants, in conjunction with the separate reactions of Marguerite and Hans inevitably brought the question of gender to the fore. In Toscan's account of the concert, Marguerite was the first to respond sexually to the performance, seemingly incapable of withstanding the emotional force of the music. His observation established a norm for the elephants that reflected and ultimately reinforced a very human stereotype of feminine behavior. Toscan and his contemporaries did not limit the characteristic inability to control one's passions to female elephants, rather they assumed this weakness to be a universal feminine condition.

A reference to the Concert for the Elephants in yet another scientific study amply demonstrated this point. In 1844, M. A. Raciborski published a monograph on female puberty that included a chapter in which he considered the effect of musical stimulation on young girls.[41] The author repeated the story of the concert experiment in support of his argument that females were more susceptible to the power of music than males. Raciborski maintained that extended exposure to music could lead to the premature development of a young girl's ovaries and early menstruation.[42] Further acceleration of this physical development occurred if a girl's musical education was accompanied by trips to the theater, where visual stimulants intensified the effect of music.[43] Raciborski employed the concert to endorse the limits placed on a young girl's musical education. As a result, culturally determined restrictions for females acquired scientific credentials designed to make these gendered constraints appear natural.

From these subsequent references to the experiment, it is evident that the ramifications of the Concert for the Elephants extended far beyond the world of music aesthetics. Nevertheless, it was a change in that world of music aesthetics that made the concert possible. If music was to be used in support of certain cultural conventions, then music needed to be defined as free from cultural constraint. For the organizers of the concert, music possessed an independent power that directly influenced animal passions. Composers and performers could channel this influence and control its application, but the music itself enjoyed an independent existence that knew no barriers, apparently not even species-related barriers. Consequently, music acquired a universality that enabled Toscan to make his observations and interpret them as if the performance was merely the vehicle for some immutable substance that affected all animals alike. In the nineteenth century this aesthetic resulted in the privileging of music as an elemental force that produced scientifically measurable effects while retaining an elusive and somewhat mystical identity.[44]

In retrospect, the Concert for the Elephants may seem, by our standards, a frivolous attempt to confirm cultural assumptions on the part of Toscan and his fellow naturalists. Nevertheless, the serious nature of their goal justified the unusual means. No society, past or present, has ever considered the process of defining and reinforcing cultural norms, whatever form it assumed, to be absurd. Too much is at risk.[45]

This leaves one final question regarding the Concert for the Elephants: Exactly who performed for whom? Certainly, the musicians offered a performance to Hans and Marguerite, but the two elephants also performed. Indeed, in this instance the audience stole the show. For it was through the elephants that Toscan was able to reify the cultural values of his own society and give those values a basis in nature, proven scientifically.

Notes

1. Pleasure gardens became something of a fad in Paris during the Directory. Their displays of fireworks, musical concerts, and dances seriously rivaled theaters as a popular form of entertainment. Claude Ruggièri, *Précis historique sur les fêtes, les spectacles et les réjouissances publiques* (Paris: Chez l'auteur, 1830), 84–107; and Marvin Carlson, *The Theatre of the French Revolution* (Ithaca: Cornell University Press, 1966), 266–67.

2. On 10 June 1793 the National Convention issued a decree that reorganized the Jardin Royal des Plantes Médicinales under the new name of Muséum d'Histoire Naturelle. Both the botanical garden and the zoo were under the direction of the Muséum. Gustave Loisel, "Histoire de la ménagerie du Muséum." *Revue scientifique* 49 (1911), 262–63. See also Paul-Antoine Cap, *Le Muséum d'histoire naturelle* (Paris: L. Curmer, 1854).

3. Performers known to have participated in the concert were Martin-Joseph Adrien (singer), François Devienne (flute), Frédéric Duvernoy (horn), Louis-Joseph Guichard (singer), Xavier Lefèvre (clarinet), and Gaspard Veillard (bassoon).

4. Animal acts were a popular form of entertainment prior to the French Revolution, and elephants were occasionally included in these performances. Robert Isherwood, *Farce and Fantasy: Popular Entertainment in Eighteenth-Century Paris* (New York: Oxford University Press, 1986), 44.

5. As the result of its victories, France annexed the Austrian Netherlands (October 1795) and oversaw the transformation of the United Provinces of the Netherlands into the Batavian Republic (May 1795). A description of the elephants and the Dutch zoo is found in André Thouïn, *Voyage dans la Belgique, la Hollande, et l'Italie*, ed. C. J. Trouvé (Paris: Chez l'éditeur,

1841), 1:255–60. Thouïn was a botanist at the Muséum who traveled extensively in order to acquire animals and plants for the Jardin. Thouïn's acquisition of the elephants for the menagerie is recorded in *Procès-verbaux du Comité d'instruction publique de la Convention nationale*, ed. M. J. Guillaume (Paris: Imprimerie nationale, 1891–1907), 6:12. The transport of the elephants from the Netherlands to Paris is described in Gustave Loisel, *Histoire des ménageries de l'antiquité à nos jours* (Paris: Octave Doin, 1912), 2:36–49. See also Jean-Pierre-Louis-Laurent Houel, *Histoire naturelle des deux éléphans mâle et femelle du Muséum de Paris, venus de Hollande en France en l'an VI* (Paris: Chez l'auteur, 1803).

6. The arrival of Hans and Marguerite was noted in the official newspaper of the Directory, *Rédacteur*, 12 germinal an VI (1 April 1798), 2–3.

7. The extent of the elephants' popularity in Paris at this time is indicated by the success of a *vaudeville* that included roles for two elephants most likely modeled on Hans and Marguerite. The play, entitled *Le Concert aux éléphans*, was the product of the collaborative team of Piis, Barré, Radet, and Desfontaines. It premiered at the Théâtre du Vaudeville on 4 July 1799. Reviews of the *vaudeville* are found in *Affiches, annonces et avis divers*, 18 messidor an VII (6 July 1799), 5565–66; and *Magazin encyclopédique* 26 (1799), 237–39. Although it received enthusiastic reviews, the play was never published, and no manuscript copy is known to survive. Despite the suggestive title, it is impossible to determine from reviews alone whether the authors made any explicit references to the concert organized at the Jardin des Plantes. The brief synopsis that is provided in the *Affiches*, however, does describe a scene in which the elephants spray water all over a zookeeper who had substituted water for the animals' daily ration of wine. This scene may have been based on an incident involving Marguerite that is mentioned in Georges Toscan, *L'Ami de la nature, ou choix d'observations sur divers objets de la nature et de l'art* (Paris: Imprimerie de Crapelet, an VIII [1799/1800]), 298–99. Marguerite apparently sprayed water all over a zookeeper who kept visitors from feeding the elephants.

8. [Georges Toscan], "Du pouvoir de la musique sur les animaux, et du concert donné aux éléphans," *Décade philosophique, littéraire et politique*, 20 thermidor an VI (7 August 1798), 257–64; and 30 thermidor an VI (17 August 1798), 321–29. I have adopted the names Hans and Marguerite for the elephants since those are the names that appear in Toscan's articles. Other sources from the late eighteenth and early nineteenth centuries referred to the female as Parkie or Perkai, while the male's name was occasionally spelled as Hanz or Heinz.

9. Toscan, "Du pouvoir," 323–29. There was a long European tradition of attributing human characteristics to animals and to elephants in particular. See Donald Lach, "Asian Elephants in Renaissance Europe," *Journal of Asian History* 1 (1967), 133–76.

10. Jacques-Henri Bernardin de Saint-Pierre, "Mémoire sur la nécessité de joindre une ménagerie au Jardin des plantes de Paris," in *Oeuvres complètes de Jacques-Henri Bernardin de Saint-Pierre*, ed. L. Aimé-Martin (Paris: Méquignon-Marvis, 1818), 12:631–70. Bernardin briefly served as director of the Jardin des Plantes from July 1792 to June 1793. He wrote the "Mémoire" during that time.

11. Ibid., 12:661–66. The menagerie was established in 1794. The first animals it acquired were from the royal zoo at Versailles. Loisel, *Histoire des ménageries* 2:158–64.

12. Toscan and a number of his associates at the Museum of Natural History had a strong interest in music. In his memoirs Louis-Marie Larévellière de Lépeaux described *soirées musicales* at which Georges Toscan, André Thouïn, and other scientists from the Museum performed alongside musicians such as the prominent composer Etienne-Nicolas Méhul. Larévellière de Lépeaux, one of France's five Executive Directors from 1795 to 1799, was a trained botanist and frequently socialized with the Museum's naturalists. Louis-Marie Larévellière de Lépeaux, *Mémoires de Larévellière-Lépeaux, membre du Directoire exécutif de la République francaise et de l'Institut national* (Paris: E. Plon, 1895), 2:412–13.

13. Prior to the concert for the elephants, Toscan had published an essay on Jean-Baptiste Lemoyne's opera *Nephté* in which he discussed the rhetorical power of harmony. [Georges Toscan], *De La Musique et de Nephté* (Paris: Imprimerie de Monsieur, 1790).

14. Michel-Paul-Gui de Chabanon, *De La Musique considérée en elle-même et dans ses rapports avec la parole, les langues, la poésie et le théâtre* (Paris: Pissot, 1785; reprint, Geneva: Slatkine, 1969). Toscan was aware of Chabanon's essay and included a brief quote from it in his own essay. [Toscan], "Du pouvoir," 326.

15. Chabanon, *De La Musique*, 62–68.

16. Ora Frishberg Saloman, "Chabanon and Chastellux on Music and Language, 1764–1773," *International Review of the Aesthetics and Sociology of Music* 20 (1989), 109–20; Saloman, "French Revolutionary Perspectives on Chabanon's *De La Musique* of 1785," in *Music and the French Revolution*, ed. Malcolm Boyd (New York: Cambridge University Press, 1992), 211–20; and William Weber, "Learned and General Musical Taste in Eighteenth-Century France," *Past and Present* 89 (1980), 58–85.

17. Saloman, "French Revolutionary Perspectives," 219–20.

18. James H. Johnson, "The French Musical Experience from the Old Regime to Romanticism" (Ph.D. dissertation: University of Chicago, 1988), 231–36, offers a clear discussion of the scientific context in which the Concert for the Elephants was performed. The scientists' choice of elephants as the animals most suitable for this musical experiment may have been influenced by Chabanon who described pachyderms as highly sensitive to music. Chabanon, *De La Musique*, 41.

19. *Esprit des Journaux*, fructidor an IX (August/September 1800), 201–204; Marie-Jacques-Armand Boieldieu, *De L'Influence de la chaire, du théâtre et du barreau dans la société civile* (Paris: Demonville, an XII [1803/1804]), 46–128; Jean-Marie Mauduit-Larive, *Réflexions sur l'art théâtral* (Paris: Rondonneau, an IX [1800/1801]); Gabriel-Raimond Olivier, *L'Esprit d'Orphée, ou l'influence respective de la musique de la morale et de la législation* (Paris: Pougens, 1798–1804), 3:47–53.

20. Olivier, *L'Esprit d'Orphée* 1:36–69; James A. Leith, *The Idea of Art as Propaganda in France, 1750–1799: A Study in the History of Ideas* (Toronto: University of Toronto Press, 1965), 98–124; Leith, "Music as an Ideological Weapon in the French Revolution," *Canadian Historical Association Annual Report* (1966), 126–40; Noel Parker, *Portrayals of Revolution: Images, Debates and Patterns of Thought on the French Revolution* (Carbondale: Southern Illinois University Press, 1990), 68–69.

21. "La musique perfectionna, ou corrompit les nations, selon que les gouvernans se proposèrent leur liberté ou leur asservissement. Sous le règne des tyrans, elle énerva et fit des esclaves; sous l'empire des moeurs, elle trempa l'âme et fortifia l'amour des vertus et de la patrie." Jean-Baptiste Leclerc, *Essai sur la propagation de la musique en France sa conservation, et ses rapports avec le gouvernement* (Paris: Imprimerie nationale, prairial an IV [1796]), 7. For contemporary reviews of Leclerc's essay see *Censeur des journaux*, no. 298, 19 June 1796, 2–3; no. 299, 19 June 1796, 1–2; *Esprit des journaux*, November 1796, 96–104; *Magazin encyclopédique* 8 (1796): 363–65.

22. "Ce n'est point une erreur de dire que la révolution opérée par Gluck dans la musique aurait dû faire trembler le gouvernement: ses accords vigoureux réveillèrent la générosité française; les âmes se retrempèrent, et firent voir une énergie qui éclata bientôt après: le trone fut ébraulé." Leclerc, *Essai*, p. 10.

23. I explore this theme further in my dissertation: "Politics, Performance, and the Public Sphere: Revolution, the Théâtre Feydeau, and French Musical Culture, 1789–1801" (Ph.D. dissertation, University of North Carolina at Chapel Hill, 1994).

24. For this reason, Leclerc ardently supported the development of national schools of

music and demanded government involvement in the organization and regulation of cultural institutions, such as the lyric theaters, which influenced the relationship of a society to its government. Isolating the practice of music within state-sponsored conservatories and government-monitored theaters safeguarded musical aesthetics from dangerous, counterrevolutionary influences. Through these institutional means music could be controlled and used appropriately in support of the Republic. Leclerc, *Essai*, 14–24. For a discussion of Leclerc's model of music education and his influence on the Conservatoire see Cynthia M. Gessele, "The Conservatoire de Musique and National Music Education in France, 1795–1801," in *Music and the French Revolution*, ed. Malcolm Boyd (Cambridge, Eng.: Cambridge University Press, 1992), 201–204.

25. "[L]es hommes s'en sont servis [. . .] pour se civiliser eux-mêmes et régler leurs propres moeurs." Toscan, "Du pouvoir," 323. Following this assertion, Toscan quotes a brief portion of Leclerc's essay in which that author described the use of music to control and direct the actions of farm animals.

26. Johnson, "French Musical Experience," 226–29.

27. The elephants' compound consisted of an outdoor park connected to a two-room enclosure. A sliding door, which the elephants themselves could open with their trunks, separated the rooms. The concert took place inside the enclosure. The compound is described in Toscan, *L'Ami de la nature*, 294–97.

28. Toscan, "Du pouvoir," 258.

29. "[S]es caresses étaient plus démonstratives, ses agaceries plus piquantes; souvent elle s'éloignait rapidement du mâle, et revenant à reculons, elle lui détachait lestement des coups de pied de derrière, pour l'avertir qu'elle était là." Ibid., 260–61.

30. "[E]lle tombait à terre sur sa croupe, jetant en l'air les pieds de devant, et s'appuyant du dos contre les barreaux de la loge [. . .] jeter les cris du désir." Ibid., 262.

31. "[L]'instant d'aprés, comme si elle eût été honteuse d'une action qui avait tant de témoins, elle se relevait et reprenait sa course cadencée." Ibid.

32. "Attentif, immobile, il écoutait. Cependant les feux de l'amour s'insinuaient dans ses veines; trahi par des signes extérieurs." Ibid., 321–22.

33. "[L]a femelle renversée à terre et couchée tout de son long sur le dos: le mâle debout au-dessus d'elle, les jambes écartées et se donnant du mouvement." Ibid., 328.

34. Ibid., 329.

35. Toscan intended this description of elephants copulating in the missionary position as proof of a hypothesis that Buffon had advanced in an early volume of his celebrated study of natural history. Buffon himself had later retracted this assertion in a supplement to the same study. See Georges Buffon et al., *Histoire naturelle, générale et particulière* (Paris: Imprimerie royale, 1750–1804), 11:61–63; and Suppl. 3:295–96. A few years after the concert, two other naturalists associated with the Museum of Natural History in Paris corrected Toscan. See Bernard Lacépède and Georges Cuvier, "L'Eléphant des Indes," in *La Ménagerie du Muséum national d'histoire naturelle, ou les animaux vivants peints d'après nature* (Paris: Miger, 1801), 2:6. These two naturalists confidently stated that "cet accouplement [des éléphants] est entièrement semblable à celui du cheval et dure à-peu-près autant de temps."

36. [Toscan], "Du pouvoir," 326. See also Chabanon, *De La Musique*, 43.

37. [Toscan], "Du pouvoir," 327. See also André-Ernest-Modeste Grétry, *Mémoires, ou essais sur la musique* (Paris: Imprimerie de la République, 1797), 2:100–101.

38. François Fournier de Pescay, "Musique," *Dictionaire [sic] des sciences médicales, par une société de médecins et de chirurgiens* (Paris: C. L. F. Panckoucke, 1812–22), 35:42–80.

39. Ibid., 35:58.

40. Ibid., 35:59.

41. M. A. Raciborski, *De la Puberté et de l'âge critique chez la femme* (Paris: J.-B. Baillière, 1844), 46–53. I am indebted to Sharon Marcus of Johns Hopkins University for bringing this study to my attention.

42. Ibid., 50.

43. Ibid., 50–51.

44. This concept of music is evident in the work of Saint-Simon and his disciples. See Ralph P. Locke, *Music, Musicians, and the Saint-Simonians* (Chicago: University of Chicago Press, 1986), 53–67.

45. The twentieth century has produced its own version of the Concert for the Elephants. In 1940 Tommy Dorsey's band performed a variety of swing selections for animals at the Philadelphia Zoo. The chimpanzees showed a particular fondness for the ballad, "I'm Getting Sentimental Over You." Charles Panati, *Panati's Parade of Fads, Follies and Manias: The Origins of Our Most Cherished Obsessions* (New York: Harper, 1991), 222.

PROGRAM FOR LE CONCERT POUR LES ELEPHANTS

Jardin des Plantes, Paris
10 Prairial, An VI (29 May 1798)

Part I:

1. "Trio de petits airs variés," B major, string trio.
2. C. W. Gluck, "Air de danse" from *Iphigénie en Tauride* (Act I), B minor, orchestra.
3. P.-A. Monsigny, "O ma tendre musette," C minor, bassoon solo.
4. "Ça ira," D major, orchestra.
5. A. Sacchini, "Mânes plaintifs," *Dardanus* (Duet, Act I), B-flat major, orchestra with bass soloists.
6. "Ça ira," F major, orchestra.
7. J.-J. Rousseau, Overture from *Le devin du village*, orchestra.*
8. Henri IV (attributed to), "Charmante Gabrielle."**
9. "Ça ira," D major, orchestra with vocal soloists.

Part II:

1. F. J. Haydn, *Symphony*, C major [possibly No. 82, or No. 90], orchestra.
2. N.-M. Dalayrac, "Air de musette" from *Nina*, clarinet.*
3. P.-A. Monsigny, "O ma tendre musette," D minor, clarinet.
4. "Ça ira," cor-de-chasse.*

*The key of the piece is not identified.
**The key of the piece and the instrumentation are not identified.

Notes on Contributors

Philip Brett, Professor of Music and Chair of the Music Department at the University of California, Riverside, is general editor of *The Byrd Edition*, co-editor of *Queering the Pitch*, and compiler of the Cambridge Opera Handbook on Benjamin Britten's *Peter Grimes*.

Ellen Brinks, a doctoral candidate at Princeton University, is finishing a dissertation on gender and sexuality in the gothic narratives of English and German Romanticism. She lives just up the street from the apartment featured in *Single White Female*.

Jennifer DeVere Brody teaches African American literature, Victorian theater, and cultural studies in the English Department at the University of California, Riverside. She has published essays on race and sexuality in the work of Nella Larsen and Ann Petry.

Sue-Ellen Case, Professor of English at the University of California, Riverside, is the author of *Feminism and Theatre* and editor of *The Divided Home-Land: Contemporary German Women's Plays* and *Performing Feminisms: Feminist Critical Theory and Theatre*. She is the co-editor of *The Performance of Power: Theatrical Discourse and Politics*.

Brian Currid is a graduate student in the Department of Music at the University of Chicago. His main research interests include queer(ing) popular musics and the place of subcultures in the history of mass-mediated musical practice.

Michael Davidson is Professor of Literature at the University of California, San Diego. He is the author of *The San Francisco Renaissance: Poetics and Community at the Mid-Century* and seven books of poetry, including *The Landing of Rochambeau* and *Post Hoc*.

Jane C. Desmond is Associate Professor of American Studies and Women's Studies at the University of Iowa. Her work on the cultural politics of the body stems from an earlier career as a professional modern dancer and choreographer. She is the author of *Physical Evidence: Bodies in Contemporary American Performance*.

Susan Leigh Foster, choreographer, dancer, and writer, is Professor and Chair of the Department of Dance at the University of California, Riverside. Her book, *Reading Dancing: Bodies and Subjects in Contemporary American Dance*, received the De La Torre Bueno prize for scholarship on dance.

Cynthia J. Fuchs teaches in the English Department and Film and Media Studies Program at George Mason University, and is working on a manuscript entitled *Identity Effects*, about contemporary U.S. media culture, race, and sexualities.

Ellis Hanson teaches lesbian and gay studies at Sarah Lawrence College.

Michael E. McClellan is a Ph.D. candidate at the University of North Carolina at Chapel Hill. He is currently completing his dissertation, "Politics, Performance, and the Public Sphere: Revolution, the Théâtre Feydeau, and French Musical Culture, 1789–1801."

Ricardo L. Ortiz is Assistant Professor of English at San Jose State University. He has published work on *Tom Jones* and contemporary gay and Latino writers. He is at work on a book on John Rechy and Reinaldo Arenas.

Richard Rambuss teaches English and Gay Studies at Tulane University. His work includes *Spenser's Secret Career* and essays on early modern literature and culture. He is completing *Closet Devotions*, a book on devotion, sexuality, and the erotic Christ.

Parama Roy is Assistant Professor of English at the University of California, Riverside. She has published essays on Victorian fiction and colonial discourse, and the essay appearing in this volume is drawn from her forthcoming book, *Indian Traffic*.

Marta E. Savigliano is Assistant Professor of Dance at the University of California, Riverside. She is the author of *Tango and the Political Economy of Passion*.

Katrin Sieg is Assistant Professor in the German Department at Indiana University. She is the author of *Exiles, Eccentrics, Activists: Women in Contemporary German Theater*, as well as articles on the performance of gender and sexuality in the context of German and U.S. cultures.

Index

ACT UP, 38, 41, 72, 83
activism, 38, 41, 72, 79, 83, 154. *See also* feminists; politics
Adam, Helen, 198
Adams, Robert Martin, 76, 80
adulthood, 15. *See also* family
African American(s): as hyphenated culture, 151–52, 156; Michael Jackson as, 13–27; phone sex use by, 36; relation of with house music, 165–92. *See also* blackness; minorities
After Lorca, 211
aggression, 220–21, 234–35. *See also* violence
AIDS, 34, 38–43, 51, 83, 169
AIDS and Its Metaphors, 34
Akerman, Chantal, 82
Almodóvar, Pedro, 45, 78
Altman, Robert, 38
ambivalence, 180–82
animal tourism, 217–35
animals: music for, 237–44; sexual arousal in, 240–42
anonymity, in phone sex, 36
anthropomorphism, 217–35, 237–44
apathy: as aspect of passion, 141, 143. *See also* emotion
appearance. *See* look
Approaches to Teaching the Metaphysical Poets, 81
Armstrong, Nancy, 204
Ashbery, John, 209
asocials: homosexuals as, 102, 103; women prisoners as, 95, 96
assimilation: compared to difference, 149–50, 158; as evil, 209–10; resistance of queer community to, 165–92
audience: at Sea World, 218, 224, 229; of Michael Jackson, 17, 18, 20, 21, 25, 26; for pornography, 61; spectator as, 179–92; of Swami Vivekenanda, 119. *See also* performance; spectator
auto-exoticism, 131, 132

Baker, Houston, Jr., 166
Baker, Nicholson, 36, 44
Ballad of Ravensbrück, The, 95–106

Barthes, Roland, 42, 67, 177–78
Bataille, Georges, 135
Baudrillard, Jean, 135, 136
becoming: as aspect of identity, 4, 9–10, 41. *See also* identity; self; transformation
Bernhard, Sandra, 184–85, 186
Between Men, 200
Bhabha, Homi, 16, 158, 178, 180
The Birds, 45
bisexuality, 38
Black Mountain poets, 195–214
blackness, 18, 188; compared to whiteness, 23, 151; and mysticism, 135; in relation to house music, 165–92. *See also* African Americans; minorities
blends, 154; cross-species, 224
Bly, Robert, 199
Bodies that Matter, 20–21
body: black, 187, 189, 190; of Christ, 73–77; desire for, 72; female, 6; male, 214; Michael Jackson's problems with, 13–27; permeability of, 76–78, 85; in religious poetry, 71–86; as site of identity, 17, 72, 221, 231; transcendence of, 115–16
bonding, homosocial, 197–214
Boorstin, Daniel J., 151–52, 155
boundary: between nature and culture, 217, 220; between self and other, 154, 158; lack of in male body, 76–77; of Michael Jackson's sexuality, 22, 25; violation of, 4, 46. *See also* difference; other
bourgeois society: acceptance of tango by, 131; gender concerns in, 113, 124–25; homosocial bonding in, 201–14; legitimization of passion in, 120, 131, 138; relation of to queer society, 173. *See also* class; professional class
breeding: as family discourse, 231. *See also* family; heterosexuality
Brideshead Revisited, 201
Buchmann, Erika, 96
Buddhism, 115
Bury, Chris, 16
butch-femme, 8, 105, 157
butch male, 72, 83, 84

Butler, Judith, 18, 20–21, 66, 135, 165, 166, 213
Bynum, Caroline Walker, 74

Campbell, Naomi, 25–26
capitalism: effect of on sexual identity, 6–7, 10–11, 22, 49, 101; culture of, 130, 197, 203; sponsorship of nature by, 218–19. *See also* dominant culture; materialism
Case, Sue-Ellen, 157, 165
castration, 9, 39, 82. *See also* penis
celibacy, 115, 120
Cement, 97
Chesley, Robert, 43
child: Michael Jackson as, 19, 21. *See also* family; father; mother
child abuse: effect of on gay men, 36, 50; involving Michael Jackson, 13, 14, 18, 24
Christ: erotic representation of, 71–86; union with body of, 115. *See also* religion
Christianity, 71–86, 115, 117, 121, 137, 228
City of Night, 64
civil rights, 52. *See also* minorities
Cixous, Hélène, 51
class: in Britain, 201; effect of on sexual identity, 4–11, 14, 93–95, 201; as identity, 100, 133, 151. *See also* bourgeois society; professional class
Clément, Catherine, 51
closet: epistemology of, 17, 71–72; prayer, 74, 79, 84, 86; sexual, 3–12, 24–27, 53, 103
clothing: as sexual identity, 3–11, 116, 118; of Vivekenanda, 118. *See also* drag
Cochran, Johnnie L., 14
Cocteau, Jean, 42, 45
Coiro, Ann Baynes, 81
collectivity: private property in, 10–11; as sexual norm, 97, 103
Colo, Papo, 154
colon: as homosexual reference point, 60–61. *See also* genitals; scatology
colonial subject, 142, 159; Michael Jackson as, 16. *See also* capitalism; race
colonialism, 142, 143, 204; intellectual, 130, 131, 132; and nationalism, 112–26. *See also* politics; state
commodity: community as, 169; desire for, 9–10; identity as, 6–7; Michael Jackson as, 16, 18; nature as, 217–18; sexuality as, 34–35, 166. *See also* private property; repetition
communism, 48, 95
community: at Sea World, 219; as commodity, 169; identity within, 165–92

consumption: of passion, 131; spectator as, 180; universalization in, 9
control. *See* power
The Conversation, 45, 48–49
copy. *See* imitation
Crashaw, Richard, 72–86
Creeley, Robert, 202
Crimp, Douglas, 40–41
Culkin, Macaulay, 23
cultural pluralism, 149–59
culture: of capitalism, 130; clothing in, 4–5; Michael Jackson affecting, 13, 17, 21–22; nature differentiated from, 217, 220–21; nature of, 220–29; of pornography, 67; race as, 153; state control of, 239. *See also* dominant culture; multiculturalism

Dancer from the Dance, 173, 185
Dawson, Fielding, 205, 206
death: of God and Man, 139; relation of telephone to, 41, 42, 43. *See also* murder
Derrida, Jacques, 59, 67, 135
desire: affecting sexual identity, 8, 11, 41, 45, 49, 211; attrition of, 120; heterosexual, 115, 116; homosexual, 51, 72, 79, 82, 205, 212; illicit, 182; in love, 97; mimetic, 7–11; postmodern, 130–31, 137, 138; in religious poetry, 72–86; transformed by telephone, 34, 46, 51
deviants. *See* queers
devotion, Christian, 71–86
Dial M for Murder, 45, 46
Dick, Philip K., 35, 36
difference: compared to assimilation, 149–50, 157–58; feminized space of, 205; racial and sexual, 7, 9, 16, 19–20, 135. *See also* other
discipleship, 112, 116, 120, 122, 123, 205
Discourse, 134–35
disembodied voice: of black diva, 186–87; as instrument of terror, 46–49, 96; in relation to sexuality, 34, 36, 38, 39, 43–45, 52–55, 189; of tango, 133. *See also* speech; voice
displacement: in Hindu males, 122; of "miraculist fusion," 198; telephone as device for, 38, 39, 49
dissidence: in relation to queerness, 93–106. *See also* activism; politics
Divine, 78
Doane, Mary Ann, 119
Dobie, Kathy, 155–56
dominant culture: homosexuality within, 94, 98; literary movements in, 197. *See also* capitalism; materialism

Donne, John, 72, 74, 79, 80, 81, 82
double: role of in identity, 3–12. *See also* imitation
Douglas, Jerry, 71, 83
drag, 22, 84, 166, 176. *See also* clothing
drug addiction, 35
Dunn, Joe, 211
Dyer, Richard, 82

e-mail, 36
economic factors: affecting sexuality, 6–7, 10, 34–35, 96, 103; in guru-disciple relationship, 116. *See also* capitalism; commodity
ego-identity: inherited nature of, 4; model for, 56, 120; sexual foundation of, 8. *See also* identity; self
Ehrenreich, Barbara, 155
The Elements of Style, 150
Elevator to the Gallows, 40
Eliot, T. S., 80
emotion: anthropomorphism of, 238; evaluation of, 136, 142; in phone sex, 39; suppression of, 138. *See also* love
Epistemology of the Closet, 71–72
equality: and law of equivalence, 6; in relation to eroticism, 99; in relation to sexual orientation, 7; in sadomasochism, 105–106
eroticism: gay, 177; and mysticism, 135; in relation to equality, 99; sublimation of, 119; of telephone, 34, 38–39. *See also* homoeroticism
ethnicity: American, 155–56; in relation to pornography, 67. *See also* blackness; minorities
evil, 53, 139
exhibitionism, 59–68, 79

family: commercialization of, 217–35; as paradigm of relationship, 220–30; in relation to queer community, 165–92. *See also* father; marriage; mother
Fanny Hill, 65
fantasy, 65, 221; sexual and racial, 21, 189; telephone as instrument of, 35, 37, 39, 42, 44
fascism: homosexuality equated with, 93–94, 102, 210. *See also* power; state
fashion. *See* clothing
father: fixation on, 50, 53; power of over child, 39; queer role for, 62, 64, 68. *See also* family; men
fear: of disembodied voice, 46–49, 96; in phone sex, 37; postmodern, 139, 140. *See also* paranoia
feelings. *See* emotion
femininity: black, 190; butch, 105–106; compared to masculinity, 49, 203–204; cultivation of, 51–53, 65–66, 80–82, 115–19, 207; as evil, 209; and gynophobia, 115, 117; Hindu, 120, 122; "infantile" vs. "mature," 9; of Michael Jackson, 22; in relation to phallus, 65–66; of telephone use, 46. *See also* gender; women
feminists: in communist states, 94, 99, 101. *See also* activism; politics
feminization: of black male, 167; of Hindu men, 117, 118, 119, 120; of male body, 51–53, 65–66, 80–82, 85, 115–19, 207; of space, 205, 208, 214; in tango, 133
Ferenczi, Sándor, 49, 52
fetishism: of capitalism, 22; of masculinity, 199; in phone sex, 35. *See also* sadomasochism
Fiore, Mary, 204
Fish, Stanley, 81
Foucault, Michael, 135, 139
Freud, Sigmund, 49, 50
fucking: after sex-change, 99; compared to orgasm, 82–83; fetishization of, 199; traditional, 37. *See also* orgasm

García Lorca, Federico, 211, 212
Gaynor, Gloria, 187
gays, 67, 200; in black community, 165–92; Hollywood portrayal of, 3, 9–12; house music enjoyment by, 182–83; involvement of with phone sex, 34–56; as other, 101; persecution of, 104–105; sexual definition of, 40–41. *See also* homosexuality; queers
gender, 167, 243; effect of on Michael Jackson, 13–27; in colonialism, 112; in relation to other, 81, 167; in relation to pornography, 64–67; role of in relationship, 37, 84–85, 116, 201
"gender border control," 213
Gender Trouble: Feminism and the Subversion of Identity, 66
genitals: artistic representation of, 76; flowers as representation of, 64, 65; grabbing of onstage, 17, 20; hatred of, 199, 203–205, 209, 210, 213; in relation to homosocial relations, 198. *See also* penis; phallus
German Democratic Republic (GDR), queer community in, 93–106
Gifford-Gonzalez, Diane, 157
Ginsberg, Allen, 199
Gitlin, Todd, 140–41
God: death of, 139; of mysticism, 116; relation of metaphysical poets with, 73–86; relation of Schreber with, 49–55
Gomez-Peña, Guillermo, 158

Goodman, Paul, 206–207
Gorky, Maxim, 93
Gray, Francine Du Plessix, 204
guilt, of sexual transgression, 41

Hall, Arsenio, 26
Haraway, Donna, 22, 35
Harris, Herbert, 38–39
Heller, Anges, 138
Herbert, George, 72
Herdt, Gilbert, 165
Herman, Pee-Wee, 24
hermaphroditism, 116
heterosexuality: effect on of autoeroticism, 8; as
    normative model, 81, 82, 86, 94, 103, 118,
    165–92, 197–214, 225, 242; relation of homo-
    sexuality to, 9, 17; tango as forum for, 131
Hinduism, 112–26
The History of Bodies, 135
Holleran, Andrew, 173, 185, 186, 191
Hollywood: sexual stereotypes of, 3, 119; tele-
    phone device used by, 45–46
homoeroticism: effect of on heterosexuality, 8;
    in relation to AIDS, 34; in religious poetry,
    72–86. *See also* eroticism
homophobia, 3, 10, 52, 212–13; and misogyny,
    207; recognition of lesbianism within, 7; in
    relation to Michael Jackson, 19; in relation to
    state policy, 94, 95, 96
homosexual. *See* gays; lesbians; queers
homosexuality, 83, 99; of asocials, 95, 96, 102; in
    black society, 165–92; in Britain, 201; in com-
    munist society, 93–106; compared to hetero-
    sexuality, 9, 17, 67, 199; decriminalization of,
    105; in dominant culture, 94, 98; and Michael
    Jackson, 19; narcissism as, 8, 9, 17, 204; para-
    noia as, 49–52; in religion, 72; repressed, 39,
    71, 72. *See also* gays; queers
homosociality, compulsory, 197–214
house music, 165–92; described, 169–72
The Human Voice, 42, 45
humans, relation of with animals, 218–21, 234
The Hunger, 45

identification: cultural, 158, 224; mimetic, 5, 10;
    regenerative process of, 131; in relation to
    identity, 154–55. *See also* mimetic identifica-
    tion
identity: American, 151, 153; assertion of, 101,
    180; body as site of, 17, 72; butch, 105; com-
    mercialization of, 6–7; as commodity, 6, 7; in
    communism, 95; essentialist vs. construction-

ist, 16; exchangeable, 3–12, 16; gay, 176, 184,
    210; gendered, 65–67, 117; hyphenated, 154;
    indeterminate, 18, 21, 26, 36, 66; masculine,
    200; national, 117, 120, 122, 149; performance
    of, 158; as private property, 4–5, 7, 10–11, 16,
    20; pure, 151–52; queer, 165, 184; in relation
    to work, 5–6, 103. *See also* ego-identity; indi-
    viduality; sexual identity
imitation: effect of on subject, 5, 7–10, 62–63;
    of culture, 121; music as, 238; paranoia pro-
    duced by, 4–5; of self, 17–18, 20, 21, 22, 23–24;
    as women's role, 122, 126
immigrants, 149–59
IMPACT, 165
impotence, 132
incest, 47. *See also* family; father
individuality: in communist state, 96; and hy-
    phenation, 157; in universalization, 3–12. *See
    also* identity; self
inferiority, stereotype of, 5
Innocent Angel, 102–103
intellectualism, 130, 131, 132, 134, 198, 206
intimacy: of tango, 132; telephone as device for,
    39, 44
Islam, 115

Jackson, Janet, 15
Jackson, Michael, 13–27
Jameson, Fredric, 49
Jasmine, 158
Jerker, 43
John Paul II, Pope, 38
Johnson, Samuel, 79
Jones, Grace, 18

Kantorowicz, Ernst, 208–209
Kerouac, Jack, 199
Kline, Franz, 205, 206
Klute, 45, 46
Knuckles, Frankie, 171–72
Kollontai, Alexandra, 97
Kramer, Larry, 41, 43
Kristeva, Julia, 34
Kyger, Joanne, 198

Lacan, Jacques, 55, 60, 62, 65, 130, 135, 138
language: homosexual jargon as, 60; hyphenated,
    150; of law, 67; "literary" language, 64; mi-
    metic identification as, 5; pleasure in, 45; of
    tango, 131, 132; as tool of repression, 94–95
Larue, Chi Chi, 84
Law of Desire, 45, 78

law of equivalence, 6

Lemke, Jürgen, 103

lesbians, 3, 200; in communist state, 95, 101–103; desire in, 7–11; as other, 101; sexuality in, 82. *See also* homosexuality; queers; women

Levertov, Denise, 198, 211

life, initiation into, 133

look: as aspect of identity, 4–5, 6, 8, 118–19; as class indicator, 4; as commodity, 6, 7, 64. *See also* identity; self

Lorca. *See* García Lorca, Federico

love: in accordance with desire, 97; commercialization of, 221; divine and sensual, 73, 123; equality as obstacle to, 99; free love, 93. *See also* emotion

Lyotard, Jean-François, 135

machine: as ally of death, 42, 44, 49; as dehumanizing, 97–98; as source of sex, 35, 37; use of in house music, 170. *See also* telephone

machismo, 65, 67, 209. *See also* masculinity

McQuain, Jeffrey, 154

Madonna, 17, 19, 24, 71

The Manchurian Candidate, 45, 48

Mann, Klaus, 93

Mapplethorpe, Robert, 177–92. *See also* photography

marketing: of house music, 174; of identity, 6; of Michael Jackson, 16, 18; of passion, 131; of pornography, 59. *See also* capitalism; commodity

marriage: as model of sexuality, 81, 93, 104, 120; to establish sexual credibility, 15, 27. *See also* family; heterosexuality

masculinity: African American, 14–15, 18, 19, 23–24, 167, 180; compared to femininity, 49, 203–204; and fetishism, 199; of Hindu men, 112, 117–20, 124; homosexual, 66; machismo, 65, 67; of Michael Jackson, 17, 20; performance of, 83; in telephone use, 46; transformation of into femininity, 51–53. *See also* gender; men

mass media, 14

mass production. *See* commodity; repetition

The Master as I Saw Him, 112–26

masturbation: as aspect of phone sex, 35, 39; in church, 78; as stage device, 17, 24; telephone as symbol of, 38, 43. *See also* orgasm

materialism: effect of on sexual identity, 4; in relation to religion, 115, 121. *See also* capitalism; dominant culture

Maxwell, James A., 36

Memoirs of My Nervous Illness, 49–56

memory: function of, 39, 42; loss of as spiritual command, 118; in relation to phone sex, 43, 44

men: domination of women by, 201; paranoia of, 47; same-sex bonding among, 197–214; transformation of into women, 51–53, 65–66, 80–82, 115–19, 207; as victim of women, 9. *See also* gays; homosexuality

men's movement, 199

Mercer, Kobena, 18, 23, 177, 180–82

Merleau-Ponty, Maurice, 139

Miller, Nancy K., 198

mimetic identification: in language, 5; "psychotic" principle of, 10. *See also* identification; imitation

mimetic performance, 3, 5, 11. *See also* performance

minorities, 149–59. *See also* African Americans; Native Americans

mirror stage, 5, 60, 61

miscegenation, 154. *See also* race

misogyny, 3, 10, 81, 94, 115, 199, 207

monogamy: as model of sexuality, 93. *See also* heterosexuality; marriage

morality, 117

More of a Man, 71–86

mother: fixation on, 48, 64, 65, 199; women defined as, 101. *See also* family; women

mourning: for Nazi victims, 102; in relation to telephone, 34, 40, 41–45, 49. *See also* victims

Mukherjee, Bharati, 158

multiculturalism, 149–59

Multiple Maniacs, 78

Mulvey, Laura, 180

murder: as career, 78; of gays, 3, 9, 184; in relation to sexuality, 46–47. *See also* death

music, effect of on sexuality, 240–44

mysticism, 112–14, 135

narcissism, as homosexuality, 8, 9, 17, 49, 59, 204

Naté, Ultra, 187

nationalism: identity in, 149, 151; relation of to colonialism, 112–26. *See also* politics; state

Native Americans, 151, 155

nature: cultivation of, 220; and culture, 217–18, 220–21; music not imitation of, 238; performance of, 217–35

Neale, Steve, 119

negrophobia, 182, 183. *See also* African Americans; blackness

Nietzsche, Friedrich, 137–38, 141
Nivedita, Sister, 112–26
Noble, Margaret, 112–26
nomination, relation of to denomination, 62–63
The Normal Heart, 43
normality, sexual spectrum of, 104
Numbers, 59–68

object(s): relation of to identity, 4, 7, 46, 62, 136; as simulacra of each other, 6
Olson, Charles, 197–214
orgasm: of Christ, 77; as cinematic device, 65, 66, 82, 83; Michael Jackson as, 19. *See also* fucking; genitals; masturbation
orifices: artistic representation of, 76. *See also* genitals
ostentation, grammar of, 59–68
other: boundaries for, 4, 6, 154, 158, 223; desire for, 62, 138; as enemy, 95; homosexual as, 101; Michael Jackson as, 19; passion as, 130–33, 141–43; in postmodernism, 134; for queer militants, 41; in relation to gender, 81, 167; relation of to self, 19. *See also* difference
ownership: of identity, 4–5, 10. *See also* private property

panic: as apathy control, 141; homosexual, 8, 50–51, 167; lesbian, 45; postmodern, 139, 141; in professional class, 5; sexual, 36, 48
paranoia: in gay community, 34, 35, 40, 45, 46, 54, 55; as homosexuality, 49–52; of persecution, 46–49; in postmodernism, 139; in psychosomatic transvestism, 4–5. *See also* fear; psychosis
partnering: inter-species, 225–29, 230. *See also* marriage
The Party Line, 48
passion: conquest of with reason, 137; and postmodernism, 130–43
Passion of Christ, 72–86
patriarchy: penis in relation to, 99; support of by state, 94. *See also* masculinity; men
penis: as breast, 65; of changed-sex woman, 99; cultural significance of, 15–16, 19; problems with, 13–27. *See also* genitals; phallus
performance: for animals, 237–44; of differential identity, 158; of dissidence, 101; and house music, 165–92; of hyphen, 149; of masculinity, 83; Michael Jackson as, 14, 20; mimetic, 3, 5, 11; passion as, 131, 136; sexual identity as, 53; "sexuality-performance," 20; of Shamu, 221–29; terms for, 198

performativity: normative force of, 20–21; queer, 165–92; relation of to pornography, 66
Perloff, Marjorie, 202
persecution: of homosexuals, 104–105; paranoia of, 46–49. *See also* fascism; racism
personality, as code for body, 119
perversion, 40. *See also* queers
phallus, 65–66, 82, 84, 204–205, 207. *See also* genitals; penis
phone sex, 34–56; drawbacks of, 34–35. *See also* telephone
photography, 177–92, 227–29, 233; photo collage, 181, 184
pleasure: associated with Cross, 78–79; of house music, 177–78; telephone as instrument of, 36, 37, 42, 44–45, 49, 51, 54; of voyeurism, 60, 62
poetry: religious, 72–86; of sexual politics, 197–214
police brutality, 14
politics: effect of on sexual identity, 16, 18, 67, 104–105, 122, 124, 125, 200; gendered, 137; homosexuality as liability in, 93–94; postmodern, 142–43; in relation to Michael Jackson, 16–27; in relation to music, 239–40. *See also* sexual politics
Poltergeist, 42
Pope. *See* John Paul II
pornography: homodevotion in, 71–86; representational problems of, 59–68
postmodernism: homosexuality in, 199–200; passion in, 130–43
power: class privilege for, 7, 133, 143, 150, 152; of humans over nature, 220; loss of, 234–35; of male speech, 204–205; in master-disciple bond, 116, 122–23; of music, 237–44; of passion, 131, 132; telephone as instrument of, 37, 39, 42, 46–47, 49. *See also* class
Presley, Lisa Marie, 13, 19
privacy, 55
private: in relation to public, 5–6, 17, 104. *See also* identity
private property: identity as, 4, 5, 10–11; Michael Jackson as, 16; in relation to sexual politics, 93, 105–106. *See also* commodity; ownership
professional class: compared to lower class, 4–6, 9–10; homosexuality in, 83
promiscuity: as alternative to sexual norm, 97; in time of AIDS, 36, 41, 54
prostitution, 6
protocols, as alternative performance, 102–104
psychoanalysis: of phone sex, 35, 37, 39–40; in relation to class, 5, 130

psychosis, 3, 5; "professionalization" of, 10; schizophrenia, 49–50. *See also* paranoia

public: demands of on Michael Jackson, 17; display of passion in, 131–32; homosexual encounters in, 72; in relation to private, 5–6, 17, 104. *See also* space

queer bashing, 40

queers: as dissidents, 93–106, 200; effect on of sexual stereotyping, 3; as other, 101; persecution of, 104–105; and religious poetry, 75, 79; sexual identification in, 36, 40, 41; white vs. black, 165–92. *See also* gays; homosexuality; lesbians

race: effect of on Michael Jackson, 13–27; effect of on phone sex, 36–37; as culture, 153, 155; in relation to fantasy, 21; in relation to sexuality, 18–19, 23, 191. *See also* blackness; whiteness

racism, 14, 176; in relation to hyphenation, 155–56. *See also* fascism; minorities

Ramakrishna Paramhansa, 112–17

Ransom, John Crowe, 198

rape, 78; desire for by men, 80–82, 85, 86; rape culture, 47. *See also* misogyny; violence; women

reason, compared to passion, 137

Rechy, John, 59–68

redemption, and pornography, 71–86

reference point: destruction of in capitalism, 6–7; hyphen as, 149; passion as, 131; penis as, 16; of "this" and "that," 60

regression: effect of on hyphen-nations, 151–52; in relation to homosexuality, 39–40

Reich, June, 19

religion: availability of in phone sex, 38; centrality of body in, 74; relation of to homosexuality, 71–72, 84; relation of to sexuality, 80, 120. *See also* Christ

repetition: of bodies, 75; of Michael Jackson, 20–21; in music, 166, 240; of passion, 136; reproduction as, 150; of self, 21, 25; of sexual encounters, 66; telephone as device for, 45; of voice, 104. *See also* commodity; imitation

responsibility, abdication of, 18

Rich, Adrienne, 197

Rio, Johnny, 59, 67

Ritt, Herb, 25

Ronell, Avital, 35, 37, 42, 50

sacred: in female eroticism, 81; in religious poetry, 79. *See also* religion

sadism, associated with lesbian, 95

sadomasochism: in relation to equality, 105–106; in relation to phone sex, 37; and self-mutilation, 74. *See also* fetishism

Safire, William, 153

sameness. *See* equality

San Juan, E., 153

scatology, 76. *See also* colon

Scheer, Robert, 18

schizophrenia, 49–50. *See also* psychosis

Schreber's story, 49–55

Schroeder, Barbet, 3

Sea World, 217–35

Sedgwick, Eve Kosofsky, 17, 71, 197, 200

seduction: feminine power for, 137; intellectual, 134, 135; telephone as instrument of, 35, 43

self: boundary violation of, 4; knowledge of as narcissism, 9; as pornographic object, 60–62; relation of to other, 19; split of, 16, 104, 134, 135; universalization of, 4, 10. *See also* becoming; identity

self-mutilation: religious, 74. *See also* sadomasochism

sex: mourning for in gay community, 40, 44–45. *See also specific types of sex*

Sex-Change, 98–99

sexual abuse, 52. *See also* child abuse

sexual identity: effect on of politics, 16, 18, 67, 104–105; deconstruction of, 4–12; as economic identity, 3, 5–6; as performance, 53; in relation to phone sex, 37, 40. *See also* identity

sexual liberation, in time of AIDS, 40, 45

sexual politics: effect on of economic violence, 3; effect of on gender, 99; private property concepts in, 93–94. *See also* politics

sexuality: effect of on economic factors, 6–7, 10, 34–35; effect of on Michael Jackson, 13–27; effect on of music, 240–44; black male, 14–15, 18; concepts of, 20, 82; female, 4, 82; initiation into, 133; marriage as model of, 81, 93, 104, 120; and race, 18–19, 23; in relation to disembodied voice, 34, 36, 38, 39, 43–45, 52–55, 189; and state authority, 94–97; violence in, 24, 94. *See also* masculinity

shame, 52

Short Cuts, 38

showing, in exhibitionism, 59–62

Shriver, Maria, 165

Shuger, Debora Kuller, 81

Silverman, Kaja, 6, 46, 49, 188, 189

Silverman, Martin, 38

simulacra: subject and object as, 6–7. *See also* imitation

Single White Female, 3–12
Sister Sledge, 165
Sister Souljah, 154
socialism: queer community process under, 93–
    106. *See also* capitalism
Sollers, Werner, 150
Sontag, Susan, 34
Sorry, Wrong Number, 45, 46
space: of bodies, 59, 76; classroom as, 81; cul-
    tural, 104; for disbelief, 133; domestic, 47;
    empty, 22; feminization of, 205, 208, 214; lo-
    cated by hyphen, 149; moral, 117; paranoid,
    47–48; queer, 45, 77; representational, 16; so-
    cial, 101, 172; subjective, 96; textual, 64; ur-
    ban, 64, 191
spectator: in relation to performance, 179–92.
    See also audience
spectatorship, 119. *See also* audience
speech: eroticization of, 34–56; female body as
    site of, 189. *See also* voice
Spicer, Jack, 197–214
Spillers, Hortense, 151
Spivak, Gayatri, 158
Stachura, Joseph, 43
state: control of culture by, 239; relation of to
    sexuality, 94–106. *See also* nationalism; politics
status: role of clothing in, 4. *See also* class
subject: "colonial subject," 16, 19; of Discourse,
    134; relation of to identity, 4, 7, 9–10, 46, 62,
    136; sexual, 93–106. *See also* colonial subject
subjectivity: of body, 51; creation of, 151, 157;
    feminization of, 81; in relation to identity, 4,
    17, 106; in relation to sexuality, 7, 8, 10, 46,
    177–79; in religious poetry, 72–86; of space,
    96; white, 186
submission: in master-disciple relation, 122–23;
    in same-sex relation, 5. *See also* feminization
Summer, Donna, 174
Superbowl, 20–21
symbolism: within body, 51; universalizing na-
    ture of, 5, 63, 64
Syms, Kim, 170

tango, as expression of passion, 130–43
Taylor, Elizabeth, 19, 21, 26
technology. *See* machine; telephone
telephone: as instrument of sex and death, 41–43,
    46; as phallic device, 38; and phone sex, 34–56.
    See also machine
tension: between difference and assimila-
    tion, 149–50; in phone sex, 46; in tango, 131–
    32, 134
Tesich, Nadja, 22

Theory of Feelings, 138
Thomas, Anthony, 172
Thomas, Clarence, 24
tongues, 64–65
transexuality, 16–17, 52
transference: American, 155; of homosexual de-
    sire, 51; telephone as symbol of, 38, 39
transformation: of desire, 34, 46, 51, 65; of gen-
    der, 66; of men into women, 51–53, 65–66,
    80–82, 115–19, 207; of women into men, 98–
    99. *See also* becoming
transvestism: in mysticism, 115, 116; in relation
    to class, 10; in relation to identity, 16
Tratado de la Pasión, 136
Trías, Eugenio, 136
twin. *See* double

Un-Visible Women, 102
universalization: of consumptive desire, 7, 9; in
    relation to individuality, 3–12; resistance to,
    130, 157

vicariousness, mimetic identification as, 5
The Vicious Circle, 95
victims: compared to aggressor, 14; gay men as,
    36; men as, 9; Michael Jackson as, 14–15, 18,
    21, 26, 27; of Nazis, 102; of postmodernism,
    135; women as, 48. *See also* mourning
violence: against queer community, 40, 41, 50;
    bureaucratic, 134; of class differentiation, 3, 4;
    revolutionary, 10; in sexuality, 24, 94. *See also*
    aggression; rape
Vivekananda, Swami, 112, 114, 117–26
voice: male vs. female, 188–89; in poetry, 198.
    See also disembodied voice; speech
Vox, 36
voyeurism, 8, 60, 62, 180
vulnerability: of body, 76–78; of Christ's body,
    73–86; experienced with phone sex, 39; use of
    as stage device, 26

Wagner, Tom, 43
Warhol, Andy, 50
Waters, John, 78
When a Stranger Calls, 45, 46–47, 55
whiteness, 14; "anti-whiteness" in house music,
    173; compared to blackness, 23; as minority,
    155, 156; personified in white woman, 119,
    122. *See also* bourgeois society; professional
    class
wife: as submissive identity, 5. *See also* marriage;
    women
Williams, Raymond, 217, 218, 220

Willis, Susan, 22

Winfrey, Oprah, 14–15, 17, 26

Woman and Socialism, 93

women: asocial women, 95, 96; Christ as, 84; domination of by men, 201; exchange of identities among, 3–12; Hindu women, 112, 120–22; male hatred of, 199, 203–205, 209, 213; in male homosocial groups, 198; men as victims of, 9; non-existence of, 135; as private property, 4, 105–106; "queering" of, 99–100; in rape culture, 47–48; as saints, 74; transformation of into men, 98–99; transformation of men into, 51–53, 65–66, 80–82, 115–19, 207; voices of, 188; "western" woman, 112, 119; white women, 119. *See also* femininity; lesbians; mother

Women on the Verge of a Nervous Breakdown, 45

work, relation of to sexual identity, 5–6, 99, 103, 105–106

Wright, James, 199

youth: loss of, 15; of Michael Jackson, 17, 18

zero, as objective, 62–64

Zinner, Hedda, 95